U S M C

A COMPLETE HISTORY

U S M C

A COMPLETE HISTORY

Colonel Jon T. Hoffman, USMCR, *Editor*

MARINE CORPS ASSOCIATION

HUGH LAUTER LEVIN ASSOCIATES, INC.

MARINE CORPS ASSOCIATION

At Guantanamo Bay, Cuba, on 25 April 1913, Marines of the Second Provisional Brigade formed the Marine Corps Association. John A. Lejeune, then a lieutenant colonel, headed its first executive committee. The purpose of the MCA was defined then and continues to drive the Association into the 21st century, to: "disseminate knowledge of military art and science to its members; to provide for professional advancement; to foster the spirit and preserve the traditions of the United States Marine Corps."

For all who have earned and worn the Eagle, Globe, and Anchor, the Marine Corps Association is the professional organization for all Marines—active duty, reserve, retired and Marine veterans. The MCA understands and identifies with the sacrifices made and the services rendered as a Marine to this great country. Once a Marine, always a Marine!

A member of the Marine Corps Association is part of a brotherhood rich with history, traditions, and accomplishments. Membership is the lifeblood of the MCA. Regardless of status—active duty, reserve, retired, or veteran—we urge eligible individuals to become members of the professional association of the Marines.

Individuals may learn more about the Marine Corps Association and become an MCA member at http://www.mca-marines.org.

Marine Corps Association
Box 1775
Quantico, Virginia 22134
Tel: (703) 640-6161
http://www.mca-marines.org

Published by Hugh Lauter Levin Associates, Inc.
© 2002 Marine Corps Association
Design: Charles J. Ziga
Project Editor: James O. Muschett
Illustration Editor: Beth L. Crumley
Technical Editor: Colonel John Greenwood, USMC (Ret)
Design production: Chris Berlingo

ISBN 0-88363-111-3
Printed in Hong Kong
Distributed by Publishers Group West
http://www.HLLA.com

CONTENTS

MARINES
IN THE
FIGHTING
TOPS

1775–1844

MARINES IN THE FIGHTING TOPS

1775–1844

The concept of a corps of Marines was well established when the colonies in America rebelled against Great Britain in 1775. Since the seventeenth century, the Royal Navy had used army regiments, and then its own dedicated force of sea soldiers, for a variety of specific missions. During battles at sea, Marines employed muskets against exposed enemy personnel, repelled attempts to board, and provided assistance in manning the great guns if required. For combat ashore, their skill with small arms made them the core of the landing force (with sailors often fleshing out the expedition). Marines and their muskets also enforced regulations among the crew and served as the bulwark against mutiny.

It was natural, then, that when the American revolutionaries decided to form their own navy, they made an immediate provision for Marines to help man the fleet. Thus the Continental Congress decreed on 10 November that "two Battalions of Marines be raised." Continental Navy warships subsequently recruited detachments of Marines for each cruise. State navies, privateers, and other forces such as General Benedict Arnold's flotilla on Lake Champlain, likewise provided for this necessary component of warfare on the water.

The American Marines made an immediate impact, sailing with the first Continental Navy squadron in early 1776 and leading the first amphibious landing at New Providence in the Bahamas. The auspicious beginning in the Caribbean heralded what would become the primary mission of the Corps—landings on hostile shores. It was not a natural outcome, since the Royal Marines never focused on this task to any great degree. And New Providence might have remained a rare exception, given the thorough defeat American landing forces suffered in the Penobscot Bay expedition in 1779. Nevertheless, the association of American Marines with operations across the beach was firmly ingrained.

The Continental Marines served in another role that later would prove important, even if their employment in this capacity during the Revolutionary War was inconsequential. Major Samuel Nicholas's battalion of Marines fought as part of General George Washington's army at Princeton and Trenton in the desperate period around Christmas 1776 and suffered the same hardships in winter quarters near Morristown, New Jersey. This campaign set a lasting precedent—Marines would not limit themselves to service in naval operations, but would lend a hand even in extended land operations as an adjunct of the Army.

The Continental Marines and their counterparts in the state navies ceased to exist following the end of the Revolutionary War. This had nothing to do with their utility, often demonstrated during the conflict, but came about solely because the navies which they served also went out of existence. When the Congress of the

newly established United States decided to build a navy in 1794, the lawmakers provided again for Marines. In its first few years, the new U.S. Marine Corps saw frequent action on ship as part of the Quasi War with France and the Barbary Wars. In a rare exception to this traditional role during this period, Lieutenant Presley O'Bannon and seven enlisted Marines made an epic overland march and led an attack on the fortress of Derna that helped bring a successful conclusion to the war with Tripoli. Marines also began guarding the Navy's first shore installations, and established their own first permanent facility, Marine Barracks 8th and I, in Washington, D.C.

The War of 1812 brought more of the same; frequent participation in ship-to-ship duels, punctuated by an occasional operation as a purely land force. Ships' detachments were in the thick of many famous sea battles that established the reputation of the fledgling U.S. Navy. Marines also were there with General Andrew Jackson's Army during the famous victory at New Orleans in 1815, but they played a much more prominent part in the 1814 Battle of Bladensburg. Although the latter was a crushing defeat, Marines and reinforcing sailors fought well and briefly stemmed the relentless British advance on Washington, D.C. In the long period of relative peace following the War of 1812, the Marine Corps fought on ship and shore with the Navy in suppressing piracy and the slave trade, and alongside the Army in the

Seminole Wars. The opening of the latter campaign showcased what would become another hallmark of the Corps. In a relatively short period of time, Commandant Archibald Henderson put together a regiment from ships detachments and Marine barracks and deployed it into battle.

Throughout these first six decades of the existence of American Marines, their numbers seldom rose much above 1,000 men and frequently were considerably lower. This minuscule body of Marines also had established a combat reputation, afloat and ashore, that at least matched that of their soldier and sailor compatriots. The Corps was quick to find other ways to endear itself to government leaders and the public. The Marine Band became an early fixture at social events and celebrations around the national capital, while budget-conscious commandants looked for every opportunity to trim expenditures.

The record of the Corps was not perfect, but it was largely positive and it contained nearly all the elements that would distinguish subsequent generations of Marines—courage and resourcefulness in battle, readiness for war at a moment's notice, a miserly regard for the public's tax dollars, a sense of pomp and pageantry, and a determination to perform whatever service was most needed without regard for formal roles and missions. The Corps was small, but it occupied an important niche in the armed forces of the United States.

MARINES IN THE FIGHTING TOPS

1775–1844

1775

19 April
American Revolution
The American Revolution opens with the battles of Lexington and Concord.

9 May
Lake Champlain
Soldiers from Brigadier General Benedict Arnold's Massachusetts force capture a British sloop at Skenesborough on Lake Champlain and rename her *Liberty*. Massachusetts soldiers, turned sailors and Marines, man her.

10 May
Lake Champlain
Liberty participates in the capture of Fort Ticonderoga from the British.

18 May
Lake Champlain
At St. John's on Lake Champlain, Marines from *Liberty* assist Arnold's force in capturing another British sloop. Arnold mans her with more improvised sailors and Marines and renames her *Enterprise*. The crew of the sloop was reinforced with 18 Marines in all. The first known Marine officer, listed on the payroll, was Lt James Watson.

25 May
Manpower
The first recorded mention of American Marines appears in an account describing eight Connecticut Marines escorting pay for troops to Albany, New York, for further shipment to Ticonderoga. These Marines often are referred to as the "Original Eight."

10 June
Manpower
The Continental Congress passes a resolution bringing all American forces (including Marines) operating on and around Lake Champlain under the control of the Congress and providing that they be paid from 3 May.

15 June
Atlantic
Marines participate in the action between *Katy* and *Washington* (Rhode Island Navy) and an armed tender supporting the British frigate *Rose*.

July
Atlantic
Marines in *Spy* (Connecticut Navy) participate in the capture of the Tory brig *Nancy*.

24 August
Massachusetts
Hannah, the first ship in the fleet fitted out by General Washington, goes into Continental service. Soldiers from Washington's army serve as the crew and Marines of the ship.

7 September
Massachusetts
Hannah and her Marines recapture the unarmed *Unity* off Massachusetts.

October
Atlantic
Connecticut Marines in *Spy* assist in the capture of a large British ship.

5 October
Massachusetts
The Continental Congress mentions Marines for the first time when it directs Washington to give "Proper encouragement to the Marines and seamen" serving on the two armed vessels under "Continental risque and pay."

10 October
Massachusetts
Marines participate in the action between *Hannah* and the British sloop *Nautilus* off the Massachusetts coast.

13 October
Manpower
Congress directs the acquisition, fitting out, and manning of two vessels for the Continental Navy. Since Marines are a normal part of a warship's complement, this is the first (albeit indirect) authorization for the enlistment of Continental Marines.

5 November
Massachusetts
Marines in *Harrison* (Washington's fleet) participate in the capture of the British supply vessels *Polly* and *Industry* off Boston.

7 November
Massachusetts
Lee (Washington's fleet) and her Marines recapture the sloop *Ranger* in Massachusetts Bay.

10 November
Force Structure
The Continental Congress formally establishes an organization of Marines with the following resolution:
"Resolved, That two battalions of Marines be raised consisting of one colonel, two lieutenant-colonels, two majors, and other officers, as usual in other regiments; that they consist of an equal number of privates with other battalions; that particular care be taken that no persons be appointed to office, or enlisted into said battalions, but such as are good seamen, or so acquainted with maritime affairs as to be able to serve

Opposite: *A Marine reaches into his cartridge box to reload. ("Continental Marine, 1775," Donald Dickson,* Leatherneck *magazine)*

Above: *"Continental Marine Officer, 1775," Col Donna Neary, Marine Corps Art Collection*

to advantage by sea when required; that they be enlisted and commissioned to serve for and during the present war with great Britain and the colonies, unless dismissed by order of Congress; that they be distinguished by names of First and Second Battalions of American Marines, and that they be considered as part of the number which the Continental Army before Boston is ordered to consist of."

11 November
South Carolina
Marines in *Defence* (South Carolina Navy) participate in the action against the British ships *Tamar* and *Cherokee* at Charleston, South Carolina.

17 November
Canada
Marines from *Hancock* and *Franklin* (Washington's fleet) make an unopposed landing at Charlottetown, Prince Edward Island.

19 November
Manpower
The first discord between the Army and the Marines occurs when General Washington takes issue with orders from Congress to supply

personnel from his force for the Marine battalions authorized on 10 November. The general noted that since the men "must be acquainted with maritime affairs," he would have to select from and therefore disrupt many of his units.

20 November
Canada
Marines join in the raid by *Hancock* and *Franklin* on Canso Harbor, Nova Scotia.

24 November
Massachusetts
Marines in *Harrison* participate in her fight with three British warships in Boston Bay.

27 November
Atlantic
Lee's Marines play their part in capturing the sloop *Polly* off the New England coast.

28 November
Commandants
Samuel Nicholas of Philadelphia is commissioned a captain of Marines by the Continental Congress. The senior Marine officer throughout the Revolutionary War, he is regarded as the first Commandant of the Marine Corps.

Right: *The Continental Marines of Commodore Esek Hopkins's squadron capture Fort Montagu on 3 March 1776. Contrary to the depiction here, there was no assault, as the local militiamen had abandoned the fortress. ("Marine Raid on Fort Montagu," H. Charles McBarron, Marine Corps Art Collection)*

28 November
Massachusetts
Over the next several weeks, Marines aboard ships of Washington's fleet help capture numerous British ships in the waters off Boston.

December
Force Structure
The Continental Marines form their first unit, for service on board the brig *Cabot*.

4 December
Massachusetts
Marines are among those taken prisoner when *Washington* is captured in Massachusetts Bay by two British frigates.

1776

3 March
Bahamas
At New Providence Island in the Bahamas, Captain Samuel Nicholas and a battalion of Marines and sailors land from Commodore Hopkins's squadron, seize the fort, and capture stores for Washington's army. This was the first amphibious landing by Continental Marines.

16 March
Bahamas
Hopkins's squadron and Marines withdraw from New Providence.

April
Manpower
John Martin enlists to serve on the Continental brig *Reprisal* and becomes the first black Marine.

5 April
New York
Marines participate in the capture of the British brig *Bolton* by Hopkins's squadron in the waters off New York City.

6 April
New York
Several Marines are killed or wounded during the battle between Hopkins's *Alfred* and *Cabot* and the British frigate *Glasgow* off Long Island, New York. The casualties include the first Continental Marine officer to die in battle.

7 April
Virginia
The Continental brig *Lexington* and her Marines defeat the British armed tender *Edward* off the Virginia Capes.

THE RAID ON NEW PROVIDENCE

The Continental Navy was only a few weeks old when Congress dispatched it on a mission overseas. Commodore Esek Hopkins was to take his eight ships and their Marines to New Providence Island in the Bahamas and capture a large supply of gunpowder rumored to be there. The fleet had hardly gotten into the Atlantic from Chesapeake Bay in mid-February 1776 when two of the ships collided in bad weather and had to turn back. Two weeks later, the Americans were in sight of their objective. Nassau was the main town on the island, with Hog Island offshore providing a protected anchorage for the port city. The entrances to the harbor around either end of Hog Island were guarded by Fort Nassau in the west and Fort Montagu in the east. Both were in disrepair, and the defenders consisted of a few hundred militiamen subject to call up.

The fleet put Captain Samuel Nicholas and his 234 Marines ashore two miles east of Fort Montagu at noon on 3 March. Since it was clear the townspeople had observed the approach of the ships and there would be no surprise, 50 sailors were provided as reinforcements. But in response to the drum roll to muster, only about a hundred militiamen had appeared at the rallying point at Fort Nassau. These were soon dispatched to Montagu. A militia lieutenant directed to reconnoiter the enemy marched his detail of 30 men toward the landing site and then ordered one to go forward with a flag of truce and inquire who the invaders were and what they wanted. After a brief parlay he reported back to the fort.

As the Americans approached the bastion, the British governor (also acting as commander) fired three cannon at nothing in

Left: *Continental Marines storm the beach of New Providence Island. ("Landing at New Providence," Col Charles Waterhouse, USMCR (Ret), Marine Corps Art Collection)*

Opposite: *Fifty seamen reinforce the Marines in the New Providence raid. The initial objective, Fort Montagu, is in the left background. ("New Providence Invasion," V. Zveg, Navy Art Collection)*

particular and ordered a retreat to Fort Nassau. Some of his men deserted as they passed their homes in the town. Captain Nicholas was not inclined to be aggressive either. After taking the just-abandoned eastern fort, he decided to rest his force until the next day. That evening, Hopkins issued a manifesto to the town promising not to harm people or private property, if they turned powder and arms over to him. He also kept his ships well away from the port.

The British governor, in a rare fit of boldness and energy, used the delay to load most of the 200 barrels of gunpowder at Fort Nassau on two merchant ships, which conveyed it to safety that night. With the work done and little left to defend at the fort, the remainder of the militia melted away. After ascertaining that Fort Nassau was deserted the next morning, Nicholas and his force marched to the western fortification, occupied it, and raised the Continental flag over foreign soil for the first time. Two weeks later, the flotilla sailed for home.

Although Hopkins and Nicholas had not achieved their primary aim of capturing gunpowder badly needed by Washington's army, they had acquired 46 cannon, thousands of round shot, and a considerable quantity of other military stores. It was the first landing against a hostile shore mounted by American Marines and sailors, and would presage bigger, more elaborate, and much fiercer amphibious assaults in the many decades to come.

Just two years later, in 1778, a lone Continental ship and its 28 Marines reprised the attack on New Providence, but in a much more daring fashion. Landing at night, the small detachment of Marines silently reached Fort Nassau and captured its surprised sentinels. Pretending to have a force of several hundred, Captain John Trevett bluffed Fort Montagu into surrendering the next day. The Americans then seized five merchantmen in the harbor and made off with another supply of British arms.

8 May
Pennsylvania
Marines of the Pennsylvania Navy employ row galleys to drive off two British warships in the Delaware River.

17 May
Atlantic
Marines assist *Franklin* of Washington's fleet in capturing the transport *Hope*, laden with 1,000 carbines and 75 tons of gunpowder.

29 May
Atlantic
Andrew Doria and her Marine contingent capture two British transports bearing two companies of infantry.

16 June
Massachusetts
Washington's fleet and its Marines capture two British troopships trying to reinforce Boston (already abandoned by the British army).

25 June
Manpower
Samuel Nicholas is promoted to the rank of major. Innkeeper Robert Mullan is commissioned as a captain in Philadelphia and begins recruiting enlisted men from his establishment, Tun Tavern.

29 June
New Jersey
Marines assist in the unloading of arms and gunpowder from the grounded *Nancy* under fire from the British frigate *Orpheus*.

4 July
American Revolution
The Declaration of Independence is signed.

27 July
Martinique
Marines and sailors of the brig *Reprisal* drive off the British sloop *Shark* and deliver an agent to Martinique to acquire intelligence and arms.

5 September
Uniforms
The Marine Committee of the Continental Congress decrees the first uniform for Marines— green coats faced with white, white trousers, and a single silver epaulette for officers.

20 September
Atlantic
Marines participate in the action between the sloop *Providence* and the British frigate *Milford*. Although surprised while the crew is fishing, the smaller American ship is able to escape in a day of expert sailing.

22 September
Canada
Providence and her Marines raid Canso Harbor, Nova Scotia, then strike at Isle Madame the next day, destroying fishing boats.

October
Manpower
Sergeants William Hamilton and Alexander Neilson are promoted to lieutenant. These are the first recorded "mustangs," enlisted Marines who become officers. Many Marines in the future will follow the same path.

11–13 October
Lake Champlain
Marines participate with Arnold's fleet in the Battle of Valcour Island on Lake Champlain. Although defeated, the Americans delay a British invasion until the following year.

December
Atlantic
Lexington is captured by the British frigate *Pearl*. Soon after, Marine Captain Abraham Boyce leads his men and *Lexington*'s sailors in overwhelming the small British prize crew and escaping to the harbor at Baltimore.

2 December
New Jersey
Major Samuel Nicholas and three companies of Marines are dispatched from Philadelphia to reinforce Washington's army as it retreats from New York through New Jersey.

9 December
Atlantic
Marines participate in the action between the *Alfred* and the British frigate *Milford*. The American ship outsails its better-armed opponent and escapes unharmed.

26 December
New Jersey
A portion of Washington's army crosses the Delaware River at night and defeats the Hessian forces at Princeton, New Jersey. Brigadier General John Cadwalader's division, which includes Samuel Nicholas's Marine battalion, gets across the river too late and misses the battle. The victory temporarily ends the British threat to Philadelphia, the seat of the Continental Congress.

1777

2 January
New Jersey
Major Samuel Nicholas and his battalion participate in Washington's defense of Trenton against Lord Cornwallis' British army. The Marines help hold the important Assunpink Bridge against a Hessian attack.

3 January
New Jersey
During the night, Washington's force silently departs the battlefield and marches toward Princeton. Marines assist in defeating the British garrison and capturing the town.

4 January
New Jersey
Samuel Nicholas's battalion goes into camp at Sweets Town, not far from Washington's bivouac at Jockey Hollow, Morristown, New Jersey. The American forces begin a long winter of hardship due to inadequate clothing and food.

1 February
New Jersey
The Marines transfer to Morristown and assume the role of artillerymen for the remainder of the winter.

5 February
France
Marines of *Reprisal* lead a boarding party that storms and captures the British *Swallow* in the Bay of Biscay off France.

8 March
Atlantic
The British frigate *Levant* defeats the Pennsylvania Navy ship *Montgomery* and her Marines.

20 March
Atlantic
The Connecticut Navy ship *Defence* and her Marines capture the British ship *Grog*.

7 June
Atlantic
Frigates *Hancock* and *Boston* and their Marine detachments capture the British frigate *Fox*.

14 June
Heritage
Congress adopts the Stars and Stripes as the national flag.

7 July
Atlantic
Hancock defeated by the British frigate *Rainbow*.

19 September
France

Lexington and her Marine detachment are defeated by the British cutter *Alert* near France. Captain Henry Johnson and Sergeant John Barry eventually would escape from an English prison.

27 September
Pennsylvania

Frigate *Delaware* and her Marines are driven onto a shoal in the Delaware River as they fight with British batteries guarding the approaches to Philadelphia (now occupied by the British). The ship is captured, but many of the Marines are able to escape.

1778

10 January
Mississippi River

A company of Marines under Navy Captain James Willing depart Fort Pitt (Pittsburgh) in the armed boat *Rattletrap* for an expedition to New Orleans.

15 January
Civil Support

Marines from the frigate *Randolph* help fight a blaze that destroys hundreds of buildings in Charleston, South Carolina.

4 September
Atlantic

Marines on board the frigate *Raleigh* assist in a bold attack on the British sloop *Druid* escorting a large convoy, but are unable to sink or capture any ships.

Above: *There is too little to eat and too little to wear during the hard winter at Morristown, New Jersey, in 1777. ("Marine Sentry, 1777," Col Charles Waterhouse, USMCR (Ret), Marine Corps Art Collection)*

Left: *Marines go back to the Bahamas in 1778 and raise the Stars and Stripes over foreign soil for the first time. ("Flag Raising at New Providence," Col Charles Waterhouse, USMCR (Ret), Marine Corps Art Collection)*

Right: *Naval Captain James Willing leads an expedition down the Mississippi River in 1778 in an effort to weaken Britain's hold on the waterway. He and his Marines raid Loyalist plantations along the way. ("Willing's Marine Expedition," Col Charles Waterhouse, USMCR (Ret), Marine Corps Art Collection)*

28 January
Bahamas
In a surprise night attack, Marines of the sloop *Providence* again seize the forts at New Providence Island in the Bahamas and raise the Stars and Stripes over a foreign shore for the first time. They also capture five ships in the harbor.

23 February
Mississippi River
Marines from *Rattletrap* capture the British sloop *Rebecca* on the Mississippi River and temporarily free that waterway from enemy domination.

7 March
Caribbean
Randolph and her Marines (reinforced by Continental soldiers) take on the 64-gun ship-of-the-line *Yarmouth* near Barbados. In the midst of the battle, *Randolph's* powder magazine explodes, and she sinks with the loss of 301 sailors, Marines, and soldiers.

7 March
Pennsylvania
Marines join the crewmen of two armed barges in capturing two British supply ships in the Delaware River. The barges also support General Anthony Wayne's brigade as it forages in New Jersey for food for Washington's army at Valley Forge.

9 March
Atlantic
Alfred is defeated by the British ships *Ariadne* and *Ceres* in the Atlantic, and her sailors and Marines are taken prisoner.

28 March
Rhode Island
Marines hold off an attack by Royal Marines while crewmen unload valuable equipment from the grounded *Columbus* near Newport, Rhode Island.

15 April
Atlantic
Marines participate in the actions in which the Connecticut Navy ships *Oliver Cromwell* and *Defence* capture the British letters-of-marque *Admiral Keppel* and *Cyrus*.

23 April
Great Britain
John Paul Jones and sailors and Marines of the sloop *Ranger* make a dawn raid on the British port of Whitehaven, setting fire to ships and spiking the cannon of the fort. Later that day they land at St. Mary's Isle to capture a British earl, but find him away from home and instead take the family silver.

7 August
Canada

Marines participate in *Providence*'s attack on a 30-ship convoy off Nova Scotia. They inflict damage on an armed transport carrying Highland troops.

27 September
Maine

The British ships *Experiment* and *Unicorn* engage *Raleigh* off the Penobscot River, Maine, and force her aground. Some of the Marines and sailors escape to shore, but most are captured.

24 April
Great Britain

Ranger and her Marines defeat the British sloop *Drake* in the Irish Sea.

1 May
Rhode Island

Marines assist in a night battle with the British frigate *Lark* in Narragansett Bay as *Providence* escapes the blockade and makes it to the open sea.

August
Atlantic

The brigantine *General Gates* and her Marines defeat the British letter-of-marque brig *Montague* in the Atlantic.

1779

April
Marksmanship

First recorded marksmanship practice by Marines takes place at Nantasket Beach, Massachusetts, and on board Commodore Hopkins's fleet composed of *Ranger*, *Warren*, and *Queen of France*.

6–7 April
Virginia

Off Cape Henry, Virginia, Marines assist Commodore Hopkins's fleet in capturing the armed British schooner *Hibernia*, the escort ship *Jason*, and six merchantmen carrying supplies for the British Army.

Above: *John Paul Jones inspects the Marine detachment aboard the frigate* Ranger *in 1778. (*"Marines Aboard the Ranger," *H. Charles McBarron, Marine Corps Art Collection)*

Right: *The original of this painting depicting the 1779 battle was destroyed by the terrorist attack on the Pentagon on 11 September 2001. (*"Assault on Penobscot," *Col Charles Waterhouse, USMCR (Ret), Marine Corps Art Collection)*

construction in Penobscot Bay, Maine. The fleet is composed of Continental ships *Warren*, sloop *Providence*, and brig *Diligence*, reinforced with four ships of the Massachusetts and New Hampshire state navies, a dozen privateers, and 20 merchantmen carrying supplies and troops (Continentals and state militiamen).

24 July
Maine
Marines from the Massachusetts Navy ship *Tyrannicide* land on Fox Island in Penobscot Bay to reconnoiter the area.

7 May
New Jersey
The sloop *Providence* and her Marines defeat the British brig *Diligent* off Sandy Hook, New Jersey.

18 July
Atlantic
Ranger, *Queen of France*, and the frigate *Providence* use the cover of heavy fog to cut out and capture 10 ships of a large convoy near the Newfoundland Banks.

24 July
Maine
An expedition sails from Massachusetts with the goal of destroying the British base under

26 July
Maine
Marines land on Banks Island, Maine, and install batteries to fire on British ships and positions around Penobscot Bay.

28 July
Maine
Marines land as the right flank of the American force, which successfully attacks up a steep slope and establishes a lodgment ashore near the British fort at Penobscot. The Americans settle down to build a fortified line instead of continuing the assault, which likely would have succeeded. A lack of coordination between land and sea forces contributes to the ultimate failure of the campaign.

Above: Bonhomme Richard, *under John Paul Jones, defeated HMS* Serapis *off the coast of England in September 1776. (*"The Serapis *and the* Bonhomme Richard," *William Elliott, U.S. Naval Academy Museum)*

Right: *"Bonhomme Richard and* Serapis," *J. O. Davidson, Marine Corps Art Collection*

13–15 August
Maine
After a British fleet arrives off Penobscot Bay, the American landing force re-embarks in an attempt to withdraw. The American fleet tries to evade the British, but all American ships are subsequently captured or scuttled. Escaping Marines, sailors, and soldiers start an overland trek back to Massachusetts.

10 September
Louisiana
Marines aboard an armed schooner assist in defeating and taking possession of the British sloop *West Florida* on Lake Pontchartrain near New Orleans.

23 September
Great Britain
Captain John Paul Jones's flagship *Bonhomme Richard* engages the British frigate *Serapis* off Flamborough Head. In bitter fighting, both ships are badly damaged and more than 250 men are killed and wounded. *Serapis* strikes her colors after Marines and sailors in the tops of Jones's ship use grenades and musket fire to sweep the tops and weather decks of the British ship. (*Bonhomme Richard*'s Marines were mainly Irishmen serving in the French Army.)

15–17 March
Florida
West Florida and her Marines participate in the successful Spanish attack on the British fort at Mobile.

21 March
South Carolina
Marines of the Continental fleet at Charleston are sent ashore to bolster artillery batteries defending the city against a pending British attack by land and sea.

10 May
South Carolina
Charleston surrenders after the British fleet and army completely surround the city.

2 June
Atlantic
Frigate *Trumbull* and her Marines battle the 36-gun British letter-of-marque *Watt* to a bloody draw. Three Marine lieutenants and a sergeant are among the American dead.

December
Atlantic
Marines participate in the engagement between John Paul Jones's *Ariel* and the British privateer *Triumph*.

5 January
Atlantic
Sloop *Saratoga* and her Marines defeat the 16-gun British privateer *Resolution* and the letter-of-marque *Tonyn*.

2 April
France
Marines of the *Alliance* assist in defeating British privateer brigs *Mars* and *Minerva* off the coast of France.

28 May
Atlantic
British sloops *Atlanta* and *Trepassey* surrender to

Alliance after a long fight in the Atlantic Ocean.

9 August
Atlantic
Partially dismasted by a storm, *Trumbull* and her Marines are defeated by the British frigate *Iris* off the Delaware Capes.

6 September
South Carolina
Marines on board the Pennsylvania privateer *Congress* help defeat the British sloop *Savage*, which recently had plundered General Washington's estate at Mount Vernon.

Fall
Civil Support
Major Samuel Nicholas is in charge of safeguarding the delivery from Boston to Philadelphia of a million silver coins, a loan from France to the Continental government.

1782

8 April
Atlantic
The Continental privateer *Hyder Ally* and her Marines defeat the British sloop *General Monk* off Delaware Bay.

8 May
Bahamas
Marines from the South Carolina Navy ship *South Carolina* participate in another landing at New Providence, Bahamas, that helps secure those islands for Spain.

1783

10 March
Caribbean
Alliance and her Marines engage the British frigate *Sybil* in the West Indies and inflict heavy damage on her. This is the last naval battle of the Revolutionary War.

11 April
American Revolution
The Treaty of Paris is signed to end hostilities in the Revolutionary War.

1784

26 April
Manpower
The last recorded mention of a Continental Marine is of Private Robert Stout serving in *Alliance*. With the end of the war, the Continental Navy and Marines are disbanded.

1785

3 June
Force Structure
Congress authorizes the sale of *Alliance*, the last vessel of the Continental Navy.

1790

27 August
Commandants
Major Samuel Nicholas, the senior Marine to serve during the Revolutionary War and considered the first Commandant of the Corps, dies in Philadelphia.

1794

27 March
Manpower
By the Navy Act of 1794, Congress authorizes Marines, totaling six officers and 310 enlisted men, to serve aboard the six frigates that will constitute the United States Navy, once the ships are built. This marks the rebirth of the Corps, this time designated the U.S. Marine Corps (as distinguished from the Continental Marines).

1796

20 April
Manpower
Due to lessening of tensions with the Barbary states, Congress continues construction of only three of the six planned frigates and cuts authorized Marine strength in half.

1797

4 January
Manpower
The first recorded mention is made of U.S. Marines serving on a U.S. Navy ship, the frigate *United States*. The detachment provides sharpshooters, boarders, and guards.

1 July
Manpower
President John Adams signs legislation detailing the size of Marine detachments on ships, pay scales, enlistment terms, and retirement regulations.

24 August
Uniforms
The Secretary of War prescribes the uniform for Marines: blue coats with red lapels.

1798

9 April
Force Structure
The Secretary of War recommends to Congress the raising of an additional "regiment of infantry . . . to act in the double capacity of Marines and Infantry."

30 April
Department of the Navy
Congress establishes a separate Department of the Navy to handle naval affairs.

28 May
Quasi War
The Quasi War with France officially begins when President John Adams instructs commanders of armed ships of the United States to make reprisals upon the commerce of France.

30 June
Manpower
At the end of the government's fiscal year, Marine strength stands at 25 officers and 58 enlisted.

11 July
Force Structure
President John Adams signs an act "Establishing and Organizing a Marine Corps," giving the Corps an institutional footing.

12 July
Commandants
The President commissions William Ward Burrows as a major and second Commandant of the Marine Corps.

20 November
Guadeloupe
The French frigates *L'Insurgente* and *Volontaire* force the outgunned Navy schooner *Retaliation* and her Marines to surrender. She is the only ship lost by the United States in the Quasi War.

1799

3 February
Martinique
Marines on board frigate *United States* assist in sinking the French privateer *L'Amour de la Patrie* off the island of Martinique.

9 February
Caribbean
Frigate *Constellation* and her Marines defeat the French frigate *L'Insurgente* off the island of Nevis.

2 March
Manpower
President John Adams approves legislation raising the strength of the Marine Corps to one major, 40 other officers, and 1,044 enlisted.

30 June
Manpower
The actual size of the Marine Corps is 25 officers and 343 enlisted.

18 October
Guadeloupe
Marines participate in the action between the revenue cutter *Pickering* and the French privateer *L'Egypt Conquise* off Guadeloupe.

30 December
Guadeloupe
Frigate *Connecticut* and her Marines engage the French privateer *L'Italie Conquise* off the island of Guadeloupe.

Opposite: *The artist executed this 1988 portrait of the first Commandant based on a known likeness. It replaced an earlier one done without research.* ("Samuel Nicholas," Col Donna Neary, USMCR, Marine Corps Art Collection)

Right: "American Merchant Ship Planter vs French Privateer," Marine Corps Art Collection

MAJOR DANIEL CARMICK

Daniel Carmick was born in Philadelphia in 1772 and appointed a lieutenant in the recently revived Marine Corps on 5 May 1798. He commanded the Marine detachment of *Ganges*, the first ship of the new United States Navy to go to sea, and won a quick promotion to captain in August as the fledgling Corps expanded to man the burgeoning fleet. In May 1799 he took command of the 50 Marines of USS *Constitution*.

A year later, during the Quasi War with France, Carmick led half his detachment in a foray under command of Navy Lieutenant Isaac Hull. Their objective was to seize the French corvette *Sandwich* hiding in a harbor in Santo Domingo. *Constitution* drew too much water to enter, so her captain commandeered a merchant ship. Hull and Carmick secreted their men below decks, sailed into the harbor, and drew alongside the unwary enemy. The Marines "went on board like devils" and took control of the ship in minutes. Surprise was so complete that Carmick and his men immediately rowed ashore, seized the over-watching Spanish fort, and spiked the guns, all without a shot. Then the sailors and Marines had to wait the rest of the day and night, prepared to repel boarders, until the wind and tide allowed them to sail the prize out to sea.

Carmick's reputation for audacity took him on a far different mission at home later that year. The Commandant, Major William Ward Burrows, was dismayed that a Marine lieutenant had been struck by a Navy officer. Burrows wrote the young officer and told him to challenge the

Opposite: *The Marine detachment of* Constitution *awaits its new commander in Boston. ("Captain Carmick Arrives for Inspection," Col Charles Waterhouse, USMCR (Ret), Marine Corps Art Collection)*

Right: *Marines and sailors seize a French privateer. ("Cutting Out of the* Sandwich," *Col Charles Waterhouse, USMCR (Ret), Marine Corps Art Collection)*

offending party to a duel to uphold the honor of the Corps, citing the experience of another Marine lieutenant who had shot an insolent Navy officer—"afterwards Politeness was restored." The Commandant also added that he had assigned Carmick "to call on you and be your Friend. He is a Man of Spirit, and will take care of you." The ensuing challenge and Carmick's backing brought forth an apology without a duel.

During the Barbary Wars, Carmick headed the detachment in the flagship *Chesapeake* in 1802, but saw no action. His lasting memory of the campaign was the aftermath of yet another pistol duel between Marine and Navy officers. This time a Leatherneck captain upheld his honor and that of the Corps at the cost of his life, and Carmick was "obliged to see a Brother Officer's heart cut out, that I might certify that the Ball had passed through the center of it."

In 1804 Carmick and 100 Marines helped establish U.S. authority over the just-acquired Louisiana Purchase. He remained there in command of all Marines around New Orleans, rising to the rank of major in 1809 when his force grew to 300 men. There were occasional clashes with Spanish troops from Texas and Florida, with Indians, and with pirates. In September 1814, while most American servicemen were preoccupied with the war against Britain, Carmick led his Marines and some Army reinforcements against the pirate stronghold of Barataria. They cleaned it out and burned it to the ground.

The War of 1812 came to Louisiana that December in the form of a British fleet and 9,000 soldiers. Carmick and his men participated in a spoiling attack on the night of 23 December by General Andrew Jackson's small army; it caught the British advance guard by surprise and mauled it. The invaders probed Jackson's formidable defensive line five days later and were repulsed with significant losses. The Americans suffered just 17 casualties, but one of them was Carmick, who must have exposed himself above the defensive works. He lay in a New Orleans hospital when Jackson's force resoundingly defeated the main British assault in January. The Marine major never fully recovered from his wounds and died in 1816. His New Orleans tomb bears the inscription: "Where shall we find such another?"

1800

1 February
Guadeloupe
Marines on board *Constellation* assist in defeating the French frigate *La Vengeance* off Guadeloupe. The French ship escapes in the night, but is run aground to avoid sinking.

31 March
Washington, D.C.
Marines arrive in Washington, D.C., to establish a Marine Barracks and guard the Navy Yard there.

22 April
Commandants
Congress authorizes the rank of Lieutenant Colonel Commandant for the head of the Marine Corps.

1 May
Commandants
Commandant William Ward Burrows becomes the first Marine promoted to lieutenant colonel.

11 May
Santo Domingo
At Puerto Plata, Santo Domingo, Captain Daniel Carmick and Marines and sailors from the frigate *Constitution* use the sloop *Sally* to capture *Sandwich* from the French. The Marines then land and spike the guns of a shore battery to permit a clean escape.

17 June
Guadeloupe
Marines participate in the action between the schooner *Enterprise* and the French privateer *La Cygne* off Guadeloupe.

30 June
Manpower
The Marine Corps has 38 officers and 487 enlisted on duty.

4 July
Marine Band
The Marine Band makes its first appearance in public at Tun Tavern in Philadelphia.

9 July
Guadeloupe
Enterprise and her Marines capture the French privateer *L'Aigle* off Guadeloupe.

15 July
HQMC
Lieutenant Colonel Commandant Burrows and his staff arrive in Washington, D.C., and establish a temporary headquarters in Georgetown.

23 July
Caribbean
Marine musket fire helps decide the battle between *Enterprise* and the French privateer *Le Flambeau* off Nevis Island.

1 September
Caribbean
The schooner *Experiment* and her Marines engage the French privateer *Le Deux Amis* off St. Bartholomew, West Indies.

13 September
Caribbean
Marines participate in the fighting between *Experiment* and the French privateer *La Diana* north of St. Bartholomew.

23–24 September
Caribbean
The sloop *Patapsco* bombards protective forts (recently captured by French troops) in the harbor of Willemstad, Curacao, then her Marines land

and assist Dutch forces defending the town against the French invasion.

12 October
Atlantic
Marines on board the frigate *Boston* assist in defeating the French corvette *Le Berceau* in the Atlantic Ocean. Neither ship was aware that a peace agreement recently had been signed between the two nations.

1801

1 January
Marine Band
The Marine Band plays for the first New Year's reception held at the White House in Washington.

3 February
Quasi War
The treaty ending the Quasi War with France is ratified by the U.S. Senate.

3 March
Marine Barracks 8th and I
Congress appropriates $20,000 to build a Marine Barracks in Washington. The site is chosen within the month and purchased by June.

MARINE BARRACKS 8TH AND I

The history of the Marine Barracks in Washington, D.C., is entwined with that of the national capital itself. When the federal government first moved to Washington from Philadelphia in 1800, Lieutenant Colonel Commandant Burrows and his small headquarters soon followed on 15 July. Since the city itself was being built largely from scratch, accommodations were hard to come by. Burrows and his few staff officers initially worked and lived together in a private residence in Georgetown, but he made it clear: "I care not for myself where my house is, so I can get my men comfortably provided for."

The enlisted Marines and their officers arrived soon after and first set up camp on a hill in Georgetown. After a period in another bivouac site in Washington itself, they moved into winter quarters in a rented building. Newly sworn-in President Thomas Jefferson took a keen interest in permanently settling his Marines. On 31 March 1801, Burrows recorded: "I have been all this morning engaged riding with the President looking for a proper place to fix the Marine Barracks on." The two men had focused their attention in the southeast quadrant of the city, between Capitol Hill and the new Navy Yard along what would later be named the Anacostia River. They settled on a plot bounded by 8th, 9th, G, and I Streets. It had to be purchased from a private owner at a cost of $6,247.18.

Congress already had approved $20,000 and plans for the new facility, so work quickly got underway. The contemplated barracks for 500 men and officers, plus a residence for the Commandant, was projected to cost $50,000.

The Secretary of the Navy assumed the difference would be made up by the labor of the Marines themselves, and so it was. Spurred on by an extra ration of rum per day, the men toiled at construction instead of drill. They were assisted by contractors, but the efforts of the latter did not satisfy the new Commandant, Lieutenant Colonel Wharton. He accepted the southern wing of the barracks and the Center House officers' quarters in early 1804, but the northern half of the barracks had to be taken down and rebuilt. Congress appropriated an additional $11,000 to complete the complex. The northern wing and the Commandant's house were finished around the end of 1805. The layout at that time consisted of the two-story Center House flanked by one-story barracks buildings on the 8th Street side of the lot, with the Commandant's house along G Street. Ancillary buildings housing Headquarters Marine Corps and other functions completed the perimeter of the square.

While the Commandant's residence was built with especially thick walls that have stood the test of time, the remainder of the buildings fell into poor condition by the end of the century. The offices of Headquarters Marine Corps moved out in 1901 to a building on New York Avenue. A band hall and other support facilities were completed about this time and temporarily pressed into service as barracks space while the old living quarters were demolished. New barracks went up soon after along 9th Street. The last of the current buildings around the parade deck were the quarters for senior officers built along 8th Street and completed in 1908. A new Center House in that location still serves as a gathering place for the officers of the post.

The Marine Barracks has performed a number of functions in its long history. In addition to being the home of Headquarters Marine Corps for almost a century, it early on served as the primary training ground for new officers and men. It also frequently has provided expeditionary forces in wartime. Captain Miller, the Adjutant of the Marine Corps, led the men of the Barracks into the Battle of Bladensburg in 1814. Commandant Henderson went off to Florida for the Seminole Wars, leaving behind just 16 men and the Marine Band. Subsequent organized detachments from the Barracks fought in the Mexican War, the Civil War, the Spanish-American War, and even Desert Storm.

Today, the Marines of 8th and I perform three major roles. Since 1920 they have operated the Marine Corps Institute, which educates Marines in a wide range of professional subjects via correspondence courses. The Silent Drill Platoon and the other Marines of the Barracks also perform ceremonial functions from the Evening Parades to funerals at Arlington National Cemetery. And all stand ready to play their part in providing a provisional infantry battalion if the need arises in war, just as their predecessors have done throughout the 200-year history of the "Oldest Post of the Corps."

Opposite: *"Placing the Barracks," Col Charles Waterhouse, USMCR (Ret), Marine Corps Art Collection*

Above: *The Commandant's house as it appears today. (Eric Long)*

31 March
Marine Barracks 8th and I
Lieutenant Colonel Commandant Burrows records, "I have been all this morning engaged in riding with the President [Thomas Jefferson] looking for a proper place to fix the Marine Barracks on."

14 May
Barbary Wars
Tripoli declares war on the United States, marking the formal beginning of the Barbary Wars.

21 June
Marine Barracks 8th and I
The government purchases land at the corner of 8th and I Streets in Washington, D.C., for $6,247.18 for a site for the Marine Barracks.

30 June
Manpower
The strength of the Marine Corps on active duty is 38 officers and 319 enlisted.

1 August
Tripoli
Enterprise forces the Tripolitan ship *Tripoli* to surrender after a three-hour cannonade. Marines play an important role by sweeping the enemy decks with musket fire whenever the corsair approached to board.

4 August
Marine Band
The Marine Band plays at the first inaugural parade in Washington, D.C.

29 September
Tripoli
Frigates *Philadelphia* and *Essex* and their Marines battle two gunboats near Tripoli.

1802

30 January
Budget
The Secretary of the Navy reports that the annual expense of the Marine Corps is $99,109.23.

30 June
Manpower
The strength of the Marine Corps on active duty is 29 officers and 330 enlisted.

22 July
Tripoli
Constellation and her Marines engage nine gunboats off the coast of Tripoli.

1803

9 May
Tripoli
Marines participate in the action between frigate *John Adams* and seven gunboats off Tripoli.

2 June
Tripoli
Marines and sailors from the U.S. blockading squadron land on shore in a bay near Tripoli to drive off defending soldiers while other Americans burn 10 small enemy cargo ships.

30 June
Manpower
The strength of the Marine Corps on active duty is 25 officers and 317 enlisted.

31 October
Tripoli
Frigate *Philadelphia* runs aground while pursuing a small cargo ship and surrenders when surrounded by Tripolitan gunboats. Her crew and Marines are imprisoned and the ship brought into the harbor after a storm floats her off the sandbar.

23 December
Tripoli
Enterprise and her Marines capture the ketch *Mastico*, renamed *Intrepid*, off the coast of Tripoli.

1804

16 February
Tripoli
Navy Lieutenant Stephen Decatur, 52 sailors, and eight Marines (led by Sergeant Solomon Wren) use *Intrepid* to enter Tripoli Harbor during the night and burn the captured *Philadelphia*.

7 March
Commandants
Lieutenant Colonel Burrows resigns as Commandant for health reasons.

1 April
Commandants
Captain Franklin Wharton is named the Lieutenant Colonel Commandant. He is the third Commandant of the Marine Corps.

30 June
Manpower
The strength of the Marine Corps on active duty is 25 officers and 364 enlisted.

3 August
Tripoli
As the U.S. squadron bombards the forts at Tripoli Harbor, four gunboats under command of Captain Stephen Decatur attack 11 Tripolitan boats. In close quarters fighting with muskets and cutlasses, the Americans capture three of the boats and inflict nearly 100 casualties among the enemy at a cost of one dead (Decatur's brother) and three wounded.

Right: *Marines help man 24-pounder long guns during the August 1804 sea bombardment of forts guarding Tripoli Harbor. ("Marines at the Great Guns," Col Charles Waterhouse, USMCR (Ret), Marine Corps Art Collection)*

LIEUTENANT PRESLEY N. O'BANNON

Presley O'Bannon was born on the large family homestead in Fauquier County, Virginia, sometime between 1776 and 1784. His father, William, had served as an army captain in the Revolutionary War and a maternal uncle had been a general. In 1801 the young man took a commission as a second lieutenant in the Marine Corps and also married Matilda Heard, a granddaughter of Revolutionary War hero General Daniel Morgan. O'Bannon would more than live up to his ancestral heritage.

The new lieutenant deployed to the Mediterranean Sea in 1802 on the frigate *Adams*. He and his ship spent most of the first months overseas blockading a Tripolitan warship at Gibraltar. His fellow officers found him a pleasant companion; when time dragged heavy, he would entertain them with his fiddle, playing songs such as "Hogs in the Cornfield." Even after they rejoined the squadron, there was little action under a relatively unaggressive commodore. O'Bannon's only brush with battle came in June 1803 when his ship and others sent forces inshore to burn Tripolitan merchant ships. He ended the cruise in late 1803 as a first lieutenant.

Transferred to frigate *President* the following year, he sailed again to the Mediterranean. One of the passengers was William Eaton, a former diplomat now on a mission to open a new front in the war with Tripoli. The young Marine officer was impressed by Eaton's boldness, and the respect was apparently mutual. When the ship arrived in North African waters, Eaton shifted to the brig *Argus*, and O'Bannon transferred as well to take command of the Marine detachment on that ship. Soon after, they went ashore in Egypt and launched their audacious expedition to overthrow the bashaw of Tripoli.

The close bond between the two Americans, and O'Bannon's own sense of duty and daring, came through at Bomba. Eaton's shaky army had endured considerable hardship and turmoil up to that point, and the teetering coalition hardly seemed capable of attacking and defeating an entrenched, superior force. The commodore of the U.S. squadron clearly expressed his own lack of confidence when he refused to provide any American reinforcements and in fact claimed that he needed the handful of Marines with Eaton back on the ships. O'Bannon stayed ashore and sent out a note to the captain of *Argus*: "Unwilling to abandon an expedition this far conducted, I have to request your permission to continue." The brig's commanding officer did not enforce the commodore's will. That decision was important, because the determination and discipline of O'Bannon and his seven Marines made all the difference a few days later at Derna.

Following the campaign against Tripoli, *Argus* and O'Bannon sailed back to the United States in 1806. The Virginia legislature had voted a richly designed ceremonial sword for its courageous native son in December 1805, but it was not presented to him until 1811. In the meantime, he had resigned his commission in 1807. Although there has been speculation that O'Bannon was upset at the lack of a brevet promotion or other recognition for his efforts, no one really knows why he left the Marine Corps. Soon after, he moved to Kentucky where members of his family ran a successful distillery business. O'Bannon eventually entered politics, served in the Kentucky legislature for a number of years, and died at the age of 74 in 1850.

This portrait of Lieutenant Presley O'Bannon, painted by a former editor of the Marine Corps Gazette, *was presented to the Basic School by the Warrant Officer Class of 1960. ("Lieutenant Presley O'Bannon," Donald L. Dickson, Marine Corps Art Collection)*

Legend has it that the Mameluke sword carried by Marine officers today was patterned after one given to O'Bannon by Hamet, the former Bashaw of Tripoli. In reality, the Mameluke-style sword first came into the Corps when the Marine quartermaster ordered a batch from England in 1825. Except for a brief period during and immediately following the Civil War, it has remained the sword of Marine officers ever since.

29 November
Derna
Lt Presley N. O'Bannon, former consul William Eaton, and seven Marines land at Alexandria, Egypt, with the objective of leading an assault against Tripoli in conjunction with the bashaw's brother.

1805
---

8 March
Derna
Presley O'Bannon and his landing party, reinforced by several hundred Greek and Arab mercenaries, start the 600-mile trek to Tripoli.

27 April
Derna
Supported by American warships, O'Bannon and his force storm and capture the fortress town of Derna, in western Tripoli. Two Marines are killed, and Eaton and one Marine are wounded.

13 May
Derna
O'Bannon and his Marines help repel an assault against Derna by 1,200 Tripolitan soldiers.

28 May
Derna
O'Bannon leads a small force in a spoiling attack against Tripolitan forces camped outside Derna.

4 June
Barbary Wars
Tripoli signs a peace treaty with the United States.

12 June
Derna
Marines cover the seaborne withdrawal of Eaton's force from Derna.

30 June
Manpower
Marines on active duty are 22 officers and 556 enlisted.

1806
---

30 June
Manpower
Marines on active duty are 11 officers and 307 enlisted.

15 August
Gibraltar
Marines participate in an action between *Enterprise* and Spanish gunboats in the Straits of Gibraltar.

27 October
New Orleans
The Secretary of the Navy directs the Commandant to send four officers and 74 enlisted Marines to New Orleans to replace a sickly force and defend against possible Spanish operations.

1807
---

22 June
Virginia
Marines are on board the frigate *Chesapeake* off Chesapeake Bay when she is attacked by the British frigate *Leopard* searching for Royal Navy deserters.

30 June
Manpower
Marines on active duty are 11 officers and 392 enlisted.

1808
---

8 May
South Carolina
A Marine Barracks is established at Charleston, South Carolina.

30 June
Manpower
The strength of the Marine Corps on active duty is 11 officers and 861 enlisted.

1809

3 March
Manpower
Congress authorizes an increase in the Marine Corps to 46 officers and 1,823 enlisted. The period of enlistment is changed from three years to five.

4 March
Marine Band
The Marine Band plays for the first Inaugural Ball held in Washington, D.C., for President Jefferson.

30 June
Manpower
The strength of the Marine Corps on active duty is 10 officers and 513 enlisted.

1810

24 June
Bahamas
Brig *Vixen* and her Marines are fired upon in the night by the British sloop *Moselle*. The British captain claims he thought the American warship was a French privateer, and he apologizes.

30 June
Manpower
The strength of the Marine Corps on active duty is nine officers and 440 enlisted.

7 October
Civil Support
Marines from the sloop *Wasp* assist in fighting fires in Charleston, South Carolina.

1811

4 May
Florida
Marines establish a post at Cumberland Island, off the southeast coast of Georgia, to deal with smuggling from Spanish Florida.

16 May
Atlantic
In search of an impressed American seaman, frigate *President* and her Marines engage the British sloop *Little Belt* off the east coast of the United States. The smaller British ship loses nine killed and 23 wounded in the night action, which further heightens tensions between the two nations.

THE DERNA CAMPAIGN

Early in 1805, *Argus* sailed to Egypt with William Eaton, the former consul to nearby Tunis. His mission was to find Hamet, the previous bashaw of Tripoli, who had been deposed by his brother. Eaton took along Lieutenant O'Bannon, seven enlisted Marines, and a midshipman. The party tracked down their quarry in chaotic Egypt and enlisted him in a bold scheme to overthrow the current bashaw and end the war with Tripoli. The Marine lieutenant then recruited a force of several dozen western mercenaries (from a number of countries) to reinforce 100 Arab soldiers under Hamet. Along with Eaton and a retinue of camel drivers, the tiny army set out across the North African desert on 8 March 1805. Once on the march, Eaton's outfit was swelled by another few hundred Arabs willing to fight for a fee.

Water was scarce, food ran low, the sun broiled, rumors of growing enemy opposition repeatedly surfaced, and tensions flared between the disparate groups. The polyglot expedition nearly fell apart almost every day, with camel drivers, Arab horsemen, or the mercenaries taking turns demanding additional pay or threatening to desert when the going seemed to get the roughest. O'Bannon and his Marines provided the backbone that repeatedly held the force together.

Possibly the worst moment came on 15 April when the army straggled into the Bay of Bomba, where Eaton had promised that the U.S. Navy would provide fresh supplies and reinforcements. There were no ships. The next morning, as the various contingents prepared to abandon the enterprise, *Argus* came over the horizon with food and preserved the shaky alliance one more time. But the commodore refused to lend any of his other Marines.

The army departed Bomba on 23 April and reached the hills above Derna on the evening of the 25th. The 600-mile march was finally at an end. The 800 defenders and their nine artillery pieces outnumbered and outgunned Eaton's force, which would have to attack across an open plain against a fort and a line of breastworks on the eastern edge of the city. The former consul made one last attempt at diplomacy, sending in a note that offered the city's governor the chance to continue in office under Hamet if he did not fight. The governor's bold reply presaged a tough battle: "My head or yours."

Three U.S. Navy ships arrived off Derna over the next two days. They put ashore two heavy guns, but Eaton could get only one to the front in time for the attack on the afternoon of 27 April. Hamet took most of the Arabs around to the southern flank of the city, O'Bannon led a force of about 60 men against the eastern defenses, and the ships bombarded the fort. Heavy fire initially checked O'Bannon's wing, but Eaton called for a charge. The Marines led the way, the western mercenaries followed, and the defenders cracked at the sight of bayonet-tipped muskets rushing toward them. Eaton was hit in the arm, and three Marines went down, but O'Bannon kept the remainder moving right through the breastworks and into the fort itself. There he raised the U.S. flag over foreign soil for the first time (as opposed to the first raising of the Stars and Stripes of the Continental government at New Providence, Bahamas, in 1778). Meanwhile, Hamet's force captured the governor's palace on the opposite side of town. The formerly bold governor sought refuge in a harem. At a cost of two dead Marines (Privates

John Witten and Edward Steward), Eaton had placed the bashaw's rule in jeopardy. A larger Tripolitan army tried to retake the town during the next few weeks, but failed.

On 3 June, the bashaw held on to his throne by signing a peace treaty with the United States and freeing the crew of *Philadelphia*. The news arrived by sea at Derna on 11 June. In a well-planned operation, Eaton, O'Bannon, Hamet, and the reliable elements of the force withdrew with the fleet, and the Barbary Wars came to an end.

Reinforced by a handful of mercenaries and Arab soldiers, William Eaton, Lt Presley O'Bannon, and seven enlisted Marines storm the fortress at Derna. Their victory forces an end to the war with Tripoli on U.S. terms. ("Attack on Derna," Col Charles Waterhouse, USMCR (Ret), Marine Corps Art Collection)

17 March
Marine Barracks 8th and I
The Marine Corps establishes its reputation for frugality by completing the Marine Barracks complex in Washington, D.C., for $5,571.16 less than the amount appropriated by Congress.

18 March
Florida
In order to prevent the British from taking over Florida, U.S. Marines and soldiers support an advance by "patriots" (unofficial militiamen) across the St. Mary's River into Spanish-controlled Florida.

18 June
War of 1812
The War of 1812 begins when Congress passes and President James Madison signs a declaration of war against Great Britain.

30 June
Manpower
Despite having an authorized strength of 1,869, the number of Marines on active duty consists of just 10 officers and 483 enlisted.

13 August
Atlantic
Marines participate in frigate *Essex*'s defeat of the British sloop *Alert*.

19 August
Atlantic
In the Atlantic Ocean east of Boston, *Constitution* and her Marines defeat British frigate *Guerriere*, which is so badly damaged the Americans scuttle it the next day.

12 September
Florida
While escorting a wagon convoy in Florida, Marines drive off an ambushing Indian force at a cost of two dead and six wounded.

18 October
Atlantic
The 17 Marines on sloop *Wasp* help defeat the British sloop *Frolic* southwest of Bermuda. Later that same day the American warship, as it tends to the battered *Frolic*, is captured by British ship of the line *Poictiers*.

25 October
Atlantic
Near Africa, *United States* defeats British frigate *Macedonian*, but entirely by long-range firepower, thus leaving little role for the Marines to play.

28 November
Canada
Marines and sailors join Army troops in capturing the British fort at Red House, Canada.

29 December
Atlantic
Constitution and her Marines defeat the British frigate *Java* off Brazil.

1813

9 February
Florida
Marines and soldiers destroy two Indian towns in east Florida that were home to those who had ambushed the wagon convoy in September 1812.

24 February
Atlantic
Marines assist the sloop *Hornet* in defeating and sinking the British brig *Peacock* off the coast of British Guiana.

16 April
Florida
Marines participate in the Army-Navy expedition to Mobile, but the Spanish defenders surrender without a fight in the face of superior strength.

27 May
Canada
Marines from the Lake Ontario squadron participate with an Army regiment in a landing on the Canadian shore and the subsequent seizure of Fort George.

1 June
Massachusetts
Chesapeake is defeated by British frigate *Shannon* off Boston. The American Marine force of 44 officers and men suffers losses of 14 killed and 20 wounded in close combat with British boarders.

22 June
Virginia
Fifty Marines from *Constellation* reinforce the fort on Craney Island, Virginia, guarding Norfolk Navy Yard and assist in repelling a British amphibious assault.

LIEUTENANT COLONEL JOHN GAMBLE

John Marshall Gamble came from a thoroughly military family. His father had served as a major in the Revolutionary War and his three brothers would all die while on active service with the U.S. Navy. He was born in New Jersey around 1790 and received his commission in the Marine Corps in July 1809. Two years later he took charge of the Marine detachment on frigate *Essex* under the command of Captain David Porter. Gamble and his 31 Marines were the first Leathernecks to see action in the War of 1812, participating in *Essex*'s defeat of a British ship two months after the conflict began. The fame of Porter, Gamble, and *Essex* was yet to come, but the Marine officer almost missed it. On a subsequent combat cruise, following orders to return "that night" with a boatload of provisions from the Brazilian coast, Gamble and a Navy lieutenant braved a severe storm and were tossed into the sea. The two men kept afloat for hours and swam to the ship before daylight.

Porter sailed *Essex* around Cape Horn and into the South Pacific in February 1813. He devastated the British whaling fleet there and turned two prizes into warships. In an unprecedented mark of confidence, Gamble received command of *Greenwich*. He upheld Porter's judgment on 14 July by defeating the 14-gun *Seringapatam* with astute tactical handling of his own small ship. In October, Porter took his little fleet of warships and prizes to Nukuhiva in the Marquesas Islands (far southeast of Hawaii) to refit them. The Navy officer took an interest in tribal politics, helping one group defeat another, and then subjugating a third unfriendly faction. In December Porter sailed with his two largest warships and the richest prize, leaving

Gamble with *Greenwich* and three smaller whalers. The Marine lieutenant had a force of 18 men and six prisoners. His orders were to guard the base for five months, then depart for the States with the two largest ships if Porter had not returned.

Trouble began almost immediately with the much more numerous natives. Gamble had to forcibly recover supplies stolen from his encampment, then maintain a continuous guard with his tiny force. The Marine officer was "amiable, gentle, yet firm," but nevertheless discipline was difficult to maintain as many of the men routinely gave the local women some of the limited food supplies. His force dwindled after one man drowned and four others who had been punished deserted in a small boat. As time came to depart the island, disaffection grew among the prisoners and a few of their captors.

The Englishmen incited a mutiny on *Seringapatam* and subdued Gamble and two midshipmen, shooting the Marine in the heel in the melee. At sea that night, the three were placed in a leaky boat, but they managed to make it back to Nukuhiva and rejoin the few loyal men still there. A battle with the islanders, who tried to take advantage of the weakened force, resulted in a loss of four more men. At one point in the fight, Gamble hobbled from cannon to cannon firing them alone to cover the rescue of a wounded man.

With only three of the eight men fit for duty, no charts, and a damaged ship, Gamble's force nevertheless sailed to the Hawaiian Islands over the next three weeks. Having secured food and needed equipment from friendly natives there, his plans for the next leg of the journey were dashed when the British warship *Cherub*

captured him and his band. He was detained until the war was over and did not make it back to the United States until August 1815. He spent his first day in America writing a lengthy report to the Secretary of the Navy that closed: "I arrived here last evening, and have the honour to wait either the orders of the Navy Department or of the Commandant of the Marine Corps." Gamble served the rest of his career uneventfully as a barracks commander and died on active duty as a lieutenant colonel in 1836.

Opposite: *"John Gamble, Equestrian," Anthony Lewis DeRose, Marine Corps Art Collection*

Below: *"Gamble at Nukuhiva," Col Charles Waterhouse, USMCR (Ret), Marine Corps Art Collection*

Opposite: *On board* Lawrence *at Lake Erie. ("Marines to the Rigging," Col Charles Waterhouse, USMCR (Ret), Marine Corps Art Collection)*

Left: *"Battle of Plattsburgh, Lake Champlain, 1814,"* Edward Tufnell, Navy Art Collection

Below: *"Battle of Lake Erie,"* William H. Powell, Courtesy of the U.S. Capitol

30 June
Manpower
The strength of the Marine Corps on active duty is 12 officers and 579 enlisted.

14 July
Pacific
Marine Lieutenant John Gamble, captain of the prize *Greenwich*, defeats the British armed whaler *Seringapatam* near the Galapagos Islands.

31 July
Canada
Marines and soldiers land at York and burn British barracks, naval stores, and public buildings.

14 August
Ireland
Argus and her Marines are defeated and captured by the British ship *Pelican* off the coast of Ireland.

4 September
Maine
The Marines of *Enterprise* assist in her victory over the British brig *Boxer* in the waters near Maine.

10 September
Lake Erie
Marines participate in Commodore Oliver Hazard Perry's complete victory over the British fleet on Lake Erie, thus gaining permanent control of the western Great Lakes.

24 October
Marine Barracks, Portsmouth
The Marine Barracks is established at Portsmouth Navy Yard, New Hampshire.

24 December
Marquesas
Lieutenant John Gamble leads a handful of Marines and sailors in a show of force to restore order on the Island of Nukuhiva in the Marquesas, which was serving as the base for Captain David Porter's small Pacific squadron.

1814

28 March
Chile
Essex and her Marines are defeated and captured by the British frigate *Phoebe* and the sloop *Cherub* in Chilean coastal waters.

BATTLE OF BLADENSBURG

With the end of the Napoleonic Wars in the spring of 1814, the British suddenly had substantial additional forces to throw into the fray in North America. While their primary interest remained Canada and New England, they sent major forces to attack the mid-Atlantic coast and New Orleans. General Robert Ross landed about 4,000 men on the banks of the Patuxent River off Chesapeake Bay in August. His initial target was Washington, D.C. Brigadier General Henry Winder mustered almost 6,500 soldiers (mainly militia) to defend the national capital. Winder himself was not a professional officer, and most of his units came together for the first time on the battlefield, many of them after days of hard marching in hot, humid weather.

The two forces came to grips on 26 August near Bladensburg, Maryland, where a bridge crossed over what is now the Anacostia River at a point northeast of Washington. Winder's men were arrayed more or less in three lines near the road ascending up the slope from the river. The three formations did not mutually support each other, there were almost no defensive works, and Winder gave them no plan of action.

Commodore Joshua Barney was ordered at the last minute to support Winder with roughly 400 sailors, 114 Marines under command of Captain Samuel Miller, and five artillery pieces. The naval contingent arrived as the battle was underway, and the men ran to join the middle of the third line, occupying a small hillock near the road. The Marines were on the left of Barney's position, the guns in the center, and sailors acting as infantry were on the right. Militiamen were off to the left of Barney and a body of regular soldiers to the right.

The British attacked across the shallow river and suffered some casualties from two artillery pieces in the first American line, but the militia soon pulled back in the face of the enemy's determined charge. Winder's second line momentarily checked the British thrust with musket fire, then an American regiment counterattacked and temporarily drove back the invaders. As a second British brigade crossed the river and began to envelop the second line, and frightening (but not particularly dangerous) Congreve rockets soared overhead, most of these American units broke and fled. Winder ordered his counterattacking force to withdraw, but too late for them to do so in good order.

Flushed with relatively easy success, Ross's soldiers moved boldly up the road. Barney held his fire until they were close, then unleashed grape shot from a heavy cannon. In the words of his subsequent report, that "completely cleared the road." The British recoiled, then charged twice, each time being turned back by artillery and musket fire from the naval contingent. The fourth time the enemy worked to the flanks, at which point the American forces there, which had not yet been engaged, withdrew hastily after a few volleys. With his ammunition almost exhausted, on the verge of being surrounded, and men now falling steadily to British sharpshooters, the commodore ordered his tiny force to retire from the field. Barney himself had already had his horse shot from under him and then been hit in the thigh; he was forced to remain behind. Captain Miller also had received a severe wound in the arm. Twelve other Marines were wounded, one killed, and two captured.

Afterward the British swept into Washington and burned all the public buildings, to include

"Final Stand at Bladensburg," Col Charles Waterhouse, USMCR (Ret), Marine Corps Art Collection

the Capitol and the White House. The Commandant's House and the Marine Barracks were spared, and legend has credited Ross's respect for the fighting spirit of the Marines at Bladensburg. While probably apocryphal—British forces never approached that part of the city—Ross did say later that Barney's Marines and sailors "have given us our only real fighting."

29 April
Atlantic

Marines participate in sloop *Peacock*'s defeat of the British warship *Epervier* in the Atlantic.

12 June
Maryland

Captain Samuel Miller leads a small battalion of Marines from Washington, D.C., to reinforce American units guarding the approaches to the capital along the Patuxent River.

26 June
Maryland

Marines assist Captain Joshua Barney's gunboat fleet in driving off a British attack in the Patuxent River.

28 June
Atlantic

Marines play a conspicuous role in sloop *Wasp*'s victory over the British warship *Reindeer*, repelling an attempt to board and then sweeping the enemy

decks with musket fire as American sailors counterattacked onto the British ship.

30 June
Manpower

The strength of the Marine Corps on active duty is 11 officers and 637 enlisted.

11 July
Atlantic

Brig *Rattlesnake* and her Marines are defeated and captured by the British frigate *Leander* in the Atlantic Ocean.

4 August
Lake Huron

Marines assist Lieutenant Colonel George Croghan's Army force in a landing against the British and Indians holding Fort Mackinac on Lake Huron. The Americans are forced to withdraw after significant losses.

24 August
Bladensburg

Captain Samuel Miller's force of 103 Marines and Barney's sailors beat back three British assaults during the closing stages of the Battle of Bladensburg in Maryland. The British subsequently occupy and burn Washington, D.C.

1 September
Virginia

Marines and sailors at White House, Virginia, fire artillery at British warships withdrawing down the Potomac River.

Top: *"Shipbuilding at Sackett's Harbor," Col Charles Waterhouse, USMCR (Ret), Marine Corps Art Collection*

Right: *"USS* Essex *vs HMS* Cherub *and HMS* Phoebe," *Marine Corps Art Collection*

Opposite, top: *"Wasp vs Reindeer," John Clymer, Marine Corps Art Collection*

Opposite, bottom: *"Christmas Day, 1814," Col Charles Waterhouse, USMCR (Ret), Marine Corps Art Collection*

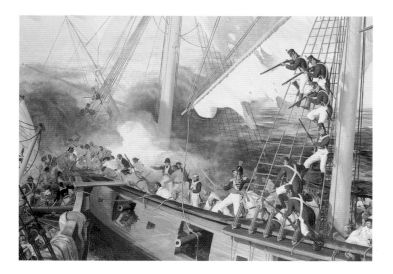

1 September
Atlantic
Wasp and her Marines sink the British sloop *Avon* in the Atlantic Ocean.

16 September
New Orleans
Marines and soldiers form the landing party that wipes out the pirate stronghold on Grand Terre Island at the mouth of the Mississippi River.

15 December
New Orleans
Marines serve aboard Navy Lieutenant Thomas Catesby Jones's small squadron of gunboats, which battle a larger British fleet of small craft and delay the enemy's advance on New Orleans.

22 December
Civil Support
Marines from the Portsmouth Barracks and *Congress* fight fires in Portsmouth, New Hampshire.

23 December
New Orleans
Marines aboard the schooner *Carolina* assist in the bombardment of the British camp a few miles below New Orleans, while a company of Marines participate in a night attack on the British force by elements of General Andrew Jackson's army.

24 December
War of 1812
The Treaty of Ghent is signed in Europe to bring the War of 1812 to an end. News of the peace is not received in the U.S. until much later.

27 December
New Orleans
Carolina duels with British shore batteries and is eventually sunk.

28 December
New Orleans
Marines with Andrew Jackson help repel a British probing attack against the defensive works along the Rodriguez Canal below New Orleans.

1815

8 January
New Orleans
Marines participate in Andrew Jackson's repulse of the British assault on his lines. The enemy lose more than 2,000 soldiers, while American forces suffer only 13 casualties.

15 January
New York
In a battle against a British squadron off Long Island, *President* and her Marines cripple the frigate *Endymion*, but suffer enough damage that they are forced to surrender to three other enemy frigates.

Opposite: *A re-created painting of the fifth Commandant, whose official portrait shows him as a much older man. Archibald Henderson took over leadership of the Marine Corps at 37 and served in that billet for 38 years. ("Archibald Henderson," Col Avery Chenoweth, USMCR (Ret), Marine Corps Art Collection)*

20 February
Atlantic
Marines on *Constitution* participate in her victory over the British sloops *Cyane* and *Levant* near Madeira Island.

3 March
Barbary Wars
President Madison signs legislation authorizing force against Algiers.

23 March
Atlantic
Sloop *Hornet* and her Marines defeat the British brig *Penguin* off Tristan d'Acunha.

17 June
Barbary Wars
Marines in Commodore Stephen Decatur's squadron assist in the defeat of the Algerian frigate *Mashuda*.

30 June
Barbary Wars
A treaty of peace is concluded with Algiers.

Manpower
The strength of the Marine Corps on active duty is eight officers and 680 enlisted.

1816

30 June
Manpower
The strength of the Marine Corps on active duty is 21 officers and 451 enlisted.

Top: *"Repulse of the Highlanders, New Orleans," Col Charles Waterhouse, USMCR (Ret), Marine Corps Art Collection*

Right: *"Defeat of the British Army at New Orleans," Heathe Laclotte, Marine Corps Art Collection*

27 July
Florida
Marines assist the crews of two gunboats in capturing and destroying a fort on the Apalachicola River in Florida, built by Indians and runaway slaves who had turned to piracy.

1817

3 March
Manpower
Congress passes the Peace Establishment Act, which sets the authorized strength of the Marine Corps at 50 officers and 942 enlisted.

30 June
Manpower
The strength of the Marine Corps on active duty is 14 officers and 652 enlisted.

23 December
Florida
Marine detachments from six Navy ships participate in a joint operation with the Army to seize Amelia Island, Florida, from pirates.

1818

30 June
Manpower
The strength of the Marine Corps on active duty is 24 officers and 536 enlisted.

19 August
Oregon
Sergeant McFadian and his Marines from the sloop *Ontario* help raise the flag along the Columbia River to strengthen the U.S. claim to the Oregon Territory.

1 September
Commandants
Lieutenant Colonel Commandant Franklin Wharton dies in office. Brevet Major Samuel Miller takes over as acting Commandant.

16 September
Commandants
Brevet Major Archibald Henderson takes over as acting Commandant.

1819

3 March
Commandants
Brevet Major Anthony Gale is appointed Lieutenant Colonel Commandant. He is the fourth Commandant of the Marine Corps.

30 June
Manpower
The strength of the Marine Corps on active duty is 21 officers and 664 enlisted.

1820

5–12 April
Slavery Suppression
Marines participate in the capture of seven slave-trading ships by the corvette *Cyane* off the coast of Africa.

30 June
Manpower
The strength of the Marine Corps on active duty is 19 officers and 552 enlisted.

30 August
Commandants
Lieutenant Colonel Commandant Gale is arrested for trial by court-martial, and Brevet Major Samuel Miller becomes acting Commandant.

16 October
Commandants
A general court-martial convicts Gale of conduct unbecoming an officer for his public drunkenness, and he is dismissed from the Corps on this date.

1821

2 January
Commandants
President Monroe appoints Brevet Major Archibald Henderson to be the Lieutenant Colonel Commandant. He is the fifth Commandant of the Marine Corps.

30 June
Manpower
The strength of the Marine Corps on active duty is 35 officers and 844 enlisted.

16 October
Cuba
Marines participate in the capture of five pirate ships by the brig *Enterprise* off Cuba.

21 December
Cuba
Enterprise and her Marines seize a pirate schooner off Cuba.

1822

8 March
Cuba
Marines and sailors from *Enterprise* land at Cape Antonio, Cuba, to pursue pirates.

June
Caribbean
Marines assist in the capture of two pirate schooners, *Shark* and *Grampus,* in the West Indies.

30 June
Manpower
The strength of the Marine Corps on active duty is 23 officers and 708 enlisted.

16 August
Caribbean
Grampus and her Marines engage the pirate brig *Palmyra* in the West Indies.

9 November
Cuba
Marines participate in the fight between schooner *Alligator* and several pirate schooners in the harbor of Matanzas, Cuba.

of the Spanish language acquired during his time in Pensacola. The Secretary of State also provided a letter of introduction to explorer John C. Fremont, who then was operating along the west coast of the continent. Fremont's father-in-law, Senator Thomas Hart Benton, entrusted a packet of family letters to the Marine.

Given the lack of cross-continental transport, Gillespie would have to go via Mexico, even though the United States was on the verge of war with that nation. He assumed the guise of a civilian merchant, sailed for Vera Cruz, and memorized and then destroyed the dispatch to Larkin. He made it by wagon to Mexico City and was waylaid there by a military coup. After more than a month's delay, he made his way overland to the Pacific coast, where he hitched a ride on a Navy sloop sailing for Hawaii (apparently to allay any Mexican suspicions). He finally arrived in Monterey, California, on 17 April 1846, and delivered his verbal message to Larkin. It was much tougher to make contact with Fremont, but Gillespie finally tracked him down near the Klamath River in the dangerous wilderness of northern California on 9 May.

By June, Fremont had recruited local Californians into a mounted battalion and made Gillespie his adjutant. Although Fremont was a brevet captain in the army engineers, Gillespie believed that the explorer had no experience as a line officer and that his own tactical knowledge would make all the difference in the subsequent campaign. His finest hour came in the battle at San Pascual in December, where he was wounded by lance thrusts, but managed to fire an artillery piece and thus help drive off the enemy.

Already a brevet captain for his early efforts in California, the Marine Corps made him a brevet major in July 1848 for his actions at San Pascual. He subsequently commanded various barracks detachments, but his service was interrupted by continuing poor health. Shortly after Gillespie was assigned to a shipboard detachment in 1854, the ship's captain charged him with swindling money. The major resigned rather than go through the ordeal of a court-martial. He retired to California and held various small government jobs until his death in 1873.

7 August
Mexico
A landing force of Marines and sailors in boats fails in an assault against Alvarado, Mexico, due to strong river currents and heavy enemy fire.

13 August
California
Marines and sailors, reinforced by volunteers, march into Los Angeles, California.

7 October
California
Frigate *Savannah*'s Marines reinforce sailors and a volunteer outfit under Gillespie. The combined force captures San Pedro, California.

8–9 October
California
Marines participate in the overland movement from San Pedro to retake Los Angeles, but the small expedition retires to San Pedro and its ships after small skirmishes.

23–26 October
Mexico
Commodore Matthew C. Perry uses Marines and sailors from his squadron to seize Frontera, Mexico, and then conduct a raid 70 miles up the Tabasco River to briefly capture the town of San Juan Bautista.

27 October
California
Marines from Commodore Stockton's squadron assist in retaking San Pedro. The town had been lost to Californians revolting against the small U.S. forces trying to hold the vast territory.

14 November
Mexico
Perry's Marines and sailors capture Tampico, Mexico.

19 November
Mexico
Marine Captain Alvin Edson leads 20 Marines and 12 sailors 80 miles upriver from Tampico to destroy enemy supplies.

6 December
California
Gillespie is wounded in the battle of San Pascual, California, in which a body of Californians engage Kearney's force of soldiers and volunteers.

11 December
California
Lieutenant Jacob Zeilin and Marines and sailors of Stockton's squadron march to the relief of Kearney.

21 December
Mexico
Perry sends ashore his ships detachments and sailors to raid the port of Carmen, Mexico.

29 December
California
Stockton leads a force of 600 men overland against Los Angeles, with the Marines of his squadron organized as a separate company under Zeilin.

1847

2 January
California
Captain Ward Marston and the Marines of sloop *Dale* defeat a force of Californians at Santa Clara.

8 January
California
Stockton's force defeats Californians in the Battle of San Gabriel.

Top: *Gillespie fights with Kearney's force against mounted Californians, resulting in a draw. ("San Pascual," Col Charles Waterhouse, USMCR (Ret), Marine Corps Art Collection)*

Right: *"Marston at Santa Clara," Col Charles Waterhouse, USMCR (Ret), Marine Corps Art Collection*

9 January
California
Marines participate in Stockton's victory over the Californians in the Battle of La Mesa.

10 January
California
Stockton retakes Los Angeles without fighting.

9 March
Mexico
The ships detachments of Connor's squadron form a battalion that lands at Vera Cruz, Mexico, as part of Brigadier General William Worth's division of General Winfield Scott's army. The Marines participate in the siege of the city, which surrenders on 29 March.

17 November
Okinawa
Sloop *Vincennes* sends Marines and seamen ashore on Okinawa to enforce treaty provisions.

1855

19 May
China
Powhatan puts her Marines ashore in Shanghai for two days due to unsettled conditions there.

30 June
Manpower
The strength of the Marine Corps on active duty is 52 officers and 1,552 enlisted.

4 August
China
British forces assist *Powhatan*'s Marines and sailors in a punitive expedition against pirates near Hong Kong.

28 August
Uruguay
Sloop *Germantown* sends her Marines into Montevideo, Uruguay, to protect American lives and property when a revolution appears imminent.

12 September
Fiji Islands
Marines from sloop *John Adams* make a show of force ashore, to prevent depredations against American trading ships.

22 September
Fiji Islands
A landing party of Marines and sailors from *John Adams* seizes the king on Viti Levu Island and convinces him to guarantee protection to American property.

3 October
Fiji Islands
After the king of Viti Levu fails to abide by the agreement, *John Adams's* Marines and sailors defeat a native force and burn a village on the island.

28 October
Fiji Islands
Continuing the Viti Levu punitive campaign, an American force burns two more villages.

25 November
Uruguay
Germantown's Marine detachment goes ashore to guard the U.S. consulate during a revolution. The Marines spend a week there and prevent a massacre of insurgents who surrender to the Uruguayan army.

1856

26 January
Seattle

Sloop *Decatur* lands her Marines, some sailors, and a howitzer to protect American settlers in Seattle from hostile Indians. In a night-long battle, the naval force drives away the threatening marauders.

30 June
Manpower

The strength of the Marine Corps on active duty is 57 officers and 1,414 enlisted.

20 September
Panama

Marines and seamen from *St. Mary's* and *Independence* guard the railroad station on the Panama Isthmus to protect American travelers from rioters.

23 October
China

Portsmouth commits her 19 Marines and 64 sailors to safeguard Americans in Canton, China, during a civil war there. They are reinforced by men from *Levant* and steam frigate *San Jacinto* on 27 October and 12 November respectively.

16 November
China

The landing force in Canton begins to return to its ships. Upriver from the city, a ship's boat is fired on from one of the Barrier Forts. *Portsmouth* engages the forts with cannon fire, and a Marine is wounded.

20 November
China

A landing party of 287 Marines and sailors attacks and captures the first of the Barrier Forts, then repels three assaults by thousands of Chinese.

21 November
China

The American force storms two more Barrier Forts and seizes both in heavy fighting. In both cases, Marine Corporal McDougal reached the walls under severe fire and planted the American colors in the midst of the assault.

22 November
China

The Marines and sailors attack the final Barrier Fort and take it, then turn back a counterattack. The naval force destroys all four stone forts and their large number of cannon. The cost is 29 killed and wounded.

1857

1 June
Civil Support
During a rancorous election in Washington, D.C., Baltimore thugs (known as "Plug-Uglies") come to the city and begin to take over the polling places. A company of Marines from the 8th and I barracks restores order as Commandant Henderson personally confronts a mob armed with a small cannon.

30 June
Manpower
The strength of the Marine Corps on active duty is 57 officers and 1,694 enlisted.

1858

2 January
Uruguay
The Marine detachment of frigate *St. Lawrence* lands alongside a British force to protect foreign lives and property during civil disorder in Montevideo. The Americans remain there until 27 January.

16 June
Civil Support
Twenty Marines help restore order at the jail in Washington, D.C.

30 June
Manpower
The strength of the Marine Corps on active duty is 52 officers and 1,555 enlisted.

2 September
Civil Support
Sixty-five Marines from the New York Navy Yard and the steamer *Sabine* protect government buildings housing yellow fever patients on Staten Island from mobs intent on burning them.

8 September
Slavery Suppression
Marines on board sloop *Marion* participate in the capture of a ship supporting the slave trade off Africa.

6 October
Fiji Islands
Marines and sailors from *Vandalia* defeat a native force on Waya Island in the Fijis, to avenge the earlier murder of two Americans.

17 October
Paraguay
A force of 300 Marines participates in a large demonstration of naval power in Paraguayan waters after troops fire on an American ship doing survey work.

1859

6 January
Commandants
Brevet Brigadier General Henderson dies in office at the age of 76. He had served as the fifth Commandant for almost 39 years.

7 January
Commandants
Lieutenant Colonel John Harris is appointed to serve as the Colonel Commandant of the Corps. He already had served 45 years as a Marine officer before becoming the sixth Commandant.

21 April
Slavery Suppression
Marion and her Marines capture a ship supporting the slave trade near the Congo River in Africa.

27 April
Slavery Suppression
Marion seizes another slave ship off the African coast.

30 June
Manpower
The strength of the Marine Corps on active duty is 47 officers and 1,804 enlisted.

31 July
China
Marines and sailors from *Mississippi* go ashore at Shanghai to protect American interests during unrest related to combat between British and Chinese forces. The naval contingent remains there three days.

18 October
Harper's Ferry
Marine Barracks 8th and I dispatches a company to put down an insurrection launched by John Brown at Harper's Ferry, West Virginia, in what was then Virginia. The force is led by Army Colonel Robert E. Lee, then home on leave in Arlington.

October
Uniforms
Among other new uniform regulations, the Mameluke sword for officers is replaced by the same sword used by U.S. Army infantry officers. It also becomes the sword for Marine NCOs.

Below: "Bombardment of Port Royal, South Carolina," Currier & Ives, Marine Corps Art Collection

1860

1 March
Africa
A landing force from *Marion* goes ashore at Kissembo, Angola, in Portuguese West Africa, to protect American lives and property from local unrest.

14 May
Civil Support
Marines from the Washington Navy Yard participate in the ceremony welcoming the first Japanese embassy personnel to the U.S. capital.

30 June
Manpower
The strength of the Marine Corps on active duty is 46 officers and 1,755 enlisted.

27 September
Panama
The Marine detachment of *St. Mary's* lands at Bay of Panama in Columbia to protect Americans and the railroad from revolutionaries.

1861

5 January
Fort Sumter
In New York City, four officers and 250 enlisted Marines board the steamer *Star of the West*, bound for the relief of Fort Sumter, South Carolina. The ship later is not allowed to land them at the fort.

5 January
Maryland
Forty Marines from the Washington Navy Yard garrison Fort Washington, Maryland, on the Potomac River.

9 January
Maryland
The Washington Navy Yard guard dispatches 30 Marines to garrison Fort McHenry in Baltimore.

THE HALLS OF MONTEZUMA

Commandant Henderson was not one to let a war pass by the Marine Corps. As the conflict with Mexico progressed into 1847, it was clear that the small regular army was woefully short of manpower. In May, the Marine general met with the Secretary of the Navy and President Polk and offered a regiment of 600 sea soldiers to the War Department under the provisions of the Act of 1834. The civilian leaders readily agreed. But even the resourceful Henderson found difficulty cobbling together enough Marines from his far-flung barracks and ships detachments. By 1 June he had mustered only about 300 officers and men. They formed a battalion under command of Brevet Lieutenant Colonel Samuel E. Watson, with Major Levi Twiggs as his executive officer. Later reinforced by an additional 60 or so Marines from Pensacola and the ships on blockading duty off Mexico, the unit landed at Veracruz on 29 June.

During the move overland to catch up with General Winfield Scott's army, the Marine battalion served as the rear guard of the reinforcing echelon. On 21 July, Watson's men fought their first battle of the war in driving off an enemy assault on the column. Upon joining Scott for the final approach to Mexico City, the Marines were brigaded with the 2d Pennsylvania Regiment, with Watson as the commander of the combined force. The division commander was Major General John A. Quitman. There was plenty of hard marching in hot, dry, ascending terrain to reach the vicinity of the enemy capital. There was hard fighting, too, but again the Marines were part of the rear guard, and this time saw no action. The brigade was in position south of Mexico City on 11 September.

Scott's plan of attack required the capture of Chapultepec Castle, a large fortified complex of walls and buildings sitting on a hill that dominated the few causeways crossing the often swampy ground southwest of the capital. A force of 800 Mexicans and several artillery pieces held the formidable position. Quitman would strike from the south, while another division attacked the western slope. The Marines received their first taste of the enemy's strength when Major Twiggs led a detachment escorting their division

Left: *("Storming of Chapultepec," C. Nebel, Marine Corps Art Collection)*

Opposite: *This drawing of Marines and soldiers in the assault was made by an observer at the battle. ("Castle of Chapultepec," J. Allison, Marine Corps Art Collection)*

15 January
North Carolina
Four hundred Marines and 1,600 sailors of the fleet participate in the ground assault on Fort Fisher. Although the naval brigade is beaten back, it diverts the attention of Confederate defenders and allows the Union army to penetrate the defenses and capture the bastion.

26 February
South Carolina
A Marine battalion occupies Georgetown, South Carolina.

9 April
Civil War
General Robert E. Lee surrenders the main Confederate army at Appomattox Courthouse, Virginia, effectively bringing the Civil War to an end.

15 April
Civil Support
Washington Navy Yard Marines take over the guard of those accused of conspiring in the assassination of President Abraham Lincoln.

30 June
Manpower
The strength of the Marine Corps on active duty is 87 officers and 3,773 enlisted.

1866

30 April
Civil Support
The Marine detachment of *St. Mary's* boards the mail steamer *Golden City* in the Caribbean at the request of her captain to quell a riot.

20–25 June
China
Marines and sailors from *Wachusett* land at Newchwang, China, to capture those responsible for an assault on the American consul.

Above: *Photo of Marine officers in 1865 (left to right): Brevet Captain William Wallace, Captain McLane Tilton, and Second Lieutenant George C. Reid. (National Archives)*

Right: *"Fort Fisher," Col Charles Waterhouse, USMCR (Ret), Marine Corps Art Collection*

CONFEDERATE STATES MARINE CORPS

The very first Marine officer to leave the service of the United States following the start of the Civil War was Second Lieutenant Calvin L. Sayre. He hailed from Alabama and tendered his resignation, after two and a half years of service, on 14 February 1861. A month later, he received a commission as a first lieutenant in the Confederate States Marines. Nineteen more Marine officers (of a total of 63) followed him south. At first, senior U.S. Marines were sympathetic to this natural pull to one's home state; Commandant Harris and others wrote recommendations for some of the initial officers who resigned. After the fighting at Fort Sumter in April, officers tendering resignations were dismissed instead and sometimes even imprisoned for a brief period. All but one of the officers who left the Marine Corps ended up joining its southern counterpart.

The Confederate States Marine Corps officially came into being on 16 March 1861, when the Southern Congress passed legislation authorizing such an outfit. Subsequent action established its strength at 46 officers and 944 men, organized into a headquarters and 10 companies. A former Army officer, Colonel Lloyd J. Beall, was appointed commandant, while former U.S. Marine Major Henry B. Tyler received the only lieutenant colonel's commission in the CSMC. Recruiting for the ranks never kept up with the demand, in part due to shorter enlistment periods and higher pay for the army and, later, the workings of the conscription law. One arm of the corps, consisting almost entirely of roughly a hundred enlisted men who had left the U.S. Marines, gathered at Richmond in the summer of 1861. Fresh recruits initially went primarily to the naval station at Pensacola for training. (A "conscript camp" eventually was established near Raleigh, North Carolina.) By October 1864, there were only 539 Southern Marines, officer and enlisted (and 67 of them were Northern prisoners of war).

The Confederate Marines served in much the same capacity as their opposites above the Mason-Dixon Line. They provided detachments on many (but not all) of the Confederate navy warships and commerce raiders, guarded naval stations, and on a few occasions operated in the field alongside the army. They participated in some of the most famous engagements of the war. Fifty-four Marines were aboard CSS *Virginia* when the ironclad battled the Union blockading fleet in March 1862. The ship's captain later noted that the "tranquil mien" of the Marine detachment commander "gave evidence that the hottest fire was no novelty to him." A contingent in CSS *Tennessee* served some of her guns when she sallied forth to take on Farragut's fleet at Mobile Bay. During the December 1864 and January 1865 assaults on Fort Fisher, a substantial number of Confederate Marines manned a battery of heavy artillery pieces. They fought from gun position to gun position as the Union army battered its way through the fortification and finally took it on the second attempt. A provisional battalion defended Drewry's Bluff below Richmond in 1862 and again in 1864.

One of the most spectacular actions of the CSMC came in February 1864, when a company of Marines participated in a raid to capture the Federal gunboat *Underwriter*, which was anchored under the Union shore batteries at New Bern, North Carolina (near the site of

present day Camp Lejeune). The Southern Marines and sailors achieved surprise and took control of the ship, but could not sail it away and ended up having to destroy it. The last battle of the CSMC took place in early April 1865 during the Appomattox campaign. Although the Marines under Major George Terrett fought well, their war came to an end when General Ewell surrendered his Confederate army, to which they were attached.

30 June
Manpower
The strength of the Marine Corps on active duty is 79 officers and 3,258 enlisted.

7 July
Civil Support
Two companies of Marines from the navy yard in Portsmouth, New Hampshire, arrive in Portland, Maine, to restore order after a fire.

14 July
China
Wachusett sends 100 Marines and sailors ashore to escort the American consul at Tung Chow Foo, China.

9 August
China
Marines from *Wachusett* land at Shanghai, China, to assist in fighting a fire.

1867

2 March
Commandants
Jacob Zeilin assumes the rank of Brigadier General Commandant.

April
Civil Support
Four companies of Marines from the Brooklyn Navy Yard assist civil authorities in raids on illegal distilleries in the city.

1 May
Japan
Marines from steamers *Wyoming* and *Shenandoah* escort the American minister to Japan during a civil war in that country.

13 June
China
A landing force of Marines and sailors from *Hartford* and *Wyoming* attempts to punish natives in southern Formosa following the murder of a shipwrecked American crew. The naval force is unable to close with the elusive enemy.

30 June
Manpower
The strength of the Marine Corps on active duty is 73 officers and 3,438 enlisted.

18 October
Alaska
Marines officially raise the U.S. flag over newly purchased Alaska at Sitka.

Left: *"Attack on Formosan Pirates," Marine Corps Art Collection*

1868

19 January
Japan
A Marine guard is posted at the residence of the American minister to Japan in Yokohama during a period of civil strife.

1 February
Japan
Steamer *Oneida* lands Marines and sailors to protect American lives during a period of hostility to foreigners at Hiogo, Japan.

7 February
Uruguay
Marines from the South Atlantic Squadron join forces from other powers in landing at Montevideo, Uruguay, during a military revolt there. Uruguayan forces lay down their arms.

8 February
Japan
Shenandoah sends Marines and sailors ashore at Nagasaki, Japan, to protect the American consul during a period of unrest.

19 February
Uruguay
Naval forces again land at Montevideo to guard the American consulate during renewed rebel activity.

March
Civil Support
Marines from the Brooklyn Navy Yard again assist local authorities in closing down illegal distilleries.

4 April
Japan
Steamers *Monocacy* and *Iroquois* land Marines and seamen at Yokohama, Japan, to safeguard American lives and property during a period of hostility to foreigners.

30 June
Manpower
The strength of the Marine Corps on active duty is 81 officers and 2,979 enlisted.

November
Civil Support
Brooklyn Navy Yard Marines make another foray into the city to enforce the distillery laws.

1869

30 June
Manpower
The strength of the Marine Corps on active duty is 70 officers and 2,314 enlisted.

Right: *The punitive assaults upon the forts along the Salee River in Korea were a small but bloody action. This scene of Marine casualties would presage even heavier combat in the region eight decades later. (Marine Corps Historical Center)*

THE FIRST BATTLE OF BULL RUN

The Marine Corps entered the Civil War hobbled by the loss of officers to the South, including such stalwarts as George Terrett of Mexican War fame and Israel Greene of Harper's Ferry, who also happened to be the only trained artillery officer. Fully one-third of its leaders departed for the Confederacy, but primarily those in the company grades who would bear the burden of frontline fighting. The rapid expansion of the Navy also drained officers and NCOs into numerous new ships detachments. An increase in authorized strength in 1861 brought a substantial number of recruits to the barracks, but there was hardly anyone to train them. At the Marine Barracks in Washington in mid-July, one officer noted that the 377 junior enlisted men "are not fit to go into the field, for every man of them is as raw as you please, not more than a hundred of them have been here over three weeks." Many of the lieutenants were equally new to the service and being trained themselves. Nevertheless, on 15 July

the Secretary of the Navy ordered Commandant Harris to form a battalion of 12 officers and 336 enlisted for service with the Army in the first offensive against the Confederacy. Of that number, only six officers, nine NCOs, and seven privates had been in the Corps before the war.

There was little time to mull over the future, as the battalion received orders to depart the next day for the field. Major John G. Reynolds, the commanding officer, recognized the shortcomings of his force and used each halt in the march on 16 July to run his men through the manual of arms. Along the way, the Marines learned they were to be part of the 1st Brigade of the 2d Division and took their assigned place behind the brigade's battery of horse-drawn artillery. The rest of the Army, largely composed of short-service volunteers, was hardly better prepared for a campaign. After a bivouac in the field that night, there was only a short advance on the 17th. Reynolds spent the balance of the day again drilling his force and kept the men at it

Left: The first battle of Bull Run, 21 July 1861, was the only extended service of the Marine Corps in joint land operations with the Union Army during the Civil War. (National Archives)

after the sun went down. The 18th brought another brief march, to Centerville, Virginia, where the division camped the next two days. Drill continued for the Marines.

The Union commander elected to attack on 21 July. The 2d Division drew the mission of flanking the Confederate line after a march starting at 0200. Surprise was lost after delays stretched the movement into daylight. The rebel forces responded to the threat, but the Union soldiers initially pushed them back in heavy fighting. The Marine battalion followed the artillery battery, which inflicted severe casualties on the enemy flank. The raw Marines kept good order when they could, but were physically drained after running to catch up with two quick moves by the heavy guns. As yet they had not played any significant role in the battle.

On Henry Hill late in the morning, the battery came under unexpected fire from a Virginia infantry regiment at close range. With gunners falling in large numbers, the artillery commander called for infantry support from the Marines and a New York regiment. At the same time, Confederate artillery fire began to strike the Marines. The inexperienced battalion wavered, with officers and NCOs forcing the weaker spirits back into line. Just then a cavalry force under Colonel J. E. B. Stuart (the same lieutenant who had served with Greene at Harper's Ferry) attacked the New Yorkers and put them to flight. Almost simultaneously, the Virginia infantry regiment advanced and directed its volley fire at the Marines. Under this determined attack, with other units around them dissolving, the battalion also broke and ran.

Marine leaders rallied the force at a nearby crossroads, and they soon advanced with another New York regiment tasked with recapturing the guns lost on Henry Hill. At first they had some success driving Confederates off the high ground, only to encounter Brigadier General Thomas Jackson's Virginia Brigade firing from a pine woods. The first volleys nearly sent them reeling, but the Marines and New Yorkers made one more push into the forest. Continuous heavy fire from the Virginians routed the Federals a second time. A surgeon with the Virginians gave the 8th and I battalion a compliment nonetheless, noting that the woods in front of his position were filled with Northern casualties, "but the only men that were killed and wounded twenty or thirty yards behind and in the rear of our lines were the United States Marines."

Reynolds corralled most of his men once more at the crossroads, and they participated in one last attack to regain Henry Hill. This time a South Carolina brigade came up and fired on the Union forces from the flank. Nearby, a fresh Federal brigade was put to flight. This time there was no stopping the disorganized Northern troops. Even that part of the Union Army that initially retreated in good order was soon put to the rout by pursuing Confederate fire. It would take days for the last stragglers to make it back to Washington for a final accounting.

Losses to the Marine battalion totaled 44 dead, wounded, and taken prisoner. Moreover, they had lost most of their equipment and arms. The Commandant lamented the embarrassment to the Corps, for "it was the first instance in recorded history where any portion of its members turned their backs to the enemy." There was one bright spot—the battalion had not lost its colors to the rebels. Harris was not about to suffer a repeat of raw troops being thrown into battle, and he asked the Secretary of the Navy to obtain the release of the Marine battalion from the War Department. The request was granted on 24 July. For the remainder of the momentous Civil War, the Corps would avoid extended service on land with the U.S. Army, a role it had successfully carried out in the Mexican War and which it would reprise with glory in World War I and subsequent conflicts.

16 July
Civil Support
Fifty Marines from Brooklyn Navy Yard take a revenue cutter to Gardiner's Island off Long Island and capture 125 men preparing to invade Cuba.

1870

January
Colombia
A detachment of 63 Marines assists an expedition surveying a possible route for an interoceanic canal through Colombia.

28 March
Civil Support
Brooklyn Navy Yard Marines, reinforced by the detachment of the *Vermont*, work with revenue agents in seizing illegal distilleries.

17 June
Mexico
Steamer *Mohican* sends Marines and sailors to Boca Teacapan, Mexico, to destroy a pirate ship.

30 June
Manpower
The strength of the Marine Corps on active duty is 77 officers and 2,469 enlisted.

11 October
Civil Support
Marines from the Philadelphia Navy Yard help quell a disturbance in the city during the first vote by black Americans following passage of the 15th Amendment to the U.S. Constitution.

2 November
Civil Support
The Brooklyn Navy Yard dispatches 245 Marines to aid local law enforcement officials in rooting out illegal distilleries in the city.

1871
---

14 January
Civil Support
Marines from the Navy Yard guard 14 legal distilleries in Brooklyn against attacks by workers from the illegal operations.

10–11 June
Korea
In response to Koreans firing on a survey party, four Marine officers and 105 enlisted men lead the landing of a naval brigade on the banks of the Salee River near Inchon. In two days of fighting, the force assaults and destroys four large forts and captures hundreds of cannon. Six Marines earn the Medal of Honor. Later renamed the Han River, this would be the scene of more Marine battles roughly 80 years in the future.

30 June
Manpower
The strength of the Marine Corps on active duty is 74 officers and 2,439 enlisted.

14 July
Civil Support
Brooklyn Navy Yard Marines quell disturbances in the city following raids on illegal distilleries.

September
Civil Support
Marines from the Brooklyn Navy Yard assist revenue agents in seizing ships with cargoes of contraband whiskey in New York harbor.

17 October
Civil Support
Brooklyn Marines guard seized illegal distilleries.

1872

30 June
Manpower
The strength of the Marine Corps on active duty is 77 officers and 2,126 enlisted.

10 November
Civil Support
Marines from the Boston Navy Yard help restore order following a destructive fire in Boston, Massachusetts.

1873

7 May
Colombia
Marines and sailors from the steamers *Pensacola* and *Tuscarora* land at the Bay of Panama in Colombia, to protect American lives and property during a period of political unrest.

Opposite: *"Korea, 1871,"* *John Joseph Capolino, Marine Corps Art Collection*

Right: *Capt McLane Tilton poses with a captured Korean flag and Medal of Honor recipients Cpl Charles Brown and Pvt Hugh Purvis of the Marine detachment USS Colorado, after 1871 landings in Korea. (Marine Corps Historical Center)*

30 May
Civil Support
Marines from the Boston Navy Yard, *Ohio,* and *Powhatan* help maintain order after a fire in Boston.

25 June
Peru
Marines from *St. Mary's* assist in putting out a fire aboard an Italian merchant ship in the harbor of Callao, Peru.

30 June
Manpower
The strength of the Marine Corps on active duty is 87 officers and 2,675 enlisted.

24 September
Panama
Steamers *Pensacola* and *Benicia* deploy Marines and sailors ashore to protect American lives and the railroad during a revolt in the Panamanian Isthmus of Colombia. The isthmus and its railroad are critical to the United States since it constitutes a key link in the quickest transportation route from the east coast to the west coast of North America.

1874

24 January
Training
The Marine detachments of the ships of the

Atlantic Squadron participate in a battalion field exercise under command of Lieutenant Colonel Charles Heywood, as the fleet awaits possible orders to intervene in disorder in Cuba.

12 February
Hawaii
To assist in preserving order during the inauguration of a new king, Marines from *Portsmouth* and *Tuscarora* go ashore at Honolulu, Hawaii.

6 June
Commandants
Commandant Jacob Zeilin is reverted to the rank of colonel due to the dwindling strength of the Marine Corps.

30 June
Manpower
The strength of the Marine Corps on active duty is 85 officers and 2,184 enlisted.

1875

30 June
Manpower
The strength of the Marine Corps on active duty is 76 officers and 2,037 enlisted.

1876

16 May
Mexico
Marines land at Matamoros, Mexico, at the request of the American consul after civil control in the city dissolves during a revolution.

30 June
Manpower
The strength of the Marine Corps on active duty is 76 officers and 1,904 enlisted.

25 October
Heritage
In commemoration of Marine service with the U.S. Army in the Mexican War, the Navy Department authorizes the Corps to adopt the motto, *"Per Mare, Per Terram"* ("By Sea, By Land").

1 November
Commandants
Commandant Jacob Zeilin retires. Colonel Charles G. McCawley assumes duties as the eighth Commandant of the Marine Corps.

1877

30 June
Manpower
The strength of the Marine Corps on active duty is 73 officers and 1,824 enlisted.

21 July
Civil Support
A battalion of Washington Navy Yard Marines under Lieutenant Colonel Heywood moves to Baltimore to protect railroad property during a major strike by rail workers. After securing the situation there, the unit moves on to Philadelphia.

26 July
Civil Support
Lieutenant Colonel James Forney forms a battalion from the Marines of the Norfolk Navy Yard and ships of the Atlantic Squadron. His force guards the arsenal in Washington and railroad property in Baltimore.

3 April
Expositions
A detachment of Marines arrives at Le Havre, France, on board *Constitution* to serve as the honor guard for the American exhibit at the Universal Exposition in Paris.

30 June
Manpower
The strength of the Marine Corps on active duty is 77 officers and 2,257 enlisted.

30 June
Manpower
The strength of the Marine Corps on active duty is 62 officers and 1,906 enlisted.

8 June
Department of the Navy
Congress establishes the office of Judge Advocate General of the Navy. Marine Captain William B. Remey is the first officer appointed to fill the billet.

30 June
Manpower
The strength of the Marine Corps on active duty is 69 officers and 1,870 enlisted.

March
Arctic
The Marines of *Alliance* participate in an attempt to locate Arctic explorers lost north of Norway.

30 June
Manpower
The strength of the Marine Corps on active duty is 70 officers and 1,832 enlisted.

30 June
Manpower
The strength of the Marine Corps on active duty is 63 officers and 1,806 enlisted.

14 July
Egypt
Marines and sailors from the Mediterranean Squadron land at Alexandria, Egypt, to protect American lives and the U.S. consulate during a rebellion against the government.

Opposite: *Marines plunge into the mud flats on the banks of the Salee River and struggle to pull a landing gun through the muck. ("The Storming of Fort Ch'ojijin," John Clymer, Marine Corps Art Collection)*

Right: *Fort Monocacy, named for one of the ships that supported Marines in its capture in Korea in 1871. (National Archives)*

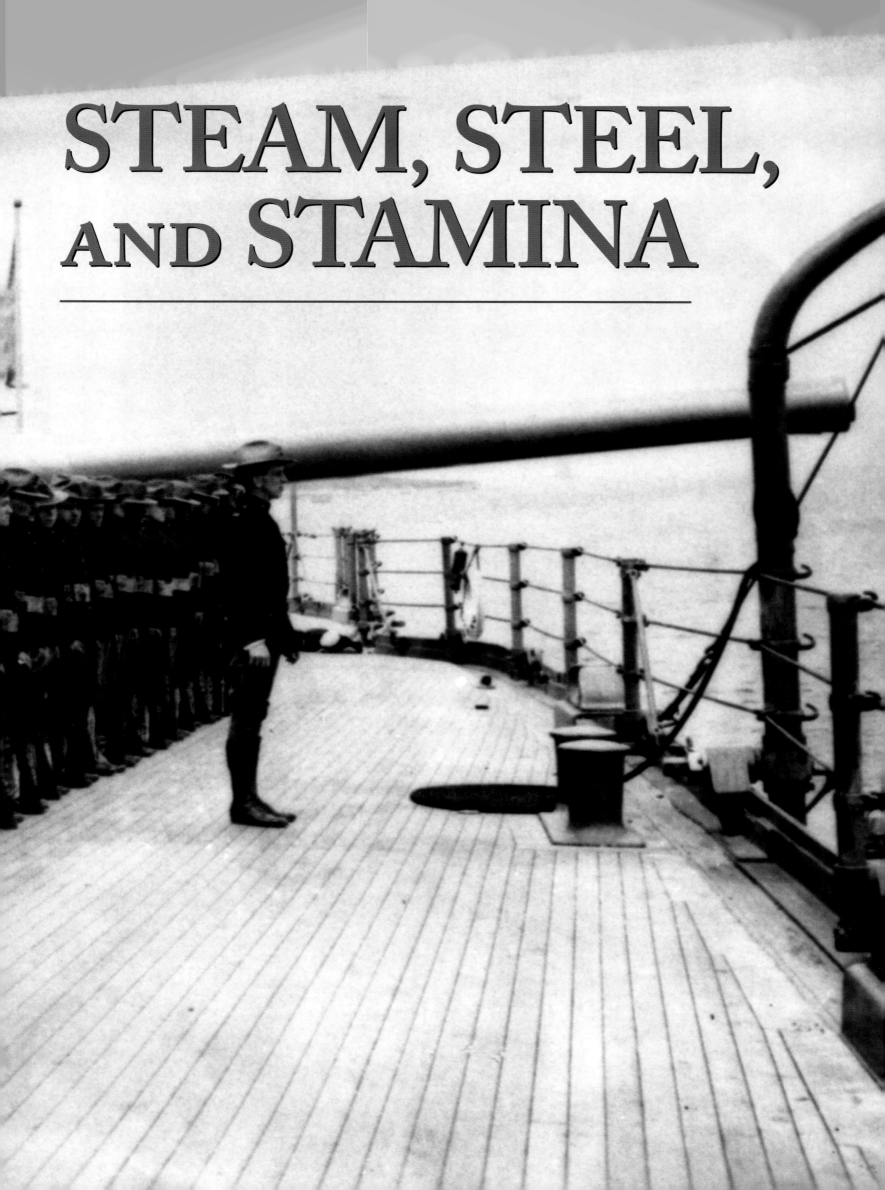

STEAM, STEEL, AND STAMINA

STEAM, STEEL, AND STAMINA

1883–1913

The three decades spanning the end of the 1800s and the beginning of the 1900s proved to be among the most important in the history of the Corps. Nearly irrelevant during the Civil War—the nation's largest conflict to date—Marines found new and vital missions and became a professional force as the new century dawned. Strangely, their existence also came under significant attack for the first time, thus giving rise to an institutional paranoia that would keep Marines looking over their shoulders from this point forward.

The transformation of the Corps during this period sometimes paralleled changes in the Navy. The Navy began acquiring its first steel ships, converting fully to steam power, and adopting Mahanian doctrine as a rationale for its growth and employment. Some influential Navy officers saw the Corps as an anachronism, since there would be no more need for men with muskets in fighting tops. In fact, the first major attempt to abolish the Marines came from within the Navy in 1890. Another, spurred by President Teddy Roosevelt, occurred in 1908. The Corps survived, but its officers saw the need to build their professionalism and to focus on a mission that made them a valuable contribution to national defense.

One of the first reforms was an improvement in officer selection and training, which took a dramatic leap forward when Naval Academy graduates began providing most new lieutenants from 1882 onward. Although this source would

decline in relative numbers and importance within two decades, it set a standard that all other officer candidates would have to meet or exceed. In 1891 the Corps instituted the School of Application to train newly commissioned officers. Enlisted men benefitted from more formalized and centralized recruit training. Participation in shooting competitions and more emphasis on marksmanship began in 1901, further refining combat skills. The Corps' first advanced professional training program, the Advance Base School, opened in 1910. The following year officers formed the Marine Corps Association to enhance professional knowledge.

The search for a mission received an enormous boost from the Spanish-American War in 1898. A Marine battalion made an amphibious landing at Guantanamo Bay, Cuba, to seize and secure an anchorage for coaling the warships blockading the Spanish fleet at nearby Santiago. In the new steam and steel navy, such expeditionary bases were a prerequisite for projecting naval power around the globe and fulfilling the strategic and doctrinal dictates of Admiral Alfred Thayer Mahan. The Marines brought two advantages over the Army in this emerging role. They had proven over the years (from Bladensburg to Harper's Ferry to the Spanish-American War) that they were able to form units and mount out ready for action on a moment's notice. Most important, the Corps was an integral part of the Navy Department and subject to naval command, which made it simple for fleet commanders to field a force that would

work ashore on their behalf. Before long, the Marine Corps adopted the advance base mission as its own, and began training and equipping a standing force dedicated to fulfilling the requirement. Since most expeditionary bases would have to be captured or occupied in a process involving some sort of amphibious landing, the Corps also renewed its interest in this type of operation. Many leading naval officers strongly supported the new Marine focus. Admiral George Dewey, the hero of Manila Bay, proclaimed that a landing force of Marines operating with his fleet would have prevented the Philippine Insurrection.

The acquisition of overseas territory as a result of the war, and America's expanding international trade, created another mission for the Corps. Suddenly there was a need for something much larger than a ship's detachment to handle crises in far-flung corners of the world. The United States had hardly driven the Spanish from the Philippines when elements of the population rose up to declare independence. The expanding Corps contributed several battalions to the fight. Trouble flared in China in 1900 and more Marines went there to help safeguard U.S. citizens and commercial interests from the Boxer Rebellion. Major interventions in Panama, Cuba, and Nicaragua followed. Although the Army contributed large forces to some of these

operations, the Corps often proved adept at getting there first with units composited from ships' detachments and overseas barracks. Marines also learned how to deal with these brush fire wars (ultimately dubbed "small wars"), which were considerably different from the major conflicts that now drew the primary attention of the Army. Simultaneously the Corps began to develop closer relations with the diplomats of the State Department, and even began guarding the U.S. Embassy in Peking, China.

These new missions had a large impact on the Corps. The service that had barely reached 3,000 men during the Civil War ended this period, when the nation was largely at peace, with almost 10,000. Marines were also becoming a professional force, improving training, education, doctrine, and manpower policies to better prepare for expanded roles. The Corps was now capable of operating in brigade strength with combined arms, to include an infant aviation element beginning in 1912. It was a far cry from the mid-nineteenth century, though one thing had not changed. Marines still had to exhibit courage and determination to carry out their missions. If anything, the requirements in that regard had increased, since the demands of chasing down opponents in the trackless jungles or rough terrain typical of small wars called for the utmost in stamina, resolve, and bravery.

STEAM, STEEL, AND STAMINA
1883–1913

1883

12 February
Hawaii
Marines from screw sloops *Lackawanna* and *Wachusett* land at Honolulu, Hawaii, to take part in the inauguration ceremonies for King Kalakaua.

3 March
Technology
Congress authorizes construction of three new protected cruisers (*Atlanta*, *Boston*, and *Chicago*) and the unprotected cruiser *Dolphin*, the first steel ships of the U.S. Navy.

30 June
Manpower
The strength of the Marine Corps on active duty is 60 officers and 1,724 enlisted.

1884

April
Greenland
Gunboat *Alert* and her Marine detachment participate in the ultimately successful attempt to rescue the Greeley Expedition west of Greenland.

30 June
Manpower
The strength of the Marine Corps on active duty is 66 officers and 1,822 enlisted.

1885

18 January
Panama
In response to revolutionary activity in Colombia and the Isthmus of Panama, Marines from gunboat *Alliance* land at Colon, Panama, to

Left: *A depiction of Heywood's battalion moving by train in 1885. ("Marines in Panama," Col Charles Waterhouse, USMCR (Ret), Marine Corps Art Collection)*

Opposite: *The Marine detachment of USS* Portsmouth *forms on her deck about 1885. (National Archives)*

protect the Caribbean end of the railroad. They remain only a few days.

16 March
Panama
Continuing political unrest brings steam bark *Galena* to Colon. Marines go ashore to protect the U.S. consulate. The revolutionaries seize the railroad and set fires in the city.

31 March
Panama
Screw sloop *Shenandoah* lands a company of Marines and reinforcing sailors at Panama City, the Pacific terminus of the rail line. Screw frigate *Tennessee* and screw sloop *Swatara* put a landing force ashore at Colon.

3 April
Panama
One day after receiving orders to form a battalion from East Coast detachments and barracks, Lieutenant Colonel Charles Heywood sails from New York with 10 officers and 212 enlisted.

7 April
Panama
A second battalion of 15 officers and 250 men departs New York along with a battalion of sailors and some artillery.

12 April
Panama
Heywood's battalion lands at Colon, takes the train to Panama City, and establishes control of the rail line.

15 April
Panama
The second battalion of Marines arrives at Colon. All Marine forces ashore are grouped into a brigade under command of Heywood. This is the first brigade-size force established by the Marine Corps in its history.

25 May
Panama
The last Marines forces depart Panama following the arrival of Colombian troops to restore government control.

30 June
Manpower
The strength of the Marine Corps on active duty is 65 officers and 1,819 enlisted.

1886
---

30 June
Manpower
The strength of the Marine Corps on active duty is 66 officers and 1,934 enlisted.

1887
---

30 June
Manpower
The strength of the Marine Corps on active duty is 61 officers and 1,870 enlisted.

1888
---

19 June
Korea
Marines and sailors from steam bark *Essex* land at Chemulpo, Korea, and march to Seoul to protect the U.S. consulate during a period of political turmoil.

30 June
Manpower
The strength of the Marine Corps on active duty is 72 officers and 1,829 enlisted.

14 November
Samoa
Steam bark *Nipsic*'s Marines go ashore at Apia, Samoa, to protect American lives and property during a time of unrest.

20 December
Haiti
Marines participate in the show of force by steam barks *Galena* and *Yantic* at Port-au-Prince to secure the release of an American commercial ship wrongfully seized by the Haitian government.

1889
---

15 March
Samoa
Marines are among those lost when the screw steamer *Trenton* and screw sloop *Vandalia* sink in Apia Harbor during a typhoon. Naval Academy cadet John A. Lejeune is one of the survivors.

land at Taku and proceed to Peking to guard the legation as the anti-foreign Boxers grow more menacing.

10 June
China

U.S. sailors reinforced by a handful of Marines participate in the first relief column destined for the entrapped foreign legations in Peking. The 2,000-man force of several nationalities, under command of British Vice Admiral Edward Seymour, finds slow going against the Chinese.

19 June
China

Major Littleton W. T. Waller and a company of Marines from the Philippines arrive at Taku.

21 June
China

In conjunction with 450 Russian troops, Waller's force attempts to seize Tientsin, but they are driven back. Chinese government forces join Boxers in laying siege to the Legation Quarter in Peking. Meyer's Marine detachment defends the Tartar Wall overlooking the compound.

22 June
China

Seymour's force falls back on a Chinese arsenal six miles from Tientsin.

24 June
China

Waller and his men, now joined with British troops and additional Russians, capture Tientsin against strong resistance.

24–26 June
China

Marines under Waller participate in the relief of Seymour. The combined force of roughly 4,000 men moves back to Tientsin.

27 June
China

A combined force of Russians, British, and American Marines captures an arsenal in Tientsin from a much larger Boxer force. In Peking,

Opposite: *A Marine sergeant balances tote bags on his Krag rifle during the Boxer Rebellion. ("The Old China Hand," Col Charles Waterhouse, USMCR (Ret), Marine Corps Art Collection)*

Top: *"Defense of the Peking Legation," John Clymer, Marine Corps Art Collection*

Right: *"Resupply at Pei-ho River," Col Charles Waterhouse, USMCR (Ret), Marine Corps Art Collection*

THE 1ST MARINE REGIMENT

The Marine Corps formed its first regimental-size unit in 1836 under Commandant Henderson for service in the Seminole War. The next leatherneck regiment, and the first to bear an official designation, was the 1st Regiment, formed in the Philippines from three battalions on 1 January 1900. Although it never took the field as a single entity during the pacification campaign, its battalions participated in the fighting throughout the island chain. That summer the regiment deployed to China, where it served in the expedition to relieve

the siege of the Legation Quarter in Peking. Transferred back to the Philippines in October, the 1st Regiment assumed responsibility for the naval station at Olongapo. It largely remained at that base until 1914.

Having just exceeded 4,000 men for the first time in 1900, the Marine Corps was still new to the business of organizing large units. Starting in 1904, things got confusing as Headquarters indiscriminately applied the designation of 1st Regiment to various outfits at overlapping times. A 1st Regiment existed briefly in Panama in 1904. Another came into being for the Cuban occupation in 1906, though it was soon styled as the 1st Provisional Regiment and lasted under that designation until the withdrawal from Cuba in 1909. Four other outfits would bear some variation of the 1st Regiment title during the period 1911 through 1913.

The direct lineal ancestor of the modern 1st Marine Regiment came into existence in November 1913 as the 1st Advance Base Regiment. It participated in the landings at Veracruz, Mexico, in April 1914. A year later it played a major role in establishing order in Haiti. In 1916, it moved next door and repeated the same mission in Santo Domingo. When not engaged in active combat operations, the regiment served with the Advance Base Force and helped develop the concepts that would contribute to the Corps' preeminent role in amphibious warfare from World War II onward.

Throughout its first decade of service, the regiment went through seven variations in title, not to mention an exchange of numbers of gasoline caught fire in the night. He rushed in to help put out the blaze. Four years later he was in Haiti fighting Caco guerrillas. On the night of 24 October 1915, Gunnery Sergeant Daly was with a patrol of 35 enlisted men and five officers, under command of Major Smedley Butler. As the force crossed a stream, a large band of Cacos ambushed it. The Marines fought forward to better ground and formed a perimeter. After taking fire all night long, at first light two officers and Daly each attacked with a squad in different directions. The surprised Cacos fled, leaving their dead and wounded behind. For this action, Daly soon received his second Medal of Honor (making Butler and him the only Marines ever to receive two such awards for separate acts of valor). On 17 November, he participated in the daring assault on Fort Riviere, which required the Marines to crawl through a drainpipe to enter the enemy-held bastion.

During World War I, Daly was the first sergeant for the 73rd Machine Gun Company, 6th Regiment, 4th Marine Brigade. He participated in most of the outfit's engagements, but seemed to be everywhere during the crucial battle at Belleau Wood, where the largely untested Marines of the brigade faced veteran German forces for the first time. On 5 June 1918, he waded into a fire in an ammunition dump and extinguished it. Two days later, under a thunderous bombardment, he moved along the front line visiting his gun crews and reassuring them. At the start of a Marine attack on the 10th, as men hesitated under withering enemy fire, he called for them to follow with a cry that has been enshrined in history: "Come on, you sons of bitches! Do you want to live forever!" Later that day, he single-handedly assaulted a German machine-gun nest with grenades and his pistol. As the fighting subsided, he went back into the open under fire and pulled wounded to safety. For these actions, he received the Navy Cross, the Army Distinguished Service Cross, and the French Croix de Guerre. He also suffered three wounds during his months of combat in Europe.

After 20 years of heroism, Daly went on the inactive list in 1920 and worked as a bank guard in New York. He officially retired from the Marine Corps in 1929 and died in 1937. Smedley Butler lauded his old comrade as "the fightingest Marine I ever knew."

Opposite: *"Private Dan Daly in China," Col Charles Waterhouse, USMCR (Ret), Marine Corps Art Collection*

Right: *The view from the Tartar Wall into the back of the U.S. Legation in Peking. (Marine Corps Research Center)*

10 October
China
With the Boxer Rebellion at an end, the 1st Regiment (the only Marine unit still in China) sails from Taku for the Philippines.

1901

1 May
Expositions
A detachment of Marines assumes guard duty for the Pan-American exposition at Buffalo, New York.

10 June
HQMC
Headquarters Marine Corps moves from Marine Barracks 8th and I to the Bond Building at 14th Street and New York Avenue in Northwest Washington, D.C.

30 June
Manpower
The strength of the Marine Corps on active duty is 171 officers and 5,694 enlisted.

24 October
Samar
A provisional battalion under Waller, composed of three companies from the 1st Regiment and a company from the 2nd Regiment, arrives on the island of Samar in the Philippines. Their mission is to deal with rebellious Moro natives that have massacred an army infantry company.

1–10 November
Samar
Marine patrols on Samar skirmish with numerous enemy bands, driving them back to a rebel stronghold dug into the cliffs along the Sohoton River.

16 November
Samar
Waller's force attacks the Moro bastion at Sohoton and routs the enemy with heavy rifle and machine-gun fire.

24 November
Panama
After a rebel faction stops rail traffic across the Isthmus of Panama, 12 Marine officers and 233 enlisted land from battleship *Iowa* (BB-4) and *Concord* at Panama City.

26 November
Panama
Marines and sailors from gunboat *Machias* (PG-5) and *Marietta* land at Colon to assist in restoring rail transportation. Both elements remain ashore until 4 December.

28 December
Samar
Ordered to map out a telegraph route through the wild heart of Samar, Waller, five officers, 50 men, and a group of native scouts and bearers, depart Lanang on the east coast.

1902

3 January
Samar
With illness and shortages of food debilitating his force, Waller sets out with the strongest Marines to find a way out of the jungle and seek help for the remainder of his beleaguered detachment.

6 January
Samar
Waller's small band reaches a safe haven on the west coast of Samar.

7–17 January
Samar
With fresh Marines, Waller searches in vain for the remainder of his force.

11 January
Samar
Another element of Waller's original patrol makes it back to the east coast of Samar.

15 January
Samar
The last survivors of the Waller expedition make it to the east coast. Ten Marines had died in the interior.

Top: *Lt Dion Williams and his detachment salute Admiral Dewey upon his first visit to the Navy Yard at Cavite, Philippines, 13 June 1898. (Marine Corps Research Center)*

Right: *Marines at Subic in the Philippines in 1901. (Marine Corps Historical Center)*

SAMAR

When the United States took the Philippines away from Spain in 1898, it had to put down a revolt throughout the island chain. The Moro population on the island of Samar proved to be among the toughest opponents. On 28 September 1901, as a company of the Army's 9th Infantry ate breakfast in their mess hall at Balangiga, a Moro force surprised and massacred the soldiers. The Navy soon dispatched Major Littleton W. T. Waller and a battalion of 14 officers and 300 enlisted men to assist in establishing firm control over southern Samar. Two companies under Captain David D. Porter landed at Balangiga in the south on 24 October, while Waller and the other two companies went to Basey a little to the northwest. The blunt instructions from the senior Army general were to destroy the insurgents and anything that might be of assistance to them.

Within days Waller and Porter were patrolling the hinterland and skirmishing with rebel bands. In the course of the campaign they followed Army practice in burning dwellings, boats, and food supplies. They also killed 39 insurgents and captured another 18. Under this pressure, the bulk of the rebel force withdrew into the interior of the island to a system of caves dug into soft rock in cliffs above the Sohoton River.

Waller's command converged there on 17 November. Porter's column reached the scene slightly ahead of Waller and managed to make its way from the rear to the top of the cliff on one side of the river. The Moro soldiers were cooking and working on the opposite bank. Supported by a Colt machine gun, the Marines opened up a devastating fire on the surprised enemy. As the Moros broke and fled, Porter's men rushed down to the river's edge, crossed on canoes and a raft tied up there, and stormed up the opposite rise. They had killed 30 rebels and broken their morale with the daring attack on the supposed bastion. One of the heroes of the assault was John Quick, of Guantanamo fame, since promoted to gunnery sergeant.

Subsequent patrolling inflicted further losses on the rebels, but Waller was intent on showing that he could go anywhere on the island. On 28 December, the battalion commander, four other officers, 50 enlisted men, two native scouts, and 33 porters set out from the east coast to find a route to the west coast. They boated up the Lanang River to its navigable head, then marched along a trail that criss-crossed the swift, swollen waterway. The rough terrain sapped the strength of the Marines, and some of their food proved to be spoiled. By 2 January, a number of men were sick or exhausted, and rations were almost gone. An attempt to construct rafts to go downriver failed for lack of material that would float.

Waller decided to continue westward with 13 of his strongest Marines, in hopes of bringing back a relief party. Porter was to follow with the weaker members of the patrol as best he could. Confusion and disaster ensued. Waller soon found a village and food, but failed to ensure that word got back to Porter. After making it to the west coast on 6 January, Waller retraced his steps the next day and searched for his men without success until the 17th. Porter had turned back and, copying his commander, finally decided to head for the east coast with the seven strongest Marines and obtain help for the others. Before the fiasco was over, 10 Marines were dead, and another had gone insane. Waller, ill and feverish, subsequently had 11 of the native porters executed on charges they had stolen provisions or otherwise undermined the patrol. He was later court-martialed for murder, but was exonerated. Still, the bravery of Sohoton and the bitter tragedy of the cross-island patrol drew admiration. It became customary among Marines in the Philippines to honor the presence of a survivor with the toast: "Stand, gentlemen, he served on Samar."

"Waller's Patrol Crossing Samar," Col Charles Waterhouse, USMCR (Ret), Marine Corps Art Collection

20 January
Samar
Major Littleton W. T. Waller executes 11 Filipinos for alleged treachery associated with his failed expedition.

24 February
Civil Support
Two thousand Marines form the honor guard for Prince Henry of Prussia on his visit to Washington.

2 March
Samar
Waller's battalion returns to Luzon.

16 April
Panama
Marines and sailors from *Machias* go ashore at Boca del Toro in the Isthmus of Panama to protect the American consulate and the shipping port of the United Fruit Company during a civil war.

18 May
Panama
Screw steamer *Ranger* lands her Marines and sailors at Panama City to protect American lives.

30 June
Manpower
The strength of the Marine Corps on active duty is 191 officers and 6,031 enlisted.

July
Commandants
Commandant Heywood is promoted to major general by special legislation, the first Marine to hold that rank.

17 September
Panama
Marines and seamen from cruiser *Cincinnati* (C-7) land at Colon to guard Americans during a rebellion against Colombian rule. U.S. interest in the Isthmus of Panama is heightened by a recent decision to build a canal there to connect the Pacific and Atlantic oceans.

22 September
Panama
A battalion of 17 officers and 325 enlisted Marines arrives at Colon from the United States.

17 November
Panama
Marines withdraw from Panama after Colombian troops restore order in the troubled province.

1903

23 March
Honduras
Marines from *Marietta* and cruiser *Olympia* (C-6) land at Puerto Cortez, Honduras, to protect U.S. interests during a period of civil strife.

28 March
HQMC
Headquarters Marine Corps moves from the Bond Building to the Mills Building at 17th Street and Pennsylvania Avenue in Northwest Washington.

1 April
Santo Domingo
Atlanta sends her Marines ashore at Santo Domingo City in Santo Domingo to protect American lives during political disturbances.

3 May
Training
The School of Application moves from Marine Barracks 8th and I to Annapolis, Maryland.

30 June
Manpower
The strength of the Marine Corps on active duty is 213 officers and 6,445 enlisted.

7 September
Lebanon
Marines and sailors from cruiser *Brooklyn* (ACR-3) land at Beirut, then part of Syria, to defend U.S. interests during a period of unrest.

3 October
Commandants
Major General Heywood retires. Colonel George F. Elliott is promoted to brigadier general and becomes the 10th Commandant of the Marine Corps.

4 November
Panama
A day after Panamanians revolted against Colombia, Marines and sailors from *Nashville* land at Colon to protect American lives and secure the railroad from use by the forces of either side.

5 November
Panama
Major John A. Lejeune's Marine battalion goes ashore at Colon from *Dixie* to reinforce the *Nashville* contingent. Colombian forces withdraw and the Marines re-embark the next day. The United States recognizes the independence of Panama on the 6th.

18 November
Ethiopia
A detachment of 20 Marines lands at Djibouti, French Somaliland, to escort a U.S. diplomatic mission to Addis Ababa for negotiations with the emperor of Ethiopia. They return to the coast on 15 January 1904.

12 December
Panama
Lejeune's battalion goes into camp near Colon.

21 December
Panama
Another expeditionary force of 11 officers and 300 enlisted Marines arrives in Colon, Panama, on board auxiliary cruiser *Prairie*.

Opposite: *Marine drummers and buglers in the Philippines, 1900. (Marine Corps Research Center)*

Right: *These Marines of the relief expedition pause during the hard campaign to rescue the Legation Quarter in Peking. (Marine Corps Research Center)*

3 January
Panama
Two additional battalions of Marines arrive in Panama to ensure the independence of that new nation. Brigadier General Commandant Elliott accompanies them and takes command of the brigade composed of the four Marine battalions in Panama.

Santo Domingo
Cruiser *Detroit* (C-10) lands her Marines at Puerto Plata to help forestall intervention by European creditor nations.

5 January
Korea
A company of Marines from the Philippines lands at Seoul, Korea, to protect the U.S. legation during the Russo-Japanese War.

17 January
Santo Domingo
Marines and sailors from screw sloops *Hartford* and *Detroit* go ashore at Puerto Plata when fighting breaks out near the city.

9 February
Hawaii
Fifty Marines establish a permanent garrison at naval facilities in Honolulu.

11 February
Santo Domingo
Newark and cruiser *Columbia* (C-12) send 300 Marines and sailors ashore at Santo Domingo City after Dominican revolutionaries fire on an American launch.

12 March
Korea
The Marine detachment of *Cincinnati* assists in the evacuation of American nationals from Chemulpo and Seoul during the Russo-Japanese War.

27 April
Samoa
Gunnery Sergeant J. F. Cox arrives at the naval station at Tutuila, Samoa, to become the first drill instructor for the "Fita-Fita" native constabulary.

30 April
Expositions
A Marine unit assumes duties at the Louisiana Purchase Exposition in St. Louis, Missouri, to conduct exhibition drills and guard displays.

May
Midway
Twenty Marines arrive at Midway Island in the Pacific to maintain order among laborers installing a transoceanic cable. The detachment remains there until March 1908.

Left: *Some of the Marines of USS* Columbia *strike a tough pose after their intervention in Santo Domingo in 1904. (Marine Corps Research Center)*

Opposite: *Buglers and drummers of the Marines of the Atlantic Squadron in camp at Pensacola, Florida, April 1898. (Marine Corps Research Center)*

30 May
Morocco
Brooklyn's Marines land at Tangiers as a show of force to convince the Sultan of Morocco to negotiate with rebel leader Ahmed Raisuli for release of an American citizen held for ransom.

30 June
Manpower
The strength of the Marine Corps on active duty is 255 officers and 7,329 enlisted.

20 December
Panama
Marine forces move into Camp Elliott, their permanent base in the Panama Canal Zone. It is located at Bas Obispo, about one-third of the way along the canal from the east coast.

1905

January
Santo Domingo
A Marine expeditionary force sails from Panama for service in politically troubled Santo Domingo.

30 June
Manpower
The strength of the Marine Corps on active duty is 270 officers and 6,741 enlisted.

6 July
Heritage
Marines and sailors from cruisers *Tacoma* (C-18), *Brooklyn*, *Galveston* (C-17), and *Chattanooga* (C-16) land at Cherbourg, France, to escort the body of John Paul Jones from Paris to the United States.

12 September
China
A detachment of 100 Marines previously stationed in the Philippines assumes duties as the Legation Guard in Peking.

December
Russia
Marines are assigned to guard the U.S. embassy at St. Petersburg.

1906

18 April
Civil Support
Marines from the naval stations at Yerba Buena Island and Mare Island aid civilians following an earthquake and fire in San Francisco.

29 May
Panama
A battalion of 229 Marines under Major Lejeune arrives in Panama to deal with civil disturbances in the Canal Zone.

June
Caribbean
A Marine battalion embarks in *Dixie* for service in the Caribbean.

30 June
Manpower
The strength of the Marine Corps on active duty is 278 officers and 7,940 enlisted.

12 September
Cuba
The *Dixie* battalion arrives in Cuban waters as the Cuban government deals with a rebellion.

14 September
Cuba
Marines and sailors from *Marietta* go ashore at Cienfuegos, Cuba, to protect American-owned sugar plantations.

16 September
Cuba
A battalion of 400 Marines sails from Norfolk to reinforce U.S. naval power off Cuba.

18 September
Cuba
Another battalion sails from Philadelphia for service in Cuba. The Marines on board *Dixie* land at Cienfuegos to reinforce the ships detachment there.

25 September
Cuba
Marines and seamen from *Marietta* move inland to protect railroad lines.

28 September
Cuba
A detachment of 31 Marines lands at Havana to guard the Cuban treasury.

29 September
Cuba
Two thousand Marines go ashore at Havana and fan out to garrison various key points in the country.

30 September
Cuba
A fourth Marine battalion departs from Boston for Cuba.

1 October
Cuba
Part of a fifth Marine battalion departs Norfolk for Cuba. A sixth battalion of 804 officers and enlisted, formed from detachments of ships in the Atlantic Fleet, arrives in Havana Harbor. Colonel L. W. T. Waller assumes command of all Marines in Cuba and organizes them into a brigade with two regiments. The eventual strength of the brigade is 97 officers and 2,795 enlisted.

10 October
Cuba
The first U.S. Army units begin arriving in Cuba and relieving Marines from garrisoning various posts.

1 November
Cuba
The remaining 1,000 Marines in Cuba are organized into the 1st Provisional Regiment. It remains there until January 1909.

1907

17 January
Jamaica
Marines and sailors from several U.S. warships land at Kingston, Jamaica, to assist in rescue efforts following a severe earthquake.

18 March
Honduras
Marietta sends her Marine detachment ashore at Truxillo, Honduras, to guard the U.S. consulate during political disturbances.

28 April
Honduras
Marines from *Paducah* (Gunboat No. 18) land at Laguna and Choloma, Honduras, to protect American lives and property during a war between Honduras and Nicaragua.

30 June
Manpower
The strength of the Marine Corps on active duty is 279 officers and 7,807 enlisted.

16 December
Virginia
Marine detachments are part of the Great White Fleet as it sails from Hampton Roads, Virginia, on a 14-month voyage around the world.

1908

21 May
Commandants
The rank of the billet of Commandant is formally established as major general for the first time, resulting in a promotion for Brigadier General Elliott.

28 May
Panama
A battalion of 17 officers and 400 enlisted men arrives in Panama to reinforce the normal Marine garrison during elections. It remains until 6 July.

June
Panama
Another Marine battalion, composed of 19 officers and 706 enlisted men, goes to Panama to assist in maintaining order during elections.

30 June
Manpower
The strength of the Marine Corps on active duty is 283 officers and 8,953 enlisted.

12 November
Roles and Missions
President Theodore Roosevelt signs Executive Order 969, which directs the removal of all Marine detachments from Navy ships. The action is rescinded by Congress in legislation passed on 3 March 1909.

1909

1 January
Training
Marine Officers School (for new lieutenants) moves to the Navy base at Port Royal, South Carolina.

30 June
Manpower
The strength of the Marine Corps on active duty is 328 officers and 9,368 enlisted.

November
Nicaragua
Major Smedley Butler's battalion boards auxiliary cruiser *Buffalo* in Philadelphia for duty in Panama. It ends up in Nicaraguan waters pending the resolution of a civil war in that nation and stays there until 16 March 1910.

December
Nicaragua
A regiment of 750 Marines departs from Philadelphia early in the month for possible duty in troubled Nicaragua. It remains on ship off the west coast port of Corinto until March 1910.

1910

22 February
Nicaragua
Butler and a few Marines land at Corinto to reconnoiter the rail lines.

19 May
Nicaragua
Marines and sailors from *Paducah* go ashore at Bluefields, Nicaragua, to protect American lives and property when revolutionary forces threaten the town.

31 May
Nicaragua
Major Butler and two companies of Marines arrive at Bluefields from Panama and remain there until early September.

30 June
Manpower
The strength of the Marine Corps on active duty is 328 officers and 9,232 enlisted.

30 November
Commandants
Commandant Elliott retires.

1911

---

3 February
Commandants
Following a long period of political indecision over the selection, President Taft confirms the acting

Commandant, Colonel William P. Biddle, as the 11th Commandant of the Marine Corps.

8 March
Force Structure
Colonel George Barnett assumes command of a provisional regiment, which eventually encamps at Guantanamo Bay, Cuba, for possible service in Mexico as a result of a revolution there.

10 March
Force Structure
Colonel Charles A. Doyen activates another provisional regiment at Mare Island, California, for potential expeditionary duty in Mexico.

Above: *Marines applying first aid while on training maneuvers, May 1913. (National Archives)*

Right: *Marines at ease with their rifles at stack arms on the deck of their battleship in 1913. (National Archives)*

MAJOR GENERAL SMEDLEY BUTLER

Smedley Darlington Butler was the product of a prominent line of eastern Pennsylvania families—the Smedleys, Darlingtons, and Butlers. His father went to Congress in 1896 and remained there for 32 years. Despite 16-year-old Smedley's youth, privileged upbringing, and Quaker religion, he rushed to the colors at the outbreak of the Spanish-American War. His father's seat on the House Naval Affairs Committee enabled the son to obtain a Marine commission. He soon reported to the battalion at Guantanamo Bay, but too late to see any action.

In the spring of 1899, Butler deployed to the Philippines with a new battalion. His first battle came in the assault on Novaleta, an important victory in the war against Filipino insurgents. Temporarily in command of a company, he led it against entrenched rebels and routed them. In June 1900, he accompanied Waller's battalion to China. During the initial operations against Tientsin, he distinguished himself by leading a group of six men to rescue a wounded Marine who had been left behind. Not quite 19, he was breveted to the rank of captain for bravery. He was wounded in subsequent fighting, but still participated in the relief expedition to Peking, where he was hit a second time.

Promoted to major in 1908 (at the age of 27), he took command of a battalion in Panama the following year. He twice deployed with his Marines to troubled Nicaragua in 1910 and 1911, but without any fighting. In August 1912 he returned, and this time bluffed his way through rebel forces to open the rail line from the port of Corinto to the capital of Managua. Pushing on to Granada in

September, he and his men were ambushed at Masaya and fought their way through. In early October, Butler's battalion played a major role in defeating the main revolutionary force at Coyotepe. In April 1914, Butler's battalion joined in the landing at Veracruz, Mexico. Once ashore, the Marines and reinforcing sailors had to fight their way house-to-house through the city. For his leadership there, he soon received the Medal of Honor. He tried to refuse it, saying that his conduct had not been sufficiently heroic, but the Secretary of the Navy ordered him to keep it.

A year later, Butler commanded a battalion during the intervention in Haiti. His most spectacular battle was the assault on Fort Riviere. While part of his force covered the approach with fire against the high walls, the major and two dozen men dashed to the face of the bastion. The only entrance through the thick masonry was via a drainpipe about three feet in width. A Caco

shooter to achieve an unprecedented level of precision in aiming. (The exception was in low-light conditions, when the front sight was more difficult to see than its fatter cousins.) The initial .30-caliber round was improved in 1906 (and quickly dubbed the "30/06") to produce a higher muzzle velocity and flatter trajectory. The combination of rifle and ammunition forged the most accurate weapon of the day. Married with the Marine emphasis on marksmanship training beginning in the first decade of the twentieth century, the result was a body of riflemen who squeezed off rounds rapidly and hit targets at extremely long ranges. (The rear sight was calibrated out to 2,850 yards, though the standard maximum range in actual use was 800 to 1,000 yards).

The Marine Corps began converting to the '03 in 1908. Marines first fired it in combat in Nicaragua in 1912. By the time of the Veracruz landing of 1914, the switch to the new weapon was just about complete. The Springfield earned its everlasting fame in World War I. Beginning on 2 June 1918, victorious German troops swept out of Belleau Wood in pursuit of reeling French forces and promptly ran into the U.S. 2nd Division and its 4th Marine Brigade. The Marines began picking off the advancing enemy soldiers at 800 yards, as veteran

NCOs called out the range, and riflemen adjusted their leaf sights. The devastating firepower put a stop to the German offensive and established the legend of Marine combat marksmanship.

During the two decades after World War I, the Marines and their '03s surpassed all their rivals in competitive marksmanship on the firing ranges. The bond—forged in war and peace—was so strong that the Corps was extremely reluctant to replace the bolt-action Springfield with the Army's M-1 Garand at the start of World War II, even though the new semi-automatic rifle provided a significantly higher rate of fire. The finely machined Springfield was unsuited to the mass production required for a global war, however, and that helped seal its demise. Most Marine riflemen who arrived in the first weeks at Guadalcanal were still armed with the trusty '03, but the Garand soon took over. The Springfield continued in service thereafter as a superior sniper rifle and also as a grenade launcher.

Opposite: *Marines put their Springfields to use on the rifle range at Quantico in August 1918. (National Archives)*

Top: *The M-1903 was adapted from a design by German Paul Mauser and manufactured at both Springfield Armory and Rock Island Arsenal. (Marine Corps Historical Center)*

FIRST
TO
FIGHT

FIRST TO FIGHT

1914–1918

While the Spanish-American War and other events around the turn of the century had given the Corps new missions and helped spur professionalization, the World War I era solidified those changes and established the status of Marines firmly in the hearts of Americans.

The Marine Corps already was fully employed when a nearly global conflict engulfed European nations and their overseas colonies in August 1914. The advent of the Panama Canal, opened that same month, focused the interest of the U.S. Navy and the Marines on protecting this waterway. The canal not only permitted the fleet to shift quickly from one coast to another, it also facilitated transportation of commerce and people from one end of the transcontinental nation to the other. It quickly became U.S. policy to ensure that no other powerful nation placed military forces in a position to interdict this vital link. The most obvious threat would be European encroachment in the Caribbean or Central America, where several chronically impoverished countries provided potentially easy inroads. This strategic situation would lead to two decades of American intervention in this often chaotic region.

The first major deployment of Marines came in 1914. Revolution had engulfed Mexico, and the U.S. government was determined to influence the outcome. When word came that arms were going to be shipped through the port of Veracruz, the

United States dispatched forces to forestall this. Elements of the fleet and embarked Marines were the first to arrive and they took control of the city a week before the first units of the U.S. Army reached the scene. This occupation was short lived, but the operation again demonstrated the readiness of the Corps.

A series of revolutions and violent changes in the government of Haiti brought U.S. intervention there the following year. Again, ships' detachments and regiments hastily formed from several Marine barracks provided the means to get American forces on the ground in a hurry. The very next year, 1916, the Marines subdued troublesome elements in Santo Domingo, the other half of the island of Hispaniola. In both cases, the Marines provided almost the entire force to accomplish the mission. And they stayed put, with the mission of bringing long-term stability to these two troubled nations.

Although the Corps already had considerable experience in small wars, Marines brought to bear a new tactic in Hispaniola. In both countries, Marines formed a constabulary force to carry out police and military functions. Marine officers and NCOs served as the leaders for units otherwise composed of recruits from the local population. As these outfits grew in size and capability, they took over most of the responsibility for maintaining order, with regular Marine units serving in the background. Constabularies proved to be an effective tool, since the local soldiers engendered

Pages 158–159: While World War I in Europe dominates this era, Marines are fighting elsewhere, as well. These Marines are engaged in Santo Domingo in 1916. (National Archives)

Right: *Training in the Overseas Depot at Quantico in 1917–18 included bayonet and hand-to-hand fighting in preparation for the trench warfare of Europe's western front. (National Archives)*

less resentment among the populace and knew the countryside and the people much better than Marines ever would.

The U.S. declaration of war against Germany on 6 April 1917 catapulted the Marine Corps to an unprecedented level. The United States had not prepared its Army for a war of this scope, so the War Department eagerly accepted the offer of a Marine regiment for service in Europe. Within weeks the 5th Marines was shipped to France as part of a token of U.S. commitment to its allies. By the fall, the 6th Marines and a machine gun battalion joined with the 5th to form the 4th Brigade of Marines, which became an element of the 2nd Infantry Division. Although another Marine brigade and an aviation force eventually would reach Europe, the 4th Brigade would bear the brunt of the Corps' participation in the war. The nearly 10,000 Marines of the brigade eventually were swamped by more than a million U.S. soldiers in Europe, but the small Leatherneck force made an outsize contribution to victory. In a month of fighting around Belleau Wood in June 1918, the 4th Brigade helped stop a German offensive threatening Paris and proved that American infantrymen were more than a match for the vaunted Germans. Although the rest of the 2nd Division also played a prominent role, a fluke in the censorship system gave the Marines the lion's share of publicity for one of the first American victories in the war. The action endeared the Corps to the nation, backed up the Marine claim of being "First

to Fight," and created a lasting and bitter rivalry with the Army.

The 4th Brigade lived up to its status as an elite fighting unit throughout the remainder of the war. In battles at Soissons, St. Mihiel, Blanc Mont, and the Meuse-Argonne, the Marines took grievous casualties but still accomplished their mission and often exceeded expectations. By the end of the conflict, the Corps had a well-deserved renown for deadly marksmanship and determined bravery. Marine airmen came late to the struggle and did not serve directly in support of their ground compatriots, but they performed well in battle, too.

World War I did more than simply burnish the standing of the Corps. Strength grew from 10,000 in 1914 to 75,000 at war's end. Although it would drop precipitously after the armistice in November 1918, it would remain double its prewar size. Aviation, previously an experiment, became a major component in the Corps. Artillery and other supporting elements also took on new importance. The Marines acquired the first bases that they could call home, at Parris Island, Quantico, and San Diego. And from its close service with the Army in a major war, the Corps also gained a greater appreciation for doctrine, tactics, and the challenges of controlling organizations at the division level and above. In four short years, in skirmishes in the jungles of the Caribbean and in epic battles in Europe, the Corps had changed dramatically and become a completely modern fighting force with an elite reputation to uphold.

FIRST TO FIGHT

1914–1918

3 January
Training
The 1st Advance Base Brigade sails from Philadelphia for field exercises at Culebra, Puerto Rico.

28 January
Haiti
The Marine detachment of battleship *South Carolina* (BB-26) lands at Port-au-Prince along with British, French, and German forces to protect foreign interests during revolutionary turmoil.

16 February
Haiti
Marines from *Wheeling* (Gunboat No. 14) go ashore at Port-de-Paix to safeguard American citizens as political unrest continues.

21 February
Haiti
Marines from *Wheeling* deploy to Cape Haitien to defend the U.S. consulate.

24 February
Commandants
Commandant William P. Biddle retires after 39 years of service in the Corps.

25 February
Commandants
Colonel George Barnett is appointed as the 12th Commandant of the Marine Corps.

16 April
Force Structure
The 4th Regiment is reactivated on the West Coast of the United States and embarks on ships of the fleet.

21 April
Veracruz
In an effort to forestall delivery of munitions to revolutionary forces in Mexico, lead elements of the 2nd Regiment go ashore at Veracruz, Mexico, from auxiliary cruiser *Prairie*. They are reinforced by Marines and sailors of the fleet. Fighting erupts in the city with Mexican soldiers.

Left: *Marines take a break from field duty in Cuba in 1914, during a period when the restive Caribbean nation was unusually quiet. (Marine Corps Research Center)*

22 April
Veracruz
The 1st Regiment, composed of 24 officers and 810 enlisted men, lands at Veracruz, Mexico, from transport *Hancock* (AP-3). Colonel Lejeune takes command of the Marine Brigade formed from the two regiments.

23 April
Veracruz
Marine and Navy forces complete the seizure of Veracruz.

Top: *Marine artillerymen train with their light field gun during the Cuban intervention in 1917. (National Archives)*

Right: *Marines on the march toward Camaguay, Cuba. (National Archives)*

24 April
Veracruz
The remainder of the 2nd Regiment arrives on board battleship *Mississippi* (BB-23).

29 April
Veracruz
Another Marine regiment created at Philadelphia arrives with 33 officers and 861 enlisted. Army occupation forces begin to go ashore.

1 May
Veracruz
Marine detachments return to the fleet and the Marine Brigade comes under command of the U.S. Army occupation forces, which remain in Mexico until November.

6 May
Santo Domingo
The 44th Company (three officers and 125 enlisted men) arrives off Puerto Plata, Santo Domingo, and remains on ship there for a month for potential deployment due to revolutionary disorder in that country.

30 June
Manpower
The strength of the Marine Corps on active duty is 336 officers and 10,500 enlisted.

Left: *Marines crowd the fantail of a ship as they mount out for the Veracruz expedition in 1914. (National Archives)*

Below: *This photo shows how a Marine carried his field gear during the landing at Veracruz. (Marine Corps Historical Center)*

7 July
Force Structure
The 4th Regiment goes into camp in San Diego after weeks of sailing off the western Mexican coast.

12 August
Force Structure
The newly formed 5th Regiment embarks on *Hancock* at Guantanamo Bay and sails to Hispaniola, where it remains offshore troubled Santo Domingo and Haiti almost continuously through mid-December.

11 December
Expositions
The 4th Regiment headquarters and its 2nd Battalion move into a model camp at the Panama-California Exposition in Balboa Park in San Diego.

17 December
Haiti
Marines from gunboat *Machias* (PG-5) escort the Haitian government's gold stocks from Port-au-Prince onto the ship for transport to New York and safekeeping there.

22 December
Expositions
The 1st Battalion, 4th Regiment embarks from San Diego to sail to Mare Island for subsequent duty with the Panama-Pacific International Exposition in San Francisco Bay.

January
Training
The Marine Corps establishes a field artillery school, its first, at Annapolis.

9 January
Aviation
The Marine Section is established at the Navy Flying School, Pensacola.

16 February
Expositions
The 1st Battalion, 4th Regiment establishes a model military camp at the Panama-Pacific Exposition in San Francisco.

2 June
Department of the Navy
Commandant George Barnett becomes an ex-officio member of the General Board of the Navy.

17 June
Mexico
Three companies of the 2nd Battalion, 4th Regiment in San Diego embark on cruiser *Colorado* (CA-7) and remain on station off the west coast of Mexico for six weeks.

30 June
Manpower
The strength of the Marine Corps on active duty is 338 officers and 9,948 enlisted.

9 July
Haiti
Cruiser *Washington* (ACR-11) lands her Marine detachment to guard a radio station at Cape Haitien. They remain there until 27 July.

28 July
Haiti
A naval regiment from *Washington*, composed of Marines and sailors under command of Marine Captain George Van Orden, goes ashore at Port-au-Prince to protect U.S. lives and property following a severe outbreak of revolutionary violence in Haiti.

29 July
Haiti
A company of Marines from Guantanamo Bay arrives to reinforce the regiment at Port-au-Prince.

Top: *Col L. W. T. Waller and his brigade staff at Veracruz. In the front row (from left) are LtCol Wendell Neville, Col John Lejeune, Waller, Maj Smedley Butler, and Maj Randolph Berkeley. (Marine Corps Research Center)*

Right: *USS* Prairie *sends the first landing party ashore in Mexico on 21 April 1914. (National Archives)*

4 August
Haiti
Five companies of the 2nd Regiment arrive in Port-au-Prince from Philadelphia.

15 August
Haiti
The 1st Regiment and the headquarters of the 1st Marine Brigade reach Port-au-Prince. The mission is to restore order in the chaotic country. The Marines move out to garrison various cities and towns.

17 August
Aviation
Secretary of the Navy Daniels asks the Secretary of War to provide instruction in flying land planes to Marine and Navy aviators. Lieutenant W. M. McIlvain is the first Marine to receive such training.

30 August
Haiti
A Marine artillery battalion joins the forces in Haiti. The brigade now has a strength of 88 officers and 1,941 enlisted.

16 September
Haiti
The United States and Haiti sign a treaty which provides for creation of a constabulary force under Marine supervision. This is the genesis of the Gendarmerie d'Haiti.

20 September
Haiti
Marine patrols engage in the first major battle with Caco bandits in northern Haiti, killing 40 at a cost of 10 wounded Marines.

24–25 October
Haiti
Major Smedley Butler and a 40-man patrol defeats a night ambush by Cacos in northern Haiti. Gunnery Sergeant Dan Daly's heroism will result in his second Medal of Honor.

25 October
Bases
After a hiatus at Norfolk, Virginia, the Marine recruit training depot returns to Port Royal, South Carolina, which is officially turned over to the Marine Corps by the Navy a few days later.

9 November
Mexico
Most of the 4th Regiment deploys at sea off the west coast of Mexico.

18 November
Haiti
Marines under Butler seize Fort Riviere, kill 50 Cacos, and break enemy resistance in northern Haiti.

Left: *"Fort Riviere, Haiti," Maj Donna Neary, USMCR (Ret), Marine Corps Art Collection*

Opposite, top: *"Charge Across the Beach, Caribbean," Sydney Riesenberg, Marine Corps Art Collection*

Opposite, bottom: *A steam launch tows Marines ashore off Santo Domingo in 1916. (National Archives)*

28 November
Mexico
Elements of the 4th Regiment embark on cruiser *San Diego* (ACR-6) and take station off the west coast of Mexico until 3 February 1916.

1916

8 January
Bases
The Navy Department directs the establishment of a permanent Marine Corps base at San Diego, California.

5 May
Santo Domingo
Two companies of Marines from Haiti on board *Prairie* and the detachment of *Castine* (Gunboat No. 6) go ashore at Santo Domingo City to protect the U.S. legation during a revolt. Additional Marines follow during the month. Their ultimate mission is to support the U.S. policy of establishing an effective government for Santo Domingo following years of instability.

1 June
Santo Domingo
The Marine detachments of battleships *Rhode Island* (BB-17) and *New Jersey* (BB-16) lead a naval battalion ashore at Puerto Plata, Santo Domingo.

17 June
Technology
Henderson (AP-1), named for the Marine Commandant and the first transport built specifically to carry Marines, is launched at Philadelphia.

21 June
Santo Domingo
Colonel Pendleton and the 4th Regiment arrive in Santo Domingo at Monte Cristi, then proceed overland toward Santiago.

27 June
Santo Domingo
Pendleton's force, with supporting fire from artillery and machine guns, assaults and seizes the dominating Las Trencheras Ridge against strong rebel opposition.

30 June
Manpower
The strength of the Marine Corps on active duty is 348 officers and 10,253 enlisted.

DE HAVILAND DH-4

An American had been the first to achieve powered flight, but the U.S. aviation community was behind its overseas competitors when the nation entered World War I. Combat had spurred inventiveness in Europe and moved those countries far ahead. Since there was no time for the United States to catch up with its own designs, a group went across the Atlantic to select Allied aircraft for manufacture by American industry. The prime candidate was the British de Haviland DH-4, a biplane bomber. The initial sample plane came to the United States on 27 July 1917. It had no engine, but luckily the newly designed American Liberty motor was a good fit for the airframe and more powerful than its British predecessor. The re-engined sample first flew on 29 October.

Production proved more difficult, in part because the plans had to be converted to standard U.S. measurements. Three companies, all formed by automakers, ended up manufacturing the de Haviland. But the wood-and-fabric DH-4s were nothing like cars, which further slowed the initial building program. Nevertheless, the three firms turned out nearly 5,000 planes at a cost of $5,500 apiece before the war ended. Very few made it to the front in time for combat, however. Among them were some of those employed by the Marine Corps Day Wing of the Northern Bombing Group (which also flew British-built airframes of the same type, plus a modified craft known as the DH-9).

The de Haviland was not particularly well designed. The main gas tank (with a capacity of 67 gallons) was located between the pilot and his observer. The resulting distance between the two men made it difficult for them to converse in flight. The heavy tank also posed a hazard to the pilot in any crash that broke it loose from its moorings. The ease with which it ruptured and caught fire

the lower wing allowed it to carry several bombs, not to exceed a total weight of about 450 pounds. With the added horsepower of the Liberty engine, the DH-4 could achieve a speed of 125 miles per hour and climb to 17,500 feet. Its speed and firepower enabled it to survive against the fighter planes of the day. Of the 196 American-built de Havilands that went into combat, 33 were downed by enemy fire, but the U.S. planes also accounted for 45 enemy aircraft. The Marines lost only one DH-4 in combat and had four confirmed kills and eight more claimed (although some were attributable to the DH-9A).

gave the DH-4 its lasting nickname, "Flaming Coffin." (A major change in the British DH-9 was swapping the location of the pilot's cockpit and the fuel tank.) The location of the wheels left the plane too heavy in front, which gave it a tendency to nose over on landing. A late-war version—the DH-4B—fixed these shortcomings, in part by copying the changes incorporated in the DH-9.

The DH-4 was relatively well-armed for the time. The pilot had two fixed .30-caliber Marlin machine guns firing through the propeller. The observer had a pair of Lewis machine guns on a ring mount. Racks under

There were so many surplus de Havilands at the end of the war, and budgets were so tight, that it served as the workhorse of Marine Corps land-based aviation for the next decade. It underwent a number of modifications to improve performance, and Boeing even built its own version with a metal-framed fuselage, designated the O2B-1. The two fixed Marlin guns were also replaced by a single Browning. The airplane proved its worth as late as 1927, when Marines providing close air support at Ocotal in Nicaragua flew the venerable DH-4Bs and O2B-1s into action.

Opposite: *Pilots and ground crew with a DH-4B. (National Archives)*

Top: *"Bombing at Thielt, Belgium," James Butcher, Marine Corps Art Collection*

Right: *A Marine de Haviland in France. (National Archives)*

3 July
Santo Domingo
The 4th Regiment defeats a sizable enemy force at Guayacanas.

5 July
Santo Domingo
Pendleton and his regiment occupy Santiago, Santo Domingo.

29 August
Manpower
The National Defense Act authorizes an increase in the Marine Corps to 597 officers and 14,981 enlisted and also allows the President to expand it further to 693 officers and 17,400 enlisted in case of a national emergency. This legislation also establishes the Marine Corps Reserve and provides money to purchase land for a base in San Diego.

29 November
Santo Domingo
The U.S. declares a military government in Santo Domingo, with the goal of establishing a stable country, thus taking on an extended occupation.

13 February
Aviation
1st Lieutenant Francis T. "Cocky" Evans makes the first successful loop in an N-9 seaplane, in the process determining how to come out of a spin after an initial failed attempt. His spin-recovery technique becomes a standard flying procedure.

25 February
Cuba
Marine detachments from U.S. battleships land at Guacanayabo Bay, Cuba, to guard American-owned sugar plantations and processing mills during a revolution. Sugar is considered a vital commodity, and the Cuban supply is important not only to the United States, but also to prospective allies in Europe.

26 February
Force Structure
1st Lieutenant Alfred Cunningham is ordered to organize an Aviation Company for the Advance Base Force in Philadelphia.

4 March
Cuba
Six companies of Marines from Haiti arrive in Cuba.

8 March
Cuba
Marines from Guantanamo Bay and three warships occupy Guantanamo City, then begin to spread out to other threatened areas. Marine forces remain in Cuban territory until 25 May.

26 March
Manpower
The President issues an executive order allowing expansion of the Corps to its maximum strength under the law passed on 29 August 1916.

29 March
Virgin Islands
Following the purchase of the Virgin Islands from Denmark (to prevent them from being used as German naval bases), a company of Marines occupies St. Croix.

6 April
World War I
The United States declares war on Germany and enters World War I.

7 April
Santo Domingo
Marine patrols defeat a large bandit force at Las Canitas in Santo Domingo.

21 April
Virgin Islands
Two companies of Marines occupy St. Thomas, Virgin Islands, and establish harbor defenses.

27 April
Force Structure
The aviation detachment with the Advance Base Force in Philadelphia is designated the Marine Aeronautic Company.

1 May
Santo Domingo
Marines establish the Guardia Nacional Dominica to begin the process of creating a stable military force for Santo Domingo.

14 May
Bases
The first detachment of Marines, from Annapolis, move to the newly leased base of 5,300 acres at Quantico, Virginia.

19 May
World War I
Secretary of the Navy Josephus Daniels offers a Marine regiment for service in France. The Secretary of War accepts the proposal on 23 May.

22 May
Manpower
Congress authorizes expansion of the Marine Corps to 1,323 officers and 30,000 enlisted.

Opposite: *A WWI Marine prepares to throw a grenade. ("Bombing," Gilbert Gaul, Marine Corps Art Collection)*

Top: *"First in France," John A. Coughlin, Marine Corps Art Collection*

Right: *"Return of the Mayflower," Bernard F. Gribble, U.S. Naval Academy Art Collection*

MARINE CORPS BASE, QUANTICO

Quantico and the surrounding area had been an important site since the early days of the colony of Virginia. The narrow flatlands where Quantico Creek flowed into the Potomac River made an ideal location from which the region's tobacco growers could ship their commodity to markets along the eastern seaboard and in Europe. But a decrease in the importance of tobacco and the silting up of the creek slowly turned Quantico into a backwater during the latter 1800s. Various speculative companies took over the land and periodically tried to market it as a commercial center, a resort destination, and finally a shipyard.

World War I brought a significant increase in the size of the Corps beyond the strength of several thousand that it had maintained since the conflict with Spain. The creation prior to World War I of the Advance Base Force, the first permanently organized peacetime Marine field unit, also brought to the fore a requirement for a place where Marines could train with their growing arsenal of heavier weapons. Simultaneously, the rapid buildup of the Navy after 1914 caused that service to take back facilities aboard naval bases previously provided for the use of Marines. These factors forced Headquarters Marine Corps to search for a suitable base of its own somewhere along the east coast.

The quest became urgent with U.S. entry into the war in April 1917. That same month, a board of senior Marines determined that the Quantico area met just about every need. There was sufficient space for units to fire their weapons and practice maneuvers, a major road and railroad running through the tract, and access for ships on the Potomac. Within days, the Marine Corps leased 5,300 acres from the company that had been trying to sell it for years. Quantico thus became the first Marine Corps base designed specifically for the use of operational units.

Opposite: *During training at Quantico, Marines race into position with crew-served weapons. (National Archives)*

Right: *Marines march through Quantico upon their return from Nicaragua in 1933. (Leatherneck Magazine)*

Other than a tiny village laid out along a single dusty street, there were absolutely no facilities on the largely wooded land. The Marines would have to build their base entirely from scratch. They wasted no time. The first troops arrived from Annapolis in mid-May. A month later, the newly organized 1st Battalion of the 5th Regiment sailed from Quantico for duty in France. Other Marines poured in just as fast as the recruit depots could churn them out. They initially lived in tents pitched in a cornfield. Civilian laborers swarmed over the site erecting single-story wood-and-tarpaper barracks and larger buildings, putting down a concrete road, and creating means to provide fresh water and dispose of waste. By fall 1917, the base was sending additional units to France and elsewhere and training all officer candidates.

Before the war was over, the Marine Corps purchased the land from the development company and even expanded the site to 7,000 acres. When Marine aviation units returned from France in 1919, they established an airfield. Major General Lejeune took command of the base during this period and soon created the Marine

Corps Schools for officers. The base did not take on its first permanent character until the late 1920s, when Congress finally appropriated money to replace the temporary wooden structures of the World War. Brick buildings began to spring up in 1928, while work got underway to create a larger airfield on filled land in the Potomac.

Quantico's use as a home for operational units came to an end with the onset of World War II. When the Fleet Marine Force expanded to division and wing strength, there simply no longer were sufficient facilities for organizations of that size. The base expanded dramatically in 1942 with the purchase of 51,000 acres west of U.S. Route 1, but newer bases on the nation's coasts provided more suitable locations for amphibious training. The regiments and aircraft groups soon left for these better sites, never to return. Quantico remained the intellectual heart of the Corps, however. It continues today to provide advanced training and education to Marine officers and senior enlisted men, and it also is home to organizations that oversee the development of doctrine and the acquisition of new equipment for the Corps.

29 May
Force Structure
Secretary of the Navy Daniels orders creation of the 5th Regiment. Commandant Barnett already has begun drawing together forces at Philadelphia from the U.S. and the Caribbean.

4 June
Manpower
The Commandant directs that all future commissioned officers for the World War come from the enlisted ranks of the Marine Corps (with the exception of Naval Academy graduates). The mechanism for turning selected enlisted men into lieutenants is Officers' Training Camp, a three-month course that soon begins at Quantico.

14 June
Force Structure
The 5th Regiment sails for France. It arrives at St. Nazaire on the 26th and comes under command of the American Expeditionary Force (AEF). The regiment is assigned to the U.S. Army's 1st Division in excess of division tables of organization.

15 June
Bases
The Navy purchases 232 acres on San Diego Bay. San Diego donates 500 acres of adjacent tidal land (to be covered by land fill) for a Marine base for the West Coast expeditionary force.

22 June
Bases
The Marine Corps redesignates the base at Port Royal as Marine Barracks, Paris Island. (Spelling would be changed to Parris Island on 3 May 1919.)

30 June
Manpower
The strength of the Marine Corps on active duty is 776 officers and 26,973 enlisted.

4 August
Force Structure
Secretary Daniels orders creation of the 6th Regiment for eventual service with the AEF.

17 August
Force Structure
The 1st Machine Gun Battalion is established at Quantico.

21 August
Force Structure
The newly organized 7th Regiment departs Philadelphia for Cuba to guard U.S. sugar interests.

5 October
Force Structure
Lead elements of the 6th Regiment arrive in France.

9 October
Force Structure
The 8th Regiment is organized at Quantico to serve with the Advance Base Force. It is soon sent to Galveston, Texas, for possible deployment to the Mexican oil fields to protect the fleet's fuel source from disruption.

12 October
Force Structure
The Advance Base Force aviation unit at Philadelphia is divided into the 1st Marine Aviation Squadron and the 1st Marine Aeronautic Company.

14 October
Force Structure
The 1st Marine Aeronautic Company deploys to Cape May, New Jersey, and specializes in seaplanes.

17 October
Force Structure
The 1st Marine Aviation Squadron transfers to Long Island, New York, and specializes in land planes.

23 October
Force Structure
The 6th Regiment joins with the 5th Regiment to form the 4th Marine Brigade. At full strength, the brigade musters 280 officers and 9,164 enlisted.

26 October
Force Structure
The 4th Marine Brigade is joined with Army units to form the 2nd Division.

20 November
Force Structure
The 9th Regiment is organized at Quantico to serve with the Advance Base Force.

25 November
Great Britain
Marine detachments sail from Chesapeake Bay on board the battleships sent to reinforce the Royal Navy's Grand Fleet in British waters.

Be Up-to-Date=Be A U. S. Marine

First to Change the Old Campaign Hat for the Modern Helmet

Enlist at

15 December
Force Structure
Captain Roy Geiger establishes the Aeronautic Detachment at Philadelphia.

Opposite: *World War I recruiting poster. ("First to Fight for Democracy," G. A. Shafer, Marine Corps Art Collection)*

Top: *World War I recruiting poster. ("Be Up To Date, Be A Marine," W. A. Rogers, Marine Corps Art Collection)*

Right: *Marine aviation in the Azores. ("Protect the Convoys," Col Avery Chenoweth, USMCR (Ret), Marine Corps Art Collection)*

PRIVATE ELTON E. MACKIN

Elton Mackin came from a working-class family in western New York, where he was born in 1898. His father died a few weeks later in an accident and his mother eventually remarried. Elton completed high school in the summer of 1917, but did not rush to the colors in the first months after the United States joined the World War. Just before Christmas, inspired in part by an article in a popular magazine of the day, he joined the Marine Corps. Five months later, he arrived in France with the 3rd Replacement Battalion. His group moved up to the front on the evening of 7 June—the second day of the Marine assault on Belleau Wood. They were fed into the lines of the 1st Battalion, 5th Regiment, which had suffered significant losses the prior day while seizing ground west of the main forest. Years later he would recall: "We didn't know how young and scared we were, nor how much we showed it."

Assigned to the 67th Company, Mackin participated in the remaining weeks of fighting to clear Belleau Wood. Near the end of the battle he was offered duty as a battalion runner, considered a suicide billet due to the requirement to frequently traverse fire-swept ground carrying messages. His fear of looking like a coward in front of a senior NCO outweighed his fear of death, and he accepted. In mid-July, he and his battalion were part of the hurried, all-night movement to reach the front lines for the attack at Soissons. The 5th Regiment caught the enemy unprepared and drove them through a wooded area. Its losses were high, but not like Belleau Wood. The St. Mihiel offensive was the easiest of all, with the Army's 3rd Brigade leading the way against a

Left: *During the Meuse-Argonne campaign, Marines pick their way through a heavily shelled landscape. (National Archives)*

Opposite: *"Forced March, Soissons," John W. Thomason, Sam Houston State University*

withdrawing enemy. Blanc Mont in October was the worst. The initial attack was too successful, and the 5th Regiment swept past its objectives in pursuit. The Marines ended up stranded in a wood, with no friendly forces to their flanks and open ground between them and the rear. Heavy German fire savaged the exposed position from three sides, and losses were the heaviest of the war for the regiment. Mackin received the Army Distinguished Service Cross and two citations (subsequently converted to Silver Star medals) for his bravery in this battle. He served as the chief of the battalion runners during the Meuse-Argonne and was one of the lucky, courageous Marines who survived crossing the footbridge over the river under artillery and machine-gun fire during the final night of the war. He also was one of the few men to live through every battle of the Marine Brigade.

Mackin was able to come home before his unit did, mustering out in the States in May 1919. He held several jobs in the 1920s, suffered like most of his countrymen during the Depression, and finally found steady employment as a government clerk with his local draft board in 1939. After World War II, he opened an appliance store, but ended his working life as a schoolbus driver and custodian. Eventually he jotted down his memories of his service, telling the personal story of a young man suddenly thrust into the maw of a cataclysmic war.

He recalled small incidents of great magnitude to those who experienced them. The new replacement, gathering up days-old dead after the battle at Belleau Wood, sickened when he picked up one head-shot Marine, whose brains then slid out of his helmet and on to the feet of the stretcher bearer. A dud shell burrowing at a man's feet, the force of its landing sending him flying through the air, the sheer fright of what might have been leaving

him "twitching horribly, his eyes rolling up and showing white." Marines watching a nearby unit take the brunt of a counterattack, for once feeling a sense of safety, only to have it shattered by the order of the sergeant to "Fix your bayonets" and move forward for their first attempt to kill a man at arm's length. A runner coming across a badly wounded German in a lonely wood and hearing long after the plaintive cries for help as he continues on his mission. A man finally receiving a long-awaited letter from home, but every page an indecipherable blob of water-soaked ink. Looking back, Mackin believed that he and many of his comrades had been "too damned young and under fire too soon," which left an emotional "brittleness that was to mark all the days of our remaining lives." He died in 1974, too soon to see his words published as one of the most searing memoirs of World War I— *Suddenly We Didn't Want to Die.*

25 December
Force Structure
The 9th Regiment arrives at Guantanamo Bay to further reinforce units guarding U.S. sugar production capability.

28 December
Force Structure
The 1st Machine Gun Battalion arrives in France and is assigned to the 4th Marine Brigade.

1918

January
Force Structure
The 11th Regiment is formed at Quantico as an artillery unit.

1 January
Force Structure
The 1st Marine Aviation Squadron departs Long Island for the Army flying field at Lake Charles, Louisiana.

14 January
Force Structure
The 10th Regiment is organized at Quantico to man tractor-mounted 7-inch naval guns.

20 January
Force Structure
The 1st Machine Gun Battalion is redesignated the 6th Machine Gun Battalion.

21 January
Azores
The 1st Marine Aeronautic Company arrives at the naval base at Ponta Delgado, Azores, and undertakes antisubmarine patrols with its 12 seaplanes and six flying boats.

5 February
Force Structure
Captain Alfred Cunningham convinces the Navy's General Board to order the creation of a bombing group to attack German submarine pens along the Belgian coast.

6 February
Force Structure
The last battalion of the 6th Regiment arrives in France, completing the organization of the 4th Marine Brigade.

7 February
Force Structure
Geiger and his Aeronautic Detachment depart Philadelphia for the Naval Air Station, Miami.

25 February
Commandants

Major General Barnett is reappointed for a second four-year term as Commandant.

17 March
Verdun

The 2nd Battalion, 5th Regiment, becomes the first Marine unit to occupy front-line positions in France, in a sector just south of Verdun.

1 April
Bases

Captain Cunningham's 1st Marine Aviation Squadron arrives at the newly established Marine Flying Field, Miami (recently acquired by Geiger's detachment).

13 April
Verdun

The 4th Marine Brigade suffers its first significant combat casualties when the 74th Company of the 6th Regiment is hit with a barrage of mustard gas prior to dawn while billeted in a reserve area near Verdun. A shell bursting inside a building where many men are sleeping results in unusually heavy casualties. Losses are nearly 300, of whom 40 are killed or subsequently die.

15 April
Force Structure

1st Marine Aviation Squadron becomes 1st Marine Aviation Force with four authorized squadrons.

23 April
Verdun

The first Medal of Honor is earned by a member of the Marine Brigade when Navy dentist Lieutenant Commander Alexander G. Lyle moves through a heavy barrage and renders surgical aid to a wounded Marine.

Top: *The scene of a vicious and bloody 1916 battle became the Marine introduction to the western front in 1918. ("Verdun," Lester G. Hornby, Marine Corps Art Collection)*

Right: *"Chateau-Thierry," Lester G. Hornby, Marine Corps Art Collection*

GENERAL GERALD C. THOMAS

Gerald Carthrae Thomas was a 21-year-old sophomore at Illinois Wesleyan University when the U.S. entered World War I. The 5-foot, 9-inch, 160-pound student had excelled as a lineman on the college football team and managed to achieve decent grades even as he worked to put himself through college. He was eager to serve his nation and tried to join an Army commissioning program. Receiving no response from an overwhelmed bureaucracy, he enlisted in the Marine Corps on 15 May 1917. Following recruit training at Parris Island, he reported to the 1st Battalion, 6th Marines, and shipped with them to France.

Sergeant Thomas participated in his battalion's attack into Belleau Wood on 10 June 1918. He was cited for bravery in brigade orders for leading a squad that wiped out German holdouts in the rear of the Marine position. During the advance at Soissons, he became an acting platoon commander due to heavy losses. Temporarily assigned as a student at a weapons course in the rear, he left without permission to rejoin his battalion when he leaned of its participation in the St. Mihiel offensive. As a newly commissioned officer, he was gassed at the start of the Meuse-Argonne offensive.

After the "war to end all wars," Jerry Thomas soon went to Haiti to help put down the Caco revolt. Initially consigned to a staff job in Port-au-Prince, he nevertheless played a major role in defeating a substantial rebel attack on the capital by establishing a hasty night ambush with a handful of Marines and destroying one of the enemy columns. There followed uneventful tours commanding a ship's detachment, serving in a Stateside Marine barracks, returning to Haiti as a staff officer, getting professional education at the Army Infantry School at Fort Benning and the Field Officers Course at Quantico, and teaching at The Basic School. He developed a reputation as an intelligent planner and confident commander who demanded the best from subordinates and peers and did not suffer fools. His most significant assignment, from a career standpoint, came when he reported in 1935 for duty with the Peking Legation Guard. His superior work as a leader and staff officer in China established him as a valued protege of Colonel Alexander A. Vandegrift. More time as a student and instructor followed.

In 1941, Thomas became the operations officer for the 1st Marine Division. Soon after, Vandegrift took over the division. In August 1942, they led the division in the assault on Guadalcanal. Thomas's resolute performance brought a spot promotion to colonel and chief of staff of the division early in the campaign. The two men were inseparable thereafter. Thomas reprised his role as chief of staff when Vandegrift took command of the I Marine Amphibious Corps and led it in the invasion of Bougainville. When Vandegrift became the Commandant in January 1944, Thomas received a second spot promotion—to brigadier general—and became the director of the Plans and Policies division at Headquarters Marine Corps. From that billet he orchestrated the manpower and materiel needed to fight through the bloody closing campaigns of the war.

13 August
Manpower
Opha M. Johnson, a civil service employee at Headquarters Marine Corps, becomes the first female to enroll in the Marines. A total of 305 are enlisted during the war.

5 September
Force Structure
The Commandant directs formation of the 5th Marine Brigade headquarters at Quantico. The 11th and 13th Regiments and 5th Machine Gun Battalion are assigned to it.

12 September
St. Mihiel
The 4th Marine Brigade serves as the reserve of the 2nd Division during the U.S. First Army's attack to reduce the St. Mihiel salient. Over the next three days, the brigade participates in reducing German pockets of resistance. Marine losses total 919.

24 September
Force Structure
Lead elements of the 5th Marine Brigade arrive in France. Its units are assigned to guard duty along the lines of communication.

25 September
Force Structure
The 2nd Division is transferred to the French Fourth Army.

28 September
France
While flying with a British squadron, Lieutenant Everett S. Brewster and Gunnery Sergeant Harry B. Wersheimer become the first Marines to shoot down an enemy plane.

1 October
Blanc Mont
The 2nd Division moves into the front lines, with the 4th Marine Brigade occupying the forward trenches.

2 October
France
Marines conduct their first aerial resupply mission, dropping food to a surrounded French regiment.

3 October
Blanc Mont
The 4th Marine Brigade attacks and seizes the Blanc Mont ridge. Corporal J. H. Pruitt and Private James J. Kelly later receive the Medal of Honor for separately destroying German machine-gun nests.

7 October
Commandants
Major General Barnett arrives in France for a month-long tour of Marine units with the AEF.

8 October
Blanc Mont
The brigade takes the village of St. Etienne, its last objective beyond Mont Blanc.

10 October
Blanc Mont
French forces relieve the 2nd Division. Marine casualties in the Blanc Mont battle total 2,369.

THE BATTLE OF BLANC MONT

In late September 1918, General John Pershing, commander of the AEF, loaned his 2nd and 36th Divisions to the battered French Fourth Army on his flank. Major General Lejeune, commander of the 2nd Division, soon learned that the French hoped to use his brigades independently as reinforcements for their weakened outfits. He countered with a bold offer—if the army commander allowed him to employ his division as a unit, he would deliver Blanc Mont in the coming offensive. Given the impregnable reputation of the high chalk ridge, long held by the Germans, the French commander accepted.

Lejeune employed unusual tactics for his attack. The 4th Marine Brigade would jump off from the left half of the division front, while the 3rd Brigade launched its assault from the trench lines of the French division on the right, thus leaving a mile of uncovered ground in between the two American outfits. The Army brigade would move diagonally into the 2nd Division zone during the assault and eventually converge with the Marine brigade. This scheme of maneuver avoided a triangle of terrain that contained the Bois de la Vipere (Snake Woods). The American infantry would avoid strong outposts in concealed positions, focus on the main

Left: *Marines mop up in the Essen Hook. ("Capture of Blanc Mont Ridge," George M. Harding, Marine Corps Art Collection)*

Opposite: *"Marine Mud and Misery," Col Charles Waterhouse, USMCR (Ret), Marine Corps Art Collection*

objective of the ridge beyond, and mop up the bypassed covering defenses later. Although an unusually large aggregation of supporting artillery (48 batteries) was available, the guns would fire only a five-minute preparation—just enough to stun and disorganize the enemy, but not provide them with any warning to move up reserves.

The operation kicked off on the morning of 3 October. The 6th Regiment led off the 4th Marine Brigade in a column of battalions, with 2/6 in the lead. The battalion made rapid progress against weakly held outposts. Two Marines, Private James J. Kelly and Corporal John H. Pruitt, helped spearhead the assault by single-handedly destroying machine-gun nests. By 0830, 2/6 had gained 3,000 yards, climbed the slopes of Blanc Mont, and seized its eastern half. But the French division on the left had not gotten through a strong position immediately to its front. Germans in the Essen Hook, as it was dubbed, poured flanking fire into Marine units moving up to support 2/6. Other enemy outfits threatened to counterattack into the yawning gap on the 4th Brigade's left flank. The 5th Regiment established a line facing perpendicular to the advance to cover this zone. Captain Leroy P. Hunt led his 17th Company against the Essen Hook. By skillful use of machine guns and maneuver, he captured the trench-and-bunker complex and its hundred surviving defenders. He turned it over to the French, who lost it soon after to a German counterattack. The 3rd Brigade achieved equal success to the right of Blanc Mont.

The French high command directed a renewed attack in the afternoon to exploit the rapid advance, but the orders came late, and the Marine brigade elected to postpone the assault until the next morning. That

night the Germans brought up strong reserves to stave off the Americans while other elements withdrew from the main defensive line, now untenable due to the loss of the area's commanding ridge. The 5th Regiment moved through the 6th Regiment and made substantial gains the next morning, but came under intense artillery and machine-gun fire from the fresh German forces on the left flank. (The French still were not keeping pace.) The result was the bloodiest day of the war for the Marines, with more than 1,100 killed or wounded.

In subsequent days of hard fighting, the Marines slogged forward against heavy resistance to clear the remainder of Blanc Mont and seize the town of St. Etienne beyond. The badly depleted 2nd Division was relieved by elements of the 36th Division by 10 October, but Lejeune's outfit had made a major contribution to the Allied offensive.

14 October
Belgium
Captain Robert S. Lytle leads Squadron 9 in the 1st Marine Aviation Force's first independent mission. The five DH-4s and three DH-9As drop 2,218 pounds of bombs on the German-held rail yards at Thielt, Belgium. Lieutenant Ralph Talbot and his observer, Corporal Robert G. Robinson, shoot down two enemy planes before landing their crippled plane. Both men later received the Medal of Honor.

17 October
Haiti
Charlemagne Peralte launches an attack against Marine-led Gendarmerie force at Hinche, Haiti, and is driven off. This marks the opening of the Caco Revolt.

22 October
Belgium
German planes shoot down the bomber of Lieutenant Harvey G. Norman and his observer, Lieutenant Caleb W. Taylor. This is the first Marine aircraft lost to enemy action. Both men die in the crash.

25 October
France
The 2nd Division is reassigned to the U.S. First Army.

1 November
Meuse-Argonne
The 2nd Division, with the 4th Marine Brigade in the lead, joins in the Meuse-Argonne offensive. The brigade attack overruns all German defensive lines and creates a salient forcing an enemy withdrawal all across the front. In pursuit, the division reaches the Meuse River on 9 November.

3 November
Cuba
The 1st Regiment departs Philadelphia for duty in Cuba to deal with revolutionary activity in that country.

10 November
Meuse-Argonne
The 4th Marine Brigade makes a night attack across the Meuse River and gains a foothold on the opposite bank by the next morning. Marine losses in the Meuse-Argonne offensive total 1,263.

11 November
World War I
At 1100, an armistice goes into effect, and World War I comes to an end. Of the roughly 32,000 Marines who served in France, 2,459 died as a result of action, 8,907 were wounded, and 25 had been taken prisoner.

Left: *Marines take a break around the time of the Meuse-Argonne offensive. ("At a Bridge Near Romagne," Lester G. Hornby, Marine Corps Art Collection)*

Opposite: *With peace only hours away, Marines conduct a last attack across the Meuse River. ("The Last Night of the War," F. C. Yohn, Marine Corps Art Collection)*

17 November
Germany
The 2nd Division begins its march toward Germany and reaches the border on 23 November.

20 November
Manpower
The Commandant issues demobilization plans that authorize the immediate release of reservists and those regulars who had enlisted for the duration of the war or who had valid personal reasons for discharge.

1 December
Germany
The 4th Marine Brigade and other Allied forces cross into Germany under the armistice terms. The brigade reaches the Rhine on 9 December.

2 December
Manpower
The Marine Corps resumes reliance on voluntary enlistments for manpower.

6 December
Force Structure
The 1st Marine Aviation Force sails for the U.S.

11 December
Manpower
The Marine Corps reaches its highest strength since its inception, with 2,462 officers and 72,639 enlisted on active duty.

13 December
Germany
The Marines occupy their portion of the bridgehead east of the Rhine, near Coblenz, Germany.

26 December
Force Structure
The battleship force and embarked Marine detachments, deployed in the British Isles for the war, return to New York harbor.

COLONEL JOHN W. THOMASON

John W. Thomason II was born to a well-off family in Huntsville, Texas, on 28 February 1893. His father was a doctor and landowner who expected his son to follow in his footsteps. Young John loved reading and showed a talent for art from his early years, but he disliked school and had no interest in any profession. After mediocre performances at three different colleges, two stints as a teacher, and a year as a reporter, he joined the Marine Corps on the day the U.S. entered World War I. Writing and art would stay with him until the day he died, but he had finally found his niche in life.

Lieutenant Thomason reported to the 4th Marine Brigade in France in April 1918. He led his platoon through the battles of Belleau Wood and Soissons, distinguishing himself in the latter when he and a NCO destroyed a pair of machine guns pinning down their company. He eventually would receive the Navy Cross and an Army Silver Star for that act of bravery. Promoted to XO of the company, he went on to fight at St. Mihiel

and Blanc Mont. Only a severe case of the flu prevented him from being one of the rare officers who lasted through to the armistice.

He first tried his hand at serious writing while he was stationed in Cuba in the early 1920s. Editors initially rejected his stories because the public supposedly was tired of reading about war. Transferred to an ammunition depot near New York City, he began to exhibit some of his artwork. A fellow Marine veteran of the great war, Laurence Stallings, launched Thomason into the literary and artistic circles of the metropolis. A national magazine published his first article, about Soissons, in the summer of 1925. "Fix Bayonets!" met rave reviews for its unvarnished depiction of men in combat and its accompanying illustrations. His own stories and his illustrations for the articles of others soon were in high demand. Before long, the Marine captain was earning far more from writing and drawing than he did as an officer, but he chose to stick with the profession of arms and pursue his other talents as a part-time avocation.

For a time, his two worlds merged, as the Commandant assigned him to write a history of the 2nd Division in the World War. But generally Thomason performed duties just like any other Marine officer. He commanded a detachment on a ship in Central American waters, served in the Legation Guard in Peking, attended the Army and Navy War Colleges, and commanded an infantry battalion in the late 1930s. In his spare time, he served as an editor for a major national magazine and published several books, ranging from

collections of short stories, to a biography of J. E. B. Stuart, to a novel.

During the interwar years, he was hospitalized for extended periods on several occasions, usually with a diagnosis of exhaustion. Although the facts are in dispute, alcoholism may have played a part in his poor health. Whatever the cause, his physical condition prevented him from playing a significant role in World War II. He served for a time as a training officer in the States, then as a planner in the Pacific theater on the staff of Admiral Nimitz. The closest he came again to the sound of guns was as an observer during the campaign against Munda Airfield on New Georgia. Invalided home for illness in August 1943, he died in March 1944 at the age of 51.

Thomason's intimate accounts, both fictional and factual, of his fellow Marines in war and peace remain among the very best descriptions of the essence of the Corps. His drawings equally capture in bold fashion the everyday life and sometimes commonplace death of Marines. His ability to translate what he saw and felt into words and art has never been matched by any other leatherneck.

Opposite: *"A small figure in a long gray cloak . . ."*
John W. Thomason, Sam Houston State University

Above: *Capt John Thomason, Jr., in a trench, Sino-Japanese War, 1932. (Marine Corps Historical Center)*

THINKERS
AND
FIGHTERS

31 March
Haiti
Squadron E arrives in Haiti to provide an aviation element to the 1st Marine Brigade.

4 April
Haiti
A Marine patrol of four officers and 51 enlisted attacks and scatters 500 Cacos near Hinche.

5 May
HQMC
Marine Corps Headquarters moves to the new Navy Building on Constitution Avenue.

20 May
Force Structure
Squadron C of the former 1st Marine Aviation Force arrives in Quantico for duty.

12 June
Bases
Marine Corps Base, Quantico leases a site for its first flying field for land planes, and construction begins on hangars and other supporting facilities.

30 June
Manpower
The strength of the Marine Corps on active duty is 2,270 officers and 46,564 enlisted.

1 July
Force Structure
Squadron C absorbs the Marine Aeronautic Section at Quantico.

11 July
Manpower
Congress completes legislation establishing the enlisted strength of the postwar Marine Corps at 27,400. The next day, Commandant George Barnett promulgates directives to speed up demobilization. The process is largely completed by the end of the year.

21 July
Force Structure
The 15th Separate Battalion is formed at Camp Pontanezan, France, from personnel of the 4th and 5th Marine Brigades, for duty in connection with a plebiscite in Germany.

23 July
Santo Domingo
The first Marine air attack on Dominican bandits is made near Meta de la Palma.

3 August
Force Structure
The 4th Marine Brigade returns to the United States from Europe.

8 August
Force Structure
The 4th Marine Brigade parades through New York City along with its parent 2nd Division. It returns to duty with the Navy Department later that day. The 5th Marine Brigade returns to the United States from Europe.

11 August
Manpower
This is the final day of active service for women Marine reservists enlisted for the World War. A total of 305 women served in clerical billets.

12 August
Force Structure
The 4th Marine Brigade parades for President Wilson in Washington, D.C., and then disbands.

26 September
Force Structure
Squadron A of the former 1st Marine Aviation Force arrives in Quantico after closing down activities at the former Marine Flying Field in Miami.

1 October
Force Structure
The 2nd Advance Base Force is activated to serve as the West Coast Expeditionary Force for the Marine Corps. Its mission is to defend expeditionary overseas naval bases.

7 October
Haiti

Charlemagne Peralte, the most important Caco leader, sends 300 of his men into Port-au-Prince prior to dawn. Marines and gendarmes defeat and drive off the rebels.

31 October
Haiti

Sergeant Herman Hanneken and Corporal William R. Button (respectively a gendarmerie captain and lieutenant) use a ruse to get their patrol into Peralte's camp and kill him.

1 December
HQMC

The Aviation Section is made a part of the newly formed Operations and Training Division at Headquarters Marine Corps.

17 December
Force Structure

The 8th Regiment is reactivated in the States and shipped to Haiti to reinforce the brigade.

23 December
Force Structure

The 15th Separate Battalion arrives in Philadelphia. It is the last Marine unit to return home from World War I.

1920

14 January
Haiti

A few hundred Cacos under Benoit Batraville move into Port-au-Prince during the night in an attempt

Top: *A 1920s recruiting poster. ("Marine on a Jaguar," James Montgomery Flagg, Marine Corps Art Collection)*

Right: *A Marine detachment moves at "doubletime" around the deck of a battleship in 1920. (Naval Historical Center)*

BRIGADIER GENERAL
HERMAN H. HANNEKEN

Herman Hanneken was born in St. Louis, Missouri, in 1893. As a young man, he went west and worked as a cow puncher. When U.S. forces seized Vera Cruz, Mexico, in 1914, he enlisted in the Marine Corps in search of greater adventure. He was not disappointed, as he deployed to Haiti at the beginning of the American intervention there in 1915. Subsequently he joined the Gendarmerie d'Haiti as a junior officer, while rising in rank to sergeant in the Marine Corps. In 1919, as disorder heated up

again in Haiti, Hanneken was posted to command of the district of Grande Riviere. He soon devised a scheme to deal with Charlemagne Peralte, the most important leader of the Caco revolt.

Hanneken enlisted two of his gendarmes and a local citizen, Jean Conze, in his plan. Conze left town loudly proclaiming his opposition to the occupation, then installed himself at a abandoned fort and rallied Cacos to join him. Private Jean Francois promptly "deserted" the gendarmerie and joined Conze. Hanneken feigned three attacks on the fort and made it appear he had been wounded during the last fight. Conze's stock with the Cacos rose, and he convinced Peralte to launch a night assault on Grande Riviere. The wily Peralte nearly spoiled the plot when he decided to await the results of the attack at a remote point, surrounded by 700 of his followers. Francois brought word of the change to Hanneken, who lay in wait outside Grande Riviere with Cpl William R. Button and 20 gendarmes, all disguised as Cacos. With Francois providing the password, the group marched on Peralte's camp. They successfully penetrated the well-guarded site. Just as the Caco leader's immediate bodyguards grew suspicious, Hanneken drew out a pistol and shot Peralte. In the confused melee that followed, the gendarmerie outfit fought off two counterattacks. The next day Hanneken brought Peralte's body into the city. When evidence of his death spread around the country, the Caco revolt lost much of its impetus.

Opposite: *PFC D. D. Pomerleau rides Vesper Belle in Peiping in 1937. (National Archives)*

Right: *Marines at the ready at a sandbagged emplacement in Shanghai. The man in the foreground has a BAR; the others aim bayonet-tipped Springfields. (National Archives)*

26 August
China
A second company of Marines reaches Shanghai to reinforce the 4th Marines.

19 September
China
The 2nd Marine Brigade headquarters and the 6th Marines arrive in Shanghai to reinforce the 4th Marines during the fighting between Japanese and Chinese forces.

1 December
Force Structure
The 3rd Marines, a reserve regimental headquarters since December 1925, is disbanded.

12 December
China
Japanese naval aircraft sink the U.S. gunboat *Panay* (PR-5) on the Yangtze River above Nanking. The Japanese government issues a formal apology two days later.

1938

13 January
Training
Marines participate in FLEX 4 at Culebra, Puerto Rico. The exercise continues through 15 March.

18 February
China
The 2nd Brigade headquarters and 6th Marines depart Shanghai after the Chinese are forced from the city by the Japanese, and the threat to the International Settlement is reduced.

28 February
China
Following the withdrawal of the Army's 15th Infantry Regiment from Tientsin, a detachment of about 200 Marines is sent from the Legation Guard at Peiping to establish a post at the former Army barracks.

15 March
Training
Marine units participate in Fleet Problem XIX in Hawaii, practicing the occupation of an advance base.

23 June
Manpower
President Roosevelt signs legislation providing that the active duty strength of the Marine Corps should be 20 percent of the active-duty enlisted strength of the Navy. That act adds 97 billets to the 27,400 already authorized for the Marine Corps. Congress does not provide sufficient funding for that number, however.

25 June
Reserve
The Naval Reserve Act reorganizes the Marine Reserve into three groups: Fleet Marine Corps Reserve (now consisting of active-duty retirees still subject to recall), the Organized Marine Corps Reserve (units), and the Volunteer Marine Corps Reserve (individuals).

30 June
Manpower
The strength of the Marine Corps on active duty is 1,359 officers and 16,997 enlisted.

HOLDING THE LINE

1939 – MAY 1943

HOLDING THE LINE

1939–MAY 1943

When World War II erupted on 1 September 1939, the United States officially stayed neutral, but began preparing slowly for the worst. The isolationist mood of the American public hampered the buildup, but the Corps came up with an idea to create defense battalions, using a name that implied no overseas entanglements. Marine leaders thus succeeded in obtaining some additional force structure. The mission of the defense battalion, of course, was to protect advance expeditionary bases, most likely occupied or seized as part of an offensive campaign.

As the war engulfed more of the globe, the amphibious assault mission grew increasingly dominant in Marine thinking. Simultaneously, the Corps grew more and more frustrated by shortcomings in transports and landing craft. This spurred further Leatherneck creativity. In addition to the acquisition of lighter equipment (such as 75mm pack howitzers initially intended for transport on mules), the Corps began to focus on light units specifically designed for easy and rapid deployment across the beach. One idea— parachutists and gliders—came from the spectacularly successful German use of these capabilities in May 1940. Another organizational adaptation soon turned into the raider battalions. Meanwhile, amphibious exercises steadily grew larger and more challenging. The Marines eventually found the landing craft they needed by adapting products on the civilian market, though

Andrew Higgins's landing boat and Donald Roebling's tracked landing vehicle would not become available in significant numbers until after the United States was in the war. The Corps did take one step backward, breaking up its air-ground teams around the time the brigades expanded into divisions and wings. They would remain largely separate throughout the war.

The Japanese raid on Pearl Harbor brought the United States into the global conflict with a thirst for vengeance. Marine heroics could not overcome surprise, and aviation units in Hawaii suffered like everyone else. Small Marine outfits in China and Guam had to surrender against overwhelming odds. The 4th Marines won a brief respite with a late November 1941 transfer from Shanghai to the Philippines, but the regiment eventually went down swinging at Bataan and Corregidor. One of the few bright spots in the early weeks of the war was the gallant defense of Wake Island. The Marine garrison turned back one Japanese amphibious assault, though it eventually succumbed to another. At Midway in June 1942, the Marines lent a hand in the Navy's defeat of the Japanese fleet.

The dispatch of a brigade to defend Iceland and two to hold Samoa depleted the Corps at a time when it needed to train cohesive divisions for future offensives. When the 1st Marine Division received orders to land on Guadalcanal, it was ill-prepared to do so. Many of the young enlisted men and officers had barely a few months in the

13 April
World War II
The Soviet Union and Japan sign a neutrality treaty.

14 April
Palmyra
Elements of the 1st Defense Battalion arrive.

18 April
Wake Island
Admiral Husband E. Kimmel, commander of naval forces in the Pacific, asks the CNO for a Marine defense battalion for Wake Island.

1 May
Bases
Marine Barracks, New River, North Carolina, is formally established. The base will eventually be named Camp Lejeune.

20 May
World War II
German airborne forces invade the island of Crete in the Mediterranean. The island falls on 1 June.

21 May
Technology
Based on tests in Louisiana, a bow-ramp version of the Higgins boat is determined to be fully functional and preferable to the non-ramp boats previously being built for the Navy. This design goes into production and becomes the forerunner of the Landing Craft Vehicle, Personnel or LCVP.

27 May
World War II
President Roosevelt proclaims an unlimited state of national emergency.

28 May
Force Structure
The 1st Parachute Battalion is established at Quantico.

29 May
Force Structure
The Joint Board approves a plan for a landing force of 28,000 troops (half Marine and half Army) under command of Major General

MARINE CORPS RECRUIT DEPOT, SAN DIEGO

Marines first came to San Diego on 29 July 1846, when they helped seize the town after war began with Mexico. The large harbor, the location near troubled Mexico, and the ready access to the Pacific made it an ideal location for an expeditionary force poised for future contingencies. Marines put it to that use for the first time in 1911, with the 4th Regiment setting up camp on North Island while revolution flared in Mexico. By 1914, the Navy Department was eying San Diego as a site for the West Coast Advance Base Force. Assistant Secretary of the Navy Franklin Roosevelt inspected the area that year and deemed it desirable. In July, a reincarnated 4th Regiment landed again on North Island and went into bivouac. This time the Marines were in San Diego to stay.

In December 1914, over half of the 4th Regiment shifted to Balboa Park in the city of San Diego, to participate in an international exposition. The following August, Commandant Barnett personally surveyed the region and determined that the best available site for a base was a relatively cheap expanse of land near the north end of the bay. The city, eager to see the development of a military installation, offered the adjacent tidal lands for free. With the backing of the local congressman, the House and Senate approved the deal in 1916. The Navy Department acquired the land in 1917, filled in the tidal flats to provide a total of more than 700 acres, and began construction of permanent buildings in 1919. The Spanish Renaissance-style barracks and support buildings rose out of the otherwise barren area, and by 1 December 1921, sufficient facilities were complete to place the base in commission.

The Advance Base Force no longer existed, but its successor, the 5th Brigade of the Marine Corps Expeditionary Force, occupied the brand-new installation. In 1923, it was joined by the recruit depot for the western United States, which moved to San Diego from Mare Island. That same year, the Navy acquired the land immediately to the west and established its own training facility there. In 1927, the city began filling other tidal land just to the east of the Marine Base and developed its new airport—Lindbergh Field—on the site. A decade later, as part of an expansion of the airport, the city traded 544 acres adjacent to the base's outlying rifle range at La Jolla for 60 acres of the main Marine base. There was a similar transfer of another 60 acres to Lindbergh Field in 1940. The only other changes to the base since the completion of the main buildings in 1926 had been the paving of the drill field.

Throughout the 1920s and 1930s, the installation continued its dual role as a recruit depot and home to operating forces. The 4th Regiment deployed from there to mail guard duty in 1926, then to China in 1927. The outfit that replaced them at San Diego—the 6th Marines—deployed from the base to reinforce the 4th Marines in Shanghai during the 1937 crisis. The major shortcoming of the facility, however, was the lack of suitable field training sites. The San Diego base had operated the rifle range near La Jolla (several miles due north) since early in its existence. Formally designated Camp Matthews in 1942 (for a distinguished Marine marksman), it remained in use until 1964, when urban development necessitated the construction of new range facilities for the recruit depot at Camp Pendleton. (Camp Matthews then provided the land for the University of California San Diego.)

Another outlying installation was Camp Kearney to the northeast. Initially acquired in the 1920s as a site for Navy dirigibles, in the first half of the 1940s it served as the nexus for a huge Marine satellite base which grew just to the east. Dubbed Camp Elliott, these 32,000 acres provided the maneuver room for field training. Although a few FMF units continued to come to life and temporarily reside at the main base, most everything related to the FMF shifted to Kearney, Elliott, and Pendleton. After World War II, Kearney became Naval Air Station, Miramar, only to return to the hands of the Corps near the end of the century. Parts of Elliott were subsumed into Miramar, while the rest returned to civilian use.

The main base underwent a construction boom beginning in 1939 to provide facilities for the vast expansion in recruit training and the FMF. When World War II ended, all FMF activities concentrated at Camp Pendleton, leaving the San Diego base entirely devoted to recruit training and a few small, specialized training facilities (such as Sea School). On 1 January 1948, in recognition of the new focus of the installation, it formally became Marine Corps Recruit Depot, San Diego. The Korean War brought more construction, mainly in the form of Quonset huts for recruit living quarters. As in World War II, and again during Vietnam, many Korean-era recruits also resided in tents due to the shortage of buildings. In the latter 1960s, the base began putting up large permanent barracks to replace tents and Quonset huts. All of the former and most of the latter were gone by 1974. Although much has changed since the base first appeared in the early 1920s, its original Spanish Renaissance architecture remains its distinctive trademark.

Right: *Current day recruits. (Rick Mullen)*

Holland M. Smith to occupy the Portuguese Azores. Although the plan is never executed, it becomes the basis for the first Marine-Army joint command of the war.

1 June
Bases

The 2nd Marine Division begins moving to Camp Elliott. Located on Kearney Mesa in the vicinity of the current Marine Corps Air Station, Miramar, part of this area had been rented from the city of San Diego since 1934. The government would purchase and use a total of 32,000 acres here before the end of World War II.

13 June
Force Structure

General H. M. Smith relinquishes command of the 1st Marine Division to become commander of the newly created I Corps (Provisional), composed of his old division and the Army's 1st Infantry Division. This force changes its name several times and ultimately is renamed the Amphibious Force Atlantic Fleet; it focuses on training for amphibious assaults.

16 June
Iceland

Following a 5 June decision by President Roosevelt to commit American forces to the defense of Iceland, the 1st Marine Brigade (Provisional) is established at Charleston, South Carolina. It is formed around the reinforced 6th Marines, newly arrived by sea from California and originally destined to reinforce the 1st Marine Division for the Azores operation. The other major elements of the brigade are the 5th Defense Battalion and the 2nd Battalion, 10th Marines. The brigade sails on 22 June. Marines receives the mission because U.S. law prevents draftees and National Guardsmen from serving overseas.

22 June
World War II

Germany invades the Soviet Union.

24 June
Force Structure

VMF-121 is organized at Quantico.

30 June
Manpower

The strength of the Marine Corps on active duty is 3,339 officers and 51,020 enlisted.

1 July
Force Structure

New designations are applied to existing squadrons: VMF-1 and 2 respectively become VMF-111 and 211; VMS-1 and 2 are now respectively Marine Scout Bombing Squadron 131 (VMSB-131) and 231; VMB-1 and 2 are now VMSB-132 and 232; VMO-1 becomes VMO-151; VMJ-1 and 2 are redesignated VMJ-151 and 252. VMS-3 in the Virgin Islands is not redesignated.

7 July
Iceland

The 1st Marine Brigade (Provisional) arrives in Iceland.

Force Structure

The 1st Marine Aircraft Wing (1st MAW) is established at Quantico by the addition of a headquarters squadron to the 1st Marine Aircraft Group.

Opposite: Marines watch their lone F4F-3 take off to battle the Japanese on 22 December 1941. ("The Last Plane," Col John W. Thomason, Marine Corps Art Collection)

Right: Marine Corps Grumman Wildcats helped stem the tide in the Pacific war. (Marine Corps Historical Center)

10 July
Force Structure
The 2nd Marine Aircraft Wing (2nd MAW) is established at San Diego by the addition of a headquarters squadron to the 2nd Marine Aircraft Group (in Hawaii).

11 July
Force Structure
VMF-221 is organized at San Diego.

15 July
London
A Marine detachment is established to guard the U.S. Embassy in London, England.

24 July
World War II
Japanese forces occupy French Indochina. In retaliation two days later, President Roosevelt orders the freezing of all Japanese funds in the United States, which brings all trade to a halt. A formal embargo on oil and aviation fuel follows on 1 August.

26 July
Philippines
President Roosevelt nationalizes the armed forces of the Philippines and places them under command of General Douglas MacArthur, commander of all U.S. forces in the Far East.

28 July
Force Structure
2nd Marine Aircraft Group is redesignated Marine Aircraft Group 21 (MAG-21).

1 August
Force Structure
The 1st Marine Aircraft Groups is redesignated Marine Aircraft Group 11 (MAG-11).

12 August
Manpower
By a one-vote margin, the House of Representatives approves the bill continuing Selective Service and extending the service of Army draftees for 18 months.

16 August
Samoa
The first man is enlisted in the 1st Samoan Battalion, Marine Corps Reserve. Its purpose is to provide an infantry element to reinforce the 7th Defense Battalion on Tutuila.

18 August
Bases
The command that will become Marine Corps Air Station, Cherry Point, North Carolina, is established. The first air operations will commence in March 1942. Cherry Point will become one of the primary Marine airfields on the East Coast.

1 October
Force Structure
The 1st and 2nd Barrage Balloon Squadrons are organized at Parris Island.

17 October
World War II
General Hideki Tojo becomes Japan's premier and minister of war in a reorganization of the government.

1 November
Force Structure
The 2nd Joint Training Force is established at Camp Elliott, California, under command of Marine Major General Clayton B. Vogel. A West-Coast counterpart of the Amphibious Force Atlantic Fleet, it is composed of the 2nd Marine Division, 2nd MAW, and the Army's 3rd Infantry Division.

2 November
Wake Island
Additional elements of the 1st Defense Battalion reach Wake Island, bringing the Marine force to 15 officers and 373 enlisted men.

3 November
Pearl Harbor
The staff of the Imperial Japanese Navy approves the plan for the attack on the U.S. Pacific Fleet at Pearl Harbor.

10 November
China
The U.S. Asiatic Fleet receives permission to withdraw gunboats and Marines from China.

26 November
Pearl Harbor
The Pearl Harbor attack force departs Japanese waters.

27 November
World War II
The War and Navy Departments send warnings of imminent war to U.S. commanders in the Pacific.

19 August
Wake Island
The advance echelon of the 1st Defense Battalion arrives at Wake Island.

September
Training
VMSB-131 participates in the Army's Louisiana Maneuvers.

11 September
Midway
The 6th Defense Battalion relieves the 3rd Defense Battalion on Midway Atoll.

24 September
Iceland
The 1st Provisional Marine Brigade is detached from the Department of the Navy for service with the Army.

27–28 November
Philippines
The 4th Marines embarks and sails from Shanghai for the Philippines. The regiment arrives at Olongapo on the 30th.

30 November
Manpower
Total strength of the active Marine Corps has grown to 65,881 officers and enlisted.

November
Aviation
Marine officers begin training as glider pilots in civilian schools to form the cadre of a Marine glider program for carrying troops into combat.

1 December
Wake Island
The 2nd and 4th Defense Battalions arrive at Pearl Harbor, destined for eventual employment at Wake Island.

Force Structure
VMO-251 is organized at San Diego.

4 December
Wake Island
Twelve F4F-3 Grumman Wildcat fighter planes of Marine Fighter Squadron 211 (VMF-211) fly from *Enterprise* to Wake Island. They begin aerial patrols the next day.

7 December
Pearl Harbor
Japanese carrier-borne aircraft attack U.S. forces on Oahu, sinking 19 ships, destroying 188 planes, killing 2,280, and wounding 1,109. Marines losses are 111 killed or missing, 75 wounded, 33 aircraft destroyed, and 12 damaged. Two Japanese destroyers bombard Midway, inflicting 14 Marine casualties.

8 December
World War II
The United States declares war on Japan. Japanese forces invade Thailand and Malaya.
Pacific
Japanese aircraft attack Wake Island (destroying seven F4F-3s), Guam, and the Philippines.
China
Marine detachments in Peiping, Tientsin, and elsewhere in China surrender to superior Japanese forces.

9 December
Guam
Japanese air attacks continue against Guam.
Wake Island
Japanese aircraft attack the island for the second day in a row and continue to do so daily until it is captured by the Japanese on 23 December.
Force Structure
MAG-11 begins moving to San Diego from Quantico.

Opposite: A portrait of an emaciated prisoner of the Japanese, by a Wake Island defender who survived the experience. ("The Long Dark," Capt James R. Brown, USMC (Ret), Marine Corps Art Collection)

Right: A view of a Japanese prisoner of war camp in Shanghai, China. ("Kiang Wong," Capt James R. Brown, USMC (Ret), Marine Corps Art Collection)

GRUMMAN F4F WILDCAT

The Grumman F4F almost didn't make it into active service, but it went on to become the mainstay of Marine fighter squadrons during the first two years of World War II. The plane emerged from a Navy design competition launched in 1935. The Grumman Corporation of Long Island, New York, initially placed its hopes on a biplane model, but switched to a monoplane in July 1936. The resulting XF4F-2 first flew on 2 September 1937. The sole prototype suffered from engine problems, culminating in a crash that damaged the plane in April 1938. Although it was a bit faster than its competitor, the Grumman airframe lost out to the then-more-effective Brewster F2A Buffalo, which received the Navy contract in June 1938.

Later that year, the Navy decided the F4F had sufficient promise to warrant development of a new version, the XF4F-3.

Among the main changes were a better powerplant and larger, square-tipped wings. The prototype made its maiden flight in February 1939. With a few modifications, it went into production six months later as a supplement to the Buffalo. The Marine Corps received its first F4F-3 in May 1941 with the formation of VMF-111, 121, and 211.

The Wildcat, as it was dubbed, weighed in at 5,238 pounds empty, had a wingspan of 38 feet, and a length of 28 feet, 9 inches. Its main and emergency fuel tanks held 144 gallons, giving it a range of 860 miles. The Pratt & Whitney 1,200-horsepower engine produced a rate of climb of 2,300 feet per minute and a maximum speed of 331 miles per hour (40 mph faster than the initial model and 50 mph more than the Brewster Buffalo). It had a service ceiling of 37,000 feet. It was armed with four wing-mounted, .50-caliber machine guns, and it could carry a

Opposite: *Outnumbered Grumman F4F Wildcats duel with Japanese Zeros over Wake Island in December 1941. ("Cat and Mouse over Wake Island," Marc Stewart, Stewart Studios)*

Left: *The Wildcat proved a sturdy plane early in WWII. (Marine Corps Historical Center)*

100-pound bomb under each wing. The pilot had to hand crank its retractable landing gear. The Navy Department ultimately purchased 380 F4F-3 variants, of which about four dozen went to the Marines.

The Wildcat saw its first aerial combat action at Wake Island (most of them at Pearl Harbor being destroyed on the ground). The Marine F4Fs on Wake shot down several Japanese planes and sank a destroyer before that battle ended with the island overrun. One of the pilots, Captain Henry T. Elrod, later received the Medal of Honor posthumously for his bravery in the air and on the ground. Other Marine Wildcats at Midway shot down more enemy aircraft in June.

By the time of the Guadalcanal campaign, the Marines were receiving a new model, the F4F-4. The main changes were folding wings for carrier service, an additional two wing-mounted, .50-caliber machine guns, and better armor. Although the Wildcat was significantly slower than the Japanese Zero in airspeed and rate of climb, the tough Grumman fighter could take a beating and bring its pilot home. Dueling with the Japanese in the immediate environs of Henderson Field, as the Marines often did, brought additional advantages. Before long, intrepid Marine pilots were racking up kills, even against the vaunted Zero.

Captain Marion E. Carl of VMF-223 became the first leatherneck ace after he shot down three enemy planes on 24 August (he already had downed two fighters at Midway). Ultimately 26 Marine pilots flying the F4F shot down five or more Japanese aircraft during the course of the war. Six of them received Medals of Honor: Lieutenant Colonel Harold W. Bauer (posthumous), 1st Lieutenant Jefferson J. DeBlanc, Captain Joseph J. Foss, Major Robert E. Galer, Major John L. Smith, and 1st Lieutenant James E. Swett. The leading Wildcat aces were Foss (26), Smith (19), Carl (16.5 in the F4F), Galer (13), and William P. Marontate (13). In one of the most spectacular aerial engagements of the war, on 7 April 1943, Swett shot down seven Japanese Val dive bombers in one mission while defending shipping around Guadalcanal. On 31 January 1943, DeBlanc downed five Zeros while escorting a bombing raid in the central Solomons. Both men had to ditch their badly damaged planes.

Although U.S. factories churned out a total of nearly 8,000 Wildcats before the war was over, the F4F was largely superseded by late 1943 by the Grumman F6F Hellcat and the Chance Vought F4U Corsair. Nevertheless, the sturdy Wildcat had served the Marines well when the odds were toughest.

10 December
Guam
A Japanese force of nearly 6,000 men lands at three points. The 153 Marines of the garrison and the 80 Chamorros of the Insular Guard, armed with rifles and four machine guns, fight back for a time, but the U.S. Navy governor of the island soon surrenders to avoid useless casualties. Marine losses are four killed and 12 wounded.

Philippines
Japanese forces land in northern Luzon.

Gilberts
The Japanese seize Makin Island.

11 December
World War II
Germany and Italy declare war on the United States.

Wake Island
The Wake Island defense force defeats an attempted Japanese amphibious assault, sinking two enemy destroyers and damaging three cruisers, two destroyers, a destroyer-transport, and a transport. Marine losses are a handful of wounded.

12 December
Philippines
Japanese forces land in southeastern Luzon. Enemy air attacks begin against Olongapo.

15 December
Johnston
Two Japanese ships bombard Johnston Island. The Marines suffer no casualties.

Above: *A 1942 recruiting poster. ("Fly With the Marines," Marine Corps Art Collection)*

Left: *Col Samuel Howard decorates two men on Bataan. He would lament at the end of the siege of Corregidor: "My God . . . and I had to be the first Marine officer ever to surrender a regiment." (National Archives)*

17 December
Midway
Led by a Navy patrol bomber, 17 SB2U-3 Chance-Vought Vindicator dive bombers of VMSB-231 make the longest mass overwater single-engined flight recorded until then, covering the 1,137 miles from Oahu to Midway Island in 9 hours and 45 minutes. They represent the first combat aircraft on the island.

20 December
Commanders
Admiral Ernest King is appointed commander-in-chief of the U.S. Fleet (COMINCH).
Philippines
The commander of the Asiatic Fleet places the 4th Marines under command of General MacArthur. Japanese troops invade Mindanao.

21 December
Force Structure
1st MAW arrives in San Diego.
Wake Island
Japanese carrier planes destroy the last remaining aircraft of VMF-211 on the island.
Philippines
Japanese forces land at Lingayen Gulf on Luzon and move toward Manila.

23 December
Wake Island
Following a dawn landing by a Japanese Special Naval Landing Force and 12 hours of fighting, the battered garrison of Wake Island surrenders. Total Marine casualties during the campaign are 56 killed and 44 wounded. A U.S. Navy relief expedition carrying VMF-221 and the 4th Defense Battalion turns back to Pearl Harbor.
Philippines
General MacArthur decides to withdraw his forces into the Bataan Peninsula.

24 December
Force Structure
The 2nd Marine Brigade is reactivated at Camp Elliot, California. It consists of the 8th Marines, the 2nd Battalion of the 10th Marines, and the 2nd Defense Battalion.
Midway
Elements of Batteries A and C of the 4th Defense Battalion reinforce the garrison on Midway.

25 December
China
The British defenders of Hong Kong surrender following a Japanese assault.

Right: *Filipino soldiers learn the intricacies of the Browning water-cooled machine gun from a Marine crew. (National Archives)*

Left: *A Marine enjoys a fresh ration of cigarettes, about the only thing besides Japanese fire that was plentiful on Corregidor. (National Archives)*

Below: *A Marine humps a machine-gun tripod up a ridge on Guadalcanal. (National Archives)*

Midway
The 14 F2A-3 Brewster Buffalo fighter planes of VMF-221 fly off *Saratoga* and land on Midway.

26 December
Midway
Battery B of the 4th Defense Battalion and the ground elements of VMF-221 arrive at Midway.
Philippines
The 4th Marines begins moving to its assigned defensive positions on the fortress island of Corregidor guarding the entrance to Manila Bay. The deployment is completed two days later. Two antiaircraft batteries of 3/4 (recently created from units of the former Marine Barracks, Cavite Navy Yard) remain on Bataan.

29 December
Philippines
Japanese aircraft begin daily attacks on Corregidor and slowly destroy its fixed fortifications.

30 December
Panama Canal
The 1st Barrage Balloon Squadron arrives in the Panama Canal Zone to assist in defending it.

31 December
Pacific Theater
Admiral Chester Nimitz assumes command of the U.S. Pacific Fleet.

<hr />

1942

10 January
Force Structure
The Glider Detachment is formed at Parris Island.

15 January
Samoa
Brigadier General Henry L. Larsen (commanding general of the 2nd Marine Brigade) is appointed the first military governor of American Samoa.

Above: *Four Marines bring in a wounded buddy on Guadalcanal. (Marine Corps Research Center)*

Right: *F4F Grumman Wildcats lined up at Ewa Field in Hawaii. (National Archives)*

20 January
Commandants
Legislation authorizes the promotion of Commandant Holcomb to lieutenant general, the first Marine of that rank.

23 January
Samoa
The 2nd Marine Brigade reaches American Samoa and joins with the 7th Defense Battalion in protecting that territory.
New Britain
Japanese forces land on the island and take the harbor of Rabaul from its small Australian garrison.

24 January
Borneo
Four destroyers score the first surface victory of the U.S. Navy since 1898, sinking four transports and a patrol vessel during a night attack on a Japanese force invading Borneo at Balikpapan Bay.

27–28 January
Philippines
Dozens of Marines from two batteries of 3/4 assist a provisional naval battalion and Philippine units in containing a Japanese amphibious landing against the Bataan coast near Mariveles.

1 February
Bases
The airfield at Parris Island is designated a full-fledged Marine Corps Air Station.
Force Structure
The 9th Defense Battalion is organized at Parris Island.

9 February
Joint Chiefs of Staff
The first formal meeting of the new military policy body, the Joint Chiefs of Staff, is held. The members are General George C. Marshall (Chief of Staff of the Army), Lieutenant General Henry H. "Hap" Arnold (Chief of the Army Air Corps), Admiral Stark (CNO), and Admiral King (COMINCH).

10 February
Midway
VMF-221 aircraft drive off a Japanese submarine after it fires two rounds from its deck gun against the atoll.

12 February
Force Structure
The 9th Marines is reactivated at Camp Elliott. The regiment is initially assigned to the 2nd Marine Division to replace the absent 6th and 8th Marines.

airfield also meant that it would take additional time for the assault force to reach the objective, while supplies dumped ashore would be far from their eventual destination. Thomas gambled that there would be no defenders this far from the airfield, and any counterattack would take longer to arrive, thus giving the assault force time to get ashore and get organized without opposition.

Tulagi was a long, slender island consisting mainly of a wooded ridge running right down to the water, except for a small saddle near its southeastern end. The only suitable beaches were on the northeastern coast at this saddle, since the rest of the island was fringed by coral. Aerial reconnaissance indicated that the Japanese had concentrated all their defenses against the obvious landing site. American planners decided to take on coral and rough terrain instead of the enemy. They would go ashore about halfway up the southwestern coast, which meant that they would have to wade in once the boats touched the reefs and they would not be able to bring artillery or other heavy equipment ashore. There was no alternative to avoid enemy defenses on Gavutu-Tanambogo, so the parachutists would have to land under enemy fire across a seaplane ramp on Gavutu. This attack would go in four hours after the 0800 assaults on Guadalcanal and Tulagi, to allow maximum naval gunfire support.

The operation went off much as the division planned it. The raiders got ashore on Tulagi without opposition, got organized, and were ready for the hard fight for the southern end of the island, which lasted for two days. The 1st and 5th Marines also landed on Guadalcanal unmolested and took the airfield the next day with little fighting. Only Gavutu went awry, since the Japanese defenders had four hours to get ready. Once

they recovered from the pre-landing naval bombardment, they savaged the second wave of landing craft. The parachutists eventually seized the high ground by evening, but took heavy casualties. Elements of 3/2 came ashore the next day to help finish the job and then take adjacent Tanambogo.

It would take six months of sometimes intense fighting before Guadalcanal was entirely secured. In the first test of the amphibious doctrine developed in the 1930s, however, the 1st Marine Division and supporting naval forces had proven that they could successfully execute these techniques against a real enemy. The Pacific campaign would bring forth many changes in amphibious tactics and technology, but the daring, pioneering efforts of the men engaged in Watchtower gave American leaders the confidence to move on to subsequent objectives all across the war-torn globe.

Above: *Marines coming ashore on 7 August from nonramp Higgins boats. (National Archives)*

ENLIST NOW
U.S. MARINE CORPS

GUADALCANAL America's World War II ground offensive began Aug. 7, 1942, when the 1st Marine Division, Reenforced, landed at Guadalcanal. Through rivers, swamps and steaming jungle the rugged, resolute Marines fought on until this first great stepping-stone to Japan was won!

PAINTING BY SGT. TOM LOVELL

3 June
Aleutians
Japanese forces attack the Aleutian Islands as a diversion from the planned assault on Midway. Ground forces eventually occupy Attu and Kiska Islands, Alaska.
Force Structure
VMSB-243 is organized at Santa Barbara.

4 June
Midway
In the initial aerial attacks of the Battle of Midway, 108 Japanese planes strike the atoll. VMF-221 loses most of its Brewsters and Wildcats, though they destroy or damage about 40 of the enemy. VMSB-241 also suffers heavy losses among its dive bombers, but fails to achieve hits on the enemy fleet. Captain Richard E. Fleming's aircraft crashes into cruiser *Mikuma*. He subsequently receives the Medal of Honor. U.S. Navy aircraft sink four Japanese carriers, and the enemy abandons the planned invasion of the atoll. Over the next two days, American planes from carriers sink and damage more Japanese ships as they withdraw. One U.S. carrier is sunk.

14 June
New Zealand
The advance echelon of the 1st Marine Division arrives in New Zealand.

15 June
Force Structure
The 11th Defense Battalion is formed at Parris Island.

16 June
Force Structure
The 3rd Marines is reactivated at New River, North Carolina.

19 June
Commanders
Vice Admiral Robert L. Ghormley assumes command of the South Pacific Area (a subset of Nimitz's Pacific Ocean Area).

26 June
Guadalcanal
The 1st Marine Division receives the warning order for an amphibious assault against the Guadalcanal-Tulagi area in the Southern Solomons.

30 June
Manpower
The strength of the Marine Corps on active duty is 7,138 officers and 135,475 enlisted.

June
Ireland
Marine Barracks, Londonderry is established in Northern Ireland to protect naval facilities.

1 July
Force Structure
VMF-213 and 214 are commissioned at Ewa, Hawaii. The 5th Barrage Balloon Squadron is organized at Parris Island.

10 July
Bases
Marine Corps Air Station, El Centro, California, is established.

11 July
New Zealand
The last elements of the 1st Marine Division arrive in New Zealand.

14 July
Force Structure
The 21st Marines, an infantry regiment, is organized at New River, North Carolina.
Bases
The Marine Corps Glider Base, Edenton, North Carolina, is established.

15 July
New Hebrides
Elements of the 4th Defense Battalion arrive at Espiritu Santo to help protect an air base there.

20 July
Force Structure
The 23rd Marines, an infantry regiment, is established at New River.

21 July
New Zealand
The 1st Base Depot establishes an advance echelon in New Zealand. Its mission is to provide logistics support to units in the area.

22 July
New Guinea
Japanese forces land at Buna on the north coast of New Guinea to begin an operation to cross the Owen Stanley Mountains and seize Port Moresby with a ground assault.

1 August
Force Structure
The 12th Defense Battalion is organized at San Diego.

2 August
New Hebrides
The first F4F-3 long-range photographic planes of Marine Observation Squadron 251 (VMO-251) land on the recently completed airfield at Espiritu Santo.

7 August
Solomons
In the southern Solomons, the 1st Marine Division (less the 7th Marines) and reinforcing elements (2nd Marines, 1st Raider Battalion, 1st Parachute Battalion, 3rd Defense Batalion) conduct Operation Watchtower, the first Allied offensive amphibious operation in the Pacific. The objectives of Tulagi, Gavutu-Tanambogo, and the half-finished airfield on Guadalcanal are all taken by the next day.

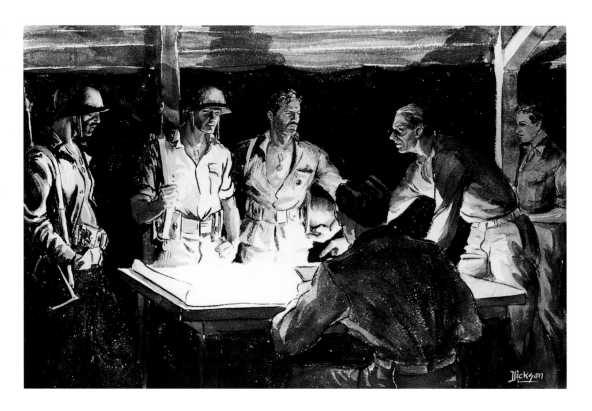

Opposite: *A 1945 recruiting poster depicts a Marine wading across a river at Guadalcanal. ("Enlist Now," Sgt Tom Lovell, Marine Corps Art Collection)*

Right: *A Marine briefs members of a patrol on their mission at Guadalcanal in 1942. ("Final Instructions," Col Donald L. Dickson, USMCR, Marine Corps Art Collection)*

Solomons without completing the unloading of Marine supplies and forces. The Marines ashore are short of critical items, including food, and begin subsisting on two meals a day to stretch out meager stocks.

12 August
Guadalcanal
Lieutenant Colonel Frank Goettge, 1st Marine Division intelligence officer, leads a 25-man patrol to the Matanikau River area of Guadalcanal to check out reports of Japanese willing to surrender. The patrol is attacked, and only three Marines escape alive.

13 August
Bases
Marine Corps Air Station, Santa Barbara, California, is established.

8 August
Guadalcanal
During the night Japanese surface forces attack the Allied naval task force off Guadalcanal, sinking four cruisers and damaging one destroyer.

9 August
Guadalcanal
The naval task force withdraws from the lower

15 August
Force Structure
Marine Aircraft Wings, Pacific, is organized at San Diego to provide administrative and logistic oversight for all MAWs.
Guadalcanal
CUB One, a Navy aviation ground support unit, arrives on Guadalcanal to provide the initial maintenance echelon for Marine aircraft.

Top: *A Marine cleans his rifle. ("Marine's Best Friend," Col Donald L. Dickson, USMCR, Marine Corps Art Collection)*

Left: *"8 August 1942, Night Action off Savo," William Draper, Navy Art Collection*

Opposite, top: *"Weary Trail," Kerr Eby, Navy Art Collection*

Opposite, bottom: *"Down the Slot: Landing of Japanese Troops on Guadalcanal," John Hamilton, Navy Art Collection*

17 August
Gilberts

Companies A and B of the 2nd Raider Battalion land from submarines on Makin Atoll to destroy enemy installations and conduct a diversionary raid in support of the Guadalcanal offensive. The Marines defeat the garrison, but heavy surf disrupts their withdrawal and delays it until the next night. Marines casualties during the raid are 18 dead, 16 wounded, and 12 missing. Of the latter, nine are captured soon after and beheaded on Kwajalein by the Japanese. Major James Roosevelt, son of the President, participates in the raid as XO of the 2nd Raiders.

18 August
Guadalcanal

Marines complete the airstrip on Guadalcanal and name it Henderson Field after Major Lofton Henderson, who died leading his Marine dive bombers against the Japanese at Midway.

Force Structure

The 51st Defense Battalion is activated at Montford Point, New River, North Carolina. It is destined to train the first African American recruits and become the first African American operational unit in the Marine Corps.

19 August
Guadalcanal

Three companies of the 5th Marines conduct attacks against Japanese forces around Matanikau and Kokumbona villages.

20 August
Guadalcanal

The first echelons of MAG-23 and 1st MAW (19 F4Fs of VMF-223 and 12 SBD-3s of VMSB-232) land on Henderson Field.

BRIGADIER GENERAL EVANS F. CARLSON

Evans Carlson got an early start in his career as a maverick. He ran away from his home in Vermont in 1910 at the age of 14, and two years later bluffed his way past the recruiters to enlist in the Army. He served four years, went into the reserves, and was recalled for duty during the Mexican Border campaign. When the United States entered World War I in 1917, he already had five years of active service under his belt. He soon won a commission, but served on the staff of a division in France that never saw combat. After the war he tried to make it as a salesman, but gave that up in 1922 and enlisted in the Marine Corps. In a few months he earned a commission again. Other than a failed attempt at flight school, his first several years as a Marine lieutenant were unremarkable.

In 1927 Carlson went over to Shanghai with the 4th Marines. There he became regimental intelligence officer and developed a deep interest in China that would shape the remainder of his days. Three years later, commanding an outpost of the Guardia Nacional in Nicaragua, he had his first brush with guerrilla warfare. That became the second guiding star of his career. In his only battle, he successfully engaged and dispersed an enemy band in a daring night attack, for which he received a Navy Cross. There followed a tour with the Legation Guard in Peking, and a stint as executive officer of the presidential guard detachment at Warm Springs, Georgia. In the latter job Carlson developed a friendship with President Franklin D. Roosevelt.

Captain Carlson arrived in Shanghai for his third China tour in July 1937. Along with "Red Mike" Edson, he watched the Japanese seize control of the city. Detailed to duty as

Left: *On 30 September 1942, on Guadalcanal, Admiral Nimitz presents a Navy Cross to LtCol Carlson for his leadership of the Makin Raid. MajGen Vandegrift is on the far left. To the right of Carlson are BGen William H, Rupertus, Col Edson, LtCol Edwin A. Pollock, and Maj John L. Smith. (Marine Corps Research Center)*

Right: *A Marine carrying a .30-caliber, air-cooled machine gun fords a stream in the South Pacific. (National Archives)*

Below: *A Stuart light tank, nicknamed "The Blizzard" by its crew, is hoisted from a cargo ship for transfer ashore at Guadalcanal. (Marine Corps Research Center)*

Force Structure
VMSB-242 and VMSB-244 swap designations.

15 September
Force Structure

VMO-151 is redesignated VMSB-151. VMD-1 and 2 become respectively VMD-154 and 254 (and soon after swap designations with each other). The new VMSB-242 becomes VMF-215.

16 September
Force Structure

The 3rd Marine Division is activated at Camp Elliott. It is initially composed of the 9th Marines, 21st Marines, 23rd Marines, 12th Marines (artillery), and 19th Marines (an engineer regiment). The 3rd Parachute Battalion is organized in southern California.

18 September
Guadalcanal

The 7th Marines land and return to the 1st Marine Division. The same ships depart with the depleted 1st Parachute Battalion.

19 September
Bases

Marine Corps Air Station, Eagle Mountain Lake is established at Fort Worth, Texas, to serve as a glider training base.

20 September
Force Structure

The 3rd Raider Battalion is organized in Samoa.

BRIGADIER GENERAL JOSEPH J. FOSS

Joe Foss grew up near Sioux Falls, South Dakota, coming to maturity during the bleak Depression years of the early 1930s. Following his father's death in Joe's junior year in high school, he ran the family farm until his brother was old enough to take over. Despite the economic hard times, he put himself through college. He also played sports in school and served in the National Guard during his senior year. The curly headed six-footer had yearned to be a flier, however, and had even paid out some of his hard-earned dollars for private pilot lessons. After graduating from college in the summer of 1940 at the age of 25, he enlisted in the Marine Corps Reserve, then soon earned an appointment as an aviation cadet. He won his wings and his commission in March 1941.

A natural pilot, Foss found himself assigned to instructor duty. His requests for transfer to a squadron got him into a photo reconnaissance unit. Finally he managed to join VMF-121 in the fall of 1942. Already a captain, he served as the executive officer. On 9 October, Foss and the 20 F4F-4s of his squadron reached Guadalcanal. He wasted no time in making his presence felt. On his fourth day, he shot down his first enemy plane—a Zero. He also almost met his own end that day. Three other Japanese fighters jumped him and shot up his oil pump. He managed to reach Henderson Field and make a dead-stick landing. That night, Japanese battleships pounded the airstrip and destroyed a majority of Cactus Air Force's planes. Foss and others gamely withstood the

Left: *"Joe Foss Downs a Zero," Robert T. Horvath, Marine Corps Art Collection*

Opposite: *Maj Joe Foss in the spring of 1944 as a squadron commander. (National Archives)*

bombardment. The next day he was aloft again and downed his second Zero. Within a few days, he added three more to his credit in a single mission—becoming an ace in his first few days of combat.

The intrepid Marine captain continued ringing up an impressive score. On 23 October he knocked down four Zeros while fending off a Japanese bomber raid. Two days later, he claimed two enemy during an initial attack, and three more in a subsequent battle that day. He had been on the island two weeks and had 16 kills. On 7 November, Foss and several of his fellow Wildcats launched with bombs under their wings to assist in attacking a reported convoy. Instead they came across six floatplane versions of the Zero. Foss got one, while his wingmates downed the others. Coming out of that melee, he saw a float biplane. The enemy pilot maneuvered deftly, giving his rear gunner a good shot. Foss's Wildcat took a beating, but gave more than it got, as the enemy aircraft went down. Limping back toward base, he destroyed a third Japanese floatplane. His engine finally gave out, and he landed on the water near the island of Malaita. Again luck was with him, as he had to scramble out of his plane after it had sunk below the surface. A missionary and natives in a dugout rescued him that night from the water.

Foss was evacuated from Guadalcanal on 19 November with a severe case of malaria. He left with 20 kills, the largest tally of any American pilot to date in the war. On the last day of 1942, he returned to Henderson Field still full of fight, but 37 pounds lighter. In the next six weeks he downed six more enemy aircraft, tying him with America's leading ace in World War I, the legendary Eddie Rickenbacker. Called back to the States, Foss received the Medal of Honor for his feat. Although he later formed VMF-

115—a Corsair outfit—and took it into battle in the Central Solomons, he found few enemy left there and did not add to his score. At the end of the war, his 26 kills ranked second among Marine aces only to Gregory "Pappy" Boyington's 28 (six of them as a Flying Tiger in China).

Following the war, Foss rose to the rank of lieutenant colonel in the reserves, but in 1947 he transferred to the Air National Guard, where he soon took command of a fighter squadron in his home state. He served in the South Dakota legislature, returned to active duty for two years during the Korean War, was elected to two terms as governor, and went on to be commissioner of the American Football League and president of the National Rifle Association. He eventually closed out his time in the Guard as a brigadier general.

22 September
New Caledonia
The 5th Barrage Balloon Squadron arrives on New Caledonia.

23–27 September
Guadalcanal
In the 2nd Battle of the Matanikau, 1/7 is briefly trapped behind enemy lines following an amphibious landing, while strong enemy defenses prevent the 1st Raider Battalion and 2/5 from crossing the river. Lieutenant Colonel Lewis B. Puller oversees a fighting amphibious withdrawal of 1/7.

24 September
Bases
Marine Corps Air Station, Mojave, California, is established.

25 September
Guadalcanal
Elements of VMF-121 arrive on the island.

Force Structure
The 13th Defense Battalion is organized at Guantanamo Bay.

1 October
Force Structure
General H. M. Smith's Amphibious Training Staff, FMF is disbanded and takes over the duties of the headquarters element of the Amphibious Corps, Pacific Fleet at San Diego. The I Marine Amphibious Corps is formed at San Diego under Major General Clayton B. Vogel. VMO-155 and VMF-441 are organized on Samoa.

3 October
Guadalcanal
Lieutenant Colonel Harold W. Bauer of VMF-212 shoots down four enemy planes and becomes an ace while making an inspection visit to Guadalcanal.

4 October
Force Structure
Headquarters, Marine Aircraft Wing, Pacific arrives at Ewa from San Diego.

October 7–9
Guadalcanal
In the 3rd Battle of the Matanikau, 3/2, 2/7, and 1/7 cross the upper Matanikau and attack toward the coast, destroying a Japanese battalion, while 2/5, 3/5, and the 1st Raider Battalion defeat a Japanese company holding the mouth of the river.

9 October
Guadalcanal
VMF-121 arrives on Henderson Field.

11 October
Guadalcanal
In the Battle of Cape Esperance, a U.S. naval force defeats a Japanese bombardment group in a night surface action.

13 October
Guadalcanal
A convoy deposits the Army's 164th Infantry regiment at Guadalcanal and takes off the depleted 1st Raider Battalion for recuperation in New Caledonia. That night, two Japanese battleships bombard Henderson Field, destroying

half of Cactus Air Force and large quantities of aviation gasoline.

14 October
Guadalcanal
Japanese planes and artillery bomb and shell Henderson Field by day, then two cruisers bombard the airstrip that night.

15 October
Guadalcanal
Cactus Air Force gets a few planes aloft to attack Japanese transports landing men and supplies on the island.

16 October
Guadalcanal
Bauer and his VMF-212 arrive after a flight from Efate, just as a Japanese air attack is ending. Despite being nearly out of fuel, Bauer engages the enemy and shoots down four dive bombers. For this feat he eventually receives the Medal of Honor. MAG-14 relieves MAG-23 as the aviation administrative and logistics element on Guadalcanal.

18 October
Commanders
Vice Admiral William F. Halsey replaces Ghormley in command of the South Pacific Area.

GUNNERY SERGEANT JOHN BASILONE

John Basilone was born on 4 November 1916 in Buffalo, New York, where his Italian-born father worked as a tailor. Later, the family moved to his mother's hometown of Raritan, New Jersey. Basilone attended a Catholic grade school, but never finished high school. After working for a few years, he joined the Army at 19 and spent his three-year tour in the Philippines. Back in civilian life in 1939, he became a truck driver in Maryland. With the war in Europe looking bleak in July 1940, Basilone went to the recruiting station in Baltimore and enlisted in the Marines. The veteran soldier soon bore the nickname "Manila John" (based on his prior service) and quickly moved up the ranks in the Corps. He made private first class in two months, corporal in eight more, and sergeant in another eight.

From the first, Basilone served with the water-cooled, .30-caliber Browning heavy machine guns of Company D, 1st Battalion, 7th Marines. His battalion commander after the summer of 1941 was none other than the already famous "Chesty" Puller. After a few months on Samoa in 1942, the 7th Marines rejoined the 1st Marine Division at Guadalcanal in September. Although Basilone and his guns missed out on the desperate fighting of the 2nd Battle of the Matanikau, he and the heavies would more than make up for it at the Battle for Henderson Field. On the night of 24–25 October, 1/7 was defending the southern zone of the Marine perimeter—a sector normally held by two battalions. It was lightly guarded because the Japanese were supposed to be attacking elsewhere. Instead, the infantrymen of the Sendai Division launched assault after assault against the Marine lines.

Basilone was leading two sections of machine guns near the left-center of 1/7's position. The Marines had one advantage— they had hacked out clear fields of fire from the jungle that fronted their position. General Vandegrift considered it to be "a machine gunner's paradise." As the Japanese swarmed forward in company-size attacks that night, Basilone's guns cut them to ribbons. When enemy grenades knocked out the two crews of one of his sections, the sergeant rushed through the fire to their gun pits carrying a fresh weapon. He got the survivors organized to man it, then put one of the original guns back into action himself. One of his fellow Marines observed the sergeant using his pistol whenever the Japanese got too close to bring the machine gun to bear. As reserves from a nearby Army regiment fed into the line to beef it up, Basilone turned over the gun to others and went back across the exposed, fire-swept ground to bring up badly needed ammunition.

The last of the enemy attacks that night petered out at dawn. During the day, the intermingled Army and Marine battalions disentangled, with 1/7 shifting to the right to concentrate on defending Edson's Ridge. That night the Japanese renewed their attack, but concentrated largely on the zone now held by the Army's 164th Infantry. But when the lines had been thinnest, Basilone and a few other stalwart Marines had held against the odds. A few days later, Puller recommended just one man—the machine gun sergeant from New Jersey—for a Medal of Honor for this critical battle that saved Henderson Field.

The Marine Corps promoted Basilone to platoon sergeant and brought him home to receive the Medal of Honor from the President. Along with other surviving heroes of early campaigns, he toured the country to help sell war bonds and motivate industrial workers. He ended up with easy duty at the Marine barracks in the Washington Navy Yard, where he could have sat out the remainder of the war. Instead, he insisted on going back to the infantry. In January 1944, he got his wish and transferred to the 1st Battalion, 27th Marines. While stationed at Camp Pendleton with the 5th Marine Division, he was promoted to gunnery

sergeant and also met and married Lena Riggi, a sergeant in the Women's Reserve.

On 19 February 1945, he was in one of the early waves of the landing on Iwo Jima. When a blockhouse barred the way forward for his company, he worked his way around to the flank under continuous fire from machine guns, mortars, and artillery. He finally reached it, clambered on top, and tossed a demolitions charge and grenades into the firing ports to silence it. Later he came upon a tank trapped in a minefield. Braving more indirect fire, he guided it back to safer ground. As his outfit moved up onto the exposed apron of an airfield, a heavy barrage came down, killing three men instantly and mortally wounding Basilone. He died soon after. For his feats that day, he was awarded the Navy Cross.

Manila John Basilone.
(National Archives)

23 October
Guadalcanal
Marine antitank guns and artillery crush a diversionary Japanese tank and infantry assault across the Matanikau.

Captain Joseph J. Foss shoots down four Zeros.
Force Structure
The 4th Raider Battalion is organized in southern California.

24–26 October
Guadalcanal
In the Battle for Henderson Field, the Sendai Division attacks the position of 1/7 south of the airstrip. Elements of the 164th Infantry reinforce Marine lines during the night and assume responsibility for the threatened zone the second

night. The Japanese are repulsed with heavy losses. Another diversionary attack across the Matanikau is defeated by 2/7. At sea, U.S. naval forces turn back a Japanese fleet in the Battle of Santa Cruz. In the air on the 25th, Joe Foss shoots down five enemy planes during two sorties, bringing his total kills to 16.

28 October
Force Structure
The I Marine Amphibious Corps (I MAC) arrives at Noumea, New Caledonia. It is initially purely an administrative command to control Marine units in rear areas of the South Pacific command.

31 October
Guadalcanal
On this day and the next, elements of VMF-211 and VMSB-132 reach Henderson Field.

November
New Hebrides
MAG-11 moves to Espiritu Santo.

1 November
Guadalcanal
VMF-112 arrives on the island.

1–3 November
Guadalcanal
With support from the division scout-snipers and 3/7 screening the flank, the 5th Marines attack

Opposite, top: *Supplies are brought ashore at Lunga Point, Guadalcanal. ("Disgorging Stores off Lunga Point," John Hamilton, Naval Art Collection)*

Opposite, below: *A Guadalcanal Marine airs his feet and cleans his Springfield. (National Archives)*

Right: *LtCol Carlson and his son, Lt Evans Carlson, both of the 2nd Raiders. (Marine Corps Research Center)*

west across the Matanikau and destroy a pocket of Japanese around Point Cruz. The 2nd Marines and 1/164 move past Point Cruz to establish a new defensive line to the west.

2 November
Guadalcanal

A battery each of Marine and Army 155mm guns arrive on the island.

Right: *Marines and soldiers offload aviation ordnance from a landing craft at Guadalcanal. (Marine Corps Research Center)*

3–9 November
Guadalcanal

The Battle of Koli Point opens with 2/7 skirmishing with Japanese reinforcements arriving by sea to the east of the Marine perimeter. The 164th Infantry and 1/7 move up to assist and help destroy part of the enemy, with the rest escaping inland.

Left: *Marines wait on the beach for a trip out to transports that will take them away from Guadalcanal in January 1943. (National Archives)*

Opposite: *A soldier bids farewell to departing Marines as the Guadalcanal campaign draws to a close. (Marine Corps Research Center)*

4 November
Guadalcanal
The 8th Marines and 1/10 arrive at Lunga Point. Two companies of the 2nd Raider Battalion secure a new beachhead at Aola Bay and are joined by the 1st Battalion, 147th Infantry, a battery of Army artillery, and a Seabee unit.

6 November
Guadalcanal
The 2nd Raider companies set out from Aola to track down enemy elements escaping the encirclement at Koli Point.

7 November
Manpower
The Marine Corps Women's Reserve is authorized by the Commandant, although actual enlistments are not taken until February 1943.

8 November
North Africa
Operation Torch begins, with U.S. and other Allied forces landing at several points along the coast of North Africa. Marine detachments serve on board the larger U.S. Navy warships and a handful of Marines participate in the landings.

9 November
Force Structure
The 6th Barrage Balloon Squadron is formed at New River.

10 November
Guadalcanal
Three more companies of the 2nd Raider Battalion land at Tasimboko and move to join the rest of the battalion.
Force Structure
The 3rd MAW is organized at Cherry Point. The 16th Defense Battalion is activated on Johnston Island.

11 November
Guadalcanal
Elements of the 2nd and 8th Marines and the 164th Infantry pull back from the Point Cruz area to the eastern side of the Matanikau in preparation for an anticipated Japanese assault on the main American perimeter. The 2nd Raider Battalion engages Japanese forces at Asamama.

12 November
Guadalcanal
Captain Foss shoots down three Japanese planes, making him the first American pilot to achieve 20 kills in the war. VMSB-131 and 142 arrive.

12–15 November
Guadalcanal
In the naval battle for Guadalcanal, U.S. surface forces drive back a Japanese bombardment group on the night of the 12th, U.S. aircraft destroy most of a large troop convoy during daylight hours on the 14th, another U.S. surface fleet beats back a Japanese bombardment force that night, and U.S. artillery and aviation destroy the remaining transports on the 15th. This is the last major Japanese attempt to retake Guadalcanal.

13 November
New Georgia
Japanese troops arrive at Munda Point, New Georgia, in the central Solomons to begin building an airfield. This will allow Japanese fighter planes to spend more time above Guadalcanal, since it is much closer to Henderson Field than existing Japanese bases at Rabaul.

16 November
Force Structure
The first Marine night fighter squadron, VMF(N)-531, is organized at Cherry Point.

18 November
Guadalcanal
MAG-23 arrives in San Diego following its stint at Guadalcanal.

24 November
Force Structure
MLG-71 moves from Parris Island to MCAS, Eagle Mountain Lake.

30 November
Guadalcanal
The 2nd Raider Battalion surprises and routs a Japanese force on the slopes of Mount Austen. A U.S. Navy task force loses one cruiser sunk and three heavily damaged while turning back a resupply run by Japanese warships in the Battle of Tassafaronga. The Japanese lose one destroyer.

1 December
Force Structure
VMF-311 is organized at Cherry Point, North Carolina.

5 December
Manpower
President Roosevelt orders the end of voluntary enlistments for those 18–37 years old for all services effective in January. Those 17, or older than 37, are still allowed to enlist. Thereafter, Marine liaisons at the draft induction centers work to arrange for draftees who want to serve in the Corps to do so.

9 December
Guadalcanal
General Vandegrift turns command of Guadalcanal over to the Major General Alexander M. Patch of the Army's Americal Division. The 1st Marine Division begins its movement to Australia, with the 5th Marines departing this day, followed soon after by the 1st Marines.

15 December
Guadalcanal
The 2nd Raider Battalion departs Guadalcanal for Espiritu Santo.

17 December
New Georgia
The Japanese complete an airstrip at Munda Point.

20 December
Bases
Marine Barracks, New River is renamed Camp Lejeune.

22 December
New Caledonia
The 1st and 6th Barrage Balloon Squadrons arrive on New Caledonia.

29 December
New Hebrides
MAG-12 begins moving to Efate. The entire group will be there by 28 January 1943.

1943

1 January
Force Structure
Marine Base Defense Air Group 41 (MBDAG-41) and VMF-113 are organized at El Toro. MBDAG-42 and VMF-422 are established at San Diego. MBDAG-43, VMF-216, and VMSB-235 are activated at El Centro. MBDAG-44, VMF-225, and VMSB-236 are formed at Mojave. VMSB-331 is organized at Cherry Point.

4 January
Guadalcanal
The command echelon of the 2nd Marine Division and the 6th Marines arrive on the island.

11 January
New Caledonia
The 2nd Parachute Battalion arrives on the island.

13 January
Guadalcanal
The 2nd Marine Division begins a coordinated attack with the Army's 25th Division to destroy remaining Japanese forces west of the American perimeter on Guadalcanal. The advance continues through 17 January.

15 January
Guadalcanal
Joe Foss shoots down three enemy planes, giving him 26 kills and tying Army Captain Eddie Rickenbacker's World War I American record. The 2nd Marines leave Guadalcanal for New Zealand.

Right: *A Stuart light tank on the ramp of a tank lighter. The Marine Corps relied on these light models early in the war because amphibious landing craft were not yet capable of bringing in heavier tanks during an assault. (National Archives)*

Force Structure
The 14th Defense Battalion is organized on Tulagi.
Manpower
Anne A. Lentz becomes the first Marine woman reservist when she is commissioned a captain following her civilian work in designing the uniforms for the Women's Reserve program.

20 January
Guadalcanal
The 6th Marines and the 2nd Marine Division artillery are joined with Army elements to form the CAM (Composite Army-Marine) Division. This organization participates in attacks designed to destroy the remaining enemy forces in western Guadalcanal. The operation continues through 8 February, when American forces reach Tassafaronga Point.
Force Structure
MAG-24 departs California for Ewa Field.

29 January
HQMC
Ruth Cheney Streeter is commissioned a major and named as director of the Marine Corps Women's Reserve.

31 January
Guadalcanal
1st Lt Jefferson J. DeBlanc of VMF-112 shoots down five enemy Zeros in a single mission over the central Solomons, giving him a total of eight kills. For this feat he will receive the Medal of Honor.

1 February
Force Structure
MAG-31, 32, 33, and 34, VMF-321, and VMSB-341 are organized at Cherry Point.

9 February
Guadalcanal
The island is declared secured. Total Marine casualties during the campaign are 1,504 killed and 2,916 wounded. Losses among Navy personnel serving with Marines units are 36 killed and 101 wounded.

13 February
Manpower
The first women are enlisted into the Marine Corps for World War II.

15 February
Solomons
All land-based aircraft in the southern Solomons are placed under a single new command, Aircraft Solomons (AirSols). This is a joint (multiservice) and combined (multinational) force.

20 February
Force Structure
The 4th Barrage Balloon Squadron is deactivated on Samoa.

21 February
Russells
The 3rd Raider Battalion makes an unopposed landing on Pavuvu Island in the Russells. The 11th Defense Battalion follows the 43rd Infantry Division ashore on nearby Banika Island.

1 March
Force Structure
VMO-351 and VMB-413 (the Marine Corps' first medium bomber squadron) are organized at Cherry Point.

Bases

Marine Corps Air Base Kearney Mesa is established adjacent to Camp Elliott, California.

8 March
Force Structure

The 1st Marine Depot Company is formed, with primarily African American enlisted Marines. It is the first of 51 such units, which have the mission of unloading supplies at the beach and moving them inland during an amphibious assault.

12 March
Technology

The first Marine F4U Chance-Vought Corsair fighter planes enter combat when VMF-124 arrives at Henderson Field.

13 March
Manpower

The first women officer candidates report for training at Mount Holyoke College in Massachusetts.

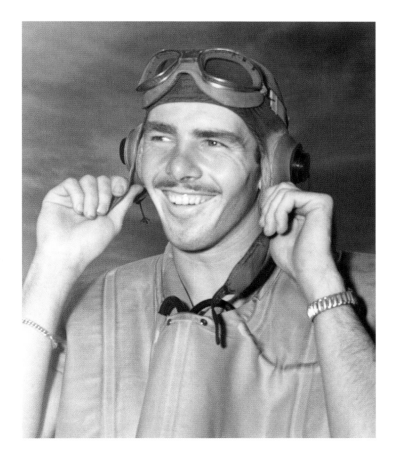

14 March
Russells

MAG-21 begins deploying to Banika Island.

15 March
Force Structure

The 1st Raider Regiment is established to command all four raider battalions. The 3rd and 4th Raider Battalions arrived in Espiritu Santo during February.

16 March
Force Structure

VMJ-353 is organized at San Diego.

17 March
Bases

Marine Corps Air Station, El Toro is formally commissioned in southern California.

Opposite, top: *Lt Merrill B. Twining. As a LtCol at Guadalcanal, he would help mastermind the operations of the 1st Marine Division. (Marine Corps Historical Center)*

Opposite, bottom: *Lt Mitchell Paige, who received the Medal of Honor as a machine-gun section leader on Guadalcanal. (National Archives)*

Top: *Lt Jim Swett. (Marine Corps Historical Center)*

Left: *Master Gunnery Sergeant Leland "Lou" Diamond, the expert mortarman of the 1st Marine Division on Guadalcanal. (Marine Corps Historical Center)*

20 March
Bougainville
Marine Torpedo-Bomber Squadron 143 (VMSB-143) conducts the first aerial mine-laying mission in the South Pacific, near Bougainville.

21 March
New Georgia
A small group of Marine scouts from the Raiders land at Segi Plantation on New Georgia to reconnoiter landing beaches for a planned invasion.

24 March
Manpower
The first women recruits report for boot camp at Hunter College in New York City. The Marine Women's Reserve training facility is co-located with the Navy's WAVEs training program at this prestigious university.

26 March
Force Structure
The 24th Marines, an infantry regiment, is organized at Camp Pendleton.

31 March
Samoa
The 2nd Marine Brigade is disbanded in Samoa.

1 April
Guadalcanal
The Japanese launch the I Operation, an aerial offensive against Guadalcanal. It lasts until 16 April.
Force Structure
MAG-51, the first Marine night fighter group, and VMF(N)-532 are established at Cherry Point. The 1st Parachute Regiment is organized at New Caledonia with the 1st, 2nd, and recently arrived 3rd Parachute Battalions.

2 April
Force Structure
MAG-35 and VMJ-352 are formed at Cherry Point. The 4th Parachute Battalion begins organizing in southern California.

4 April
Guadalcanal
MAG-12 moves to Guadalcanal in place of MAG-14, which shifts to New Zealand.

7 April
Guadalcanal
Allied fighters repel the largest Japanese air raid (about 170 planes) on Guadalcanal in months. 1st Lt James E. Swett of VMF-221 shoots down seven dive bombers before crash landing his damaged plane in the water. For this he receives the Medal of Honor.

9 April
New Caledonia
The 3rd Barrage Balloon Squadron arrives at New Caledonia.

17 April
Aleutians
Part of VMO-155 goes on board *Nassau* (CVE-16) to participate in the reconquest of Attu.

18 April
Bougainville
Army P-38s shoot down Admiral Yamamoto's transport plane over Bougainville. Marine aviators participate in planning the operation.

1 May
Force Structure
The 25th Marines, an infantry regiment, is organized at Camp Lejeune. VMSB-133 is organized at El Toro and VMTB-134 at Santa Barbara.

11 May
Aleutians
U.S. Army forces land on Attu in the Aleutians. The seizure of the island is completed on 3 June.

13 May
Solomons
1st Lieutenant Kenneth A. Walsh of VMF-124 shoots down three Zeros in the Solomons, giving him a total of six and making him the first Corsair ace.
North Africa
Allied forces complete the North African campaign following the defeat and withdrawal of the last Axis forces.

19 May
Bougainville
VMSB-143 conducts another aerial mine-laying mission in the waters around the island. Two TBF torpedo bombers are lost to heavy antiaircraft fire. Repeat attacks on 20 and 23 May complete the mission without further loss.

29 May
Force Structure
The Marine glider program is disestablished.

31 May
Force Structure
VMSB-143 is redesignated VMTB-143.

ON THE
OFFENSIVE

ON THE OFFENSIVE

JUNE 1943 – SEPTEMBER 1945

By the summer of 1943 the Marine Corps and the nation had passed through the most difficult phases of mobilization. Now it was time to switch over to full-scale offensive operations. The Corps found itself involved in two major and distinct campaigns. The first was a continuation of operations in the South Pacific theater. From Guadalcanal, U.S. and Allied forces would move north to reduce the Japanese air and naval bastion at Rabaul, on the eastern end of New Britain Island. This also would facilitate Army General Douglas MacArthur's push through New Guinea and on to the Philippines. The other main effort for the Corps was in the Central Pacific, which featured a drive straight across the Pacific toward the Japanese homeland.

The South Pacific campaign was fought on the ground mainly by the 1st and 3rd Marine Divisions, raiders, parachutists, and some of the defense battalions. The Central Pacific, which ultimately involved much bigger battles, employed all six Marine divisions. During the middle part of the war, Marine aviation was primarily engaged in the South Pacific. By the final year, Leatherneck squadrons were playing a larger role in the Central Pacific, but also supporting the Army in the Philippines and operating off Navy carriers. A smattering of Marines participated in other battles around the globe, including the campaigns in North Africa and Europe.

The Marines almost found themselves on the sidelines in the South Pacific, due to an unaggressive corps commander. An Army division was the main show on New Georgia starting in June 1943, though the raiders and defense battalions provided significant support. A revitalized I Marine Amphibious Corps (later redesignated III Amphibious Corps—IIIAC) and 3rd Marine Division spearheaded the November landing at Bougainville. The 1st Marine Division conducted the main assault on the west end of New Britain in December, then fought one of its toughest battles ever at Peleliu in September 1944 in support of MacArthur's offensive into the Philippines.

The Central Pacific campaign opened in November 1943 with the 2nd Marine Division's assault on Tarawa Atoll. Here, for the first time, tracked landing vehicles were used as amphibian troop carriers. They won their spurs hauling the initial waves of Marines across the shallow reef that guarded Betio Island. The frightful price of over 1,000 dead for the half-square-mile lump of sand shocked the American public, especially after the government released photos of Marine bodies floating off the beach. Nevertheless, the bloody battle proved that the Corps had developed the right doctrine and equipment to enable it to overcome even the strongest enemy resistance at the water's edge. The 4th Marine Division opened the Marshalls campaign in January 1944. The V Amphibious Corps (VAC—2nd and 4th Marine Divisions and Army 27th Infantry Division) landed on Saipan in June 1944, and followed up with Tinian in July. IIIAC (3rd Marine Division,

1st Provisional Marine Brigade, and Army 77th Infantry Division) assaulted Guam in July. VAC (now the 3rd, 4th, and 5th Marine Divisions) launched the epic battle of Iwo Jima in February 1945. IIIAC (now the 1st, 2nd, and 6th Marine Divisions) landed on Okinawa as part of Tenth Army in April. While both Leatherneck corps prepared in late summer for the invasion of Japan, the atomic bomb helped bring the war to an end. The cost had been high, but the Marine divisions and their supporting units had relentlessly carried the war to the enemy and rooted determined warriors out of some of the most formidable defenses ever devised.

During the last two years of the war, the Corps underwent a number of changes. As better amphibious transports and landing craft became available, the Marines acquired much heavier equipment and utilized more and more firepower. Some specialized combat forces such as the raiders, parachutists, and most of the defense battalions disappeared to free up manpower for the six divisions. Other new types of units came into being, such as the ammunition and depot companies needed to maintain the flow of material into the maw of corps-sized operations. Tables of organizations of units changed significantly, too. One of the most important innovations was the shift from the prewar unitary 8-man rifle squad to the 13-man outfit built around the revolutionary concept of the 4-man fireteam. After the demise of the raiders, the Corps developed a new light

unit devoted to amphibious reconnaissance, which later would become the forerunner of force reconnaissance. Training grew more specialized, with most every skill from cooks to communicators having a separate school. There was a training program after boot camp for infantrymen, as well, but the high rate of casualties in the latter stages of the war prevented the manpower system from letting most new Marines complete the full syllabus.

Marine aviation made use of improving communications equipment to make dramatic advances in doctrine and techniques for close air support. Regrettably, there were few opportunities to provide this tremendous capability to Marines on the ground. At Okinawa, for instance, where Marine air formed a large portion of the aviation element supporting Tenth Army, most Leatherneck fighter squadrons were assigned to combat air patrols. In many other cases, Navy squadrons on carriers supported the amphibious assaults. The Corps finally managed to get squadrons dedicated to close air support on escort carriers, but not until very late in the war. Marine air made its finest showing in the close air support role in the Philippines, perfecting the new methods in combat and setting a standard that left Army ground commanders begging for more. The Marine air-ground team was never effectively re-formed after the breakup of 1941, but the two parts were each honed to a keen edge of excellence at the end of the war.

ON THE OFFENSIVE

JUNE 1943 – SEPTEMBER 1945

1943

June
Force Structure
VMSB-131 and 232 are redesignated VMTB-131 and 232.

1 June
Force Structure
The 14th Marines (an artillery regiment) is activated at Camp Lejeune. VMF-312 is formed at Parris Island. VMSB-332 is organized at Cherry Point.

7 June
Guadalcanal
The Japanese make an unusually large aerial attack against Guadalcanal in an effort to erode growing U.S. power on the island. Allied fighter planes turn back the attack and inflict heavy enemy losses. Similar large Japanese air attacks on 12 and 16 June meet the same fate.

13 June
New Georgia
Reconnaissance patrols including men from the Marine Corps, Navy, and Army go ashore on New Georgia to survey possible landing sites for the planned invasion of the Central Solomons island.

15 June
Force Structure
The 20th Marines (a regiment of engineers and pioneers) is established at Camp Lejeune. VMJ-952 is formed at Camp Kearney.

21–22 June
New Georgia
The 4th Raider Battalion (less two companies) and two Army infantry companies land at Segi Point, New Georgia, to stave off a Japanese advance against a coastwatcher. This marks the earlier-than-planned opening of the campaign to seize the island.

26 June
Force Structure
The Army agrees to assume responsibility for all barrage balloon missions in the Pacific. The six Marine balloon squadrons gradually begin to shift over to operating 90mm anti-aircraft guns.

27 June
New Georgia
The 4th Raider Battalion (less two companies) moves by boat and overland from Segi to support a planned amphibious landing at Viru Harbor. The Raiders have several skirmishes along the way.

Left: *By the end of 1943, the gull-winged Corsair was rapidly becoming the Corps' premier fighter plane. ("F4U Corsair," 2ndLt Jesse G. Evans, USMC, Marine Corps Art Collection)*

30 June
New Georgia
The amphibious transports attempting to land an Army force at Viru Harbor are turned back by shore batteries. Army units secure Rendova Island, and the 9th Defense Battalion establishes positions there to support the pending assault against Munda Airfield on New Georgia. AirSols aircraft drive off heavy enemy air attacks against U.S. ships off Rendova. Marine fighter planes claim 58 of the 101 reported kills, with 1st Lieutenant Wilbur J. Jones of VMF-213 getting four Zeros.

Vangunu
Companies N and Q of the 4th Raider Battalion land unopposed on Vangunu Island in the Central Solomons as the vanguard for the Army's 2nd Battalion, 103rd Infantry. The two units succeed in defeating Japanese forces on the island over the next three days.

Manpower
The strength of the Marine Corps on active duty is 21,384 officers and 287,139 enlisted.

July
Manpower
The Women's Reserve officer candidate school and recruit training programs are transferred from civilian institutions to Camp Lejeune.

1 July
New Georgia
The 4th Raiders defeat the Japanese defenders of Viru Harbor.

Commanders
Major General Vandegrift takes command of I MAC in place of Major General Vogel.

Force Structure
VMF-114 and VMSB-245 are organized at El Toro, VMF-115 at Santa Barbara, VMF-217 and VMTB-242 at El Centro, VMF-218 at Mojave, and VMF-322, VMSB-342, and VMD-354 at Cherry Point.

Manpower
The Navy Department establishes the V-12 program at various universities to train enlisted sailors and Marines for commissioning.

COLONEL RUTH CHENEY STREETER

Ruth Cheney Streeter might have seemed an unlikely choice to be the first director of the Marine Corps Women's Reserve in 1943. Born to an established Boston family in 1895, she had married a successful banker and lawyer during her last year at an elite women's college, and had never held a paying job in her life. Beyond that snapshot biography, however, was a capable, determined leader. Her two brothers had joined the Army in World War I, one serving as an engineer in France and the other dying in an aviation accident. Two of her sons were Navy officers and the third had enlisted in the Army. She knew full well the cost of war. Throughout the Depression years of the 1930s, she had been active in organizations devoted to improving public health programs and assisting the elderly, the poor, and orphans—as she put it, "working with people." When World War II broke out in Europe, she prepared to do her part in a conflict that many knew would eventually embroil the United States. She learned to fly in 1940 at the age of 45, helped organize the Civil Air Patrol in New Jersey in the summer of 1941, and earned her commercial pilot's license in April 1942. Despite being a dozen years over the age limit, she tried five times to join the Women Air Service Pilots, a quasi-military group that ferried planes from factories to bases. She next looked into the Navy's reserve outfit, but rejected their limitation that she could only be a ground instructor in the aviation field. The Marines were not going to let her fly either, but they did offer her the chance to build their Women's Reserve program from the ground up. She jumped at the challenge.

The Secretary of the Navy swore in Streeter as a major on 29 January 1943. She was the second female Marine officer (the honor of being first went to Anne A. Lentz, commissioned a captain on 15 January). Major Streeter selected six other women for direct commissions as captains to fill key staff billets in her organization. Another 19 women transferred from the Navy to serve as recruiters. The Corps formally announced the establishment of its Women's Reserve on 13 February and began accepting volunteers that day. The decision to send them to formal recruit training and officer candidate programs marked a departure from World War I, when the Corps had simply given uniforms to women who already possessed the desired administrative skills. Now the Corps would train them to be Marines first, and then assign them to advanced schooling in a much wider range of occupational specialties. Major Streeter set the tone from the very first when she informed a correspondent on 14 February that there would be no catchy title (such as the Navy's WAVES) for the Corps' Women's Reserve. Commandant Holcomb seconded her instincts a few weeks later: "They are Marines. They don't have a nickname and they don't need one."

Major Streeter soon realized the limitations of her billet as director of the Women's Reserve. She would recall years later a brief conversation with her boss, the director of Reserve. To her complaint that "I've got so much responsibility and no authority," he replied: "You have no responsibility, either." Indeed, female Marines belonged to their units and the chain of command did not run

Right: *From flooded fighting holes along Bougainville's Piva Trail, men of the 2nd Marine Raider Battalion repel repeated Japanese attacks. (National Archives)*

Below: *A 40mm anti-aircraft gun crew on Bougainville sports Japanese flags on the barrel, one for each enemy plane shot down. (MacArthur Memorial)*

6 October
Samoa
MAG-31 begins operations in Samoa after its move from the United States.

8 October
Commanders
Major General Vandegrift reassumes command of I MAC following the accidental death of Major General Barrett.

13 October
European Theater
Italy declares war on Germany, although it provides no forces to join in the Allied war effort.

20 October
Force Structure
The 1st Joint Assault Signal Company (1st JASCO) is activated at Camp Pendleton. Its mission is to coordinate the fire of supporting arms, including air, during amphibious operations.
New Georgia
The commander of AirSols displaces his headquarters from Guadalcanal to Munda.
New Hebrides
The headquarters of 2nd MAW moves to Efate in the New Hebrides and begins to serve primarily as a training command.

27 October
Bougainville
The 8th New Zealand Brigade makes diversionary landings on the islands of Mono and Stirling southwest of Bougainville.
Force Structure
Marine Observation Squadron-1 (VMO-1) is activated at Quantico.

28 October
Choiseul
The 2nd Parachute Battalion makes an unopposed night landing from destroyer transports on the northwest coast of Choiseul to divert enemy attention from the pending assault on Bougainville.

30 October
Choiseul
Two companies of the 2d Parachute Battalion attack and destroy a Japanese barge staging point on the coast.

31 October
Force Structure
The 22nd Marines is detached from the Defense Force, Samoan Group, and assigned to VAC.

November
New Hebrides
MAG-12 moves from New Zealand to Efate.

1 November
Bougainville
Following air and naval bombardments (including attacks by Marine air based at Munda), the

reinforced 3rd Marine Division conducts an amphibious assault at Cape Torokina, Empress Augusta Bay, on the west coast of Bougainville. The 3rd and 9th Marines and the 2nd Raider Battalion make the main landing, while the 3rd Raider Battalion goes ashore on Puruata Island. The Marines (under command of I MAC) overwhelm the enemy company defending the Cape Torokina area and establish a beachhead perimeter. The 3rd Defense Battalion comes ashore, as well.

Force Structure
VMO-2 is commissioned at Quantico.

2 November
Choiseul
Elements of the 2d Parachute Battalion make a mortar attack on Japanese installations on Guppy Island off the coast of Choiseul. Two Navy torpedo boats (one commanded by Lieutenant junior grade John F. Kennedy) assist in returning the Marines to their main perimeter.

Bougainville
A Navy task force defeats a Japanese attempt to attack the Bougainville beachhead prior to dawn.

4 November
Choiseul
Before first light, the 2nd Parachute Battalion conducts an unopposed amphibious withdrawal from the island.

6 November
Bougainville
The second echelon of the 3rd Marine Division, including a battalion of the 21st Marines, arrives by sea at Cape Torokina.

GENERAL ROY S. GEIGER

Since the time of World War I the Marine Corps has prided itself on being the consummate air-ground team, with these two dimensions of combat power being more closely wedded than in any other armed force around the globe. One Marine more than any other epitomized that status. Roy S. Geiger not only helped lead Marine aviation to its prominent position in the Corps, he also is the only Leatherneck to ever command a field army in battle.

Geiger grew up in a small town in Florida and initially followed in his father's footsteps as an educator. Not content with that, he put himself through school to earn a law degree. A few months later he decided to look for something more adventurous. He wanted a commission in the Marine Corps, but failed the physical examination. Determined to try another route, he enlisted in the Corps a few weeks shy of his 23rd birthday in November 1907. He quickly won promotion to corporal, then a shot at taking the tests to qualify for a commission. He passed, received waivers for his physical defects, and put on his lieutenant's bars in February 1909.

There followed the usual tours with ship detachments and overseas garrisons. In late 1915, he applied for pilot training, but his physical status still dogged him. Alfred Cunningham, the first Marine aviator, listed Geiger as the sixth choice for orders to flight school, but noted that he would "place him No. 1 on the list if he can pass the physical examination." Geiger got the nod from the doctors and eventually became the fifth Marine to earn his wings. That qualification came just in time, as the United States was entering World War I. In the summer of 1918 he took command of a squadron of the 1st Marine Aviation Force. He and his outfit made it to France, but he saw almost no action, in part due to his own fault. Planes were hard to come by for the Marine unit; having just received the first for his squadron, he promptly crashed it attempting to impress British airmen with a showy take-off. Just before the end of the war, he was grounded for a time for insubordination. He received a Navy Cross, however, for his contributions as a determined leader and planner.

After the war, Geiger spent two tours in Haiti, where he had his first chance to use his planes in support of Marines on the ground. As the commander of Aircraft One (all Marine squadrons on the east coast) in the mid-1930s, he and his pilots were at the center of the development and testing of the new amphibious assault doctrine. In addition to other stints with Marine aviation units, he graduated from the Army's Command and General Staff College, the Army War College, and the Naval War College.

His fearlessness in the air and his forceful personality were just the traits required to build a small force of planes and pilots into the 1st Marine Aircraft Wing in the summer of 1941. Far more important was his clear sense that aviation's value lay not in independent action, but in working hand in glove with surface forces. The man and the moment came together at Guadalcanal in September 1942. When Geiger arrived on the island the situation was grim. His dirt landing strip suffered alternately from enemy explosives and rain. His aircraft were barely adequate to challenge the more nimble planes of the enemy. His pilots fell far short of the flying hours and combat experience of their opponents. The logistics pipeline provided only a trickle of ammunition, fuel, parts, and food. His squadrons came from all over—the Marines, the Army, the Navy, and even New Zealand. But perhaps most challenging, there was no clear chain of command. Geiger might have concentrated on his own problems and goals, but instead he melded his polyglot wing into the Cactus Air Force and placed it at the disposal of General Vandegrift. His planes fought to achieve command of the air over Guadalcanal, but they focused even more on sinking enemy ships bringing reinforcements to the island and on striking those Japanese that got ashore. The close cooperation between ground and air, in contrast with Japanese interservice rivalry, contributed significantly to ultimate victory and brought him another Navy Cross.

Geiger's ability to work with other arms and services, and his understanding of the entire spectrum of warfare, made him the only Marine aviator to command a major ground force in combat. He succeeded Vandegrift in charge of I Marine Amphibious Corps at Bougainville in late 1943 and took his outfit (redesignated III Amphibious Corps) through Guam and Peleliu the following year. In 1945 he led it into battle at Okinawa. Near the end of the campaign, he fleeted up to temporarily head the Tenth Army when the commanding general was killed. During the last few months of the war, he commanded the entire Fleet Marine Force.

He succumbed to lung cancer while on active duty in January 1947. In recognition of his outstanding service to Corps and country, a special act of Congress promoted him posthumously to the four-star rank of general.

MajGen Geiger (right) with Army LtGen Simon Bolivar Buckner, Jr., on Okinawa. Upon Buckner's death near the end of the campaign, Geiger became the only Marine ever to command a field army in combat. (National Archives)

7 November
Bougainville
A Japanese battalion lands from destroyers just west of the Marine perimeter and attacks. Artillery and the Marines of 3/9 and 1/3 turn back the enemy at the Koromokina River.

7–10 November
Bougainville
The 2nd and 3rd Raider Battalions and elements of the 9th Marines battle for control of the Piva Trail, the only route into or out of the jungle-choked eastern end of the Bougainville perimeter.

Marine dive bombers support the final attack on Piva Village on 10 November.

8 November
Force Structure
The 3rd Marine Brigade on Samoa is deactivated.

9 November
Bougainville
Major General Roy S. Geiger assumes command of I MAC and the Bougainville campaign in place of Lieutenant General Vandegrift.

13–14 November
Bougainville
In the Battle of the Coconut Grove, 2/21 defeats a Japanese force and gains control of an important trail junction on the eastern side of the Bougainville perimeter. VMF(N)-531 makes its first successful night intercept and shoots down a Japanese Betty bomber near Bougainville.

17 November
Bougainville
A Japanese air attack on a convoy results in the sinking of destroyer transport *McKean* (APD-5) and the loss of personnel from the 21st Marines.

18 November
New Hebrides
MAG-21 moves to Efate from the Russells.

19–20 November
Bougainville
In the first phase of the Battle of Piva Forks, 2/3 and 3/3 expand the perimeter to the east and seize a key ridge in the face of strong Japanese opposition.

20 November
Gilberts
The 2nd Marine Division launches an amphibious assault against Betio Island in Tarawa Atoll, Gilbert Islands, with the 2nd and 8th Marines leading the way into murderous Japanese fire. Only the use of amphibian tractors (LVTs) allows the leading waves to get through the shallow water covering the coral shelf around the island. The Marines establish a beachhead at great cost. A regiment of the Army's 27th Infantry Division makes an amphibious assault on Makin Atoll.
Commanders
Major General Ralph J. Mitchell assumes command of AirSols.

21 November
Gilberts
The 2nd and 8th Marines continue the attack on Betio and reach the opposite shore, cutting the Japanese force in two. 1/6 gets ashore relatively unscathed that evening to reinforce the assault. 2/6 lands on nearby Bairiki Island to clear it for the use of artillery. The VAC Reconnaissance Company seizes an island on Apamama Atoll in the Gilberts against light resistance.

Above: *Inside an amphibious tractor hit by a Japanese shell at Tarawa. ("Grapes of Wrath," Kerr Eby, Naval Art Collection)*

Right: *A Marine winds up to throw a grenade on Betio. (National Archives)*

21–25 November
Bougainville
During the final phase of the Battle of Piva Forks, the 3rd Marines, 2nd Raider Battalion, and 1/9 further expand the perimeter and establish firm control over the dominating high ground.

22 November
Gilberts
Reinforced by the landing of 3/6, the 2nd Marine Division seizes all of Betio except for a small pockets near the original landing beaches and the long narrow tail of the island. That night 1/6 repels enemy counterattacks coming out of the Betio tail. Organized Japanese resistance on Makin Atoll ceases.

23 November
Gilberts
The 2nd Marine Division completes the seizure of Betio.
Bougainville
The 1st Parachute Battalion arrives at Cape Torokina from Vella Lavella.

24–27 November
Gilberts
The 2nd Marine Division Scouts and 2/6 complete the conquest of Tarawa Atoll. Total

Above: *A Corsair downs a Japanese fighter. ("What a Helluva Thing," Paul J. Clinkenbroomer, Marine Corps Art Collection)*

Left: *"Dangerous Duty," George Harding, Marine Corps Art Collection)*

Marine casualties for the battle are 1,085 dead or missing and 2,233 wounded. Losses among Navy personnel serving with Marines units are 30 killed and 59 wounded.

24 November
Gilberts
The 2nd and 8th Marines depart Tarawa for a new base camp in Hawaii. The 2nd Defense Battalion arrives on Tarawa from Samoa.

25 November
Gilberts
The VAC Reconnaissance Company completes its conquest of Apamama Atoll.

29 November
Bougainville
The 1st Parachute Battalion, reinforced by Company M of the 3rd Raider Battalion, makes an amphibious raid at Koiari, about 10 miles east of the Bougainville perimeter. They encounter a large Japanese force and make an amphibious withdrawal under pressure late in the day.

30 November
Gilberts
The scout company of 2nd Tank Battalion searches for enemy on Abaiang and Makakei

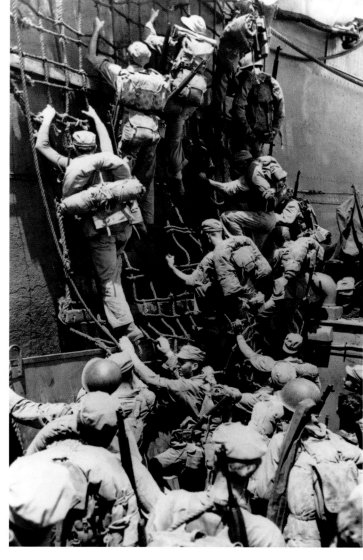

Above: *On Christmas Day 1943, Marines climb up cargo nets onto a transport to sail away from Bougainville. (National Archives)*

Right: *Marine reinforcements march toward the battle for Hill 660 at Cape Gloucester on New Britain. ("Moving Up," Master Technical Sergeant Victor P. Donahue, USMC, Marine Corps Art Collection)*

Atolls north of Tarawa and finds only five Japanese. The first Marine aircraft (six SBDs of VMSB-331) arrive on the Betio airstrip (named after 1st Lieutenant William D. Hawkins, posthumous recipient of the Medal of Honor for his actions in the battle).

December
Manpower
The first Reserve Officer Class is formed for newly commissioned women lieutenants.

1 December
Gilberts
The scouts of 2nd Tanks land at Maiana Atoll and determine it is not occupied by enemy forces.
Force Structure
Making use of lightweight search radars, the Marine Corps creates the first air-transportable air warning squadron, AWS(AT)-5, at Cherry Point. VMO-3 is organized at Quantico.

3 December
Bougainville
The 1st Marine Parachute Regiment headquarters and weapons company and its 3rd Battalion arrive at Cape Torokina.

7–15 December
Force Structure
The 1st, 3rd, 5th, and 6th Barrage Balloon Squadrons are deactivated and most of their personnel are assigned to defense battalions.

9 December
Bougainville
The ground echelons of VMF-212 and 215 reach Bougainville and move to the airstrip under construction at Cape Torokina.

9–10 December
Bougainville
The 1st Parachute Regiment and its 3rd Battalion begin an attack to seize Hellzapoppin Ridge, a

heavily defended spur east of the Bougainville perimeter. The parachutists are relieved by 1/9 and 1/21 on the night of 10 December.

10 December
Bougainville
The Cape Torokina Airfield is declared operational. The F4U Corsairs of VMF-216 fly in to make it their home, but for the near future, aircraft based in New Georgia will simply stage through this intermediate base for refueling.

11–18 December
Bougainville
The 21st Marines take Hellzapoppin Ridge in eight days of fighting, with the help of close air support by Marine planes on 13, 14, 15, and 18 December.

15 December
New Britain
The campaign on New Britain begins with Marine amphibian tractors from the 1st Marine Division carrying the Army's 112th Cavalry Regiment in the assault against Arawe Peninsula

on the southern coast of the large island. The Army's XIV Corps headquarters assumes command of the Bougainville campaign in place of I MAC.
Force Structure
The 52nd Defense Battalion is formed at Montford Point.

LANDING VEHICLE, TRACKED

As the Marine Corps grew increasingly interested in amphibious operations after World War I, it wrestled with the need for special craft and vehicles to carry men and equipment from ocean-going transports to the shore. While the primary focus was always on boats that could land and retract at the waterline, there was occasional interest in a machine that could swim in the water and then drive right up onto the beach—a true amphibian. The first significant experiment in the latter realm came in 1924, when the Marines tested an amphibian tank invented by J. Walter Christie. It used a propeller in the water and tracks on land, but was not sufficiently seaworthy for actual use in a landing.

The Marine Corps proved to be more lucky than prescient when it came to amphibian vehicles. Following a devastating hurricane in Florida in 1932, Donald Roebling (grandson of the builder of the Brooklyn Bridge) started designing a vehicle that could perform rescue operations in swampy terrain. Within two years he built a prototype consisting of a buoyant aluminum hull that relied on cleated tracks to propel itself on water and land. By 1937 he had perfected a version that could achieve a speed of eight miles per hour in the water. The Marines discovered his work when a national magazine printed a story about the vehicle that fall. Initially the inventor had no interest in dealing with the military, but following the outbreak of war in September 1939, he agreed to develop a more advanced model. It rolled out of his shop in 1940 and participated in maneuvers in Culebra. A steel version, designated the Landing Vehicle, Tracked (LVT-1), went into production at the Food Machinery Corporation (FMC) factory in Dunedin, Florida, in 1941. The vehicle was 21 feet, 6 inches long, and 9 feet, 10 inches wide, weighed in at 18,500 pounds, and could carry a load of 4,500 pounds. A subsequent design based on early experience in training resulted in creation of the LVT-2, though it would not join the Marines for duty in significant numbers until 1943.

The Marine Corps acquired the LVT-1 for a very specific purpose—to reduce the onerous requirement for men to unload supplies from landing craft at the beach and manhandle them into trucks for transport to where they were needed ashore. The amphibian LVT could be loaded at the ship, cross the beach, and drive inland to its destination, saving precious time and manpower. The tables of organization provided a battalion of amphibians (100 vehicles) for each division.

As early as the summer of 1941, the Marine Corps decided that the amphibian tractor could serve as a fire support vehicle during a landing. Roebling and FMC designed the LVT(A)1, which added light armor, plus the 37mm gun and turret of the Stuart light tank to the basic LVT-2 model, but it didn't get into production until mid-1943. It was not until the 2nd Marine Division began its planning for the invasion of Tarawa Atoll in August 1943, however, that Marines first saw the most important tactical role of the LVT. Confronted with a coral reef surrounding the main objective of Betio Island, the senior leaders of the division realized that traditional landing craft could not get the troops anywhere close to the beach. Their tentative answer was the

4 February
Marshalls
The 7th Infantry Division completes the conquest of Kwajalein Island.

5 February
New Britain
The 5th Marines begins an advance eastward along the north coast of New Britain using landing craft for shore-to-shore movements.
Marshalls
Based on the quick conquest of Kwajalein Atoll, senior leaders decide to use the VAC reserve, Tactical Group 1 (built around the 22nd Marines), to attack Eniwetok Atoll months ahead of schedule. D-Day ultimately is set for 17 February.

7 February
Marshalls
Ground elements of the 4th Marine Base Defense Air Wing arrive at Roi.

8 February
Marshalls
The 4th Marine Division begins to depart Kwajalein Atoll. The 25th Marines is temporarily detached to remain behind as the garrison force.

Force Structure
The 28th Marines is organized at Camp Pendleton to round out the 5th Marine Division.

12 February
Marshalls
A Japanese air raid strikes an ammunition dump on Roi. The resulting explosions kill 26, wound 130, and destroy large quantities of supplies.

15 February
Marshalls
The first aircraft of MAG-31 arrive on Roi. They include 10 planes of VMF-224 and seven of VMF(N)-532.
Force Structure
VMF-451 and 452 are commissioned at Mojave. VMF-512 and 513 are organized at Oak Grove. VMF(N)-541 is formed at Cherry Point. VMO-5 is established at Quantico

17 February
Marshalls
The VAC Reconnaissance Company and the scout company of the 4th Tank Battalion occupy three small islands in Eniwetok Atoll. Marine and Army artillery batteries follow and setup to support the main landings the next day.

18 February
Marshalls
The 22nd Marines assaults Engebi Island in Eniwetok Atoll and overrun it by mid-afternoon.

19 February
Marshalls
Two battalions of the Army 106th Infantry assault Eniwetok Island. During the afternoon, 3/22 goes ashore to lend support. The ground echelon of MAG-22 goes ashore on Engebi Island, with the rest of the group to follow later.
Rabaul
In the last significant aerial battle over Rabaul, an AirSols 139-plane strike tangles with 30 enemy fighters and claims 23 kills. The Japanese withdraw their remaining planes from Rabaul. Air attacks continue for the remainder of the war against ground targets at the sprawling Japanese base complex.

20 February
Marshalls
3/22 and 1/106 complete their task of clearing the southern end of Eniwetok Island. 3/106 continues the attack to capture the northeastern end.
Force Structure
VMF-514 is organized at Cherry Point.

21 February
Marshalls
Army units complete the seizure of Eniwetok Island. VMSB-231 flies onto the airfield at Majuro Atoll.
Rabaul
AirSols bombers sink two Japanese merchant ships attempting to evacuate ground crews.

22 February
Marshalls
The 22nd Marines, reinforced by a 500-man provisional infantry battalion formed from elements of the 10th Defense Battalion, assaults Parry Island. The Marines overrun Japanese defenders that day, completing the seizure of Eniwetok Atoll. Marine casualties during the Eniwetok campaign total 254 killed and 555 wounded. Losses among Navy personnel serving with Marines units at Kwajalein, Majuro, and Eniwetok are six killed and 36 wounded.

24 February
New Britain
Elements of the 5th Marines seize the Iboki Plantation on the north-central coast of New Britain.

25 February
Marshalls
The 10th Defense Battalion assumes garrison duties for Eniwetok Island.

26 February
Marshalls
VMSB-331 arrives on Majuro Atoll. The 22nd Marines arrives on Kwajalein Atoll to relieve the 25th Marines from garrison duty there.

27 February
Ellice Islands
The 51st Defense Battalion relieves the 7th Defense Battalion in the Ellice Islands.

29 February
Force Structure
The 1st Parachute Regiment and its subordinate battalions officially disband. Their personnel are transferred to form the core of the infantry regiments of the 5th Marine Division.

1 March
Marshalls
MAG-22 planes begin to arrive on Engebi Island.
Force Structure
MBDAG-46 and VMSB-454 (later redesignated VMTB-454) are commissioned at El Toro.

2 March
Ellice Islands
The 5th Defense Battalion departs the Ellice Islands for Hawaii.
Gilberts
The headquarters of MAG-15 departs San Diego for Apamama.

4 March
Marshalls
The 4th Marine Base Defense Air Wing, recently arrived in Kwajalein, begins its campaign against Wotje, Jaluit, and other atolls in the eastern Marshalls with attacks by VMSB-331. The aerial neutralization campaign continues until the surrender of Japan.

Above: *Marines take cover as a water-cooled M1917A1 machine gun duels with the Japanese on Parry Island. (National Archives)*

Right: *Infantrymen of the 22nd Marines scan for snipers on Parry Island on 22 February 1944. (MacArthur Memorial)*

MONTFORD POINT MARINES

A small handful of black men served in the Continental Marines during the Revolutionary War. When Congress formally reestablished the Corps in 1798, the first regulations specifically forbid the enlistment of African and Native Americans. No such rules applied to the Army and the Navy, and both of those services included racial minorites in their ranks for most of their history, though almost always in segregated units or in strictly limited specialties. Although the Corps had not created the initial policy of exclusion, senior leaders never made an effort to alter it, despite the successful record of Marines training, leading, and fighting alongside Caribbean blacks and Indians in the constabularies of Santo Domingo, Haiti, and Nicaragua.

Things began to change within the Marine Corps only after President Franklin Roosevelt directed on 25 June 1941 that "all departments of the government, including the Armed Forces, shall lead the way in erasing discrimination over color or race." The Corps bowed to this decree and initially planned to recruit 1,200 blacks, who would train at Montford Point, a part of what would soon be called Camp Lejeune. The first men enlisted on 1 June 1942 and began reporting to the North Carolina base in late August.

The ultimate objective was to form the men into the 51st Defense Battalion, which would be led by white officers but otherwise would consist entirely of black enlisted men. This policy of unit segregation did possess one positive aspect, since it ensured the creation of black NCOs at a pace faster than might be expected otherwise. White sergeants trained the first recruit platoons in the fall of 1942. By April 1943, new black NCOs were leading the recruit platoons. Many of these first NCOs had prior service in the Army or Navy or advanced education and were thus more than ready for the responsibility despite

Left: *African American recruits drill at Montford Point, North Carolina, in March 1943. (Library of Congress)*

Opposite: *Marines in the depot and ammunition companies saw duty in the thick of the fighting at Peleliu (pictured here) and elsewhere. (National Archives)*

their short time as Marines. Men such as Gilbert H. Johnson and Edgar R. Huff would go on to distinguished careers and rise to the very top of the enlisted ranks of the Corps. The Marine Corps began sending black enlisted Marines to officer training programs in 1944, with some going to the Navy's V-12 program and others to the Platoon Commanders Class in Quantico. It was not until November 1945, however, that a black Marine, PFC Frederick C. Branch, was able to overcome all the hurdles in his path and earn his commission as a second lieutenant.

The end of voluntary enlistments in all the services in December 1942 radically changed the plans of Headquarters Marine Corps. From then on, about 10 percent of all recruits would be black, a number reflecting the makeup of the population. To absorb this much greater influx, the Corps soon established the 52nd Defense Battalion, plus a large number of depot and ammunition companies, and a stewards' branch, as well. The depot units would provide a labor pool to unload supplies from landing craft during amphibious assaults, while the ammunition outfits would handle the flow of that critical commodity into the beachheads. As fate would have it, these logistics outfits would be the ones that saw the most action.

By the time the defense battalions made it overseas in 1944, their capability had limited utility. There was still a requirement to garrison captured bases, but the likelihood of Japanese counterattacks against them was remote. The 51st served in the Ellice Islands and then at Eniwetok and Kwajalein, but never fired a shot in combat. The 52nd went to Guam, where its patrols did engage small bands of Japanese soldiers still hiding out on the island. In contrast, depot and ammunition companies landed on the first day of amphibious assaults against Saipan, Tinian,

Guam, Peleliu, Iwo Jima, and Okinawa. They did far more than heavy labor, often serving as stretcher bearers in the front lines, or repelling enemy counterattacks and mopping up infiltrators and bypassed defenses. They took their share of casualties and performed heroically, earning a number of unit and individual awards.

The end of World War II did not bring an end to the policy of segregation within the Corps. Recruit training continued at Montford Point and graduates went to a handful of remaining units manned entirely by black enlisted men. It took another president, Harry Truman, to force the next step forward. On 26 July 1948, he ordered the military services to end bias against minorities in their ranks. By the fall of 1949, the Corps had ended segregated recruit training, accepted the first black women, and ordered black Marines to previously all-white units. The most symbolic turning point came when the recruit training facility at Montford Point ceased to exist on 9 September 1949. The Marines who had gone through their transformation from civilian life there had mixed emotions about its demise, but all could look back with pride on the pioneering role they had played. There was more for the Corps to do to achieve complete integration, but the process finally was well on its way.

6 March
New Britain
The 5th Marines, with 1/5 in the lead, conducts an amphibious assault against the Willaumez Peninsula in north-central New Britain. In three days of fighting, the regiment clears the area of Japanese forces.
Force Structure
VMF(N)-542 is organized at Cherry Point.

9 March
Ellice Islands
The 7th Defense Battalion departs the Ellice Islands for Hawaii.

12 March
Force Structure
The JCS direct the return of the 1st Marine Division from MacArthur's Southwest Pacific Area to control of CINCPAC.

15 March
Commanders
Major General Mitchell ends his tour as commander of AirSols; the billet goes to an Army Air Forces general.
Emirau
Admiral Halsey, commander of the South Pacific area, orders the seizure of Emirau Island on 20 March. Located 230 miles northwest of Rabaul, it would complete the mission of surrounding the Japanese bastion. The 4th Marines receives the assignment, draws up plans, and embarks within two days.
Force Structure
MAG-52 is organized at Cherry Point. VMF-461 is organized at El Centro.

20 March
Emirau
The 4th Marines lands on Emirau without opposition.
Marianas
Plans for the invasion of the Marianas assign VAC (with the 2nd and 4th Marines Divisions) the mission of seizing Saipan and Tinian, while

Right: *Marines with fixed bayonets prepare to advance during the assault on Roi in the Marshall Islands, February 1944. (National Archives)*

Below: *A rifleman scans the blasted terrain of Eniwetok Island for the enemy. (MacArthur Memorial)*

IMAC (3rd Marine Division and 1st Provisional Marine Brigade) tackles Guam. Major General H. M. Smith doubles as overall commander of Expeditionary Troops (both corps) and commander of VAC. The Army's 27th Infantry Division is tasked as the Expeditionary Troops reserve, while the Army's 77th Division is held in Hawaii as the theater reserve.

21 March
Marshalls
3/22 seizes Ailinglapalap Atoll in the southern Marshalls after a brief fight.

22 March
Force Structure
The 1st Provisional Marine Brigade headquarters is activated at Pearl Harbor. The primary components of the brigade will be the 4th Marines (on Emirau) and the 22nd Marines (on Kwajalein).

23 March
Marshalls
Elements of 3/22 attack Ebon Atoll and clear it of the enemy.

28 March
Marshalls
A reinforced company of 2/22 lands on Bikini Atoll and raises the U.S. flag.

29 March
Force Structure
Admiral King, COMINCH/CNO, authorizes Major General Smith to exercise administrative and logistical control over all FMF units in the Central Pacific. This is the beginning of the establishment of a FMF Pacific headquarters.

31 March
Force Structure
MacArthur asks to retain the 1st Marine Division until late June.

Force Structure
VMF-481 is organized at El Toro.

6 April
Force Structure
VAC orders establishment of a Marine Administrative Command, composed of a headquarters and the Marine Supply Service, to perform administrative and logistical services for both VAC and IMAC. This marks the birth of the command that will later be called FMF Pacific.

7 April
Force Structure
VMF-482 is organized at El Toro.

1 April
Force Structure
The 9th MAW is established at Cherry Point. Its mission is to train and equip aviation units for deployment to combat theaters. MAG-61 departs Cherry Point, ultimately bound for the Pacific. MAG-93 is organized at Bogue Field. VMF-521 and 522 are formed at Cherry Point.

10 April
Force Structure
The Marine Administrative Command is created. VMSB-474 and 484 are organized at El Toro. VMB-621, VMF-924, and VMSB-944 are formed at Cherry Point.

5 April
Emirau
The lead elements of MAG-12 arrive on Emirau.

11 April
Emirau
Army forces arrive to relieve the 4th Marines on Emirau and the regiment begins its movement back to Guadalcanal.

Above: *Curtiss SB2C Helldivers based on Eniwetok Atoll cruise high over the Pacific. (National Archives)*

Left: *Marines clamber over the carcass of a Japanese twin-engine bomber destroyed on the ground at Eniwetok Atoll. (MacArthur Memorial)*

12 April
Force Structure
Major General H. M. Smith divides his VAC headquarters into two staffs, one for his role as VAC commander and the other for his role as Expeditionary Troops commander.

14 April
Marshalls
VMF(N)-532 flew its first successful night intercept in its F4U fighters near the Marshalls.

15 April
Force Structure
IMAC is redesignated III Amphibious Corps (IIIAC). VMF-462 is formed at El Centro. VMSB-464 is organized at El Toro. VMF(N)-543 and VMSB-931 are commissioned at Cherry Point.

22 April
New Guinea
Company A, 1st Tank Battalion, 1st Marine Division, supports Army assault forces in the landing at Tanahmerah Bay, part of MacArthur's campaign around Hollandia, New Guinea.

23 April
New Britain
The Army's 40th Division begins to arrive at Cape Gloucester to relieve the 1st Marine Division.

24 April
New Britain
The 1st Marines sails from Cape Gloucester for Pavuvu Island in the Russells.

27 April
Force Structure
MAG-35 arrives at the newly designated Marine Corps Air Facility Corvallis, Oregon.

Above: Another view of SB2C Helldivers, underpowered dive bombers that came to the Corps in the middle of the war, but never performed well. (National Archives)

Right: A Navy chaplain reads the funeral service as the burial party prepares to bury fellow Marines at sea. (Marine Corps Historical Center)

Left: *A Japanese tank, dug in as an anti-boat gun, lies destroyed on Engebi Island. (MacArthur Memorial)*

Below: *A Marine leader motions for his men to stay low in a shell hole, which provides temporary cover during their attack on Namur Island. (National Archives)*

28 April
New Britain
The 1st Marine Division hands over responsibility for western New Britain to the 40th Division.

May
Force Structure
The 29th Marines (infantry) is organized at Camp Lejeune.

1 May
Force Structure
VMF(N)-544 is formed at Cherry Point.

2 May
Emirau
VMF-115 is the first flight element of MAG-12 to arrive on Emirau.

4 May
New Britain
The last elements of the 1st Marine Division sail for Pavuvu. Marine casualties for the New Britain campaign totaled 275 dead and 948 wounded. Losses among Navy personnel serving with Marine units are 12 killed and 30 wounded. The 12th Defense Battalion remains on New Britain.

5 May
Force Structure
The Marine Corps promulgates the new F-series tables of organization for its divisions. The main changes include enlargement of the rifle squad from 12 to 13 and the adoption of the four-man fire team, removal of the amphibian tractor battalion, deletion of the infantry battalion weapons company (with its machine guns and mortars dispersed to other companies), and abolition of the engineer regiments (though not its component engineer and pioneer battalions). The divisions implement the changes over the coming months. VMF-523 is formed at Cherry Point.

Right: A gun crew stands by with their M1919A4 Browning on Namur Island. (MacArthur Memorial)

Below: Marines climb down a cargo net from their Navy transport into a waiting landing craft. (National Archives)

8 May
Force Structure
3rd MAW arrives in Hawaii and assumes control of all Marine aviation units there. MAG-23 departs Hawaii for Midway.

10 May
Force Structure
VMF-524 and VMB-622 are organized at Cherry Point.

15 May
Force Structure
VMF-471 is organized at El Centro. VMB-623 and VMSB-932 are formed at Cherry Point.

20 May
Force Structure
VMS-3 is deactivated on the Virgin Islands.

21 May
Mishap
Following amphibious exercises, a Landing Ship Tank (LST) carrying ammunition explodes in Pearl Harbor and destroys five adjacent LSTs. Just over 200 men in the 2nd and 4th Marine Divisions are killed or wounded.

23 May
Bougainville
Marine and Navy torpedo bombers from Cape Torokina mine the waters off the Japanese-held southern end of Bougainville.

25 May
Force Structure
The 16th Marines is disbanded as part of the reorganization of the Marine divisions.

27 May
New Guinea
MacArthur's forces land on Biak Island off New Guinea and soon run into a tough fight for the island.

1 June
Force Structure
VMF-472 is organized at El Centro.

3 June
Force Structure
The designation of Marine transport squadrons is changed from VMJ to VMR.

4 June
European Theater
The U.S. Fifth Army enters Rome.

5 June
Force Structure
Admiral King designates Major General H. M. Smith as commander of all Marine ground forces in the Pacific theater and authorizes establishment of a headquarters FMF Pacific (FMFPAC), to include an Administrative Command, FMFPAC.

6 June
Normandy
The largest amphibious operation of the war begins, with General Dwight D. Eisenhower's Allied army landing on the Normandy Peninsula of France. Marine ships detachments participate from their stations in the fleet, while a number of officers are assigned as observers with various army and naval commands.

12 June
Force Structure
The Marine Administrative Command of VAC becomes the Administrative Command, FMFPAC. Two days later, the Marine Supply Services, VAC, becomes Supply Services, FMFPAC.

15 June
Saipan
The 2nd and 4th Marine Divisions launch their amphibious assault on the west coast of Saipan. They meet strong resistance, including an unusually profuse Japanese employment of artillery. Following an amphibious feint against the north coast of Saipan, the reserve regiments of both divisions are committed ashore. Despite heavy casualties (over 2,000 dead and wounded), the divisions seize a firm beachhead by nightfall, then drive off enemy counterattacks.
Japan
China-based Army Air Forces B-29 bombers launch their first attacks on Kyushu, thus opening an air offensive against the Japanese home islands.
Pacific Theater
The South Pacific theater is revamped, with some forces and territory going to MacArthur's command.

Left: *A Coast Guard-manned LCVP takes a boat-load of Marines toward shore during the assault on Saipan. (MacArthur Memorial)*

Right: *Men of the 2nd Marine Division under heavy fire on the beach at Saipan. An LVT(A)4, with its short-barreled 75mm howitzer, sits in the background. (National Archives)*

Force Structure

AirSols is redesignated as Aircraft, Northern Solomons. Its new commander is Major General Ralph Mitchell. Of its 40 flying squadrons, 23 are Marine.

16 June
Guam

Vice Admiral Raymond A. Spruance, overall commander of the Marianas operation, cancels the Guam landing planned for 18 June upon learning that the Japanese fleet has sortied from the Philippines.

Saipan

The 2nd and 4th Marine Divisions expand their beachhead against continuing fierce resistance. As part of the redeployment of the fleet for battle, most transports are due to withdraw on 17 June, so Smith orders two-thirds of the 27th Infantry Division landed. That night, the Japanese launch a major counterattack against the 2nd Marine Division with 44 medium tanks and 500 infantrymen. The enemy are repulsed with a loss of 31 tanks and 300 men.

17 June
Saipan

American forces on Saipan resume their attack, with the Army's 165th Regiment taking over the right flank of the 4th Marine Division zone. Progress remains slow and averages a thousand yards across the extended front.

18 June
Saipan

The 105th Infantry enters the fight on the right flank of the 165th Infantry, placing all eight U.S. infantry regiments on Saipan on the front lines. The 4th Marine Division reaches the east coast at Magicienne Bay, thus cutting the Japanese garrison in two, while the 27th Infantry Division captures Aslito Airfield.

19–20 June
Marianas

In the Battle of the Philippine Sea (also called the Marianas Turkey Shoot), Spruance's Task Force 58 decisively defeats the Japanese fleet in an aerial battle. American planes shoot down 424 enemy aircraft and sink a carrier and tanker.

20 June
Saipan

The 4th Marine Division reorients its lines to drive north on Saipan in conjunction with the 2nd Marine Division. The 27th Infantry Division's third regiment comes ashore and the division continues its attack to the southeast against enemy bottled up in Nafutan Point.

Tinian

An Army artillery battery on Saipan opens the bombardment against Tinian. By the time Marine forces launch the Tinian assault, 13 battalions of artillery will be executing preparation fires on that objective.

Force Structure

MAG-91 and VMB-624 are organized at Cherry Point. VMSB-933 is formed at Eagle Mountain Lake.

21 June
Bougainville

The 3rd Defense Battalion departs Bougainville; it had been the last Marine ground unit in action there.

22 June
Saipan

Following a day of consolidation, the 2nd and 4th Marine Divisions gain ground in their drive north

on Saipan and come up against the enemy's new defensive line. The 6th Marines seizes Mount Tipo Pale. The 105th Infantry holds its position around Nafutan Point, while the remainder of the 27th Infantry Division becomes the corps reserve. The Army Air Forces 19th Fighter Squadron lands on Aslito Airfield.

23 June
Saipan

The 27th Infantry Division assumes responsibility for the center of the corps zone on Saipan. All three divisions make minimal progress.

24 June
Saipan

The 4th Marine Division wheels east to clean out Kagman Peninsula on Saipan. Disappointed by the performance of the 27th Infantry Division, Major General H. M. Smith relieves its commander, Army Major General Ralph C. Smith.

25 June
Saipan

The 2nd Marine Division captures Mount Tapotchau, the key point for observers controlling Japanese artillery fire on Saipan. The 4th Marine Division completes its mission of destroying enemy forces in the Kagman Peninsula. U.S. destroyers disperse a Japanese attempt to reinforce Saipan from Tinian with 11 troop-laden barges.

Force Structure

VMB-453 is organized at Cherry Point. VMF-911 is formed at Kinston, North Carolina.

26 June
Saipan

During the night, 500 Japanese troops infiltrates the lines of the Army battalion at Nafutan Point and conduct attacks against Aslito Airfield, artillery positions, and a Marine regiment in reserve. The enemy force is destroyed by dawn the next day.

27 June
Saipan

The 4th Marine Division resumes its position on the right flank of the corps front on Saipan.

30 June
New Hebrides

The headquarters of 2nd MAW moves from Efate to Espiritu Santo.
Manpower

The strength of the Marine Corps on active duty is 32,788 officers and 442,816 enlisted.

July
Bougainville

The headquarters of MAG-25 moves to Bougainville from New Caledonia.

1 July
Force Structure

VMSB-943 is formed at Santa Barbara.

3–4 July
Saipan

Following the enemy's withdrawal the previous day from his main defenses, VAC forces make significant progress on Saipan. The town of Garapan falls to the 2nd Marine Division, which then is pinched out of the corps front.

6 July
Guam

Major General H. M. Smith attaches the 77th Infantry Division to IIIAC for the Guam operation.

Above: *Red Beach 2 on Roi Island shows the effects of the heavy pre-landing bombardment. (National Archives)*

Right: *The crew of a Browning air-cooled machine gun waits for orders on the beach at Namur Island. (National Archives)*

7 July
Saipan

Prior to dawn, about 3,000 Japanese launch a last-ditch banzai attack that falls primarily on the 105th Infantry. After overrunning the Army positions, the enemy strike batteries of the 10th Marines. Marines and soldiers defeat the attack by noon, but American casualties exceed 1,000.

8 July
Saipan

The 2nd Marine Division passes through the 27th Division and reassumes responsibility for the left flank of the corps front.

9 July
Saipan

The 4th Marine Division reaches Marpi Point, the northern end of Saipan, and all organized Japanese resistance is finished. Among the Japanese dead is Admiral Chuichi Nagumo, leader of the Pearl Harbor raid.

10 July
Marshalls

The Army's 305th Regimental Combat Team (305th RCT) on Eniwetok is assigned to the 1st Provisional Marine Brigade.
Force Structure
VMF-912 is organized at Cherry Point.

10–11 July
Tinian

Elements of the VAC Amphibious Reconnaissance Battalion and Underwater Demolitions Teams 5 and 7 scout the Tinian landing beaches.

12 July
Command

Major General H. M. Smith relinquishes command of VAC to Major General Harry Schmidt and becomes the first commander of FMFPAC.
Emirau
MAG-61 departs Espiritu Santo for Emirau, where it will remain for the rest of the war.

Above: *Marines carry in the body of a dead buddy on Saipan. (National Archives)*

Left: *Action on Saipan, 6–7 July 1944. ("Counterattack by Japanese Troops Defending Saipan," John Hamilton, Naval Art Collection)*

Right: *The morning after the Japanese banzai charge on Saipan. ("Aftermath of Battle, Saipan," William Draper, Naval Art Collection)*

Below: *These three Marines, all Navajo Indians, served as "code talkers" on Saipan. Selected words in their language provided an unbreakable code for tactical communications. (National Archives)*

13 July
Saipan
3/6 conducts a shore-to-shore amphibious assault and seizes Maniagassa Island off the coast of Saipan. The 2nd and 4th Marine Divisions begin recuperating and preparing for the Tinian assault. Marine casualties on Saipan total 3,152 dead and 8,575 wounded. Losses among Navy personnel serving with Marines units are 77 killed and 337 wounded.

15 July
Force Structure
VMF-913 is commissioned at Greenville, North Carolina. VMSB-941 is organized at Bogue Field.

18 July
Japan
As a result of the loss of Saipan, the cabinet of Premier Tojo leaves office and a new government is installed in Japan.

20 July
Force Structure
VMB-463 is commissioned at Cherry Point.

21 July
Guam
IIIAC (also designated the Southern Troops and Landing Force) assaults the west coast of Guam. The 3rd Marine Division goes ashore north of Orote Peninsula with all three regiments abreast, while the 1st Provisional Marine Brigade lands to

Left: *Marines get briefed on their mission just prior to the invasion of Guam. (MacArthur Memorial)*

Below: *Marines display an American flag recaptured on Guam, while a Japanese battle standard lies in the dust. (MacArthur Memorial)*

Opposite, top: *Marines use flamethrowers to rout out entrenched enemy on Tinian. (National Archives)*

Opposite, bottom: *A wounded Marine doubles over as others react to sniper fire on Saipan. (MacArthur Memorial)*

the south of the peninsula with the 4th and 22nd Marines in the lead and the 305th RCT in reserve. By the end of the day, the corps has two separate beachheads on either side of Orote. The brigade fights off a strong Japanese counterattack that night.

22 July
Guam
Elements of the 9th Defense Battalion land on Guam to provide assistance to other IIIAC forces.

23 July
Guam
Elements of the 3rd Marine Division complete the seizure of Cabras Island off the coast of Guam. The 14th Defense Battalion assumes control of the island. The 77th Infantry Division begins going ashore and replacing elements of the Marine brigade in the southern perimeter.

24 July
Tinian
The 4th Marine Division conducts an amphibious assault on the northwest coast of Tinian, while the 2nd Marine Division makes an amphibious feint in the south. The Japanese conduct a major banzai attack against the beachhead that evening and suffer severe losses.

25 July
Tinian
The 2nd Marine Division comes ashore and begins to assume responsibility for the eastern half of the corps zone. The 8th Marines captures Ushi Point Airfield.
Guam
The Marine brigade seals off the base of Orote Peninsula and positions itself with both Marine

regiments abreast to assault the peninsula the next day. The 77th Infantry Division assumes complete responsibility for the rest of the southern beachhead facing toward the remainder of Guam. That night, the Japanese launch a strong counterattack, mainly against the northern beachhead, but the 3rd Marine Division repulses it.

Force Structure

MAG-94 and VMB-473 are commissioned at Cherry Point. VMSB-934 is organized at Bogue Field.

26 July
Guam

The Marine brigade launches its assault on Orote Peninsula.

Tinian

The 2nd and 4th Marines Divisions drive south on Tinian, with the latter organization seizing Mount Lasso, the highest terrain on the island.

27 July
Tinian

Ushi Point Airfield goes into operation.

28 July
Guam

The 22nd Marines captures the old Marine Barracks on Orote Peninsula. The 3rd Marine Division and 77th Infantry Division expand their beachheads and link them in one solid perimeter. The 395th Infantry captures Mount Tenjo.

29 July
Guam

The Marine brigade defeats the last organized Japanese resistance on Orote Peninsula.

30 July
Tinian

The 4th Marine Division captures Tinian Town.

Guam

The airfield on Orote Peninsula goes into operation when aircraft from VMO-1 land on it.

31 July
Tinian

The 2nd and 4th Marine Divisions meet stiff resistance along an escarpment in southern Tinian. By the end of the day, the 8th Marines has a toehold on the high ground.

THE BATTLE OF TINIAN

Most Pacific theater battles in the latter stages of World War II pitted American foot soldiers and firepower against Japanese fortifications and fatalism. U.S. forces won every time, but always at a high cost in lives. The conquest of Tinian was a welcome exception to that rule.

Geography had made Tinian a strategic objective of the first order by 1944. The new long-range B-29 bombers of the Army Air Forces could reach distant Tokyo from this 50 square mile mesa of an island in the middle of the Pacific. Its level surface and location thus made it a massive aircraft carrier awaiting only a little engineering, some planes, and their supporting elements to become a mortal threat to the Japanese homeland.

Geography also partially accounted for the relative ease with which Marines would seize the island. Its northern end was only four miles south of Saipan, which V Amphibious Corps had captured in a bitter battle that

ended on 9 July 1944. From that close range, U.S. forces executed a pre-landing bombardment against Tinian and its 9,000 defenders that was unmatched in scope and ferocity. Naval forces had begun their preparation fires on Tinian on the same day that the assault forces went ashore at Saipan— 11 June. Once the latter island was secured, the fleet turned the full fury of its guns and carrier planes on their second objective. In addition to that 44-day blitz from the sea, the Americans were able to bring to bear artillery and land-based air once the southern end of Saipan was cleared early in that battle. By 24 July, 13 battalions of artillery were focusing their attention across the narrow waters. Planes took off regularly from a hastily rehabilitated airfield and flew the short distance south to drop their loads, which included a new munition—napalm-filled canisters. The jellied gasoline burned off concealing vegetation even when it didn't inflict casualties.

Vigilant Marines try to coax Japanese soldiers out of a bunker on Tinian. (MacArthur Memorial)

Right: *Marines turn a captured Japanese Taisho 3 Model 1914 machine gun (a modified Hotchkiss) against its former owners. (National Archives)*

Below: *Men of the 4th Marine Division climb toward the Quarry on the right flank of the Iwo Jima landing beaches. (National Archives)*

27 January
Philippines
VMSB-241 flies its first sorties in support of Army ground forces on Luzon. MAG-32 arrives at Mangalden Airfield.

31 January
Force Structure
VMO-155 is redesignated VMF-155 on Kwajalein. VMO-251 is redesignated VMF-251 on Samar. VMB-621 is redesignated VMTB-621 at Cherry Point.

1 February
Philippines
The Army's 1st Cavalry Division launches a rapid attack from Lingayen Gulf designed to free internees near Manila. MAG-14 provides air liaison parties on the ground and continuous sorties overhead during the daytime to cover the flanks and front of the fast-moving ground columns. The Marine dive bombers help the division reach Manila on 3 February and achieve its mission.

3 February
Carrier Air
VMF-216 and 217 begin going on board carrier *Wasp* (CV-18) at Ulithi, as part of the program to add fighter planes to fleet carriers to deal with the kamikazes. VMF-511 goes aboard escort carrier *Block Island* (CVE-106), the first results of the program to provide Marine air support for amphibious assaults.

8 February
Carrier Air
Forward echelon of VMF-452 joins carrier *Franklin* (CV-13).

CORPORAL TONY STEIN

Tony Stein was born in Dayton, Ohio, on 30 September 1921. After graduating from Kiser High School, he became a toolmaker. Just eight days shy of his 21st birthday in 1942, he enlisted in the Marines. He quickly sought out the most hazardous duty, volunteering for the parachutists. By April 1943, he was in the South Pacific as a demolitions man with the 3rd Parachute Battalion (oddly enough at Camp Kiser on New Caledonia). He and his battalion deployed to Bougainville in early December and participated in the hard fighting at Helzapoppin Ridge during 7–10 December. Stein and his demolitions platoon were called on to plug a gap in the regiment's lines and stop a Japanese attack on the 9th.

He returned to the United States in January 1944 along with the rest of the 1st Parachute Regiment. Upon the disbandment of the parachute program the following month, he became part of the cadre of the brand-new

Tony Stein, pictured here as a PFC wearing his jump wings. The intrepid Marine seemed to be everywhere during the first few days of the battle on Iwo Jima. (National Archives)

5th Marine Division, ending up in Company A, 1st Battalion, 28th Marines. In July he got married, just before the division moved to Hawaii for final training for the Iwo Jima landing. In Hawaii, the former toolmaker obtained a stripped-down machine gun of the type used on fighter planes. He modified it into his own unique handheld infantry weapon, which he dubbed the "stinger."

The 28th Marines formed the very left flank of the amphibious assault on Iwo Jima on 19 February 1945. The 1st Battalion led the way ashore, with B and C Companies charging across the narrow neck toward the opposite shore. Company A landed behind them, then turned left to protect the flank against enemy forces holding Mt. Suribachi. Although initial opposition was not especially heavy, the Japanese opened an increasingly severe bombardment with mortars and artillery as subsequent waves crowded into the narrow beachhead. In the move toward the looming height at the southern end of the island, Company A also encountered the band of pillboxes guarding Suribachi's approaches.

Corporal Stein used the heavy firepower of his stinger to cover his platoon as it moved forward. When intense machine-gun fire from the defenders pinned down his fellow Marines, the former paratrooper stood up, fully exposed to bullets and shrapnel, to pinpoint the source. As the enemy zeroed in on him, he dashed forward and single-handedly attacked the fortifications one by one, until he had killed 20 Japanese soldiers and enabled his unit to regain the initiative. In the process, he exhausted his ammunition for his special weapon. Without hesitation, he stripped off his helmet and shoes to improve his mobility, picked up a wounded Marine, and took him to the beach. Then he returned with enough rounds to resume the fight. Before the day was over, he made seven more trips to the rear under fire, each time carrying or assisting a wounded Marine to the beach and bringing back a fresh supply of ammunition. When a halftrack arrived on the scene, he moved alongside the vehicle to direct its fire and assist in destroying another Japanese fortification. By the time evening approached, his furious assault had carried the platoon into exposed territory, so he covered its withdrawal to the company's night position with his unerring fire. Twice during the course of the day, bullets had knocked the stinger from his hands, but he had not received a scratch.

For his "aggressive initiative, sound judgment, and unwavering devotion to duty in the face of terrific odds" on D-Day, he later would be awarded the Medal of Honor. At the moment, though, there was still plenty of fighting before the battle would be won. The next day his luck temporarily ran out and he was struck by a bullet. He sustained another hit on 21 February and finally reported to the beach for treatment. The wounds to his neck and right arm were not serious, however, and he was back in the front lines three days later.

He remained undaunted by the heavy enemy fire that met every attack on the island. On 1 March, his company tried to attack through a draw toward Nishi Ridge, which was holding up the advance of the regiment. Pinned down by positions cleverly concealed in a cliff forming one side of the draw, Stein volunteered to lead 20 men to root out the opposition. Only seven returned from the unsuccessful mission. Corporal Stein was among the dead, from a gunshot wound in the right side of his chest.

Tony Stein's body came home to Dayton, Ohio, in December 1948, for permanent burial. In 1970, his audacious courage in the bloodiest battle of the Corps was honored when the Navy commissioned a brand-new destroyer escort USS *Stein* (DE-1065).

10 February
Carrier Air
Task Force 58 (TF 58) sails from Ulithi. Four of its fast carriers host 144 Marine Corsairs (16 percent of the fighter planes in the task force).
Force Structure
VMB-623 is redesignated VMTB-623.

13 February
Kwajalein
MAG-94 arrives on Kwajalein.

15 February
Force Structure
VMB-624 is redesignated VMTB-624.

16 February
Philippines
U.S. Army parachute troops assault Corregidor.

16–17 February
Carrier Air
Marine planes of TF 58 participate in air strikes in the Tokyo area. Marine pilots claim 21 Japanese aircraft shot down and another 60 destroyed on the ground.

19 February
Iwo Jima
Under the overall command of Lieutenant General H. M. Smith's Expeditionary Troops headquarters, VAC's 4th and 5th Marine Divisions lead the amphibious assault on the southeast coast of Iwo Jima. The 28th Marines reaches the western shore at the narrow neck of the island and seals off Mt. Suribachi before the end of the day, while the 27th and 23rd Marines make it to the edge of Airfield No. 1. Heavy Japanese artillery, mortar, and rocket fire, aided by mines and machine guns, inflicts over 2,400 casualties on the assault divisions. Marine aircraft aboard TF 58 participate in air strikes in support of the landing, and continue to do so through 22 February.
Philippines
Forty-eight Marine aircraft from Mangaldan strike derelict ships in Manila harbor to silence enemy opposition to Army forces.

20 February
Iwo Jima
The 28th Marines begins the assault on Mt. Suribachi. The 4th Marine Division and the remainder of the 5th Marine Division capture Airfield No. 1 as they begin the drive north.

Left: *Marines patrol the rugged terrain of Iwo Jima in search of Japanese survivors on 8 April 1945. (National Archives)*

Right: *A flame-throwing tank in action. These modified Sherman tanks were one of the key weapons in defeating Japanese burrowed deep into Iwo Jima's volcanic rock. (National Archives)*

Force Structure
VMB-453 is decommissioned at Cherry Point.

21 February
Iwo Jima
VAC commits the 21st Marines of the 3rd Marine Division from corps reserve to reinforce the 4th Marine Division. That night, the Japanese launch the only major kamikaze attack of the campaign, against the U.S. fleet off Iwo Jima.

22 February
Iwo Jima
Elements of the 8th Field Depot begin going ashore on Iwo Jima to manage the flow of supplies onto the island.
Philippines
Marine air liaison parties join up with Filipino guerrillas operating behind Japanese lines in northern Luzon.

23 February
Iwo Jima
Elements of the 28th Marines seize the crest of Mt. Suribachi and hoist an American flag over the summit. Soon after, five Marines and a corpsman replace it with a larger national ensign. Joe

Rosenthal's photograph of this flag raising electrifies the United States and becomes the symbol for the 7th War Bond drive.
Philippines
VMF-115 Corsairs sink a midget submarine off Cebu. MAG-32 headquarters and its squadron ground echelons (the squadrons now assigned are VMSB-142, 236, 243, and 341) begin to move from Mangaldan for sea transport toward Zamboanga on the island of Mindanao in the southern Philippines.

24 February
Iwo Jima
The 3rd Marine Division (less the 21st Marines already ashore and the 3rd Marines still held as Expeditionary Troops reserve) begins to go ashore on Iwo Jima.

25 February
Iwo Jima
The 3rd Marine Division assumes responsibility for the center of the corps front on Iwo Jima, with the 4th Marine Division on its right and the 5th Marine Division on the left. VAC slugs its way slowly forward through the heaviest belt of Japanese defenses.

Carrier Air
Marine aircraft participate in TF 58 strikes around Tokyo.

26 February
Iwo Jima
Two planes from VMO-4 land on Airfield No.1 to begin spotting for artillery and naval gunfire.

27 February
Iwo Jima
The 9th Marines completes the seizure of Airfield No. 2 and also takes Hill Peter and Hill 199 Oboe, key terrain dominating the exposed strip. Army forces of the Island Command begin to come ashore. Planes of VMO-5 begin arriving.

28 February
Iwo Jima
The 21st Marines captures Motoyama Village and the high ground overlooking Airfield No. 3 on the northern plateau of Iwo Jima.
Force Structure
VMB-463 is decommissioned.

Above: *A Marine of Easy Company, 9th Marines, dashes across the open terrain leading to Iwo's Airfield #2. Men armed with flamethrowers were primary targets for Japanese gunners. (National Archives)*

Left: *A squad from 3/28 attacks up a rocky slope on Iwo Jima. (Marine Corps Research Center)*

1 March
Carrier Air

Marine aircraft participate in TF 58 strikes on Okinawa.

Iwo Jima

Transport planes of VMR-952 make the first Marine air drops of supplies on Iwo Jima. VMR-253 and 353 join in over the next few days.

Force Structure

VMSB-332 is redesignated VMTB-332. VMF-472 is reactivated at Mojave.

2 March
Iwo Jima

The 28th Marines captures Hill 362-A, the heavily fortified western anchor of the Japanese main cross-island defensive belt. Elements of the 24th Marines seize Hill 382, the highest elevation in northern Iwo Jima.

3 March
Iwo Jima

The 3rd Marine Division clears Airfield No. 3 and captures Hills 357 and 362B.

Above: *Marines bow their heads in prayer at the dedication of the 4th Marine Division cemetery on Iwo Jima. (National Archives)*

Right: *A rifle, stuck in the ground by its bayonet and topped by a helmet, marks the hasty grave of a Marine near the frontlines. (National Archives)*

Left: *A chaplain gives communion on Iwo Jima. (National Archives)*

Below: *A wounded man moves to the rear with the aid of a fellow Marine. (National Archives)*

Opposite, top: *A Marine crouches low as he dashes forward under fire on Iwo Jima. (Marine Corps Research Center)*

Opposite, below: *A tank lumbers up Iwo's sandy beaches with Suribachi looming in the background. (National Archives)*

Philippines
The U.S. Sixth Army wrests the last of Manila from the Japanese.

4 March
Iwo Jima
Although Marine gains have been measured in yards on Iwo Jima, at this point in the battle VAC has blasted and bled its way through most of the main Japanese defensive line. The first B-29, damaged during a strike on Japan, lands on Iwo Jima.

5 March
Iwo Jima
Lieutenant General H. M. Smith orders his Expeditionary Troops reserve, the 3rd Marines, to sail for Guam, despite the pleas of the VAC commander for use of the fresh regiment.

6 March
Iwo Jima

Following a day to consolidate and incorporate replacements, all three divisions of VAC renew the offensive behind a massive artillery, air, and naval bombardment. Gains remain small and hard-won in the extremely broken terrain falling away from Iwo Jima's northern plateau. Army Air Forces fighter squadrons begin to arrive on Iwo Jima.
Carrier Air
VMF-512 joins escort carrier *Gilbert Islands* (CVE-107) in San Diego.

7 March
Iwo Jima
Hill 362-C falls to the 9th Marines.

8 March
Iwo Jima
Army Air Forces fighter planes on Iwo Jima begin to assume combat air patrol over the island and to fly some close air support missions. Elements of VMTB-242 also arrive from Tinian to assist. Aircraft from VMR-253, 353, and 952 begin landing on Iwo's airstrips to deliver supplies and evacuate wounded. That night, the 4th Marine Division repulses a large-scale enemy counterattack, the first since the battle began.

9 March
Iwo Jima
Patrols from the 3rd Marine Division reach the northeast coast of the island.

10 March
Iwo Jima
The 4th Marine Division eliminates the Amphitheater-Turkey Knob salient that has been holding it up in the center of its zone since 25 February and makes substantial gains. The 3rd Marine Division largely clears the remainder of its

zone. Navy escort carriers depart Iwo Jima, leaving aerial support in the hands of Army squadrons on the island.
Philippines
Elements of U.S. Eighth Army land at Zamboanga on Mindanao. MAG-12 furnishes air support for the operation, while forward elements of its ground echelons go ashore to begin manning an existing airfield.
Carrier Air
VMF-124 and 213 are detached from *Essex* and depart for the United States. A portion of the maintenance crews remain on board to service replacement Navy squadrons in subsequent operations.

11 March
Iwo Jima
The 3rd and 4th Marine Divisions drive to the coast in their respective zones, leaving only a few pockets of organized resistance remaining on the island.

12 March
Iwo Jima
The 9th Marines surrounds and compresses Cushman's Pocket, one of the last major Japanese strongholds on the island. Operations continue against this zone for the next several days.

13 March
Carrier Air
At Ulithi, VMF-216 and 217 are detached from *Wasp*, although some maintenance personnel remain on board.

14 March
Iwo Jima
As the official flag raising on Iwo Jima is held at the VAC command post, the flag raised on 23 February over Suribachi is lowered. Army aircraft fly the last close air support mission on the island since the remaining areas under Japanese control are too small to permit further attacks.
Carrier Air
TF 58 sails from Ulithi Atoll. With the addition of *Franklin* and her two Marine Corsair squadrons (VMF-214 and 452), there are six Marine squadrons in the task force.

15 March
Philippines
VMF-115 aircraft of MAG-12 land on San Roque airfield at Zamboanga and begin operations the next day.

Force Structure
MAG-92 and VMB-473 and 483 are deactivated.

16 March
Iwo Jima
The 9th Marines completes the reduction of Cushman's Pocket, while the 21st Marines cleans out the approaches to Kitano Point. The 4th Marine Division overruns the last area of resistance in its zone along the eastern coast. Iwo Jima is declared secure, though combat operations are not yet entirely complete.

17 March
Iwo Jima
The 26th Marines reaches the coast near Kitano Point, thus closing the ring on Death Valley, the gorge where the Japanese commander is holding out with the last of his forces. VAC Artillery units complete embarkation and depart Iwo Jima.

18 March
Carrier Air
Marine aircraft participate in TF 58 strikes against Kyushu Island, Japan. Marine pilots claim 14 of the 102 Japanese planes shot down, plus a share of 275 destroyed on the ground.

19 March
Carrier Air
Franklin is hit by bombs from a Japanese plane and is severely damaged. Among the 772 dead in her crew, 65 are Marines from the two Corsair squadrons. Marine planes from other carriers shoot down 18 enemy aircraft. VMTB-233 (formerly VMSB-233) goes aboard *Block Island*, which sails from San Diego.
Iwo Jima
The 4th Marine Division completes embarkation and departs Iwo Jima for Hawaii.

20 March
Iwo Jima
The 147th Infantry arrives on Iwo Jima as the garrison force and is temporarily attached to the 3rd Marine Division.

21 March
Commandants
Commandant Vandegrift is promoted to general, the first Marine to hold four-star rank on active duty.

Opposite: *Volcanic steam piped to the surface by Japanese engineers provides hot coffee for two Marines during a break in the fighting on Iwo Jima. (Marine Corps Research Center)*

Right: *A Marine throws a grenade while his team provides covering fire. (National Archives)*

23 March
Carrier Air
Marine aircraft of TF 58 participate in air strikes against Okinawa.

24 March
Philippines
The four squadrons of MAG-32 begin flying to Zamboanga to marry up with their ground echelons and support the Eighth Army campaign in the southern Philippines. The movement is complete two days later.

25 March
Iwo Jima
The 5th Marine Division wipes out the last resistance in Death Valley. This marks the end of organized Japanese control of any terrain on Iwo Jima.
Gilberts
MAG-15 begins transferring to Ewa Field, Hawaii.

26 March
Iwo Jima
Prior to dawn, over 200 Japanese launch a surprise attack on Marine, Navy, and Army rear-area elements on the island. Marine units involved are the 5th Pioneer Battalion and the 8th Field Depot. The pioneers, including many black Marines, provide the first organized resistance and lead the effort to destroy the infiltrators after first light.

VAC turns over control of the island to the Army and begins departing.
Okinawa
Elements of the Army's 77th Infantry Division seize islands in the Kerama Reto group off the coast of Okinawa.
Philippines
MAG-14 planes support the landing of the Americal Division on Cebu.

26–27 March
Okinawa
The FMF Reconnaissance Battalion lands on four islets of Keise Shima near Okinawa, finds no enemy, and reembarks.

27 March
Iwo Jima
The 3rd and 5th Marine Divisions begin departing the island. Total Marine casualties during the battle are 5,931 dead and 17,272 wounded. Losses among attached Navy personnel are 209 dead and 641 wounded.

28 March
Carrier Air
Marine aircraft participate in TF 58 strikes against Kyushu.
Force Structure
VMD-954 is redesignated VMD-254.

29 March
Okinawa
The 77th Infantry Division completes the conquest of the Kerama Retto group. The FMF Reconnaissance Battalion scouts two islands between Kerama Retto and Keise Shima.
Philippines
MAG-14 supports the landing of the 40th Infantry Division on Negros Island.

30 March
Philippines
VMB-611 arrives on Mindanao.

April
Carrier Air
VMF-351 (formerly VMO-351) joins escort carrier *Cape Gloucester* (CVE-109).

1 April
Okinawa
Tenth Army launches its amphibious assault against the west coast of Okinawa, with IIIAC taking the left or north beaches and the Army's XXIV Corps attacking the right or south beaches. Within IIIAC, the 1st Marine Division lands on the right and the 6th Marine Division is on the left. The 2nd Marine Division conducts an amphibious feint off the southeast coast of the island. The initial landing is lightly opposed with casualties totaling about 150. The 4th Marines seizes Yontan Airfield and the XXIV Corps takes Kadena Airfield. VMF-221 and 451 fly missions to soften up the landing beaches prior to the assault.

2 April
Okinawa
XXIV Corps elements reach the eastern coast of Okinawa, cutting the island in two. One Yontan airstrip is made ready and a light plane from a Marine observation squadron is able to land. The Tactical Air Force (TAF) headquarters begins setting up ashore. The 2nd Marine Division repeats its amphibious feint off the southeast beaches. MAG-43 (formerly MBDAG-43) headquarters arrives on Okinawa to provide the administrative echelon of the Air Defense Command for TAF.
Philippines
The ground echelons of MAG-24 begin moving to the coast for transport by sea to Mindanao.

3 April
Okinawa
The 1st Marine Division reaches the east coast of the island and seals off the base of the Katchin Peninsula. *Bunker Hill*'s Marine Corsairs down 11 Japanese aircraft attempting to raid the Okinawa beachhead. Spotter planes from VMO-2, 3, and 6 are operating from Yontan airfield.

4 April
Okinawa
The 1st Marines clears out the Katchin Peninsula while the 6th Marine Division completes its wheel to the left and begins its drive north. XXIV Corps continues its drive south.
Iwo Jima
The 147th Infantry assumes responsibility for the ground defense of the island and the 9th Marines begins departing.

5 April
Okinawa
XXIVth Corps begins to meet serious resistance in the south as it runs up against the outposts of the main Japanese defenses, known as the Shuri Line. The 1st Marine Division begins mopping up rear areas while the 6th Marine Division exploits light opposition and moves rapidly northward. The FMF Reconnaissance Battalion lands on Tsugen Shima off the east coast and uncovers significant enemy defenses, then withdraws.
Japan
The Japanese cabinet installed after the defeat on Saipan resigns.

Opposite: *An amphibious tractor loaded with men of the 8th Marines heads for Iheya Shima off Okinawa. (National Archives)*

Right: *A unit of the 5th Marines lands in the fourth wave at Okinawa on 1 April 1945. (National Archives)*

Below: *Marines in later waves transfer from an LCVP into an LVT for the run into the beach. (National Archives)*

6 April
Carrier Air
The Japanese begin launching large-scale kamikaze attacks against U.S. ships around Okinawa. Marine planes of TF 58 shoot down 22 of the enemy. The Japanese suicide missions recur on a frequent basis over the next few weeks. One Marine pilot from *Bennington* achieves a bomb hit on battleship *Yamato*, which sinks under a rain of Navy bombs and torpedoes as it sorties toward Okinawa.

7 April
Okinawa
The FMF Reconnaissance Battalion scouts the remaining islands off the east coast of Okinawa and finds them free of the enemy. IIIAC artillery begins providing support to XXIV Corps along the southern front. The first Marine aircraft of TAF (MAG-31's VMF-224, 311, and 441 and VMF(N)-542) begin operating ashore on Okinawa.
Iwo Jima
Army P-51s from Iwo Jima provide the first land-based fighter escort for B-29s bombing the Japanese home islands.

8 April
Okinawa
The 6th Marine Division seals off the base of the Motobu Peninsula on the northwest coast.

9 April
Okinawa
The 22nd and 29th Marines launch patrols to determine the disposition of the strong Japanese force defending the Motobu Peninsula. The 11th Marines begins moving south to add its fires in support of XXIV Corps. Kadena Airfield is opened for operational use by MAG-33 (VMF-312, 322, and 323 and VMF(N)-543).
Philippines
Marine aircraft support the landing of the Army's 41st Infantry Division on Jolo Island.

10 April
Iwo Jima
VMB-612 arrives on Iwo Jima and begins making night anti-shipping attacks as far away as Japan.
Force Structure
VMSB-933 is decommissioned.

11 April
Okinawa
The 2nd Marine Division departs Okinawan waters and sails back to Saipan

12 April
United States
President Roosevelt dies and Vice President Harry S. Truman is sworn in as his successor.
Carrier Air
Marine Corsairs of TF 58 shoot down 51 kamikazes, while squadrons based on Okinawa get 16 more.

Major Herman A. Hansen, Jr., the 25-year-old CO of VMF-112, destroys three, making him an ace. Major Archie Donahue scores five kills, giving him a total of 14. Over the remainder of the month, Marine planes on the carriers rack up 30 additional kills. VMTB-143 goes on board *Gilbert Islands*.
Iwo Jima
The last elements of the 9th Marines depart after assisting in mopping up operations.

13 April
Okinawa
Patrols from the 6th Marine Division reach the northern tip of Okinawa. The FMF Reconnaissance Battalion occupies Minna Shima, an island off the northwest coast. TAF flies its first close air support missions for Tenth Army.

14 April
Okinawa
The 4th and 29th Marines launch an attack to destroy enemy forces concentrated around Mt. Yae Take on the Motobu Peninsula.
Philippines
The aircraft of MAG-24 begin their movement from Luzon to Mindanao. They arrive at Malabang on that island on 20 April.

15 April
Okinawa
Another large kamikaze assault begins and lasts through the next day.

16 April
Okinawa
The 4th Marines seizes Mt. Yae Take. The 77th Infantry Division launches an amphibious assault on Ie Shima, off the west coast of Okinawa. TAF Marine pilots score 38 kills and carrier-based Marines get another 10. VMF-441 claims 17 of the enemy. Lieutenant William W. Eldridge kills four, while Captain Floyd C. Kirkpatrick and Lieutenant Selva E. McGinty get three each.

18 April
Okinawa
Transport planes of VMR-252 make their first flight to Okinawa with vital supplies. VMR-253, 353, and 952 join in over the next four days.

19 April
Okinawa
XXIV Corps launches a major assault on the Shuri Line, employing three divisions abreast.

20 April
Okinawa
The 6th Marine Division completes the reduction of enemy defenses on the Motobu Peninsula.

21 April
Okinawa
The 77th Infantry Division completes the conquest of Ie Shima.

22 April
Okinawa
VMTB-232 (formerly VMSB-232) arrives on the island. Marine pilots of TAF down 33 enemy planes during a kamikaze attack. Major Jefferson D. Dorroh gets six, while Major George C. Axtell, Jr. and Lieutenant Jeremiah J. O'Keefe score five each.
Philippines
MAG-32 aircraft conduct a major close air support mission for the Army 41st Infantry Division that breaks the center of Japanese resistance on the island of Jolo. MAG-24 launches its first missions from the Malabang Airfield.

24 April
Okinawa
The 1st Marine Division is assigned the role of Tenth Army reserve. Prior to dawn, the Japanese

withdraw to the second layer of their Shuri Line defenses.

26 April
Okinawa
XXIV Corps opens a three-division assault against the second ring of Shuri Line defenses.

28 April
Okinawa
During another large kamikaze attack at Okinawa, TAF Marines shoot down 35 planes, while Marines on the carriers get another 14.
European Theater
Benito Mussolini is killed by Italian partisans.

30 April
Okinawa
The 1st Marine Division is attached to XXIV Corps and begins moving forward to replace the 27th Infantry Division in the front lines. The 77th Infantry Division replaces the 96th Infantry Division at the same time.
European Theater
Adolf Hitler commits suicide as Berlin is being overrun by Soviet forces.

May
Force Structure
VMSB-141 is redesignated VMTB-141.

1 May
Okinawa
With the 1st Marines on the right and the 5th Marines on the left, the 1st Marine Division is in position on the right of the XXIV Corps front.

2 May
Okinawa
The 1st Marine Division launches its first attacks against the Shuri Line.
European Theater
Berlin falls to the Soviets. German forces in Italy surrender.

3 May
Okinawa
In the evening, a massive Japanese kamikaze attack begins against the U.S. fleet, designed to coincide with the upcoming ground assault on Okinawa. TAF Marines splash 60 enemy planes, with Lieutenants Robert Wade, John W. Rushman, Joseph V. Dillard, and William P. Brown getting four each.

4 May
Okinawa
The Japanese launch a major daylight counterattack against XXIV Corps and continue into the night, but the Marines and soldiers defeat it and inflict heavy casualties on the enemy.
Guam
The 52nd Defense Battalion arrives on the island.

5 May
Okinawa
The 1st Marine Division reaches its initial objective, the northern banks of the Asa River.

Above: *Marines move past a dead Japanese soldier on Okinawa. (National Archives)*

Left: *Infantrymen negotiate a destroyed stone wall. (National Archives)*

Opposite, top: *LtCol Richard P. Ross, Jr., plants the U.S. flag on the ramparts of Shuri Castle. (National Archives)*

Opposite, below: *Marines get a welcome ride on a tank during the dash into northern Okinawa. (National Archives)*

19 June
Okinawa

Roy Geiger is promoted to lieutenant general and designated as commander of Tenth Army. He becomes the first Marine to command a field army.

21 June
Okinawa

Organized resistance in IIIAC's zone ends when the 1st Marine Division takes Hill 81 and the 6th Marine Division reaches the southernmost point of Okinawa. General Geiger announces that the island is secure that afternoon.

23 June
Okinawa

Army General Joseph W. Stilwell arrives on the island and assumes command of Tenth Army in place of General Geiger. The 1st and 6th Marine Divisions participate in a mop up of southern Okinawa, in which the five assault divisions turn about and slowly begin to sweep over the ground they had taken in preceding weeks. In the evening, the Japanese launch their tenth wave of kamikaze attacks.

30 June
Okinawa

The mop up of southern Okinawa is completed. Marine casualties during the campaign are 3,443 dead and 16,017 wounded. Losses among Navy personnel serving with Marines units are 118 killed and 442 wounded. At sea, the Navy loses nearly 10,000 personnel killed and wounded, almost entirely due to kamikaze attacks.

Manpower

The strength of the Marine Corps on active duty is 37,067 officers and 437,613 enlisted.

1 July
Okinawa

Marine Corsairs escort the first Army Air Forces medium bomber attack on the Japanese home islands since the carrier-launched Doolittle Raid of April 1942. The 8th Marines departs Okinawa to rejoin the 2nd Marine Division on Saipan.

Carrier Air

Marine pilots and MASG-48 headquarters on *Block Island* and *Gilbert Islands* support the landing of the Australian 7th Division on Balikpapan in Borneo.

Force Structure

VMTB-453 is organized at El Toro.

2 July
Okinawa

IIIAC is released from mop up operations on Okinawa.

4 July
Okinawa

The 6th Marine Division begins moving from Okinawa to Guam. *Cape Gloucester* and her two Marine squadrons arrive off Okinawa.

Opposite: *A Thompson submachine gunner covers the forward rush of a BAR man on Wana Ridge. (National Archives)*

Right: *A wounded Marine awaits evacuation from the frontlines of Okinawa by a Consolidated OY-1 Grasshopper. (National Archives)*

13 July
Okinawa
Many IIIAC corps-level units begin re-deployment to Guam. The 1st Marine Division, IIIAC Artillery, and the 1st Armored Amphibian Battalion remain on Okinawa and go into rehabilitation camps on the Motobu Peninsula.

14 July
Okinawa
TAF is dissolved and all Marine aircraft in the Okinawa area revert to control of 2nd MAW.

15 July
Force Structure
IIIAC is detached from Tenth Army and comes under control of FMFPAC. The corps headquarters begins displacing to Guam. VMTB-463 is organized at Santa Barbara.

16 July
Technology
The first atomic bomb is successfully tested at Alamogordo, New Mexico.
Force Structure
VMSB-133 and 241 of MAG-24 are decommissioned.

24–26 July
Carrier Air
Marine squadrons on board *Vella Gulf* fly sorties against Pagan and Rota Islands north of Guam.

29 July
Okinawa
The medium bombers of VMB-612 arrive on Okinawa and begin flying anti-shipping missions off Kyushu.

31 July
Force Structure
MAG-43 and MAG-62 are deactivated.

1 August
Okinawa
Most of 2nd MAW passes under the control of the Far East Air Forces (FEAF).
Carrier Air
Cape Gloucester and her Marine squadrons sail from Okinawa for the East China Sea to cover minesweeping operations and launch strikes near Shanghai.
Philippines
MAG-32's four dive bomber squadrons cease tactical operations in the Philippines and prepare for return to the United States.
Force Structure
VMTB-473 is organized at El Centro. VMF-481 is reactivated at Santa Barbara.

6 August
Japan
A B-29 drops an atomic bomb on Hiroshima, Japan.

Left: *A flamethrower team moves forward into the smoke. (National Archives)*

Opposite: *Cpl Robert E. Lowe and Dutch, veterans of Peleliu and Okinawa. During the latter battle, Dutch alerted his Marines to a hidden platoon of Japanese at a range of 150 yards. (National Archives)*

8 August
Japan
The Soviet Union declares war on Japan.

9 August
Japan
A B-29 drops an atomic bomb on Nagasaki, Japan.
Rabaul
Marine PBJ bombers of VMB-413, 423, and 443 conduct the last Marine air strikes on Rabaul.
China
Soviet forces invade Manchuria.

10 August
Pacific Theater
Japan offers to surrender unconditionally. FMFPAC directs the 6th Marine Division to provide a regimental combat team to the Third Fleet for possible occupation duty in Japan.

11 August
Japan
A Fleet Landing Force headquarters is formed with a Marine staff for future occupation duty. IIIAC makes preliminary plans for Task Force Able, to consist of an infantry regiment, an amphibian tractor company, and a medical company.

12 August
Carrier Air
VMTB-144 goes on board *Salerno Bay* (CVE-110).
Manpower
Plans are initiated for the establishment of separation centers at Great Lakes, Illinois, and Bainbridge, Maryland, to speedily demobilize eligible personnel.

13 August
Wake Island
Marine aircraft make their last raid on Wake Island's Japanese garrison.

14 August
Pacific Theater
President Truman announces that a cease fire is in effect with Japan. He also appoints General MacArthur as Supreme Commander Allied Powers, with authority to accept the surrender of Japan on behalf of the United States, the Soviet Union, Great Britain, and the Republic of China.

15 August
Manpower
The Commandant and the Undersecretary of the Navy approve a point system to guide demobilization. Points are awarded for time in service, for time deployed overseas, for combat awards, and for minor children. Those with the most points will be separated from active duty first.

16 August
Vietnam
Ho Chi Minh, leader of the Viet Minh movement, declares an independent Democratic Republic of Vietnam. His guerrilla forces have gained control of the northern half of the country from the defeated Japanese. British, Indian, and Free French forces soon occupy the southern half of the country, a pre-war French colony.

19 August
Japan
Task Force 31 is formed in Guam for the mission of occupying Japan. The headquarters of 1st MAW and MAG-61 complete their movement to the Philippines.

20 August
Force Structure
The reinforced 4th Marines joins TF 31 in Guam.

23 August
Japan
Aircraft FMFPAC assigns MAG-31 on Okinawa as the air component of the Marine occupation force for Japan.

NORTH AMERICAN B-25 MITCHELL

Marine aviation in World War II is best known for its top-notch fighters such as the Chance Vought F4U Corsair and its workhorse dive bombers such as the Douglas SBD Dauntless. Almost forgotten are the 12 squadrons that operated the North American B-25 Mitchell, the only medium bomber ever flown in combat by the Corps.

The plane (named for Billy Mitchell, the Army general who was court-martialed in the 1920s for his outspoken advocacy of air power) is often credited as being the best medium bomber in World War II. It was developed on a crash basis as conflict loomed on the horizon. The Army requested ideas for a two-engine bomber in March 1939, North American began designing it in August of that year, it first flew in August 1940, and the Army immediately adopted it for service and placed it in production. It gained widespread attention in April 1942 when Army Lieutenant Colonel Jimmy Doolittle flew a squadron of them off the aircraft carrier *Hornet* to bomb Japan. Although it underwent a number of changes during the war, the basic airframe was twin-engined and twin-tailed, with a wing span of 67 feet, and a length of 53 feet. It had a top speed of 284 miles per hour, a ceiling of 24,000 feet, and a range of 1,500 miles. Depending on the variant, it could carry up to 4,400 pounds of bombs and 13 .50-caliber machine guns. The B-25H model boasted a 75mm cannon in the nose.

The United States produced the Mitchell in such numbers (nearly 10,000 before the war ended) that the Army Air Forces could not use all of the airframes flowing off the assembly lines. The Marines gladly absorbed some of the excess as the Corps' aviation arm expanded exponentially in 1943. Redesignated the PBJ-1 in Marine service, the first squadron (VMB-413) organized at Cherry Point on 1 March 1943. It had 15 planes and 30 aircrews of six men each. Equipped with the B-25D, it deployed to the Treasury Islands in March 1944 and participated in the ongoing neutralization of Rabaul. It subsequently moved to other locations in the northern Solomons to operate against other bypassed Japanese garrisons. Colloquially dubbed "milk runs," these missions were hardly easy or safe. The squadron lost five planes and 32 men in its first three months in action. VMB-423, 433, and 443 all made it to the South Pacific in 1944 and conducted similar neutralization attacks until the end of the war. VMB-611 arrived in Emirau in December 1944 and flew against Rabaul until March 1945, when it shifted to the airfield at Zamboanga in the Philippines to support operations by the U.S. Army and Filipino guerrillas. VMB-613 made it to Kwajalein in December 1944 and launched attacks against enemy-held portions of the Marshalls until the end of the war.

VMB-612 drew the most complicated and challenging mission of all the PBJ squadrons. Formed on 1 October 1943 at Cherry Point, it was equipped with H and J models. These received special modifications including the addition of a nose-mounted radar and launching rails for eight rockets under the wings. The squadron trained for the mission of attacking Japanese shipping at night. The

commander for most of the outfit's life was Lieutenant Colonel Jack R. Cram. He had achieved fame in the Corps piloting General Geiger's personal PBY-5A Catalina flying boat at Guadalcanal. During the desperate fighting of mid-October 1942, Cram's ground crew affixed two torpedoes under the wings of the lumbering amphibian and he fought through anti-aircraft fire and a fighter screen to loose them at Japanese transports delivering reinforcements to the island. Now in command of VMB-612, he finally had a proper steed for hunting enemy ships.

Cram's squadron arrived on Saipan in October 1944. To give his planes the range and endurance to operate around Iwo Jima, the top turret and other equipment was removed to reduce weight. From November until the invasion of Iwo Jima in February 1945, VMB-612 flew 334 missions to slow the flow of men and supplies into the critical island. These flights produced 49 contacts and the crews claimed two ships sunk and another 27 hit.

The cost was three planes and 13 men lost. Once Iwo Jima was secured, the squadron moved onto its airfields in April and began operating in waters around the Japanese home islands. In a third of the 251 sorties from Iwo, VMB-612 found targets. The squadron estimated hits on 53 ships and it lost seven more planes. At the end of July, Cram moved his outfit forward to Okinawa to continue its mission. They flew 31 sorties and claimed 20 hits before the end of hostilities arrived.

During the course of the war, the VMB squadrons collectively lost 45 of their PBJs (26 of them in combat operations) and a total of 173 crewmen. With the exception of VMB-612, their activities were not particularly glamorous, but they had performed significant missions and contributed to the ultimate victory over Japan.

A PBJ of VMB-611. ("Marine Bombers Over Emirau," Robert T. Horvath, Marine Corps Art Collection)

27 August
Philippines
The forward echelon of VMB-611 departs the Philippines for Peleliu to join 4th MAW there.

28 August
Japan
The ships of TF 31 enter Tokyo Bay and anchor off the naval base at Yokosuka.

29 August
China
Plans are issued for IIIAC to move to northern China, with a tentative departure date of 15 September.
Japan
Naval forces begin operations to rescue Allied prisoners of war held by the Japanese.

30 August
Japan
The 4th Marines, the Fleet Marine Landing Force (a three-battalion regiment composed of the 2,000 men in the fleet's Marine detachments), U.S. and British sailors, and Royal Marines go ashore at Yokusuka, while the Army's 11th Airborne Division lands at Atsugi Airfield. General MacArthur lands at Atsugi Airfield. As SCAP, he becomes the virtual ruler of Japan.

31 August
Force Structure
The Headquarters and Service Battalion of FMFPAC is disbanded.
Japan
A company of 3/4 lands at Tateyama Naval Air Station at the mouth of Tokyo Bay.

1 September
Bases
Marine Barracks Guantanamo Bay is redesignated as a Marine Corps Base.

2 September
Pacific Theater
Japanese representatives sign the formal surrender documents on board battleship *Missouri* (BB-63) in Tokyo Bay. The ship's Marine detachment and Marines on several senior staffs are present.
Manpower
The Marine Corps is at its peak strength of the war (and all time) with a total of 485,833 officers and men.
Japan
U.S. Army occupation forces begin to arrive in Tokyo Bay. Japanese garrisons all over the Pacific begin surrendering.

Left: *Men of the 6th Marine Division cast shadows on a damaged LVT as they march past on Okinawa. The special tracks that power the vehicle on land and water are clearly visible at right. (National Archives)*

Opposite: *A night patrol of 3/29 is silhouetted on an Okinawan ridge as it prepares to depart. (National Archives)*

4 September
Marianas
A force of Marines and Seabees moves on to Rota Island in the Marianas and begins repairing its airstrip.
Wake Island
The Japanese garrison on Wake Island formally surrenders to Brigadier General Lawson H. M. Sanderson, commander of 4th MAW.
Carrier Air
VMF-511 and VMTB-233 on *Block Island* assist in rescuing Allied prisoners of war from Formosa.
Force Structure
The Marine Corps replaces the F-series tables of organization (adopted in early 1944) with the G series. The change increases the size of a full-strength division by 1,700 men (much of it due to beefed-up service and support elements in light of the planned disbandment of corps-level reinforcing units).

6 September
Japan
Nearly all elements of the Fleet Marine Landing Force have been relieved of occupation duties and returned to their ships. The 4th Marines parades for 120 former members of the regiment who had survived Japanese imprisonment since the fall of Corregidor.

7 September
Japan
The headquarters of MAG-31 and the planes of VMF-441 fly onto the Yokosuka Airfield and become the first U.S. aviation unit to operate from Japan. They are followed in the next few days by VMF-224, VMF-311, VMF(N)-542, and VMTB-131.

10 September
Force Structure
Over the course of the next two weeks, the Marine Corps decommissions MASG-51, VMD-154, VMSB-142, 243, 341, and 484, and VMF-112, 123, 221, 451, 462, 471, 481, 521, and 522.

20 September
Japan
The advance echelons of MAG-22 fly onto Omura Airfield on Kyushu.

22 September
Japan
The VAC headquarters and the 5th Marine Division arrive at the Sasebo naval base on Kyushu Island, Japan. The 5th Marine Division assumes responsibility for occupying the northern half of the island.
China
1st MAW begins to move from Mindanao to China via Okinawa.

23 September
Japan
The lead squadron of MAG-22, VMF-113, lands on Omura airfield. It is followed in the next few days by VMF-314 and 422 and VMF(N)-543. The 2nd and 6th Marines land at Nagasaki and relieve the Marine detachments of the cruisers *Biloxi* (CL-80) and *Wichita* (CA-45). The 2nd Marine Division has responsibility for occupying the southern half of Kyushu Island. VAC assumes command of the 2nd and 5th Marine Divisions.

24 September
Japan
The 8th and 10th Marines and VMO-2 come ashore at Nagasaki. The U.S. Sixth Army assumes control of all ground forces in Japan.

30 September
China
IIIAC arrives at Tangku, China. 2/7 lands and secures the city. 3/7 goes ashore and boards a train for Tientsin.

HOT OPENING
TO A
COLD WAR

OCTOBER
1945–1953

HOT OPENING TO A COLD WAR

OCTOBER 1945–1953

At the end of World War II, the Marine Corps had attained a strength of a half million, but those numbers melted away quickly in the postwar drawdown. The 3rd and 4th Marine Divisions and the 3rd, 4th, and 9th MAWs disbanded almost immediately. The 1st and 6th Marine Divisions and 1st MAW moved into China to oversee the surrender of Japanese forces, while the 2nd and 5th Marine Divisions occupied Japan and 2nd MAW remained on Okinawa. Within weeks of the end of the war, even the occupation forces began to go home, and the last Marines left Japan in June 1946. A few months later, the Corps had reached its planned peacetime force level of 7,000 officers and 100,000 enlisted. Simultaneously, Marine Corps Reserve units slowly came back into existence and began rebuilding.

Despite its outstanding wartime contributions—in terms of doctrine, equipment, and battlefield success—the Marine Corps found itself threatened institutionally as soon as the guns fell silent. An Army plan to unify the services would have resulted in air, sea, and ground forces, but no dedicated amphibious element. In secret papers exchanged between the War and Navy Departments, Army leaders envisioned a Corps limited, if it existed at all, to operating landing craft. An impassioned speech by General Vandegrift in May 1946 temporarily delayed Congressional action, but it took a strong lobbying and public relations effort the following year to

secure language protecting the Corps in the 1947 National Security Act. President Truman, a strong proponent of the merger, never forgave Marines for blocking his aims. Congress had to step in again in 1949 to prevent aviation from being stripped out of the Corps.

Internally, Marines knew they had to develop new methods if they wanted to maintain the viability of the amphibious assault in the face of nuclear weapons. The result was a new doctrine based on helicopters, even though there were then no machines capable of carrying a payload. The Corps was again operating on blind faith that technology would catch up, as it had in the late 1930s. Budget constraints also caused the Corps to continue shrinking, to the point where it numbered less than 75,000 officers and enlisted in the spring of 1950. In addition, manpower policies changed significantly with the partial integration of women into the regular component and the complete racial desegregation of the armed forces. Despite the challenges seemingly affecting all aspects of the Corps, the Marines pursued the amphibious mission with single-minded determination. Marine ground units began deploying as a ready landing force in the Mediterranean, and the air wing pressed forward with the development of helicopters and associated tactics.

A shrinking Marine presence in North China in the late 1940s attempted to stem the civil war going on there, but in the first hints of what would become the Cold War, the Chinese

Pages 406–407: *Marines trudge along the narrow mountain road on 9 December 1950 as they fight their way south from the Chosin Reservoir. (National Archives)*

Right: *Company E of 2/1 attacks North Korean positions on 13 September 1951. ("Assault on Hill 749," Col Charles Waterhouse, USMCR (Ret), Marine Corps Art Collection)*

Communists proved uncooperative and initiated several skirmishes with Marines. The Soviet Union, meanwhile, raised the Iron Curtain and divided Europe. This tense atmosphere exploded into war in June 1950 when Communist North Korea invaded the South in an attempt to reunify the peninsula by force. A wider war might have ensued, but the Chinese and Soviets initially stood by as the United States and elements of the United Nations rushed forces to save South Korea. In a sign that the Corps was determined not to repeat what had happened in World War II, it formed the air-ground 1st Provisional Marine Brigade for immediate deployment to Korea. Marines had doggedly maintained a high state of preparedness for combat throughout the period after the defeat of Japan and it showed as the brigade mounted out in a hurry and then played a major role in staving off defeat in the Pusan Perimeter. The rebuilding of the skeletonized 1st Marine Division and its sterling performance in the dramatic amphibious assault at Inchon turned the tide of the war and enshrined the Corps as the nation's premier force in readiness. The Reserves, heavily salted with World War II veterans, played a significant part, but only as individuals fleshing out regular units. The eventual result would be major changes in the reserve program, including attendance at boot camp and specialty training for reserve recruits and weekend drill training thereafter, so that reserve units could be mobilized ready to fight.

Marine performance on the battlefields of Korea more than matched the success and courage of earlier generations of Leathernecks. The brigade's counterattacks along the Naktong River, the division's landing at Inchon, the drive through Seoul, the fighting breakout from Chinese encirclement at the Chosin Reservoir, and the close air support provided by 1st MAW all added to the sterling reputation of the Corps. In the see-saw fighting along the central front during the last two years of the war, the 1st Marine Division proved itself to be the most powerful and successful outfit in Korea. Regrettably, the Air Force pursued its doctrine for centralized control of aviation and diverted much of the effort of 1st MAW during this period to deep interdiction missions, but Leatherneck airmen continued to perfect close air support tactics and techniques whenever they could. Marine innovation also came to the fore again as the Corps conducted the first tactical helicopter operations in combat and deployed the first infantry flak jackets and effective cold weather boots.

President Truman's criticism of the Corps early in the war only served to highlight for the public what Marines had accomplished. In June 1952, their elected representatives further strengthened the Corps by legislating a minimum size of three divisions and three wings, emphasizing its status as a separate service within the Navy Department, and giving the Commandant more of a role in the Joint Chiefs of Staff.

HOT OPENING TO A COLD WAR

OCTOBER 1945–1953

1945

1 October
China
1/7 arrives at Chinwangtao and arranges a halt in fighting between Communist Chinese forces and Japanese troops and their allies (forces of the former Japanese puppet government in north China). 3/7 arrives in Tientsin to secure the city. The 1st Marines follows soon after to assume occupation of Tientsin. The primary mission of Marine forces in north China is to accept the surrender of Japanese forces and oversee their repatriation to Japan. Marines also assume security for the vital coal trains that carry fuel to power the urban areas of China. They become involved inevitably in the ongoing Chinese civil war between the Nationalists and Communists, each of whom hopes to take over Japanese-controlled territory and arms.

6 October
China
The 5th Marines begins landing at Tangku and moving out toward Peiping. Headquarters of 1st MAW shifts to Tientsin from Okinawa. IIIAC, in command of Marine forces in north China, accepts the surrender of 50,000 Japanese troops in the Tientsin-Tangku-Chinwangtao area. An engineer unit and a rifle platoon of the 1st Marines are fired upon by Chinese Communist forces on the road to Peiping.

7 October
China
A stronger Marine force removes roadblocks on the road to Peiping without opposition. The 5th Marines reaches the Chinese capital. Transport aircraft of MAG-25 (VMR-152 and 153) begin arriving at Tientsin.
Japan
MAG-31 at Yokosuka is returned to naval control by Fifth Air Force.

8 October
Okinawa
A typhoon strikes Okinawa and damages many 1st MAW planes over the next two days.

10 October
Manpower
Marine separation centers are established at Navy training bases in Bainbridge, Maryland, and Great Lakes, Illinois.

Left: *6th Marine Division tanks roll through the streets of Tsingtao on 13 October 1945 as Chinese civilians look on. (National Archives)*

Opposite: *Marines prepare to disembark as they pull alongside the dock at Taku, China, on 1 October 1945. (National Archives)*

Japan

1/3 begins landing on Chichi Jima as part of the occupation of the Bonin Islands.

11 October
China

The 6th Marine Division (less the 4th Marines in Japan) begins going ashore at Tsingtao, China.

12 October
China

Aircraft of VMO-6 land at an airfield near Tsingtao.

13 October
China

Elements of the 1st Marines disperse Chinese mobs attacking Japanese civilians in Tientsin.

15 October
Force Structure

VMF-155, VMF-324, VMF-523, VMF-524, and VMSB-934 are deactivated.

17 October
China

VMF(N)-533 and 541 of MAG-24 begin operating from an airfield at Peiping.

18 October
China

Marines guarding the rail lines to Peiping kill six Chinese Communist soldiers firing at their train.

19 October
Force Structure

The 26th Marines is detached from the 5th Marine Division and placed under direct control of FMFPAC.

Roles and Missions

The Senate Military Affairs Committee begins hearings on proposed legislation that would merge the War and Navy Departments into a single agency. First proposed by Army Chief of Staff General Marshall in 1942 and again on 19 September 1945, this unification of the services poses a threat to the continued existence of the Corps, since Marines supposedly duplicate the capabilities of the Army.

21 October
Peleliu

The 26th Marines (less the 2nd Battalion, which is to be disbanded on 30 October) departs Sasebo for the Palau Islands.

China

The flight echelons of MAG-32 arrive at Tsingtao.

25 October
China

MAG-12 (VMF-115, 211, and 218) flight echelons arrive at Peiping.

Japan

MAG-22 at Sasebo is returned to naval operational control by Fifth Air Force.

26 October
Peleliu

The 26th Marines arrives on Peleliu and relieves the Army's 111th Infantry of garrison duties. The Marines will oversee repatriation of Japanese troops located throughout the Palaus and the Western Carolines.

31 October
Force Structure

Marine Air Support Group 42 (formerly MBDAG-42) and MAG-41 (formerly MBDAG-41) are deactivated, as is VMO-4.

November
Force Structure
The 51st Defense Battalion departs Eniwetok Atoll for the United States. VMF-111 is deactivated.

1 November
Japan
Eighth Army gives control of the 4th Marines to the U.S. Navy command at Yokosuka.
Force Structure
VMSB-333 is deactivated.

3 November
Force Structure
The last elements of the 4th Marine Division arrive in the United States from Hawaii. Its units are disbanded over the course of the month at Camp Pendleton.

6 November
China
The 6th Marine Division provides 1/29 to reinforce 1st Marine Division rail guards on the lines near Peiping.

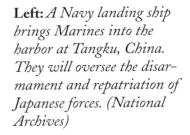

Left: *A Navy landing ship brings Marines into the harbor at Tangku, China. They will oversee the disarmament and repatriation of Japanese forces. (National Archives)*

Opposite: *Men of the 1st Marine Brigade rest on 22 August 1950 during a brief respite from the fighting in Korea's Pusan Perimeter. They have just driven North Korean troops out of the Naktong Bulge. (MacArthur Memorial)*

9 November
China
1/29 takes up station in Peitaiho.
Force Structure
VMTB-132 and VMF-351 are deactivated.

10 November
Manpower
Frederick C. Branch is commissioned a second
lieutenant. A veteran of the 51st Defense
Battalion, he is the first black Marine to achieve
officer rank in the Corps.

12 November
Force Structure
The Marine detachment at Londonderry,
Northern Ireland, is disbanded.
Japan
After flying their Corsairs to Okinawa for storage
and returning to Kyushu, the pilots and ground
personnel of MAG-22 sail from Japan.

13 November
Force Structure
VMF-215 and VMTB-332 are deactivated.

14 November
China
Chinese Communist troops fire on a train carrying
the 1st Marine Division commander.

16 November
Force Structure
VMTB-131 and 232 and VMO-7 are deactivated in
California.

17 November
Force Structure
VMSB-245 is deactivated at San Diego.

21 November
Force Structure
VMSB-331 and VMB-613 are deactivated.

23 November
Japan
As U.S. Army forces arrive to assume the primary
role in the occupation of Japan, the 5th Marine
Division begins to reduce its area of responsibility
on Kyushu and transfer its personnel to the 2nd
Marine Division.

Force Structure
VMTB-242 is deactivated at San Diego.

25 November
Truk
2/21 arrives to occupy the island, formerly the main Japanese fleet base in the Pacific. The battalion will garrison the key naval installation and repatriate Japanese troops.

28 November
Force Structure
The 4th Marine Division is disbanded at Camp Pendleton. MAG-45 is decommissioned.

30 November
Force Structure
MAG-13, recently returned to San Diego from the Marshall Islands, is deactivated. VMO-8, VMB-413, VMB-423, VMB-433, VMB-443, and VMB-611 are decommissioned.

1 December
Japan
1/4 sails from Yokosuka for the United States, where it will be disbanded.

5 December
Japan
MAG-22 arrives in the United States from Japan. Elements of the 5th Marine Division begin sailing for home.

6 December
China
Following frequent incidents of ground fire against Marine aircraft on reconnaissance flights over north China, IIIAC issues authorization for return fire, albeit on a very restricted basis.

8 December
Mishap
Six SB2C-5s of VMSB-343 are lost while flying in a snowstorm in north China. Ten of the 12 crew members die in the crashes.

9 December
Force Structure
VMTB-144 and VMF-514 are deactivated.

15 December
Force Structure
The 3rd Marines (less 1/3) arrives at Camp Pendleton.

19 December
Japan
The last elements of the 5th Marine Division sail from Sasebo for the United States.
Roles and Missions
President Truman addresses Congress and advocates the merger of the War and Navy Departments. The Secretary of the Navy orders Navy and Marine officers not to speak out against unification. Following a backlash in the media, the directive is modified the next day to allow service personnel to voice their concerns if they are stated as personal views.

20 December
Force Structure
The 21st Marines is deactivated on Guam.

24 December
Force Structure
VMF-472 and VMB-621 are deactivated.

28 December
Force Structure
The 3rd Marine Division is disbanded on Guam, with discharge-eligible Marines and some unit flags returning to the States, while Marines with obligated service remaining head to China as replacements. The exceptions are 1/3 in the Bonin Islands and 2/21 on Truk. VMB-614 is deactivated.

31 December
Force Structure
3rd MAW is decommissioned in Hawaii. The 9th Marines is deactivated at Camp Pendleton.
Japan
The U.S. Eighth Army assumes command of all occupation forces in Japan and formally relieves VAC headquarters of its occupation responsibilities. The 2nd Marine Division now reports to the Army's I Corps headquarters.

1946

1 January
Japan
3/4 assumes all security duties at Yokosuka in place of the 4th Marines.
Force Structure
2/4 sails for the United States and disbandment.

Right: *A Marine fires his M3 submachinegun at a target in the upper story of a building during street fighting in Seoul in September 1950. (National Archives)*

NCOs in Hawaii present a petition to General Geiger (commanding general of FMFPAC) calling for a speedier return to civilian life. Geiger demotes all of them to private on the spot. There are no recurrences of unrest anywhere in the Corps.

11 January
Civil Support
Marines from Marine Barracks 8th and I serve as the honor guard for the ceremony in which the Magna Carta is removed from its storage vault at the Library of Congress in Washington, D.C. (where it was kept for safety during the war) and presented to the British Ambassador for return to Great Britain.

13 January
Force Structure
The 3rd Marines is deactivated at Camp Pendleton.

14 January
Wake Island
A Marine detachment is activated to garrison Wake Island.

15 January
China
MAG-25 transports assist in moving truce teams around China and dropping leaflets announcing the cease fire.

22 January
Force Structure
Commandant Vandegrift orders the organization of a special infantry brigade at Quantico to stand in readiness for possible expeditionary service in troubled parts of the Caribbean.

28 January
Force Structure
The headquarters of the 1st Special Marine Brigade and two battalions are formed at Quantico, while a third battalion forms at Camp Lejeune. The battalions are designated as the 1st, 2nd, and 3rd Battalions; there is no regimental headquarters. VMF-321 and VMTB-454 are deactivated.

6 January
Japan
The headquarters element of the 4th Marines departs Yokosuka for Tsingtao, China.

8 January
Japan
The last corps-level elements of VAC sail from Japan, with most returning to the States and a few units shifting to Guam. The 2nd Marine Division continues on occupation duty and gradually assumes complete responsibility for all of Kyushu.
Force Structure
The 12th Marines is deactivated at Camp Pendleton.

10 January
China
General George Marshall (former Amy chief of staff and now the U.S. special envoy to China) mediates a cease fire agreement between the Chinese Nationalists and Communists. It is to take effect at midnight on 13 January.
Manpower
Imitating the widespread unrest in the Army over the pace of demobilization, a group of Marine

31 January
Force Structure
The 51st Defense Battalion is disbanded at Montford Point. VMO-5, VMF-124, VMTB-622, VMF-913, VMF-914, VMSB-932, VMSB-931, and VMD-954 are decommissioned.

4 February
Force Structure
Brigadier General O. P. Smith assumes full control of the 1st Special Marine Brigade, which also now includes MAG-11.
Japan
Elements of the British Commonwealth Occupation Force begin arriving on Kyushu to assist the 2nd Marine Division in controlling the island.

5 February
Force Structure
With most of its subordinate elements already disbanded, the 5th Marine Division headquarters is deactivated at Camp Pendleton.

10 February
Wake Island
The Wake Island Marine detachment is ordered to shift to Eniwetok and remain there through the completion of upcoming atomic bomb tests at Bikini Atoll.

15 February
Force Structure
VAC headquarters is disbanded at San Diego and the corps ceases to exist. The headquarters of 2nd MAW departs from Okinawa for Marine Corps Air Station Cherry Point. VMR-353 is deactivated.
Japan
In Yokosuka, 3/4 is redesignated as the 2nd Separate Guard Battalion (Provisional), with primary duty as the security force for the naval base.
Okinawa
MAG-14 and 33 depart for the United States from Okinawa.

19 February
Reserve
The Secretary of the Navy authorizes establishment of the Marine Air Reserve Training Command (MARTC) to administer and direct the training of Marine Corps Reserve aviation units.

26 February
Reserve
MARTC is activated at Glenview Naval Air Station in Illinois.

27 February
Force Structure
2/21 sails from Truk for Guam, where it will be disbanded on 5 March.

Opposite: *Chow and smokes lift the spirits of Marines taking a break as the chill of winter settles on North Korea late in 1950. (National Archives)*

Right: *Sgt Roger J. Hooper, SSgt Frank C. Kerr, and Cpl Robert L. Miller warm themselves and heat coffee over a fire on 6 November 1950. (National Archives)*

Left: *A patrol marches through a South Korean village during the Pohang Guerrilla Hunt in early 1951. (MacArthur Memorial)*

8 March
China
The headquarters of the 4th Marines is formally rejoined to the 6th Marine Division in north China. Its subordinate elements will be gradually reconstituted from personnel of other division units that are disbanded.

10 March
Force Structure
VMTB-143, VMF-216, VMF-217, VMTB-233, VMTB-464, VMF-511, and VMB-624 are deactivated.

13 March
Force Structure
The 52nd Defense Battalion and the headquarters of 4th MAW depart Guam for the United States.

15 March
Force Structure
The 26th Marines is deactivated on Peleliu. Some personnel are reformed as a provisional Marine detachment to continue garrisoning the island. MAG-46, VMB-612, and VMF-912 are decommissioned.

20 March
Force Structure
VMSB-231, VMTB-234, VMTB-463, VMTB-473, VMTB-623, and VMF-911 are deactivated.

22 March
Force Structure
The Marine Corps issues Basic Post-War Plan No.2. It sets the desired strength of the Corps at 100,000 enlisted and 8,000 officers (8 per 100 enlisted—an increase from the prewar ratio of 5 per 100). The FMF will consist of two subordinate headquarters, one each for the Pacific (FMFPAC) and Atlantic (FMFLANT) fleets. The ground forces will be comprised of two divisions (one each at Camp Lejeune and Guam) and a brigade at Camp Pendleton. Marine aviation will have two wing-size commands. Aircraft FMFPAC will control all ground-based squadrons in the Pacific, while another headquarters will be responsible for six Marine carrier groups.

26 March
Force Structure
4th MAW headquarters arrives in San Diego and is disbanded.

31 March
Force Structure
9th MAW headquarters is disbanded at Cherry Point. 1/29 is disbanded in China.

April
China
MAG-12 headquarters returns to the United States from China. The group's former squadrons remaining in China transfer to MAG-24.

Manpower

Congress sets the postwar strength of the Marine Corps at 7,000 officers and 100,00 enlisted.

1 April
China

The 6th Marine Division is deactivated and replaced in north China by the newly activated 3rd Marine Brigade. It consists of the 4th Marines and supporting units—all the remaining elements of the 6th Marine Division.

11 April
Force Structure

VMF(N)-543 is deactivated.

15 April
Force Structure

The provisional Marine detachment on Peleliu is designated a Marine barracks. To achieve peacetime manning levels, the 1st Marine Division disbands one battalion in each of its three infantry regiments and one firing battery in each of the four battalions of the 11th Marines.

20 April
Force Structure

VMF(N)-544 is deactivated.

24 April
Force Structure

VMF-213 is deactivated.

30 April
Force Structure

Following their return from China, VMTB-134 and VMF(N)-541 are deactivated at San Diego. VMF-422 is decommissioned.

May
China

MAG-32 returns to the United States from China.
Training

The 1st Special Marine Brigade conducts the Corps' first postwar training exercise (the only one in 1946), an operation in the Caribbean.

1 May
China

Operational control of Marine forces shifts from the theater command, which is dissolved, to the U.S. Seventh Fleet.
Reserve

Marine Corps Reserve Bulletin No. 1 advises all personnel being released from active duty that they can retain their connection to the Corps through membership in its reserve component.

Right: *Marines question a Korean about the enemy. (National Archives)*

2 May
Civil Support
Marines assist civilian police in putting down a prison riot in the federal penitentiary on Alcatraz Island in San Francisco Bay.

6 May
Roles and Missions
Commandant Vandegrift testifies before the Senate Naval Affairs Committee against the unification bill. In his presentation he argues against an emasculated role for the Marines:

> "The bended knee is not a tradition of our Corps. If the Marine as a fighting man has not made a case for himself after 170 years of service, he must go. But I think you will agree with me that he has earned the right to depart with dignity and honor, not by subjugation to the status of uselessness and servility planned for him by the War Department."

His powerful words help stop consideration of the proposed legislation for that session of Congress. In response to a question, he also reveals the existence of the classified 1478 papers, in which Army leaders had plainly stated their desire to reduce the Marine Corps to a small force operating landing craft.

10 May
Force Structure
VMF-512 is deactivated.

15 May
Force Structure
The 52nd Defense Battalion is redesignated the 3rd Antiaircraft Artillery Battalion at Montford Point.

20 May
Force Structure
The 8th Military Police Battalion (Provisional) is redesignated Marine Barracks Okinawa.

21 May
China
In one of the rare instances of fighting involving Marines since the onset of the truce in China, Communist forces clash with a 1st Marines patrol near Tientsin and one Marine is killed. He is the only fatal combat loss in the first six months of 1946 in China. Violations of the truce between the Communists and Nationalists grow more frequent as summer approaches.

1 June
Force Structure
1/3 is disbanded on Chichi Jima in the Bonin Islands. The 1st Base Headquarters Battalion becomes Marine Barracks Guam.

6 June
China
MAG-25 departs Tsingtao for El Toro.

Left: *This North Korean soldier, a casualty of the fighting along the Naktong River in late summer 1950, has been booby trapped with a grenade placed beneath his head. Marines had to be wary, even of the dead. (National Archives)*

Right: *Marine Peter Pender, nicknamed "Peepsight" for his skill as a sniper with George Company, 3/1, aims in on a target in Korea in 1952. ("The Sniper," Col Charles Waterhouse, USMCR (Ret), Marine Corps Art Collection)*

10 June
China
The headquarters of IIIAC is disbanded and the headquarters of the 1st Marine Division assumes a dual role as Marine Forces, China. The headquarters of the 3rd Marine Brigade in Tsingtao is also disbanded, with the 4th Marines (Reinforced) assuming its functions.
Force Structure
The 5th Military Police Battalion (Provisional) is redesignated Marine Barracks Saipan. VMSB-343 is deactivated.

13 June
Japan
The first elements of the 2nd Marine Division (primarily the 2nd Marines) begin sailing from Kyushu for the United States.

15 June
Japan
The 2nd Marine Division turns over responsibility for the occupation of Kyushu to the Army's 24th Infantry Division. The 8th Marines departs Japan for the United States. The 2nd Separate Guard Battalion (Provisional) at Yokosuka becomes a Marine Barracks.

20 June
Japan
MAG-31 embarks at Yokosuka for the United States. It is the last Marine occupation unit on Honshu.
Force Structure
The Marine Detachment (Provisional) in Samar is redesignated as a Marine Barracks.

23 June
Japan
The 10th Marines sails for the United States.

24 June
Japan
The headquarters of the 2nd Marine Division sails from Kyushu for the United States.

25 June
Force Structure
VMSB-142 is reestablished as VMF-142 in the Reserve at Miami.

27 June
Reserve
In a move boosting the status of the Marine Corps Reserve, the Division of Reserve is moved from the Personnel Department and now reports directly to the Commandant.

30 June
Manpower
The strength of the Marine Corps on active duty is 14,208 officers and 141,471 enlisted. The Marine Corps' participation in the Navy's V-12 officer program comes to an end.

1 July
Technology
The U.S. conducts its first test of an atomic bomb at Bikini Atoll, to determine the effectiveness of an air burst against surface ships and other military targets.
Japan
Elements of the 6th Marines sail from Kyushu for the United States.
Force Structure
VMF-112, 121, 124, 321, 251, 351, and 451 and VMTB-132, 144, and 234 are reactivated as Reserve fighter squadrons. Marine Corps Air Station Eagle Mountain Lake in Texas is deactivated and several auxiliary strips around the country are also closed.
Manpower
Draftees and reservists with 30 months of active duty become eligible for discharge regardless of the number of points they possess.

2 July
Japan
The last major elements of the 2nd Marine Division depart for the United States.

4 July
Japan
MAG-31 returns to the United States from Japan.

5 July
Force Structure
VMTB-141 is reactivated as a Reserve fighter squadron.

7 July
China
The Chinese Communist Party issues a manifesto attacking U.S. support of the Nationalist government.

11 July
Force Structure
VMF-441 is deactivated.

13 July
China
Communist forces capture seven Marines visiting

Right: *Artillerymen shield their ears as a barrage of 4.5-inch rockets launch toward Communist positions. (National Archives)*

10 October
Manpower
The first contingent of American war dead returns to the United States from Pacific battlefields on the Army transport *Honda Knot*.

12 October
Philippines
Corregidor Island is formally returned to control of the republic of the Philippines.

24 October
Force Structure
VMF-122, the first Marine jet squadron, is organized at Cherry Point under command of Major Marion Carl. It is equipped with McDonnel FH-1 Phantoms.

10 November
Training
The 1st Marine Division begins a large-scale amphibious exercise off the coast of southern California that lasts for five days.

14 November
Korea
Despite a Soviet boycott, the United Nations approves establishment of the Korea Commission to hold elections in Korea (currently divided into two zones based on postwar occupation by Soviet forces in the north and American troops in the south).

1 December
Force Structure
The first experimental Marine helicopter squadron, HMX-1, is commissioned at Quantico. It is eventually equipped with the Sikorsky HO3S-1 (a utility/observation helicopter) and the Piasecki HRP-1 (a small transport helicopter dubbed the "Flying Banana" for its unusual shape).

25 December
China
Five Marines on a hunting expedition cross into territory controlled by the Communists. In a subsequent firefight, one is killed and the others are taken prisoner.

31 December
Commandants
General Alexander A. Vandegrift relinquishes his post and General Clifton B. Cates becomes the 19th Commandant. Vandegrift will remain on active duty until 1 April 1949.

MAJOR GENERAL MARION E. CARL

Marion Carl came from a determined, unflinching family. His parents had gotten their start in life living in a tent on wooded land in the untamed Willamette Valley of Oregon. They slowly cleared acreage for farming and a dairy herd, until they finally could afford to build a house. Mister Carl died when Marion and his two siblings were still young. They pitched in to help their mother not only keep the farm going, but make it even more successful. In turn, she made sure all of them went off to college.

Marion helped put himself through school with summer jobs, but also found time to participate in the Army's Reserve Officer Training Corps. In the fall of 1937, he took private flying lessons and soloed. Upon graduation in 1938, the Army gave Carl and all his contemporaries reserve commissions, because it obtained all the regular officers it needed from West Point. The Marine Corps took advantage of the situation throughout the latter 1930s and offered the top Army ROTC graduates regular commissions and orders to active duty. Carl was one of those who jumped at the chance. He then earned his wings at Pensacola in late 1939.

Already a captain by May of 1942, he was flying one of the handful of VMF-221 Wildcat fighters at Midway Island during the Japanese attempt to take it in June of that year. In a large-scale melee with enemy fighters and bombers, he led his section against a numerically superior force of much-vaunted Japanese Zeros, shooting down one and damaging two others. Transferred to VMF-223, he and his squadron flew into

Guadalcanal on 20 August, the first element of what would become Cactus Air Force. In his first successful action on the island, just four days later, he shot down two Betty bombers and a Zero. On 26 August, he got two more fighter planes, making him the first Marine Corps ace in history. He raised his score to nine by the end of the month with three more Zeroes.

His rapid rise as an ace nearly came to an end on 9 September. Just recuperating from a bout with dysentery, he led a flight against a formation of bombers attacking U.S. shipping in Ironbottom Sound. He and his men broke up the attack and he got two bombers, but his Wildcat was crippled by a Zero in the process. He bailed out and ended up in the water far away from friendly lines. He managed to stay afloat until rescued by natives in a canoe. There were too many Japanese troops around the perimeter to get back by land, so ultimately he made it home in a small boat powered by a decrepit engine, which he had to put in working order himself. In the intervening five days, his squadron mates had written him off for dead. By the end of the month, he had claimed two more enemy planes and joined in destroying a third. He also received his first Navy Cross, for his actions during the current campaign. He scored his last kill at Guadalcanal on 3 October, downing another Zero.

The Marines brought him back to the States soon after to take advantage of the fame he had gained as a leading ace. During a national tour selling war bonds, he proved to be equally successful in love as in war— meeting, wooing, and marrying Edna Kirvin,

Maj Marion Carl during his second combat tour in the Pacific in January 1944. He had just run up his score to 18 kills. (Marine Corps Historical Center)

a New York model. Before he headed back overseas in command of his old squadron, he also was promoted to major and given a second Navy Cross, for his daring intercept at Midway. Now flying the much more powerful Corsair out of Vella LaVella, he fought several aerial battles over Rabaul and raised his total score to 18 planes by out-dueling three more enemy pilots. In early 1944 he turned over command of his squadron and eventually transferred back to the States. Not content to rest on his two Navy Crosses, three Distinguished Flying Crosses, and 13 Air Medals, he became a test pilot. With just seven years in the military, he made lieutenant colonel in September 1945.

Carl continued his pioneering ways after the war. He became one of the first jet pilots in the Corps. In a remarkable show of the range of his aerial skills, he also became one of the earliest Marine helicopter pilots (and

the first one formally designated as such). He earned his fourth Distinguished Flying Cross in 1947 while piloting a test jet to a world speed record. After a stint in command of the Corps' first jet squadron, he returned to head a test unit at the Navy's Patuxent River facility. In 1953, piloting a rocket-powered craft dropped from a bomber, he set an unofficial world altitude record of 83,235 feet. In the process, he successfully tested a special pressurized flight suit and gained a fifth Distinguished Flying Cross.

The intrepid pilot went on to command the air-ground 1st Marine Brigade and the 2nd MAW. He retired in 1973 with 13,000 flight hours and moved back to Oregon. In 1998, an intruder broke into his home. General Carl stepped between the armed man and his wife of 55 years and was killed by a shotgun blast. He died at the age of 82, courageous to the very end.

1948

1 January
Bases
Marine Corps Base San Diego is redesignated as Marine Corps Recruit Depot San Diego.

5 January
Mediterranean
The 2nd Marines (a reinforced infantry battalion under the J-series T/O) departs Morehead City, North Carolina, on the Navy transports *Bexar* and *Montague* for extended service in the Mediterranean Sea. Once in the Mediterranean, the Marines will shift to carrier *Midway* (CVB-41) and cruisers *Portsmouth* (CL-102), *Providence* (CL-82), and *Little Rock* (CL-92). They will remain afloat until 12 March. This initiates what will become a routine and near-continuous deployment of a Marine landing force as an element of the Sixth Fleet.

7 January
Mediterranean
Fleet Admiral Chester Nimitz announces that the presence of the 2nd Marines with the Sixth Fleet will serve as a warning to Yugoslavia not to menace the 5,000 U.S. Army troops in the Free Territory of Trieste.

11 January
Reserve
As part of the rebuilding of its reserve forces after WWII, the Marine Corps holds a rally and celebration in Philadelphia to inaugurate National Marine Corps Reserve Week and spur reserve recruiting.

31 January
China
A Marine patrol engages in a firefight with Chinese Communist forces near Tsangkou airfield, the home of the aviation elements of FMFWESPAC.

February
China
Early in the month, Marine transport planes evacuate U.S. and British nationals from Changchun in Manchuria, just before it falls to Communist forces.

9 February
Technology
HMX-1 receives the first Marine helicopters, two Sikorsky HO3S-1s.

13 February
China
Communist forces confirm that they had captured five Marines on 25 December 1947 and that one of them had died soon after of wounds received. The Chinese demand an official apology for what they claim was U.S. participation in the ongoing civil war with the Nationalists.

20 February
Mediterranean
The 8th Marines (a reinforced battalion) departs Morehead City as the intended relief on station for the 2nd Marines deployed with the Sixth Fleet. They will remain afloat until 28 June.

11 March
Roles and Missions
Forrestal and the Joint Chiefs of Staff (JCS) meet in Key West, Florida, to discuss the roles and missions of the services. Four days later, they

Opposite: *An HRS-1 helicopter skims over the mountainous terrain of central Korea. (National Archives)*

Right: *"On The Deck," Col H. Avery Chenoweth, USMCR (Ret), Marine Corps Art Collection*

specifically prohibits any alteration in the missions of the services assigned in the original act of 1947.

11 August
Middle East
Marine Brigadier General William E. Riley is assigned as chief of staff of the United Nations Palestine Truce Mission, which oversees the truce between Israel and her Arab neighbors.

20 August
Force Structure
VMO-3 is deactivated.

6 September
Mediterranean
The 21st Marines departs Morehead City to become the landing force of the Sixth Fleet. It will remain afloat until 26 January 1950.

8 September
Manpower
Annie E. Graham becomes the first black female to enlist in the Marine Corps.

9 September
Manpower
Montford Point Camp is deactivated at Camp Lejeune and black Marines located there are transferred to other units on the base. At roughly the same time, black recruits are integrated into regular training platoons at Parris Island.

1 October
Force Structure
The Marine Corps replaces the J-series tables of organization, reestablishing true regiments and reverting infantry units to historic nomenclature. The 1st Marine Division converts first, with the 1st, 6th, and 7th Marines (J-series battalions) being re-formed into the headquarters of the 5th Marines, 1/5, and 2/5. The 3rd Marines is deactivated at Camp Pendleton.
China
Mao proclaims the People's Republic of China in Peking (formerly Peiping). The last territory in southern China falls into Communist hands before the end of the month, with the Nationalists retreating to the island of Formosa.

11 October
Aviation
Brigadier General Vernon A. Megee, assistant director of Marine Corps aviation, tells the House Armed Services Committee that the Air Force is neglecting the close air support mission.

12 October
Manpower
Congress passes the Career Compensation Act. Among other provisions, it turns the existing enlisted pay grade structure on its head. Henceforth privates are E-1s and master sergeants E-7s, instead of the other way around.

17 October
Force Structure
The 2nd Marine Division sheds the J-series T/O. The 4th and 9th Marines (J-series battalions) are deactivated at Camp Lejeune to fill out the 2nd Marines to full regimental strength. The 6th Marines is reactivated as a skeleton regiment.
Roles and Missions
Commandant Cates testifies before Congress that the Marine Corps is being reduced to irrelevance despite the intent of the National Security Act of 1947. He argues that without a Marine voice in the JCS, the budget and manpower of the Corps are being drastically curtailed. Under current limitations, the Corps will have only 67,000 men by June 1950 and will be able to field only six infantry battalions. The Navy also is dedicating all the training time of its amphibious ships in the coming year to Army exercises and attempting to relegate the Commandant to the equivalent of one of the Navy bureau chiefs subordinate to the CNO.

21 October
Roles and Missions
Secretary Johnson assures Congress that the Marine Corps will continue in existence. There is conflicting testimony over the reason for the forced resignation of former Navy Secretary John

L. Sullivan, who claims he was pushed out in April 1949 because he was opposed to the abolition of Marine and Navy aviation and the "slow death" of the Marine Corps.

25–26 October
Training
In the largest post-WWII amphibious exercise to date, Navy, Army, and Marine forces launch a simulated assault on Hawaii to liberate it from an aggressor.

30 October
Manpower
DOD announces that a number of Navy ships will be placed in mothballs in line with plans to reduce Navy and Marine Corps personnel by nearly 55,000 by 1 July 1950. To accommodate the reductions, Marine infantry battalions shrink to two rifle companies of two rifle platoons each.

5 November
Aviation
Marine enlisted pilots begin training in jet aircraft at El Toro, flying the Lockheed TO-1 Shooting Star.

18 November
Manpower
The Marine Corps issues policy to implement Truman's executive order banning racial discrimination in the military services. One of the primary points is the adoption of assignment to units without regard for race, which spells the formal end of segregated outfits in the Corps.

30 November
Force Structure
VMF-322 is deactivated.

31 December
Force Structure
VMF-218, VMF-222, and VMF-452 are deactivated.

Opposite: *Marines lift a wounded buddy onto a Bell HTL-4 for a quick trip to a hospital in the rear. (National Archives)*

Right: *A Marine fires a 3.5-inch rocket launcher against an enemy bunker. (National Archives)*

1950

5 January
Force Structure
The last FMF units (3/5 and VMF-218) depart Guam for their new home stations in California.

6 January
Mediterranean
1/6 (Reinforced) sails from Morehead City to become the landing force of the Sixth Fleet. It will remain afloat until 23 May.

9 January
Manpower
President Truman's budget for the fiscal year beginning in July 1950 reduces Marine Corps personnel by about 10,000 to 74,396.

14 January
Training
Air Force, Navy, and Marine flyers stage the first unified air maneuvers in Miami.

1 February
Force Structure
MAG-25 is reactivated at El Toro to control VMR-152 and 352.

3 February
Force Structure
3/5 rejoins the 5th Marines at Camp Pendleton and VMF-218 reports to El Toro.

25 February
Training
U.S. forces begin their first large-scale amphibious-airborne peacetime exercise, PORTEX, which involves an assault on Vieques Island in the Caribbean. It is also the largest peacetime amphibious exercise to date, with 80,000 personnel from all four services, 160 ships, and over 700 planes. The exercise concludes on 11 March. During its course, seven personnel die in various accidents.

28 February
Force Structure
VMF-461 is deactivated.

1 March
Roles and Missions
The House Armed Services Committee issues a report calling for the inclusion of the Commandant of the Marine Corps on the JCS, more joint training, and the assignment of important air warfare roles to naval aviation.

10 March
Force Structure
The Marine Corps Schools at Quantico are reorganized into the Marine Corps Development Center (focusing on new equipment and doctrine) and the Marine Corps Educational Center (focusing on education and training programs).

4 May
Mediterranean
3/6 (Reinforced) departs Morehead City to become the landing force of the Sixth Fleet. It is scheduled to remain at sea until 18 August.

9 May
China
The Communist government releases two airmen (including a Marine) it had been holding since 19 October 1948, when their plane had gone down in Manchuria.

9 June
Aviation
Secretary Johnson announces that due to budget limitations, the armed forces will not participate in the National Air Races.

15 June
Roles and Missions
In an attempt to convince President Truman that the Corps is deserving of a bigger budget, Marine infantrymen and aviators put on a demonstration of a helicopter assault for him at Quantico.
Force Structure
VMR-253 is commissioned at El Toro.

25 June
Korea
Eight divisions of the Communist North Korean People's Army (NKPA) sweep over the 38th Parallel into South Korea and begin to roll over their weaker neighbor.

Opposite: *"That Way," Col H. Avery Chenoweth, USMCR (Ret), Marine Corps Art Collection*

Right: *The 1st Marine Brigade moves up to the front in early August 1950. (National Archives)*

27 June
Korea
The United Nations Security Council authorizes member states to help South Korea repel the invasion. President Truman immediately orders air and naval forces to intervene under the command of General Douglas MacArthur in Japan.

28 June
Korea
The NKPA captures Seoul.

30 June
Korea
Truman authorizes the use of U.S. ground forces in South Korea and air attacks against North Korea. Congress also approves the call-up of reserve forces for up to 21 months of active duty.
Manpower
The strength of the Marine Corps on active duty is 7,254 officers and 67,025 enlisted.

1 July
Force Structure
VMF-216 is reactivated.

2 July
Korea
General MacArthur requests immediate dispatch of a Marine Corps regimental combat team and associated aviation for duty in Korea. FMFPAC issues a warning order to the 1st Marine Division to prepare for embarkation. The first U.S. Army ground troops arrive in Korea from occupation duty in Japan, lightly armed and ill-trained. Senior commanders feed these and subsequent units into battle piece-meal over the next several days and they are overrun by the NKPA.

3 July
Korea
The JCS agree to meet MacArthur's request for a Marine air-ground force.

5 July
Force Structure
1st MAW forms the 1st MAW (Forward Echelon), built around MAG-33, under the command of Brigadier General Thomas J. Cushman.

7 July
Force Structure
The 1st Provisional Marine Brigade is activated at Camp Pendleton under command of Brigadier General Edward A. Craig (ADC of the 1st Marine Division). Its components are the 5th Marines (the sole infantry unit of the division), 1st MAW (Forward Echelon), and supporting elements. The three battalions of the 5th each have only two rifle companies hurriedly brought up to normal strength of three rifle platoons each. HQMC directs HMX-1 to transfer pilots and maintenance men to VMO-6 to provide a helicopter element to the observation squadron and the brigade.
Korea
The United Nations authorizes the United States to establish a combined command for U.N. forces in Korea. Truman names MacArthur to command this headquarters.

10 July
Korea
MacArthur asks for additional reinforcements, to include a complete Marine division and associated aviation support.

12 July
Korea
The 1st Provisional Marine Brigade begins sailing from California for Korea. The last ships will depart on 14 July. On the battlefield, the NKPA have occupied half of South Korea and U.S. and South Korean forces continue to retreat. MacArthur names Army Lieutenant General Walton H. Walker commander of Eighth Army, which controls all U.S. ground forces in Korea.

15 July
Korea
FMFPAC warns the 1st Marine Division to prepare for expansion to full strength. The Marine Corps provides two transport squadrons to support airlift operations to Korea.

16 July
Korea
The Republic of Korea (ROK) places all its military forces under control of Eighth Army.

19 July
Manpower
President Truman calls the Organized Marine Corps Reserve to active duty.

22 July
Korea
Commandant Cates directs the formation of third rifle companies and the provision of individual replacements to bring the 1st Provisional Marine Brigade to full strength. They are to be ready to depart California by 10 August.

25 July
Korea
The JCS approves MacArthur's request for a full Marine division, but it will include the brigade already on its way to Korea. The Commandant orders the 1st Marine Division brought to full war strength, in preparation for departure for Korea beginning on 10 August. Units of the 2nd Marine Division (primarily the 2nd Marines, 1/6, and supporting elements) depart Camp Lejeune for Camp Pendleton, where they will form the base for rebuilding the 1st Marine Division. The CNO authorizes a 50 percent reduction in the strength of Marine security forces at Navy bases, with this manpower going to the 1st Marine Division and 1st MAW.

27 July
Manpower
President Truman signs legislation lifting the legal limit on the size of the U.S. armed forces and extending for one year enlistments due to expire in the next 12 months.

31 July
Japan
MAG-33 begins to arrive in Kobe. VMF(N)-513 sets up at Itami Airfield, its initial base of operations.
Force Structure
President Truman authorizes the Marine Corps to expand to its two divisions to full war strength (about 23,000 men each). Secretary Johnson approves an increase in Marine aviation to 18 squadrons.

2 August
Korea
The ground elements of the Marine brigade arrive at the port of Pusan in southeast Korea and begins unloading.

3 August
Korea
MAG-33's day fighter squadrons will operate from Navy carriers to reduce their range to the battlefield. VMF-214 flies from Itami airfield in Japan on to escort carrier *Sicily* (CVE-118). After refueling and arming on the ship's deck, eight of the Corsairs launch the first Marine offensive against the North Koreans, bombing and strafing Communist forces that evening. The brigade moves out from Pusan and assumes defensive

positions near the southwest corner of what is dubbed the Pusan Perimeter. It is the 60-mile-wide by 90-mile-long toehold of U.N. forces in the southeast corner of the country, its western flank mainly by the Naktong River.

Force Structure
Infantry units begin arriving at Camp Pendleton by train from Camp Lejeune. The next day, they are redesignated to form the reactivated 1st Marines, under command of Colonel Chesty Puller. The regiment is filled out to war strength by regulars reporting in from other duties and by reservists.

The 1st Marines also forms and takes under its wing the third rifle companies for the 5th Marines.

4 August
Korea
The HO3S-1 observation helicopters and light OY planes of VMO-6 begin to support the brigade. The helicopters evacuate their first casualties.

5 August
Korea
Sicily moves into the Yellow Sea and VMF-214 makes the first Marine attacks on the Inchon-Seoul region. VMF-323 flies from Itami airfield on to escort carrier *Badoeng Strait* (CVE-116). It launches its first air strikes the next day.

7 August
Korea
On the eighth anniversary of the Guadalcanal landings, the Marine brigade launches its first counterattack, to relieve pressure on the southern flank of the Pusan Perimeter. The Marines move southwest to clear a peninsula, while Army units drive due west on their right flank. The objective is the town of Chinju, 25 miles to the west. The offensive runs right into NKPA soldiers resuming their attack on the perimeter.

Manpower
The Marine Corps alerts its 80,000 individual reservists for call up to active duty. The first men and women will report on 15 August.

Above: *The 1st Marine Brigade moves up to the Naktong again. (MacArthur Memorial)*

Left: *Marine Corsairs over Mt. Fuji, Japan. (National Archives)*

8 August
Korea
An HO3S-1 helicopter of VMO-6 makes the first night evacuation of a casualty from a brigade aid station near Chindong-ni.

10 August
Korea
The first Marine heliborne rescue operation takes place when a VMO-6 bird picks up a Marine pilot forced to ditch his aircraft after the engine fails. The 1st Marine Division begins embarking on ships at San Diego. The last elements of the 1st Marines will sail by 22 August. The 7th Marines, yet to form, will not complete embarkation until 1 September.

11 August
Korea
A Marine artillery bombardment rousts a large North Korean motorized force from the town of Kosong. Marine air destroys roughly 100 trucks, jeeps, and motorcycles retreating along the road. The brigade takes the town that morning.

12 August
Korea
The Marine brigade advances to the village of Changchon, several miles south of Chinju. Although the Army-Marine counterattack is short of its objective, it is called off as a Communist attack pierces the Naktong River line and threatens the Pusan Perimeter.

14 August
Korea
The Marine brigade begins a movement by truck, train, and ship to the Naktong Bulge, the NKPA salient on the eastern side of the river, about halfway up the Pusan Perimeter.

16 August
Korea
MacArthur forms X Corps, under command of his chief of staff, Army Major General Edward S. Almond. It consists of the 1st Marine Division and the Army's 7th Infantry Division, and reports directly to MacArthur, not Eighth Army. Its mission is to conduct an amphibious assault at Inchon and outflank NKPA forces around the Pusan Perimeter.

17 August
Korea
The Marine brigade opens a counterattack to regain the Naktong Bulge and drive the NKPA back across the river. The Army's 24th Division attacks on the Marine right flank.
Force Structure
The 7th Marines begins forming around remaining elements (the regimental headquarters and one

under-strength battalion) of the redesignated 6th Marines. 3/6, then afloat in the Mediterranean, will join at sea off Korea to provide the basis of the 7th's third infantry battalion.

18 August
Korea
The 5th Marines complete the seizure of Obong-ni Ridge, the first objective of the counterattack, at mid-morning. The enemy break under the fierce pursuit of Marine infantrymen and Corsairs, and the Marines sweep forward to take their second and most of their third objective. Major General O. P. Smith, commander of the 1st Marine Division, arrives in Japan by air to confer with Eighth Army planners. He learns for the first time that his division will spearhead an amphibious assault at Inchon, Korea, on 15 September.
Manpower
To spur enlistments, the Marine Corps reduces the minimum contract from four years to three, and also recruits men into the Volunteer Reserve for immediate active duty, which will allow the enlistees to revert to reserve status as soon as the war is over.

19 August
Korea
The 5th Marines cleans out the remainder of the Naktong Bulge.

20 August
Korea
The Marine brigade reverts to Eighth Army reserve and moves to the coastal town of Masan, where it goes into bivouac in a field, soon to be dubbed the Bean Patch.

24 August
Korea
Elements of the remainder of 1st MAW begin sailing from San Diego for Japan and Korea.

27 August
Indochina
A dozen Marines arrive in Saigon to guard the U.S. Embassy.
Force Structure
Representative Carl Vinson, Chairman of the House Armed Services Committee, announces that he believes the Corps should have four divisions and 26 squadrons.

29 August
Korea
The first elements of the 1st Marine Division arrive in Japan and go ashore to conduct training prior to the Inchon landing.
Technology
HMX-1 conducts the first test firing of a 3.5-inch rocket from a bazooka mounted on the landing skid of a Bell HTL-3 utility helicopter.

1 September
Korea
Elements of four NKPA divisions force another crossing of the Naktong River and begin driving the Army's 2nd Division out of the Naktong Bulge. That afternoon, the Marines are on the move back to the bulge. The last elements of 1st MAW ship out from California for Japan and Korea.
Mediterranean
3/6 detaches from the Sixth Fleet and sails through the Suez Canal toward its eventual rendezvous with the 7th Marines.
Force Structure
President Truman announces a plan to expand U.S. military forces from 1.5 million personnel to 3 million.
Roles and Missions
Representative Gordon L. McDonough inserts in the Congressional Record a letter he received from

assault, ROK forces already had taken the objective by land on 10 October. VMF-312, VMF(N)-513, and ground crews of MAG-12 had begun flying into the city's airfield on 14 October.

21 October
Korea
General MacArthur publicly announces that the end of the war is near.

26 October
Korea
Following two weeks of mine clearing offshore by the Navy, the 1st Marine Division makes an administrative landing at Wonsan. The mission of X Corps is now to assist ROK forces in clearing northeast Korea, while Eighth Army does the same in northwest Korea.

27 October
Korea
The 5th Marines assumes responsibility for controlling the 50 miles of territory between Wonsan and the port of Hungnam to the north. The 7th Marines moves north to relieve ROK forces at Sudong, 30 miles northwest of Hungnam. 1/1 relieves Korean soldiers in the town of Kojo, 25 miles south of Wonsan. That night, NKPA forces attack 1/1. Losses in the fighting total 27 dead and missing and 47 wounded.

28 October
Korea
3/1 moves 30 miles west of Wonsan to occupy the town of Majon-ni. ROK forces engage Chinese Communist forces (CCF in American parlance of the time) at Suding and capture 16 prisoners.

2 November
Korea
NKPA forces attack a Marine patrol near Majon-ni and ambush a Marine convoy bringing supplies to the town. Losses are 25 killed and 41 wounded. For the moment, 3/1 is isolated. The 7th Marines relieves ROK forces near Sudong and begins an advance up a narrow mountain road to the Chosin Reservoir (also known as the Changjin Reservoir). That night, CCF elements launch strong attacks on the positions of the 7th Marines, but are repulsed.

4 November
Korea
In moving upward as the road rises through Funchilin Pass, the 7th Marines encounters the 124th CCF Division. The regiment fails to dislodge the enemy in three days of heavy fighting, but the Chinese withdraw on the night of 6–7 November. Marine losses total about 50 killed and 200 wounded, while Chinese casualties are estimated at 2,000.

PRIVATE FIRST CLASS HECTOR A. CAFFERATA, JR.

Hector Cafferata was born in New York City on 4 November 1929, but his family soon moved to New Jersey. Too young to fight in World War II, he went to work at the age of 14, spending his evenings in a factory making aircraft instruments while his father was in the Army in the European theater. Following the war, the strapping youngster played tackle for his high school football team, then went on to a semi-pro league when he graduated in 1948. He enlisted in the Marine Corps Reserve the same year. In those days, reserve recruits learned how to be Marines in on-the-job instruction during drill meetings and summer camp. An avid fisherman and hunter, he at least knew his way around in the backwoods.

Cafferata's unit was mobilized in early September 1950 and reported to Camp Pendleton. He had far less than the minimum reserve training needed to go oversees and was slated for transfer to boot camp, but he already had missed one war and wasn't about to let another pass by him. A sympathetic sergeant got him on the ship for Korea. He arrived there as a replacement in October 1950 and joined the 2nd Battalion, 7th Marines, as a rifleman as it fought its way up to the Chosin Reservoir. He got his infantry training the hard way, under real fire in combat.

On 27 November, 2/7's Fox Company received the mission of holding an outpost in critical Toktong Pass as the 5th and 7th Marines moved forward in the attack from Yudam-ni. The company commander, Captain William E. Barber, picked a hill just off the road. He assigned his 3rd Platoon to hold the summit, while the other platoons tied in on the flanks and carried the lines down toward the road. The 2nd Platoon, including Cafferata, was on the left. Reinforcing detachments of heavy weapons from the rest of the battalion held the part of the perimeter along the road. The Marines fortified their lines as best they could, since the ground was too frozen for digging. As darkness came on, they hunkered down against the cold as the temperature dropped below zero.

Cafferata, Private First Class Kenneth R. Benson, and two other men had been sent a little ways forward of the lines as a listening post. While two men watched, the other two tried to sleep. Around 0230 the sound of close-in gunfire snapped the New Jersey reservist awake. By the time he got out of his bag, he saw Chinese all around him, rushing toward the Marine perimeter. He and Benson crawled back toward friendly lines and into a small gully that served as a trench for some 3rd Platoon Marines. In his haste, he had left behind his shoe pacs (the ineffective cold weather boot then being used by Marines).

The four Marines already in the position were wounded. The Chinese, attempting to break through the seam between the 2nd and 3rd Platoons, were focusing their attack just to the left of the gully. Cafferata and Benson fired as fast as they could load and threw every grenade they had. To obtain a better field of fire, the 6 foot-3 inch Cafferata stood upright in the shallow depression as he engaged the onrushing enemy. He killed at least 15 of them and helped drive off the determined assault.

After a lull, the Chinese renewed the attack. When a grenade came flying into the gully, Cafferata grabbed it and threw it back. As it left his hand it exploded, tearing some flesh from the end of his finger. He ignored the minor wound and kept on fighting. Benson tossed back another enemy grenade, but he wasn't so lucky. The ensuing blast close at hand knocked off his glasses and blood in his eyes temporarily blinded him. As Cafferata kept up the battle, Benson sat in the hole, pressing clips into an M-1 rifle and handing it up to his partner.

The Chinese pulled back by dawn. After first light, Cafferata went forward in search of his missing shoes pacs, his feet encased in frozen socks. The enemy finally got him, drilling him in the arm and chest. He crawled back the way he had come the night before, this time dragging a useless hand that felt like he was gripping a live electric wire. Marines carried him to the company aid station, where the corpsmen did the best they could for him.

In one night of action, Fox Company had lost 20 dead and 54 wounded, but had held off a Chinese regiment. The saga was not yet over. The enemy would come back every night, until 1/7 reached Fox Hill from Yudam-ni and linked up with the beleaguered outfit around noon on 2 December. Captain Barber, himself wounded, had suffered total casualties of 29 killed or missing and 89 wounded—half of

his 237-man outfit. Many others suffered from varying degrees of frostbite or weather-induced ills. Cafferata and the other casualties finally were evacuated. The badly wounded private ended up in Japan, then all the way back in the States. The Marine Corps retired him medically as a private first class on 1 September 1951. A little over a year later, the Nation recognized his valiant actions at Toktong Pass with its highest award, the Medal of Honor.

PFC Hector Cafferata received the Medal of Honor for his heroic defense of his post at Toktong Pass. (National Archives)

Left: *A Charlie Company tank splashes ashore from an LSU at Wonsan in October 1950. (National Archives)*

5 November
Korea
After having been repulsed the day before, Captain Robert Barrow's Company A, 1st Marines, destroys the North Korean roadblock on the way to Majon-ni, killing 51 enemy.

9 November
Sweden
The Marine detachments of *Columbus* (CA-74) and *Furse* (DD-882) participate in the funeral of King Gustav V in Sweden.

10 November
Korea
The 7th Marines occupies the village of Koto-ri at the top of Funchilin Pass. From here a plain leads to the Chosin Reservoir several miles to the north.
Heritage
To celebrate the 175th anniversary of its birth, the Marine Corps opens an exhibit of its historical documents and artifacts at the Navy Museum in the Washington Navy Yard. Colonel Katherine Towle wears the first evening dress uniform for women to the HQMC birthday ball. It is patterned after the male uniform.

15 November
Korea
The 7th Marines occupies Hagaru-ri, at the southern end of the Chosin Reservoir. The remainder of the division is slowly beginning to close up behind the 7th, on the single road (dubbed the Main Supply Route or MSR) from Hungnam to the reservoir.

20 November
Korea
41 Independent Commando of the Royal Marines (a company-sized force commanded by Lieutenant Colonel Douglas B. Drysdale) is attached to the 1st Marine Division.

23 November
Korea
1/1 assumes the mission of garrisoning Chinhung-ni, a town on the MSR just north of Sudong.

24 November
Korea
The 5th Marines moves up the eastern side of the Chosin Reservoir. The headquarters of the 1st Marines and 2/1 take over responsibility for protecting Koto-ri.

25 November
Korea
The 7th Marines reaches Yudam-ni, a village west of the Chosin Reservoir. Charlie and Fox Company of the 7th each hold outposts in Toktong Pass, about halfway between Hagaru-ri and Yudam-ni. An Army battalion relieves the 5th Marines east of the Chosin Reservoir and the regiment begins to move through Hagaru-ri and up toward Yudam-ni. Chinese forces attack II ROK Corps on the right flank of Eighth Army (in the center of the country, about 70 miles west of Yudam-ni) and practically destroy it.

26 November
Korea

3/1 (less G Company) becomes the defensive force for Hagaru-ri, site of the forward division command post, supply dumps, and an airfield under construction. The Chinese attack extends all along the front of Eighth Army, which begins to retreat in the face of overwhelming numbers and an open right flank. The U.S. Army 2nd Division is ambushed on the road as it withdraws in a massive convoy and suffers grievous losses in men and equipment.

27 November
Korea

2/5 attacks west from Yudam-ni in accordance with X Corps orders. It meets strong Chinese resistance and makes little headway. The remainder of the 5th Marines joins the 7th Marines in the town during the day. That night, as the temperature drops to 20 below zero, eight Chinese divisions (with four more in reserve) open a counterattack against U.S. positions in the reservoir area. The 5th and 7th hold on against heavy assaults, as do the two company outposts in Toktong Pass but Army units (two infantry battalions and reinforcing elements) east of the Chosin suffer heavy losses and are partially overrun. Throughout the Chosin Reservoir campaign, Marine aviators, sometimes reinforced by Navy and Air Force pilots, support the division with attacks against the CCF.

28 November
Korea

Smith halts his division's attack beyond Yudam-ni and concentrates the efforts of his Marines in opening up the MSR, now cut in several places by the Chinese. 1/7 succeeds in linking up with its C Company and bringing it back into the Yudam-ni perimeter. That night, the Chinese hit Hagaru-ri and renew their attacks on Fox Company. In addition to 3/1, division support elements and small numbers of U.S. soldiers man the Hagaru-ri perimeter and largely hold off the CCF, although losing some ground on East Hill (the key terrain feature dominating the town).

Heritage

As U.S. and British Marines fight together in Korea, the Royal Marines present the Canton Bell, captured by them in China in 1875, to the U.S. Marine Corps for display in the museum at Quantico.

29 November
Korea

1/1 launches a spoiling attack to drive off enemy forces gathering outside Chinhung-ni. Task Force Drysdale (41 Commando, 3/1's G Company, Marine tanks, and an Army infantry company) attempts to escort a convoy of headquarters and support elements from Koto-ri to Hagaru-ri. The convoy and the Army company are stopped on the road that night and overrun by the Chinese. The Communists attack Koto-ri, but are beaten back by 2/1.

Right: *Men of the 7th Marines get mail as they move up through Koto-ri in November 1950. (National Archives)*

30 November
Korea
MAG-12 and its squadrons begin shifting from Wonsan to Yonpo airfield, near Hungnam. The move is completed the next day. The Chinese again make a night attack on Hagaru-ri, but without success.

1 December
Korea
The 5th and 7th Marines begin their break-out from Yudam-ni toward Hagaru-ri. That night, 1/7 begins a cross-country night attack to relieve Fox Company in Toktong Pass. The first C-47 cargo plane lands on the partially completed runway at Hagaru-ri. Thereafter daily runs bring in replacements and needed supplies and take out wounded. East of the Chosin Reservoir, the Army force (dubbed Task Force Faith) is overrun by the Chinese during its attempt to reach Hagaru-ri. Of the original strength of 2,500 on 27 November, barely 1,000 survivors make it to Marine lines, and only 40 percentof those are still in condition to fight.

2 December
Korea
Prior to dawn, the rear guard Marines at Yudam-ni defeat CCF attacks against the perimeter. 1/7 links up with Fox Company, which has lost more than half its men killed and wounded during nightly attacks by the Chinese.

3 December
Korea
The 5th and 7th Marines link up with 1/7 and Fox Company in Toktong Pass. By evening, the head of the column reaches Hagaru-ri. There is constant fighting along the MSR as the CCF seeks to prevent the Marines from reaching the sea at Hungnam.

4 December
Korea
The tail end of the 5th and 7th Marines column reaches Hagaru-ri. VMF-212 flies out of Yonpo to Itami to re-equip with newer model Corsairs.

6 December
Korea
The 1st Marine Division launches its attack down the MSR from Hagaru-ri. Its vehicle train numbers over a thousand. Marine, Navy, and Air Force air support sorties now reach 200 per day. To control them, a Marine R5D transport plane is rigged as a flying tactical air direction center, to relieve ground units of that burden. It is the first-ever use of a transport plane in this role. That night, Marines and soldiers beat back a fierce CCF assault on East Hill.

7 December
Korea
The tail of the 1st Marine Division column reaches Koto-ri. Air Force cargo planes drop bridging sections for the division to span a blown bridge in Funchilin Pass. Engineers install the bridge when the site is retaken on 9 December. VMF-214 flies out of Yonpo and returns to *Sicily*.

8 December
Korea
The 1st Marine Division continues its push south, with the lead elements fighting their way out of Koto-ri. 1/1 meanwhile attacks north into Funchilin Pass to help clear the way.

10 December
Korea
The front of the 1st Marine Division column reaches Chinhung-ni while the rear guard is still in Koto-ri. That night, the brakes of a tank lock on the one-lane road and ultimately seven M-26 Pershings are abandoned at the tail of the column. VMF-311 arrives at Yonpo airfield and flies the first Marine Corps jet combat missions with its F9F-2 Panthers.

11 December
Korea
The last elements of the 1st Marine Division reach the Allied perimeter at Hungnam. As part of an amphibious withdrawal, the division begins embarking the next day.

12 December
Korea
VMF-212 flies on to carrier *Bataan* (CVL-29), joining VMF-214 on *Sicily* and VMF-323 on *Badoeng Strait* in providing support to X Corps during the evacuation of Hungnam.

14 December
Korea
VMF-311 shifts from Yonpo to K-9 airfield near Pusan.

15 December
Korea
With the exception of the 1st Amphibian Tractor Battalion, the last elements of the 1st Marine Division depart Hungnam.

16 December
Korea
The 1st Marine Division command post opens at the Bean Patch in Masan, the same rest area used by the 1st Provisional Marine Brigade during the Pusan Perimeter campaign. Most elements of the division immediately begin patrolling a wide belt around the town to search for bandits and guerrillas in the area.

17 December
Korea
Remaining MAG-12 units depart Yonpo airfield for South Korea. Marine losses during the fighting from 26 October until this date total 908 dead and missing, 3,508 wounded, and 7,313 nonbattle casualties (mostly frostbite or severe illness due to the weather). Enemy losses approach 40,000.

18 December
Korea
The 1st Marine Division is assigned to Eighth Army reserve.

23 December
Korea
General Walker dies in a traffic accident. Lieutenant General Matthew B. Ridgway is appointed to succeed him as commander of Eighth Army and arrives in country on Christmas Day.
Indochina
The United States signs a mutual defense agreement with France, Vietnam, Cambodia, and Laos to provide indirect U.S. military aid to the three countries of Indochina. France is still fighting Ho Chi Minh's Viet Minh, which dominates the countryside of northern Vietnam.

24 December
Korea
Elements of the 1st Amphibian Tractor Battalion are the last to depart Hungnam at the completion of the Allied amphibious withdrawal from that port city.

28 December
Aviation
Marine R5Ds fly their first mission transporting other aircraft, bringing Bell HTL helicopters from the States to Japan for eventual use in Korea.

31 December
Korea
Eighth Army and X Corps occupy a defensive line roughly along the 38th parallel. That night, Communist forces attack the ROK 1st Division and drive it back. This forces the U.N. line to withdraw below Seoul starting on 3 January. The Marine squadrons on the escort carriers and at K-9 fly missions in support of forces on the ground throughout this period, though under Air Force direction, most strikes are against the enemy rear rather than along the frontlines.

Left: *Dead Marines await burial in the frozen ground at Koto-ri in December 1950. (National Archives)*

Right: *1st MAW aviators provide unerring support to Marines on the ground during the fighting withdrawal from the Chosin Reservoir. (National Archives)*

1951

1 January
Korea
VMF-212 and its carrier shift from the east coast of Korea to the west to help stem the Communist onslaught in that area.

2 January
Department of Defense
Congress passes a supplemental defense appropriation bill adding $20 billion to the DOD's budget of $14 billion for fiscal year 1951.

3 January
Force Structure
The JCS authorize the Marine Corps to add three aviation squadrons for a total of 21.

4 January
Korea
General Ridgway orders a fresh withdrawal to Line D, roughly 50 miles south of the 38th parallel. Communist forces capture Seoul as U.N. troops fall back. Eighth Army and X Corps are in position on 7 January.

7 January
Korea
The three carriers hosting Marine squadrons withdraw from Korean waters. VMF-212 and

Bataan return within a week, but VMF-214, 323, and 311 end up at Itami, mainly due to the lack of good airfields in the remaining territory under U.N. control.

8 January
Korea
A Communist attack near Wonju in east-central Korea forces the U.S. 2nd Division to fall back The U.N. line now has a salient roughly 20 miles deep. Large numbers of North Korean soldiers penetrate the gap and begin operating as guerrillas in the U.N. rear. Ridgway alerts the 1st Marine Division for movement toward this threatened zone.

10 January
Korea
The 1st Marine Division begins a movement north from the Bean Patch to the vicinity of Pohang, a port on the east cost of South Korea. A major airlift effort, much of it provided by VMR-152 and 352, brings over a thousand replacements for the division from the States to Korea.

12 January
Korea
The U.N. cease-fire committee floats a proposal to end the fighting in Korea.

Left: *The pioneers—Marines ride into history during the first heliborne troop lift in combat.* (National Archives)

15 January
Department of Defense
President Truman asks Congress to authorize another defense budget supplement of $41.4 billion.
Force Structure
Marine Helicopter Transport Squadron 161 (HMR-161) is organized at El Toro. It is the first nonexperimental squadron of its type in the world.

16 January
Korea
Due to continuing severe maintenance problems, the jets of VMF-311 are grounded pending trouble-shooting by the manufacturer.

17 January
Korea
China rejects the U.N. peace proposal of 12 January.

18 January
Korea
The 1st Marine Division begins operating in a 1,600-square-mile area north and west of Pohang with the missions of keeping the main road open, clearing out Communist guerrillas, and being prepared to counterattack any penetration of the U.N. line in that region. The division assigns each of its regiments and combat support elements a zone of action. Combat patrols search for enemy forces.

21 January
Korea
The 1st Korean Marine Corps (KMC) Regiment is attached to the 1st Marine Division.

22 January
Korea
VMF(N)-513 begins operating from K-9 in place of grounded VMF-311. China makes its own peace offer, which is rejected by the United States.

23 January
Korea
MAG-33 and VMF-312 move to newly rebuilt Bofu airfield in Japan, which places them in reasonable range of Korea. 1st MAW and VMF-214 and 323 arrive the next day.

24 January
Korea
The most substantial fighting of the Pohang guerrilla hunt occurs after North Koreans attack the 7th Marines command post on the night of the 24th and the regiment pursues them over the next two days. The 7th Marines kills or captures 168 enemy.

25 January
Korea
Eighth Army launches an offensive on the left flank of the U.N. line that gains ground. By the

28th, all Marine squadrons in Korea and Japan are supporting the advance.

8 February
Korea
VMF-323 flies into K-1 airfield, near Pusan. VMF-214 and 312 follow over the next two days.

10 February
Korea
The U.S. 24th Division recaptures Inchon and Kimpo Airfield.

11 February
Korea
A Communist counter-offensive in the middle of the line defeats two ROK divisions and forces the retreat of the IX Corps. The drive wanes soon after.

12 February
Korea
The 1st Marine Division receives orders to begin moving to Chungju in preparation for an attack (part of Operation Killer) to regain the ground lost along the central front. Marine losses during the Pohang guerrilla hunt total 36 dead and missing and 148 wounded.

13 February
Korea
MAG-33 sets up its command post at K-3 airfield near Pohang. The squadrons at K-1 soon transfer

Right: *Under fire, Marines peer over the crest of a ridge as they advance in central Korea. (National Archives)*

there. VMF-311 and its jets, restored to good condition after a month of work, also begin moving to K-3. VMF(N)-513 and 542 are scheduled to arrive at the field before the end of the month.

21 February
Korea
The 5th Marines leads off the division attack from Wonju. The objective is high ground near the town of Hoengsong. There is no significant fighting until 23 February and the division seizes its objective on the 24th despite rain and heavy mud.

24 February
Korea
The commanding general of IX Corps dies in a helicopter accident and is temporarily replaced by Marine Major General O. P. Smith. Brigadier General Chesty Puller moves up to temporary command of the 1st Marine Division.

1 March
Korea
Eighth Army resumes Operation Killer. The 1st Marine Division jumps off from its positions near Hoengsong and after some heavy fighting achieves its objectives beyond the town on 4 March. This battle highlights the shortcomings of the Air Force's Joint Operations Center, which centralizes control of all air missions, most of which it directs toward deep targets. Requests for close air support

missions by the Marines on the ground go largely unmet, and 1st MAW's skill in that area is not utilized. Marine commanders discuss the issue with the commander of Fifth Air Force, who begins to divert more Marine aircraft to the support of the division.
Force Structure
VMF-451 is reassigned from the Reserve to permanent active duty.

5 March
Korea
An Army general arrives to assume command of IX Corps and Smith returns to the 1st Marine Division.
Mediterranean
2/6 departs Morehead City to become the landing force for the Sixth Fleet. It will remain afloat until 6 July.

7 March
Korea
Eighth Army launches a new offensive dubbed Operation Ripper. The 1st Marine Division's mission is to capture the town of Hongchon,

north of Hoengsong. Opposition is relatively light at the Communists fight small delaying actions and withdraw.

12 March
Korea
VMF(N)-542 departs for the United States, where it will transition to F3D all-weather jet fighters.

14 March
Korea
The 1st Marine Division takes Hongchon. ROK forces retake abandoned Seoul.

15 March
Force Structure
MAG-13 is reactivated at El Toro.

15–16 March
Korea
The 1st and 7th Marines encounter tough resistance in a series of hills north of Hongchon, but seize them in close-in combat with grenades.

31 March
Korea
U.S. Army forces cross to the north of the 38th parallel for the first time since the retreats of December.

1 April
Force Structure
Force Troops, FMFLANT, is organized at Camp Lejeune to provide combat and support units to reinforce a Marine division for extended operations.

5 April
Force Structure
HMR-261 is established at Cherry Point.

7 April
Korea
1st MAW receives responsibility for the air defense of the Pusan-Pohang area.

8 April
Korea
After a period of increased support to the 1st Marine Division, the JOC again begins to divert nearly all 1st MAW sorties to other missions.

10 April
Manpower
DOD issues an order lowering the intelligence standards for enlistment in the Air Force, Navy, and Marines to those of the Army. The plan also calls for these three services to also take draftees for the first time since WWII.

11 April
Korea
President Truman relieves General MacArthur of command following his repeated statements undermining U.S. official policy in the war. Ridgway is elevated to replace MacArthur as the theater commander. Army Lieutenant General James A. Van Fleet takes charge of Eighth Army.

15 April
Manpower
The Marine Corps convenes its first Officer Candidate School since World War II, at Parris Island.

21 April
Korea
In the first Marine air-to-air action of the war, Captain Philip C. DeLong of VMF-312 and *Bataan* shoots down two Communist Yak fighters and his wingman, 1st Lieutenant Harold D. Daigh, gets another. DeLong had scored 11 kills during World War II. Chinese anti-aircraft grows increasingly effective. During the first three weeks of this month, 16 Marine aircraft are downed by ground fire, with the loss of nine pilots killed and one captured.

22 April
Korea
The 1st Marine Division and attached 1st KMC regiment reach the Hwachon Reservoir, an advance of 45 miles since the inception of Operation Killer in February. That night, the Chinese launch their spring offensive. They rout the ROK 6th Division on the immediate left of the Marines. The 7th Marines and 1st KMC hold against heavy enemy attacks while the 1st Marines refuses the division's left flank.

23 April
Korea
Eighth Army orders the 1st Marine Division and other units to withdraw due to the holes in the U.N. line. 1st MAW launches 205 sorties all along the front, of which the Marine division receives an unusually high 42. That night the Chinese come on again and 1/1 fights a fierce battle to hold Horseshoe Ridge.

26 April
Force Structure
VMF-251, recently brought back onto permanent active duty from reserve status, is redesignated as VMA-251.

30 April
Korea
The U.N. withdrawal ends. The 1st Marine Division is now near Hongchon, roughly half of the way back to Wonju, where it had started in February.

1 May
Force Structure
VMF(N)-543 is reactivated at NAS Glenview, Illinois.

5 May
Roles and Missions
Despite strong opposition from the Navy and Army, the Senate unanimously passes a bill calling

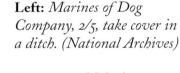

Left: *Marines of Dog Company, 2/5, take cover in a ditch. (National Archives)*

Opposite: *A Marine moves up through the smoke of battle. (National Archives)*

for a 400,000-man ceiling for the Corps and giving the Commandant a non-voting seat on the JCS when issues arise concerning the Corps. Soon after, the House votes 253–30 for a bill giving the Corps a strength of 300,000 and the Commandant full membership in the JCS. Both bills die when Congress adjourns its session without being able to reach a compromise.

9 May
Korea
1st MAW Corsairs and Panthers participate in a raid by more than 300 U.S. aircraft against Sinuiju, North Korea's temporary capital and the site of key bridges spanning the Yalu River to China.

15 May
Force Structure
VMF-121 is redesignated VMA-121. It is equipped with the Douglas AD Skyraider, a propeller attack plane that can carry over 5,000 pounds of bombs.

16 May
Korea
The Communists launch an offensive focused on two ROK divisions to the east of Marine positions. The South Koreans are defeated and the Chinese soon create a hole 20 miles wide and 30 miles deep in the U.N. line. The 1st Marine Division defeats two regimental-sized attacks in its zone.

20 May
Korea
Eighth Army reserves stabilize the Chinese penetration.

23 May
Korea
Eighth Army counterattacks against Communist forces weakened by losses sustained in their spring offensives. The 1st Marine Division drives north in a zone just to the east of the Hwachon Reservoir. Opposition is sporadic and large numbers of the enemy surrender. Within days, U.N. forces regain and cross much of the 38th parallel. Fifth Air Force begins Operation Strangle, which focuses on shutting down Communist supply lines deep behind the front. 1st MAW receives the mission of shutting down key roads in the Iron Triangle, the

area near the formal North Korean capital city Pyongyang. In the next seven weeks, 20 Marine aircraft are downed by flak, with 14 pilots killed or captured. Only a third of 1st MAW sorties go to close air support during this period.

27 May
Korea
VMF-214 and 323 begin using the K-46 dirt strip near the front lines as a forward base, rotating up to a dozen Corsairs there from the main K-1 base, as a means to cut down response time for close air support missions. 1st MAW also begins to use transport aircraft to drop flares at night in support of Marines on the ground.

31 May
Legal
The new Uniform Code of Military Justice replaces separate Army-Air Force and Navy-Marine legal systems.

1 June
Force Structure
As part of an authorized buildup beyond its current two divisions, the Marine Corps establishes the 3rd Marine Brigade at Camp Pendleton. It will be built around the 3rd Marines.

Manpower

The Marine Corps begins to release mobilized reservists. Nearly 2,200 officers and men are allowed to return to civilian life during this first month of the program.

6 June
Korea

The 1st Marines opens the fight for a dominating ridge north of the Hwachon Reservoir. The division is engaging primarily North Korean forces during this period.

10 June
Korea

Using well-coordinated artillery and close air support from VMF-214 during the day and VMF(N)-513 at night, the 1st Marines finally seizes the ridge near the Hwachon Reservoir in close combat with grenades and bayonets. After six days of inconclusive fighting for key terrain overlooking the Punchbowl (a gigantic volcanic crater), the 1st KMC conducts a night attack that sweeps away the NKPA defenders. The 7th Marines is engaged in equally tough fighting to capture the ridgeline between the 1st Marines and the 1st KMC.

14 June
Mediterranean

1/8 (Reinforced) departs Morehead City to become the landing force of the Sixth Fleet. It will return on 30 September.

15 June
Training

FMFPAC units conduct an amphibious exercise dubbed Operation LEX in southern California.
Force Structure

VMR-253 is reactivated at El Toro.

16 June
Korea

Having gained the most defensible terrain along a line running from the Hwachon Reservoir northeast to the Punchbowl, the 1st Marine Division receives orders to dig in and hold.

19 June
Manpower

President Truman signs legislation lowering the draft age to 18 years and 6 months.

20 June
Mishap

During a 2nd Marine Division training exercise at Camp Lejeune, eight Marines are killed and 25 injured when two mortar shells fall short into a battalion command post.
Force Structure

The 3rd Marines is reactivated at Camp Pendleton as part of the 3rd Marine Brigade.

25 June
Korea
The Chinese publicly endorse the idea of truce talks.

30 June
Korea
A Marine F7F Tigercat of VMF-513 achieves the Corps' first kill by this aircraft, shooting down an enemy biplane making night nuisance raids against U.N. forces near Seoul.
Manpower
The strength of the Marine Corps on active duty is 15,150 officers and 177,770 enlisted.
Force Structure
HMR-162 is activated at Santa Ana, California.

6 July
Manpower
President Truman extends for a year the enlistments of more than 300,000 personnel due to expire before 1 July 1952.
Force Structure
VMF-322 is reactivated as a Reserve squadron at Squantum, Massachusetts.

10 July
Korea
Truce talks begin between military representatives of the two sides at Kaesong.

Manpower
The Marine Corps is forced to make arrangements to take 7,000 draftees during August, its first since WWII, because voluntary enlistments are slowing just as the Corps is trying to build up its strength.

Opposite, top and bottom: *Marines pause during the battle in June 1951. (National Archives)*

Above: *A flamethrower burns off cover. (National Archives)*

Right: *Marine artillery in action. (National Archives)*

14 July
Korea
MAG-12 ceases use of K-46 airfield because the dirt runway causes too many maintenance problems. The group shifts its forward base to K-18, on the east coast near the 38th parallel.

15 July
Korea
The U.S. 2nd Division begins relieving the 1st Marine Division in the front lines and the Marines go into reserve for X Corps.

25 July
Korea
The truce talks produce an agenda for further discussion. The main items were decision on a line of demarcation and the return of prisoners of war.

18 August
Korea
1st MAW aircraft evacuate to Japan for three days due to a typhoon threatening the Korean Peninsula.

23 August
Korea
The Communists break off the truce talks.

27 August
Korea
The 1st Marine Division begins moving back into the lines southeast of the Punchbowl.

31 August
Korea
The 1st Marine Division launches an attack to seize a high ridge forming the northeast rim of the Punchbowl. The objective is achieved on 3 September by the 1st KMC and 7th Marines. HMR-161 arrives in Korea with 15 HRS-1 helicopters, each capable of carrying about 1,500 pounds of cargo or four to six troops. In the next ten days it moves to airfield X-83 close to the front lines, sharing it with VMO-6.

1 September
Force Structure
HMR-262 is established at Cherry Point.

2 September
Mediterranean
1/6 departs Morehead City to assume duty as the landing force of the Sixth Fleet. It will remain afloat until 12 February 1952.

7 September
Vietnam
The United States signs an agreement to provide economic assistance to the French-controlled government of Vietnam.

11 September
Korea
The division opens a new assault to take the next ridgeline to the north. After getting bogged down

part way up the forward slope, the 7th Marines sends 2/7 in a night move between the two assault battalions to infiltrate the enemy rear. The left half of the position falls to the Marines the next day, but at a cost of 250 casualties. The enemy has used the lull of the truce talks to build strong defenses. The Communists also now bring to bear almost as much mortar and artillery fire as American forces.

13 September
Korea
The 1st Marines renew the attack to seize the right half of the ridgeline. In a battlefield first, HMR-161 brings ten tons of supplies up to the frontlines to help keep the offensive moving forward. It simultaneously removes 74 casualties.

16 September
Korea
The 5th Marines passes through the division lines and keeps up the pressure, taking Hill 812 the next day.

20 September
Korea
The 1st Marine Division ends the attack begun on the 11th. Although it is not known at the time, this marks the end of true offensive warfare on the part of U.S. forces in Korea. Henceforth the only assaults made are to gain local positional advantage to better defend front lines existing on this date. The division also begins to assume control of terrain on its right flank in relief of the ROK 11th Division. This extends the division front by 9,000 yards to a total of nearly 23,000 yards (13 miles). VMF-323 debarks from *Sicily* and moves in the next two days to Pusan.

21 September
Korea
In another helicopter first, HMR-161 transports 224 men of the division reconnaissance company, reinforced by a heavy machine gun platoon of 2/7, to occupy Hill 884. The helicopters deposit men and supplies in two very small zones on the rugged terrain, accomplishing in less than four hours what would have required 15 hours of difficult overland movement. VMF-212 departs Itami on board *Rendova*.

26 September
Manpower
DOD announces plans to increase the number of women in the armed forces. Current Marine numbers of 63 officers and 2,187 enlisted are projected to rise to 100 and 2,900 respectively.

27 September
Korea
The division rehearses its plan to bring a reserve company from the rear by helicopter to reinforce any threatened point on its long front. The night troop movement of 223 men is made in two hours and 20 minutes.

29 September
Manpower
The draft calls scheduled for November and December are supposed to provide a total of 19,900 men for the Corps, which has grown to 211,000 personnel since June 1950. President Truman has authorized a fresh increase to 236,000.

30 September
Korea
Fighting through enemy defensive positions during September brought the third highest monthly casualties of the war (2,416), exceeded only by December 1950 and June 1951.
Technology
Marines introduce the use of the MPQ-14 radar system to drop bombs based on guidance from the ground-based radar.

1 October
Doctrine
The Joint Landing Force Board is formed at the Marine Corps Schools. The first president of the board is Marine LtGen Franklin A. Hart.

11 October
Korea
In 156 sorties, HMR-161 makes the first battalion-sized troop lift in history, moving the 958 men of 3/7 over 17 miles from a reserve position to the front lines, to effect the relief in place of another battalion.

13 October
Technology
Tests of a flak jacket designed to protect the wearer from shrapnel and low-velocity bullets are completed with a handful of Marines and soldiers in Korea. The Navy-designed vest is soon slated for production.

21 October
Commandants
General Cates announces that he will not retire at the completion of his term as Commandant. At 58, he is short of the statutory retirement age of 62.

22 October
Korea
VMA-121 arrives at K-3 airfield from the U.S.
Force Structure
VMF-441 is reestablished as a reserve squadron at Niagara Falls, New York.

25 October
Korea
For the first time, a flight of Corsairs on a mission over North Korea encounters enemy MIG jets.

2 November
Manpower
DOD issues a large draft call of nearly 60,000 men for January. 11,650 will go to the Corps.

4 November
Korea
Captain William F. Guss of VMF-311 becomes the first Marine pilot to shoot down a Chinese MIG jet.

8 November
Korea
VMF-214 embarks for return to U.S. from Japan.

much larger-scale casting for what will become the Marine Corps War Memorial in Arlington, Virginia.

15 November
Technology

The 1st Marine Division finishes issuing the new thermal boot to all its personnel. This footgear has a pocket of air between two layers of rubber, which helps retain the wearer's body heat. The bulky boots are awkward for marching, but prevent frostbite and are especially effective in the static tactical situation facing the division.

27 November
Korea

The truce talks yield one point of agreement, the line of demarcation, should hostilities be brought to an end. It largely will be the current line of contact. Beyond that, little progress is being made.

1 December
Force Structure

HMR-163 is activated at Santa Ana, California.

10 November
Heritage

A limestone version of Felix de Weldon's statue of the Iwo Jima flag raising is unveiled at the front gate of the Quantico base. The sculptor is working on a

8 December
Manpower

The announced draft call for February of 55,000 men will provide 14,000 to the Corps.

Opposite: *"Drag To Safety," Col Charles Waterhouse, USMCR (Ret), Marine Corps Art Collection*

Top: *"Communicators," Col H. Avery Chenoweth, USMCR (Ret), Marine Corps Art Collection*

Right: *"Helicopter Relief of Lines," MSgt John DeGrasse, Marine Corps Art Collection*

31 December
Korea

The division maintained patrol operations and made occasional trench raids throughout the month, but casualties declined markedly, totaling only 171.

Commandants

General Lemuel C. Shepherd, Jr., assumes duty as the 20th Commandant of the Marine Corps. Cates returns to the rank of lieutenant general and takes command of the Marine Corps Schools.

1952

2 January
HQMC

In an early move, Commandant Shepherd orders a partial adoption of a general staff system (G-1, 2, 3, 4) at HQMC in place of the old Division of Plans and Policies, but other divisions such as Aviation and Personnel remained.

7 January
Korea

HMR-161 successfully completes Operation Muletrain, during which it provides all supplies required for a frontline battalion for a week.

Force Structure

The 3rd Marine Brigade is redesignated the 3rd Marine Division. Its regiments will be the 3rd, 4th, 9th, and 12th Marines (the latter an artillery outfit). Only the 3rd Marines is fully formed as of this date.

8 January
Mediterranean

Battalion Landing Team 3/8 sails from Morehead City to assume duty as the landing force Sixth Fleet. It will return on 20 May.

31 January
Technology

The first 500 of the new flak vests are delivered to the 1st Marine Division in Korea and put into immediate use by troops most exposed to enemy fire. They immediately prove their worth.

Training

In Operation HELEX I, HMR-261 and 262 lift 1/8 from *Siboney* (CVE-112) and place it ashore at Camp Lejeune in an elapsed time of four hours and 25 minutes.

1 February
Force Structure

3rd MAW and VMF-314 are reactivated at Cherry Point.

10 February
Korea

The entire Eighth Army front conducts Operation Clam-Up, which involves a feigned withdrawal in order to lure enemy patrols to positions from which prisoners can be taken. That night Marine elements engage such patrols and inflict casualties, but get no prisoners.

11 February
Korea
VMF-312 leaves Itami airfield and goes on board *Bairoko* (CVE-115), which deploys to the west coast of Korea. It is replaced the next day by the lead elements of VMF-115, which soon joins MAG-33 at K-3 airfield near Pohang, Korea.

23 February
Training
LEX Baker One begins in southern California with the reinforced 3rd Marines and HMR-162. It is the largest amphibious exercise on the West Coast since 1949 and a major test of employing helicopters in that role.

25 February
Force Structure
The 1st MAW photographic unit is redesignated as Marine Photographic Squadron 1 (VMJ-1).

26 February
Korea
VMF-115 arrives at K-3 airfield.

28 February
Force Structure
HMR-361 is activated at Santa Ana, California.

1 March
Force Structure
VMF-312 in Korea is redesignated as Marine Attack Squadron 312 (VMA-312). MAG-16 is activated at Santa Ana, California.
Aviation
Following the second hard landing of an HMR-161 helicopter due to mechanical failure, the entire squadron is grounded for two weeks until re-designed tail pylons are received.

11 March
Manpower
The Marine Corps announces that it will no longer take draftees after 30 June because voluntary enlistments are again beginning to meet its requirements. By the end of this month, the Corps will have taken in 73,430 draftees.

12 March
Korea
1st Marine Division receives orders to prepare to shift its position from the east-central front to the west. This is part of a larger switch involving many elements of Eighth Army.

17 March
Korea
The 1st Marine Division commences its 140-mile move to the west with the 1st KMC regiment.

Right: *An infantryman awaits the helicopter that will take him up to the front lines in January 1952. (National Archives)*

Left: *A heliborne medevac. (National Archives)*

Opposite, top: *Marines of 3/5 work on their bunker in March 1952. (National Archives)*

Opposite, bottom: *Easter services 1952. (National Archives)*

Force Structure

The 9th and 12th Marines are reactivated at Camp Pendleton as part of the 3rd Marine Division. VMA-324 is reactivated at Cherry Point.

22 March
Force Structure

The Corps activates six battalions and a new air group on the west coast to reach its full complement of three divisions and three wings.

25 March
Korea

The 1st Marine Division is completely established in its new position astride the primary route of attack toward Seoul. As part of the shift, the division is now part of I Corps. The division front totals 32 miles, but much of the left portion of this is along the Han and Imjin rivers, which provide a substantial defensive barrier. Chinese forces man the opposite trench lines in this sector, which also includes the truce corridor at Panmunjom.

30 March
Korea

VMF(N)-513 begins redeploying from the east coast of Korea to K-8 airfield near Kunsan, on the west coast about 100 miles below Seoul.

1 April
Korea

Chinese forces launch strong attacks against the KMC portion of the 1st Marine Division line and are repulsed.

5 April
Korea

HMR-161 and 2/7 conduct Operation Pronto, which simulates a reserve force counterattacking an enemy landing along the coast.

15 April
Korea

In what will become a hallmark of the last year of the war, a platoon of Easy Company of 2/5 defeats a Chinese attempt to seize its outpost on a hill forward of the main line of resistance (MLR). The reinforced platoon loses 11 killed and missing and 25 wounded, while inflicting more than 70 casualties on the enemy. Before the month is over, the 1st Marine Division withdraws its permanent outposts and shifts to a policy of occupying them only during the day.

19 April
Mediterranean

3/6 departs Morehead City to become the new landing force of the Sixth Fleet. It will return on

Marines and four are Navy corpsmen. The rest of MAG-12 (VMA-212 and 323) shift to K-6, near Pyongtaek about 30 miles below the capital.

Training

The 3rd Marine Division begins PACPHIBEX-II, a full-division amphibious exercise that lasts until 10 May. It includes helicopters, simulated use of atomic weapons by both sides, and a rehearsal landing on the Silver Strand at Coronado Island off San Diego.

Mediterranean

2/6 (Reinforced) leaves Morehead City on its way to becoming the landing force of the Sixth Fleet, It will return on 26 October.

29 April

Manpower

Colonel Katherine Towle becomes the first female line officer to retire from the U.S. military. She is succeeded as director of Women Marines by Lieutenant Colonel Julia E. Hamblet.

30 April

Department of Defense

President Eisenhower submits a defense reorganization plan to Congress designed to strengthen the power of the Secretary of Defense.

1 May

Korea

The U.S. 25th Division begins relieving the 1st Marine Division on the MLR. The shift is complete on 4 May, except that the 11th Marines and the 1st Tank Battalion remain to provide fire support for the soldiers. The 1st Marine Division becomes the corps reserve and begins a period of recuperation and training at Camp Casey, 15 miles behind the lines.

13 May

Korea

As part of the division training program, the 5th Marines conducts an amphibious exercise. Other regiments take their turns soon after.

25–29 May

Korea

The 1st Marines and division reconnaissance company move up toward the MLR as a reserve force during extremely heavy Chinese attacks in and around the Nevada Cities complex. VMA-121, 212, and 323 fly numerous missions in support of the 25th Division, while the 11th Marines and 1st Tank Battalion add their weight to the battle. To avoid greater casualties, Eighth Army gives up these hotly contested outposts on 29 May.

Opposite: *A white phosphorous shell ("willie pete") bursts in front of Marine lines. (National Archives)*

Right: *Tanks still proved their worth even in the hilly terrain of Korea. (National Archives)*

29 May
Korea
VMA-332 arrives in Korea from MCAS Miami to replace VMA-312 on *Bairoko*. The relief is completed on 10 June.

10–17 June
Korea
As Communist forces launch a large offensive against ROK forces in the center of the U.N. line, 1st MAW squadrons conduct an unusually high number of sorties, including a one-day record of 283 on 15 June.

18 June
Korea
Marines help stop anti-Communist POWs from breaking out of a U.N. prison camp near Inchon.

24–30 June
Korea
During another Communist offensive against ROK forces, 1st MAW breaks its sortie record with 301 on 30 June, accounting for 28 percent of Fifth Air Force close air support missions and 24 percent of interdiction attacks.

30 June
Manpower
The strength of the Marine Corps on active duty is 18,731 officers and 230,488 enlisted.

3 July
Korea
VMA-323 depart Korea for rotation back to the United States.

6 July
Korea
The 1st Marine Division begins moving back into its old positions on the west flank of the Eighth Army line.

7–8 July
Korea
After dark, a Chinese battalion attacks Outposts Berlin and East Berlin while Marines are relieving the Turkish troops defending them. The Marines and Turks fight side by side and hold Berlin. A morning counterattack on the 8th recaptures East Berlin. That night the Marines turn back fresh assaults. The 7th Marines loses 21 killed or missing and 140 wounded.

Left: *Weary Marines of 3/1 just after a stint at the Boulder City outpost. (National Archives)*

Opposite: *A DUKW-load of 3/7 Marines ride up the ramp of an LST following a 1953 amphibious exercise in Korea. (National Archives)*

11 July
Korea
Major John F. Bolt becomes the first (and only) jet ace in the Marine Corps when he shoots down his fifth and sixth MIGs while flying with an Air Force squadron. He had downed six Japanese Zeroes during World War II.

12 July
Korea
VMA-251 joins MAG-12 in Korea as the replacement for VMA-323.

17 July
Mishap
A Marine C-119 transport plane crashes near Milton, Florida, claiming the lives of the four crewmen and 38 NROTC midshipmen.

19 July
Korea
A Chinese battalion conquers the Berlins in a night attack, completely destroying the two Marine platoons defending them. Following the loss of these two outposts, the Marine division begins to adopt a defense-in-depth, relying on supplementary positions behind the lines to block penetrations rather than relying on outposts in front of the lines to blunt attacks before the MLR.

20 July
Korea
Major Thomas M. Sellers, flying on an exchange tour with the Air Force, brings down two MIG-15s before he himself is shot down and killed.

22 July
Korea
Major John H. Glenn, flying with an Air Force squadron, downs his third MIG in 10 days, tying him with Major Gillis as the second-leading Marine scorer in Korea.

24–27 July
Korea
On the night of 24–25 July, two Chinese battalions attack Boulder City, a hill on the MLR, while other units strike Outposts Esther and Dagmar elsewhere along the Marine line. All assaults are repulsed. They come back again the next two nights, again without success. Marine losses are 43 killed and 316 wounded.

25 July
Force Structure
President Eisenhower announces that the 3rd Marine Division and MAG-11 of 3rd MAW will move to Japan to provide a ready amphibious force in the Far East.

27 July
Korea
At 1000 the two sides sign the armistice agreement at Panmunjom. The cease fire goes into effect at 2200 that night. The accord establishes a 4,000-yard-wide demilitarized zone (DMZ) between the frontlines and sets the stage for political talks to achieve a peace agreement. (No such agreement is ever signed.) During the course of the war, Marine units had lost 4,262 killed in battle and 26,038 wounded. Their sacrifice paved the way for an independent and eventually democratic South Korea.

28 July
Korea
The 1st Marine Division reorganizes its defenses, with one regiment manning the forward line and the remainder (including the 1st KMC) providing a defense-in-depth.

29 July
Department of Defense
Congress passes a defense budget of more than $34 billion for fiscal year 1954.

5 August
Korea
Operation Big Switch begins. The Communists return 157 Marines—129 from the division and the rest from 1st MAW—plus six corpsmen. Of the 221 Marines believed to have been captured during the war, 20 had escaped, 174 had been released, and 27 died in captivity. Nearly a quarter of these men had fallen into enemy hands on 29–30 November during the attempt of Task Force Drysdale to reach Hagaru-ri.

6 August
Manpower
The Marine Corps extends the standard tour of duty with units in Korea to 14 months from 11.

7 August
Manpower
Staff Sergeant Barbara O. Barnwell becomes the first female Marine to earn the Navy-Marine Corps Medal for Heroism, by saving a fellow Marine from drowning.

13 August
Japan
The headquarters of the 3rd Marine Division departs Camp Pendleton for Japan. Its subordinate elements also shift during the month. MAG-16 (a helicopter transport group) arrives in Japan with HMR-162 and 163, both flying the HRS-2.
Force Structure
As part of the transfer to Japan, the 4th Marines disbands 4/4 and the fourth rifle company in 3/4.

16 August
Japan
VMR-253 arrives at Naval Air Station Atsugi. The squadron is equipped with R4Q Fairchild Packets, which can carry 42 Marines.

14–19 August
Greece

BLT 2/6, with the Sixth Fleet, assists in rescue and relief operations following an earthquake in the Ionian Isles of Greece.

6 September
Korea

The exchange of POWs willing to be repatriated is completed.

10 September
Japan

MAG-11 arrives at Atsugi. Its three squadrons, VMF-222, 224, and 314, are all equipped with F9F Panther jets.

Mediterranean

1/2 (Reinforced) departs Morehead City to serve as the landing force of the Sixth Fleet. It will return on 4 February 1954.

30 November
Manpower

The total strength of the Marine Corps is 251,770, its maximum during the Korean War era.

Top: *Machine gunners provide long-distance support to advancing infantry. (National Archives)*

Right: *Sgt Sylvester Jarvis of 2/5 test fires his flame thrower. (National Archives)*

homicide and drinking on duty in the incident that took the lives of six recruits.

17 August
Manpower
The title of Marine Gunner is restored for warrant officers serving in nontechnical fields.

29 October
Morocco
A company of Marines from 2/2 flies to Port Lyautey to reinforce the Marine Barracks at the Naval Air Station there during a period of friction between the French and Moroccans.

30 October
Suez
Following the Israeli invasion of the Sinai Peninsula the day prior, RLT-2 goes on alert for possible deployment to reinforce 3/2 in the Mediterranean. The alert for RLT-2 ends on 27 November.

1 November
Suez
After British and French forces begin attacking Egypt on 31 October, BLT 3/2 and the Sixth Fleet evacuate over 1,500 people (mostly U.S. citizens) from Alexandria, Egypt, as well as a U.N. observer force from the Gaza Strip.

11 November
Morocco
BLT 3/3 on Okinawa is dispatched for Port Lyautey to further reinforce the base as tensions rise due to the Suez crisis. Before the Marines make it to the Mediterranean, a ceasefire ends the fighting in Egypt and BLT 3/3 is diverted to a goodwill tour of Asian ports.

31 December
Force Structure
The HMR squadrons are redesignated as Marine Light Helicopter Squadrons—HMR(L)—in anticipation of the acquisition of larger "medium" helicopters.

1957

January
Technology
VMA-224 receives the Marine Corps' first Douglas A-4 Skyhawks. The small delta-wing attack planes prove to be nimble and rugged.

7 January
Force Structure
The report of the Hogaboom Board is accepted by Commandant Pate. Its main recommendations are to add a fourth rifle company to the infantry battalion, shift the tank battalion from the division to Force Troops, and add an antitank battalion of 45 Ontos vehicles (small tracked vehicles mounting six 105mm recoilless rifles) to the division. This new M-series table of organization, designed to enhance the helicopter transportability of the division, is fully implemented by fall 1958.

Right: *Four jets of VMA-214 fly over the mountains of Japan in 1958. The squadron is flying the North American FJ-4 Fury, a naval version of the Air Force's F-86. (National Archives)*

MARINE CORPS RECRUIT DEPOT PARRIS ISLAND

Parris Island opened its recorded history as a military installation. French troops landed there in 1562 and built a small fort. They lasted only a few months before heading back to Europe, but Spanish soldiers followed a few years later. The Union Navy was next on the scene, taking over nearby Port Royal early in the Civil War and maintaining a small naval station in the area through the 1880s. In searching for a place to build permanent facilities, the Navy settled on Parris Island in 1883, purchasing 37 acres for $5,000. The first Marines, a small guard detachment, set foot on the base on 26 June 1891. In a foretaste of the island's future reputation as a tough environment for recruits, these men lived in tents until winter set in and a number of them became sick. The Navy then transferred them to quarters in a coal shed for a year before finally building a barracks.

The Corps' first major activity on the island began on 1 January 1909, when the Marine Officers School (what would later become The Basic School) moved there. On 1 June 1911, the east coast recruit training program shifted to Parris Island from Norfolk. That lasted only a few weeks, as the Navy decided to turn the base into a disciplinary barracks. Both new officers and recruits departed on 30 August 1911, transferring back to Norfolk. A Marine detachment remained to guard the base and its prisoners.

Recruit training returned to Parris Island for good on 25 October 1915. The Navy was closing down its facilities, and it completely turned over ownership of the base to the Corps three days later. With the arrival of World War I, the Marines needed much more than the 78 acres they had. Pursuant to legislation passed 1 July 1918, the President ordered the government to take over the entire island and reimburse its owners. There were 6,000 acres in all, about half of it in marsh land. (As occurred at the base in San Diego, much of this swampy ground would be filled in over the years.) The Navy Department put up more than 500 temporary structures. The recruits pouring onto the island provided the labor to create the rest of the base, building roads and other facilities as part of the process of building their muscles and stamina. At the height of the war, Parris Island had 13,286 men in training, compared to its prewar level of 835. The burgeoning base underwent name changes, as well. It had started out as Port Royal, after the nearby town, but became Paris Island to avoid confusion in mail delivery, only to switch soon after to the correct spelling of Parris Island.

After World War I, boot camp varied in length depending on the circumstances; from a high of 12 weeks during the doldrums of the 1920s, to a low of 24 days during the expansion of the Corps in the late 1930s. One of the biggest changes on the island took place in 1928 upon the completion of a causeway and bridge to connect it to the mainland. Before that, enlistees arrived on the island by barge. Preparations for war prior to Pearl Harbor enlarged a program already underway to replace the temporary buildings of World War I with permanent brick barracks and support facilities. Up through World War

Recruits at Parris Island learn the basics of marksmanship with M1 rifles as they prepare for the rifle range. (Marine Corps Historical Center)

II, the base also hosted an airfield and occasionally a number of FMF units.

The onset of American participation in World War II brought another staggering increase to recruit training. In January 1942, 22,686 men joined the Corps, 11 times the number of enlistees in November 1941. Boot camp was temporarily reduced to five weeks in duration and many recruits went to Quantico to shoot for qualification. The cycle eventually returned to 12 weeks. To accommodate the influx in personnel, the base received a new wave of temporary buildings, this time metal Quonset huts.

The base received another name change shortly after World War II. As its role outside recruit training declined to insignificance, its status as a Marine barracks disappeared. On 1 December 1946, it became simply Marine Corps Recruit Depot, Parris Island.

Parris Island received unwelcome notoriety in April 1956 following the drowning deaths of six recruits in Ribbon Creek. The resulting national attention brought significant changes in recruit training. The Commandant established recruit training commands headed by general officers at both Parris Island and San Diego. The selection and schooling of drill instructors also became more intense.

In the last decades of the 20th century, new waves of construction brought numerous new structures to the island, replacing many of the temporary facilities of four major wars. But the building of Marines at Parris Island (and San Diego) has remained unchanged in most respects— the depots still take in young men and women and turn out well-disciplined, motivated, toughened privates more than capable of handling the nation's foes.

12 January
Force Structure
The Marine Corps forms its first medium helicopter squadron, HMR(M)-461, at New River, North Carolina. It will receive the Corps' first medium helicopters, the Sikorsky HR2S-1 (later redesignated the CH-37). By far the largest U.S. helicopter to date, it can carry nearly 8,000 pounds of cargo or 23 Marines at a speed of 100 knots.

30 January
Morocco
Company H of 3/6 flies to Port Lyautey to replace Company E, 2/2.

1 February
Bases
29 Palms, located in the desert of southeastern California, becomes a Marine Corps base.

13 February
Technology
The Corps takes delivery of its first Sikorsky HUS-1 utility helicopters, which can carry nearly 6,000 pounds of cargo or 12 Marines at a speed of 90 knots.

14 February
Indonesia
The 3rd Marines and HMR-162 take up station 550 miles northeast of the island of Sumatra in readiness to evacuate U.S. citizens during a rebellion there.

17 March
Philippines
HMR(L)-162 assists in rescue operations after an aircraft carrying Philippine President Ramon Magsaysay crashes on a flight from Cebu to Manila.

15 May
Training
The 4th Marine Provisional Exercise Brigade (composed of BLT 2/5, MAG 26, and VMA 223) takes part in atomic exercise Operation Plumbbob at Desert Rock, Nevada. The operation continues through 5 July.

18 May
Morocco
Company D, 2/2 lands at Port Lyautey to relieve Company H, 3/6 of security duties there. It will remain there until 1 October.

23 May
Sergeants Major
Sergeant Major Wilbur Bestwick is appointed as the first Sergeant Major of the Marine Corps, the Commandant's senior enlisted advisor.

Left: *Dominican Republic 1965. ("Checkpoint Charlie," John Groth, Marine Corps Art Collection)*

Opposite: *Sgt Duane T. MacBeth of 3/6 in Lebanon. (Marine Corps Historical Center)*

1 June
Spain
Marine Barracks Rota is established at the Spanish port.

19 June
Force Structure
The 1st Amphibious Reconnaissance Company at Camp Pendleton is redesignated the 1st Force Reconnaissance Company.

30 June
Manpower
The strength of the Marine Corps on active duty is 17,434 officers and 183,427 enlisted.

16 July
Aviation
Major John H. Glenn, Jr., breaks the transcontinental speed record by crossing from Los Alamitos, California, to Floyd Bennett Field, New York, in 3 hours and 23 minutes in a Chance Vought F8U-1P Crusader (photo reconnaissance variant).

12 August
Manpower
Due to budget constraints, the Secretary of the Navy directs a reduction in strength in both the Navy and Marine Corps over the next two fiscal years. The Corps is slated to end up with 175,000 personnel by mid-1959.

20 August
Mediterranean
In an unusually large deployment, the headquarters of the 6th Marines, HMR(L)-261, and HMR(L)-262 depart Morehead City, North Carolina, for duty with the Sixth Fleet. This marks one of the first deployments afloat for Marine helicopter squadrons.

30 August
Mediterranean
The remainder of the 6th Marines sails for duty with the Sixth Fleet. The regiment will return to Camp Lejeune on 18 November, but 1/6 will remain with the fleet until 6 February 1958.

22 September
Training
RLT 6, MAG-26, VMF-312, and the 2nd Amphibious Reconnaissance Company conduct a landing exercise at Saros Gulf, Turkey.

16 October
Spain
HMR(L)-262, flying from *Lake Champlain* (CV-39), evacuates flood victims and distributes emergency supplies at Valencia.

3 November
Force Structure
HMR(M)-462 is commissioned at Santa Ana.

December
Technology
VMF(AW)-122 takes delivery of the Marine Corps' first Chance Vought F8U Crusader.

1 December
HQMC
The duties of Assistant Commandant and Chief of Staff are divided into two separate billets, each held by a lieutenant general.

18 December
Indonesia
RLT 3 and HMR(L)-162 deploy from Okinawa toward the waters off Indonesia for possible

evacuation of U.S. citizens during continued unrest there. RLT 3 remains offshore until 6 January 1958.

26 December
Ceylon
HMR(L)-162 is temporarily diverted from Indonesia on board *Princeton* (CV-37) to assist flood victims in Ceylon over the next few weeks.

31 December
Bases
The Marines assume command of Naval Air Station Iwakuni, transforming it into a Marine Corps facility.

1958

16 January
Force Structure
The 3rd Antitank Battalion, equipped with the Ontos, is activated at Camp Hansen, Okinawa.

21 January
Venezuela
When mob violence erupts in Caracas during the overthrow of dictator Perez Jimenez, a provisional company of Marine Barracks Guantanamo embarks on *Des Moines* (CA-134) and deploys off the coast to protect American interests. It remains offshore for a week.

25 January
Bases
The Marine Corps breaks ground for the construction of Camp Futema, which will house MAG-16, presently stationed in Oppama, Japan.

28 January
Training
RLT 2 and MAG-24 participate in PHIBTRAEX 1-58 at Vieques, Puerto Rico. The amphibious exercise continues through 17 March.

11 February
Training
RLT 3 and MAG-16, with 3/1 acting as aggressors, conduct PHIBLEX 58M in the Philippines. The exercise lasts until 13 March.

14 February
Civil Support
The 6th Truck Company, a reserve unit located in Scranton, Pennsylvania, assists in the rescue of motorists stranded on the Pennsylvania Turnpike by a severe blizzard.

9 March
Indonesia
Company C, 1/3, VMA-332, and HMR(L)-163 deploy with elements of the Seventh Fleet off Indonesia to protect U.S. citizens and interests.

10 April
Training
RLT 4 begins a three-day anti-guerrilla field exercise in the Kahuku Training Area in northern Oahu, Hawaii.

23 April
Reserve
Commandant Pate orders the formation of 12 helicopter (HMR-761 through HMR-772) and 9 fixed-wing (VMF-131, 133, 134, 413, 511, 534, and VMA-243, 341, 611) squadrons in the Marine Corps Reserve. The helicopter squadrons are the first of their type in the Reserve

25 April
Civil Support
Company M, 3/2 helps fight brush and forest fires in Hyde County, North Carolina.

1 May
Mediterranean
BLT 2/2 and HMR(L)-262 deploy as the landing force Sixth Fleet. This marks one of the infrequent deployments of helicopters with the landing force. The two units will return home on 17 October.

13 May
Venezuela
BLT 1/6 and elements of MAG-26 and MAG-35 deploy with a naval task force off the coast to protect Vice President Richard M. Nixon and party after Venezuelan mobs threaten them during a state visit.

14 May
Mediterranean
Due to deteriorating political conditions in Lebanon, BLT 1/8 remains on station at the conclusion of its normal tour with the Sixth Fleet to reinforce newly arriving BLT 2/2.

1 June
Force Structure
The 2nd Amphibious Reconnaissance Company at Camp Lejeune is redesignated the 2nd Force Reconnaissance Company.

27 June
Cuba
A group of Marines and sailors returning from liberty are kidnaped by Raul Castro, brother of rebel leader Fidel Castro. The Americans are held until 18 July.

30 June
Manpower
The strength of the Marine Corps on active duty is 16,471 officers and 172,754 enlisted.

1 July
Bases
Marine Corps Air Station Miami is closed.

12 July
Civil Support
More than 1,500 Marines from the 1st Marine Division and Camp Pendleton help Forest Service personnel in fighting fires in California's Cleveland National Forest.

14 July
Lebanon
President Camille Chamoun appeals to the United States and Britain for assistance in combating Syrian influence in his country and preventing civil war between Christian Maronites and Muslims.

President Eisenhower orders the three Marine BLTs afloat in the Mediterranean to intervene.

15 July
Lebanon
BLT 2/2 lands at Red Beach, just south of Beirut. The rifle companies set up a perimeter just inland at the city's international airport. BLT 2/8 begins an air movement toward Lebanon.

16 July
Lebanon
BLT 3/6 goes ashore at Red Beach and assumes control of the airport, as BLT 2/2 moves north to take over the port facilities and secure the U.S. Embassy and key bridges.

18 July
Lebanon
BLT 1/8 lands near Juniyah, four miles north of Beirut. BLT 2/8 and the Army's 24th Airborne Brigade begin arriving at the airport.

21 July
Lebanon
BLT 3/3 sails from Okinawa for the Mediterranean, but never goes ashore in Lebanon.

14 August
Lebanon
Following elections on 31 July that ease tensions, BLT 2/2 goes back on board ships and reconstitutes the landing force of the Sixth Fleet.

23 August
Heritage
The Marine Corps Drum and Bugle Corps, the Marine Corps Recruit Depot Parris Island band, and a ceremonial troop unit deploy to Scotland to participate in the annual Edinburgh Tattoo. The Marines return home on 13 September.

1 September
Force Structure
HMR(M)-463 is commissioned at Santa Ana, California.

2 September
Training
RLTs 1 and 5, 3/7, and MAGs 33 and 36 participate in PHIBLEX 2-59 at Camp Pendleton. The exercise lasts through 14 September.
Force Structure
HMR-773 and 774 are activated as part of the Marine Corps Reserve.

22–24 August
Training
Operation Charger, the largest reserve exercise conducted to date, takes place at 29 Palms. It involves 13 ground units and 9 squadrons, plus regular forces from Force Troops, 1st Marine Division, and 3rd MAW.

5 September
Aviation
LtCol Thomas H. Miller sets a new world speed record of 1,216.78 miles per hour over a 500-kilometer course in a McDonnell F4H-1 Phantom II.

11 September
Mishap
Hurricane Donna causes a half million dollars of damage to Camp Lejeune.

12 September
Heritage
The Marine Corps Museum is officially opened at Quantico.

14 September
Caribbean
VMF-122, already deployed in support of the 8th Marine Expeditionary Unit, takes up station at Roosevelt Roads, Puerto Rico, and remains there until 11 June 1961.

17 September
Technology
The Navy launches *Iwo Jima* (LPH-2), its first helicopter carrier built from the keel up. In addition to an entire squadron of helicopters, it can carry 2,000 Marines.

1 October
Force Structure
VMA-242 is reactivated at Cherry Point.

6 October
Manpower
Unaccompanied tours (without dependents) with FMF units in the Far East are reduced from 15 months to 13.

12 October
Force Structure
1st Force Reconnaissance Company begins to deploy elements as part of the transplacement rotation of units to Okinawa.

20 October
Caribbean
BLT 2/2, VMA-331, and HMR(L)-261 depart for standby duty at Vieques. They will return to North Carolina on 17 January 1961.

15 November
Force Structure
The 24th Expeditionary Unit is activated at Camp

Lejeune. It consists of an infantry battalion and a provisional MAG with a light helicopter squadron and a fixed-wing attack squadron.

30 November
Africa
Company G of 2/6 and HMR(L)-264 sail from North Carolina to conduct Operation Solant Amity, a goodwill tour of the continent. They will return to the United States on 15 May 1961.

15 December
Training
The Marine Corps abolishes drill based on eight-man units (the old squad prior to WWII) and reestablishes drill as conducted in the Landing Party Manual.

23 December
Technology
VMF-334 receives the Marine Corps first 2N model of the Chance Vought F8U Crusader.

1961

1 January
Force Structure
In a change to the transplacement rotation system, infantry battalions joining the 3rd Marine Division in Okinawa must now swap designations with the unit they are replacing. Although it solves the confusion inherent in a battalion serving with a different regiment (such as 1/5 under the 3rd Marines), it undercuts the traditional ties between personnel and an identified unit history.

3 January
Cuba
The United States formally terminates diplomatic relations with the Castro regime, as a result of ever-increasing tensions with the Caribbean nation. President Eisenhower already has vowed to defend the base at Guantanamo Bay with force, if necessary.

Opposite: *Troops rush from their helicopters into the landing zone. (National Archives)*

Right: *A patrol searches a village for Viet Cong in 1965. (National Archives)*

22 April
Vietnam
On Easter Sunday, HMM-362 conducts its first combat operation, lifting elements of the Vietnamese 7th Division.

23 April
Vietnam
HMM-362 makes its first sorties in support of Vietnamese Marines.

28 April
Sports
Marine Dave Tork of Camp Pendleton sets a world record in the pole vault with a jump of 16 feet, 2 inches, at the Mt. San Antonio Relays in Walnut, California.

9 May
Vietnam
Eight Marine helicopters are hit by small arms fire during a landing on the Ca Mau Peninsula.

12 May
Indochina
In response to an alarming string of Communist military victories during May in Laos, President Kennedy orders U.S. forces toward Southeast Asia.

18 May
Indochina
The 3rd MEB begins arriving in Thailand as part of the task force sent to Indochina in response to the deteriorating situation in Laos. The first elements on the ground at the Udorn airfield are the 20 A4 Skyhawks of VMA-332, which fly in from the Philippines. The Seventh Fleet landing force (BLT 3/9 and HMM-261) goes ashore at Bangkok and moves to Udorn.

1 June
Force Structure
1/22 is reactivated at Camp Lejeune.

29 June
Sergeants Major
Sergeant Major Thomas J. McHugh succeeds Sergeant Major Bauber as the third Sergeant Major of the Marine Corps.
Technology
VMF(AW)-314 at El Toro is the first Marine squadron to receive the F4H-1 Phantom II fighter.

30 June
Manpower
The strength of the Marine Corps on active duty is 16,861 officers and 174,101 enlisted.

1 July
Reserve
The entire Marine Corps Reserve is restructured from independent battalions and squadrons to form a complete 4th Marine Division and 4th MAW that can be activated as fully manned complements to the three regular division-wing teams. Among the newly reestablished units are the division and wing headquarters, the 23rd, 24th, and 25th Marines (infantry), the 14th Marines (artillery), and MAG-41, 43, and 46.
Indochina
Roughly 1,000 Marines of 3rd MEB in Thailand move back on board their ships as part of negotiations for a settlement in Laos.

14 July
Okinawa
Camp Koza, former home of the 3rd Pioneer Battalion, is returned to civilian control and use.

27 July
Indochina
As part of a settlement guaranteeing the future neutrality of Laos, U.S. forces resume their withdrawal from Thailand. The last Marines depart three days later.

1 August
Vietnam
HMM-163 replaces HMM-362 as the Shufly squadron.

4 September
Vietnam
The Shufly force begins displacing to Da Nang in the I Corps Tactical Zone in northern South Vietnam. The move is complete on the 20th.
30 September
Force Structure
HMM-265 is commissioned at New River.

6 October
Vietnam
Five Marines and two Navy medical personnel die in an accidental crash of a Shufly helicopter. They are the first Marines to die in the Vietnam War.

19 October
Cuba
Following the discovery of Soviet offensive nuclear missiles in Cuba, Marine units begin to receive alert orders. Nine hours after that order, 2/1 is ready to fly from El Toro and it does so the next day.

21 October
Cuba
Elements of the 1st and 2nd Marine Divisions begin arriving at Guantanamo Bay to reinforce the garrison there.

22 October
Cuba
President Kennedy publicly announces a quarantine to force Soviet withdrawal of missiles

Left: *A patrol from 2/3 moves along a shallow river in Vietnam. (National Archives)*

Opposite: *Marines sweep toward a Vietnamese village in June 1965. (National Archives)*

from Cuba. The 5th MEB (over 11,000 troops) is prepared to sail from San Diego for the Caribbean.

28 October
Cuba
5th MEB sails from San Diego. Most of the 2nd Marine Division and major elements of MAG-14, 24, 26, 31, and 32 are deployed to Key West and the Caribbean for a possible invasion of Cuba.

2 November
Aviation
Lieutenant Colonel John Glenn is the first recipient of the Cunningham Trophy, presented by the First Marine Aviation Force Veterans Association to the outstanding Marine pilot of the year.

13 November
Guam
400 Marines of 3/4 fly from Hawaii to Guam to provide assistance following a typhoon.

20 November
Cuba
The United States ends the naval quarantine following an agreement for the withdrawal of Soviet offensive missiles. Marine units deployed for the Cuban Missile Crisis soon begin returning to their home stations.

1963

11 January
Vietnam
HMM-162 replaces HMM-163 in the Shufly force.

6 February
Heritage
As part of his emphasis on national physical fitness, President Kennedy challenges Marine officers to fulfill President Theodore Roosevelt's 1908 executive order that Marine officers serving in Washington complete a 50-mile hike within 20 hours of marching over three days. Twenty officers at Camp Lejeune immediately make plans to take on the challenge.

13 February
Africa
Fifty-three Marines from Camp Lejeune deploy on board *Spiegal Grove* (LSD-32) for a 14-week goodwill tour of the continent dubbed Solant Amity IV.

29 March
Force Structure
VMGR-353 is deactivated at Cherry Point. It is reactivated on 3 August as a reserve squadron.

13 April
Vietnam
Marine transport helicopters conduct their first mission with U.S. Army UH-1B helicopter gunships.

30 April
Haiti
The Marine Corps training mission is withdrawn at the request of the Haitian government.

4 May
Haiti
BLT 2/2, while on a training cruise in the Caribbean, takes station off the coast of Haiti during political unrest there. It remains in the area for five days.

8 June
Vietnam
HMM-261 replaces HMM-162 as the Shufly force.

15–24 June
Training
The 11th MEB, including RLT 3 (USMC) and RLT 2 (KMC), conducts a joint amphibious exercise around Pohang, South Korea.

30 June
Manpower
The strength of the Marine Corps on active duty is 16,737 officers and 172,946 enlisted.

1 July
Force Structure
VMF(AW)-114 is deactivated in Japan. HMM-365 is activated at Santa Ana.

1 August
Force Structure
Marine all-weather squadrons equipped with the F4B Phantom are redesignated as fighter/attack squadrons. They become VMFA-314, 513, and 531.

2 October
Vietnam
HMM-361 replaces HMM-261 as the Shufly force.

7 October
Bases
The Marine Corps' Cold Weather Training Center at Bridgeport, California, is renamed the Mountain Warfare Training Center.

Left: *Marines take a knee as they approach suspected Viet Cong positions. (National Archives)*

Opposite: *Sgt David K. Costa of 3/4 crosses a foot bridge near Phu Bai. (National Archives)*

1 February
Vietnam
HMM-364 replaces HMM-361 as the Shufly force.

6 February
Cuba
The Cuban government cuts off the water supply to the U.S. base at Guantanamo Bay.

3 March
Training
VII MEF (composed of units from the 1st and 3rd Marine Divisions, the 1st Marine Brigade, and 1st MAW) joins with Nationalist Chinese forces to conduct Exercise Backpack in Taiwan.

23 March
Training
The 1st Marines engage in a 12-day counter-guerrilla exercise on board Camp Pendleton.

April
Technology
The mortar batteries of 1/12 and 3/12 on Okinawa receive the new M98 107mm mortar, dubbed the Howtar for its artillery-like wheeled mount.

27 April
Vietnam
HMM-364 lifts Vietnamese troops during Operation Sure Wind 202 in northern II Corps.

30 April
Heritage
The last Marine officer to serve during WWI retires. Chief Warrant Officer Percy L. Smith had enlisted in April 1916 at the age of 16.

20 May
Vietnam
Marine Advisory Team One arrives in Vietnam. Headed by Major Alfred M. Gray, Jr., its 30 communicators and 76 infantrymen (the latter of Company G, 2/3) become the first Marine ground unit to operate as a unit in the Vietnam War. It provides radio support to South Vietnamese forces.

20 October
Haiti
HMM-162 arrives in Port-au-Prince Bay on board *Thetis Bay* to deliver food and supplies to hurricane-stricken areas of southern Haiti.

1 November
Vietnam
The government of South Vietnam is overthrown in a military coup and President Diem is killed.

15 November
Vietnam
USMACV announces that 1,000 of the 16,575 U.S. military personnel in Vietnam will be withdrawn due to progress made in training the South Vietnamese armed forces. The first 220 servicemen depart on 3 December.

24 November
Vietnam
Two days after President Kennedy's assassination, President Lyndon B. Johnson affirms continued military support for South Vietnam against Communist aggression.

31 December
Commandants
General Shoup retires and is replaced by General Wallace M. Greene, Jr., the 23rd Commandant of the Marine Corps. One of Greene's first official duties is a trip to South Vietnam.

1–20 June
Training
Company I, 3/6 participates in a NATO exercise dubbed Northern Express in Norway, 300 miles above the Arctic Circle.

4 June
Training
A massive amphibious and airborne assault on the island of Mindoro caps SEATO Exercise Ligta. U.S. Marines and troops from Australia, France, New Zealand, the Philippines, and Great Britain participate.

20 June
Commanders
Army Lieutenant General William C. Westmoreland assumes command of USMACV in Vietnam.

21 June
Vietnam
HMM-162 replaces HMM-364 as the Shufly force. The latter squadron turns over all its helicopters to a Vietnamese air force squadron.

28 June
Aviation
VMFA-531 arrives for duty in the Far East after flying from its home station of Cherry Point, with stops at El Toro, Hawaii, and Wake Island, and aerial refueling across the rest of the Pacific.

30 June
Manpower
The strength of the Marine Corps on active duty is 16,843 officers and 172,934 enlisted.

1 July
Force Structure
HMM-164 is activated at Santa Ana, California. It will receive the new Boeing CH-46 Sea Knight helicopter.

7 July
Vietnam
HMM-162 participates in the relief of the Nam Dong Special Forces Camp.

17 July
Vietnam
Marine Advisory Team One fends off a Communist assault on its perimeter atop Tiger Tooth Mountain.

28 July
Vietnam
The United States announces it will send an additional 5,000 troops to South Vietnam.

30 July
Cuba
The Guantanamo Bay Navy base dedicates a new plant that produces fresh water.

1 August
Training
The Marine Corps Schools renames the Senior Course as Marine Corps Command and Staff College and the Junior Course as Amphibious Warfare School.

2–5 August
Vietnam
North Vietnamese patrol boats attack U.S. warships in what will become known as the Tonkin Gulf Incident.

Opposite: *A Marine from 2/9 searches a house south of Da Nang in 1965. (National Archives)*

Right: *A sniper with a Winchester Model 70 rifle scans for a target. (National Archives)*

5 August
Vietnam
In retaliation for the naval attacks, U.S. aircraft bomb North Vietnamese naval targets and an oil storage depot.

7 August
Vietnam
Congress passes the Tonkin Gulf Resolution, which authorizes President Johnson to use military force in Vietnam.

17 August
Bases
Edson Range opens at Camp Pendleton as a replacement for Camp Calvin B. Matthews, closed four days later due to urbanization around the San Diego area weapons training facility.

13 September
Vietnam
Marine Advisory Team One dissolves and departs the country.

8 October
Vietnam
HMM-365 replaces HMM-364 as the Shufly force.

14 October
Sports
First Lieutenant Billy Mills wins the gold medal in the 10,000 meter race at the Tokyo Olympics.

26 October
Training
Exercise Steel Pike I begins in Spain with 22,000 Marines, 33,000 sailors, and 2,000 Spanish Marines.

17–23 November
Vietnam
HMM-365 off *Princeton* and HMM-162 assist flood victims in central South Vietnam.

26 November
Egypt
A mob protesting U.S. policies in the Congo attack the U.S. Embassy compound, burning portions of, including the Marine Guard facility.

1965

1 February
Training
Operation Snowfex-65 begins at Fort Drum, New York, and lasts for a month. It is billed as the largest Marine Corps cold weather training exercise on the east coast since the 1940s. Participating units are 1/8, VMGR-252, and HMM-265.
Force Structure
MAG-42 is reactivated at Alameda, California, as part of 4th MAW.

8 February
Da Nang
Following Viet Cong attacks on U.S. forces and camps in South Vietnam, President Johnson orders the deployment of the 1st LAAM Battalion to the Da Nang area. Battery A arrives this day.

12 February
Training
In the largest Marine exercise since WWII, 25,000 Marines and 20,000 sailors conduct Operation Silver Lance at Camp Pendleton. It lasts through 9 March.

17 February
Vietnam
HMM-163 relieves HMM-365 as the Shufly force.

A company of the 7th Engineer Battalion arrives in Da Nang.

8 March
Da Nang
The 9th MEB begins arriving in Vietnam with the mission of defending the airbase at Da Nang. BLT 3/9 comes by sea and BLT 1/3 follows by air from Okinawa. The MEB is the first U.S. ground combat unit in country.

9 March
Da Nang
HMM-163 of Shufly and 1st LAAM Battalion are placed under operational control of the MEB. HMM-162 arrives. All three units become part of MAG-16.

29 March
Saigon
Following a bomb explosion outside the U.S. Embassy, the Marine Security Guard detachment restores order and safeguards the compound.

10 April
Da Nang
BLT 2/3 goes ashore to reinforce 9th MEB, while VMFA-531 flies onto the airfield. A company of 2/3 helicopters to the airbase at Phu Bai, about 50 miles north of Da Nang, near Hue City.

12 April
Da Nang
The headquarters of the 3rd Marines joins the brigade to serve as the command element of the BLTs.

13 April
Vietnam
VMFA-531 flies its first combat missions in Vietnam.

14 April
Phu Bai
BLT 3/4 arrives and relieves the company of 2/3 around the air base.

16 April
Da Nang
The electronic countermeasure EF-10B Skyknights of Marine Composite Reconnaissance Squadron 1 (VMCJ-1) arrive.

20 April
Vietnam
General Westmoreland authorizes 9th MEB forces to conduct aggressive patrolling and prepare to act as a mobile reaction force. The MEB now numbers more than 8,600 men.

22 April
Da Nang
In 9th MEB's first significant contact, a patrol engages Viet Cong forces, killing one enemy and suffering one wounded. A company of 1/3 sent to reinforce the patrol makes the first Marine helicopter assault of the war.

27 April
Dominican Republic
Following a coup and fighting, HMM-264 evacuates 556 American citizens to U.S. warships off the coast.

28 April
Dominican Republic
Elements of BLT 3/6 goes ashore by helicopter to guard the U.S. Embassy and protect American lives in the city of Santo Domingo. The remainder of the BLT lands the next day. U.S. Army forces also begin to deploy soon after.

30 April
Dominican Republic
Two Marines are killed in street fighting as BLT 3/6 seeks to clear part of the city of Dominican fighters.

1 May
Dominican Republic
4th MEB begins arriving by sea and air from North Carolina. It brings the total Marine force in country to over 5,500 men. Another Marine is killed and three wounded.

3 May
Dominican Republic
The Marine detachment of *Newport News* goes ashore to reinforce 3/6. It is the first ship's detachment to land in a combat role since 1945.

6 May
Vietnam
9th MEB dissolves and III MEF assumes command of Marine forces in the I Corps zone. The 3rd Marine Division headquarters assumes command of ground elements. The MEF is redesignated as III Marine Amphibious Force (III MAF) the next day. Amphibious is substituted for expeditionary in all Marine designations as a result of a request from General Westmoreland due to the connotations of the French Expeditionary Force in an earlier Vietnam intervention.

7 May
Chu Lai
The 3rd MAB (RLT 4, MAG-12, 3rd Reconnaissance Battalion, and Naval Mobile Construction Battalion 10) begins landing at Chu Lai, on the coast about 50 miles south of Da Nang. The MAB will construct an expeditionary airfield here.

11 May
Da Nang
Elements of 2/3 clear the village of Le My and establish a civic action program to assist the population. The 1st MAW headquarters arrives to assume command of Marine aviation elements.

12 May
Chu Lai
With the arrival of BLT 3/3, all of 3rd MAB is in country. It is dissolved and its forces assigned to III MAF. Marine forces in Vietnam now total over 17,500.

25 May
Dominican Republic
U.S. mediation leads to a truce between Dominican factions. Marine units begin departing the next day.

1 June
Chu Lai
Skyhawks of VMA-225 and 311 land on the recently completed SATS field, the first use of this concept in a combat theater. They conduct air strikes from their new base this same day.

3 June
Dominican Republic
President Johnson orders the withdrawal of the 2,100 Marines remaining in country. Total Marines casualties during the intervention were nine dead and 30 wounded.

4 June
Commanders
Major General Lewis W. Walt assumes command of III MAF and 3rd Marine Division.
Vietnam
In several company-sized actions around Da Nang and Phu Bai, Marines engage in their first major ground combat. At a cost of two dead and 19 wounded, they kill 79 Viet Cong.

15 June
Da Nang
VMFA-513 relieves VMFA-531, which departs Vietnam.

17 June
Da Nang
1/9 relieves 3/9, which returns to Okinawa.

21 June
Da Nang
HMM-261 relieves HMM-163, which becomes the transport squadron for the Special Landing Force at sea.

25 June
Mishap
A Vietnam-bound military transport plane crashes after takeoff from El Toro, killing 79 Marines.

30 June
Manpower
The strength of the Marine Corps on active duty is 17,258 officers and 172,955 enlisted. There are 18,156 Marines in Vietnam, with a total U.S. deployment there in excess of 50,000.

120 wounded.

7 March
Manpower
Secretary of Defense Robert McNamara requests an increase in the Corps to 278,184 Marines by mid-1967. If approved, this would make the Corps the only service to grow larger than its maximum size during the Korean War.

8 March
Da Nang
HMM-164 arrives in country with the first CH-46 helicopters to reach Vietnam.

8–17 March
Training
3/6 operates above Norway's Arctic Circle in Winter Express, the largest cold weather exercise held by NATO to date.

9–12 March
A Shau Valley
Communist forces overrun a Special Forces camp. Helicopters of HMM-163 and VMO-2 take losses in pulling out many of the survivors under heavy antiaircraft fire.

10 March
Vietnam
Following the dismissal of the Vietnamese general commanding I Corps Zone, political unrest

sweeps over South Vietnam. It lasts into June and seriously hampers the war effort.

15 March
Vietnam
III MAF stands up Force Logistics Command, composed of the 1st and 3rd Service Battalions and elements of 3rd Force Service Regiment, to support Marines in country.

20–25 March
Operation Texas
Along with an ARVN regiment, 3/7, 2/4, and 3/1 engage elements of two Communist regiments deeply entrenched in a village northwest of Quang Ngai. With the assistance of air and artillery support, the Marines kill 283 enemy at a cost of 99 dead and 212 wounded.

26 March
Operation Jack Stay
The SLF, BLT 1/5, conducts the first Marine ground action in the Saigon area, clearing enemy from the river delta southeast of the Vietnamese capital. The heliborne and riverine operation lasts through 6 April.

29 March
Chu Lai
The 1st Marine Division headquarters formally begins to operate in Vietnam. For the first time since WWII, the Corps has two of its divisions

SERGEANT MAJOR EDGAR R. HUFF

A natural leader, SgtMaj Edgar Huff served in combat in WWII, Korea, and Vietnam and earned a lasting reputation as one of the outstanding staff noncommissioned officers in the long history of the Corps. (National Archives)

Edgar Huff was born on 2 December 1919 near Gadsden, Alabama. His father, who had served in the Army Signal Corps in World War I, died soon after from complications arising out of being gassed in combat. Huff grew up in poverty, and had to quit school at 16 to help out when his mother fell ill. He was walking five miles to work each day at a steel mill in 1942 when President Roosevelt decreed that the Marines would begin enlisting African-Americans. Huff was one of the first to join. When things seemed toughest in the first few days at Montford Point, North Carolina, and drill instructors dared the new enlistees to quit, the tall burly Alabaman convinced his fellow recruits to persevere with the vow that he himself would "stick to it like a bulldog to a dug in on Hills 861, 881 South, and 881 North lasts through 13 May. The Marines kill 940 enemy and capture six at a cost of 155 dead and 425 wounded. 1st MAW flies over 1,100 close air support sorties, while artillery units fire 25,000 rounds.

26 April
Vietnam

The headquarters of the 26th Marines arrives in country.

28 April
Operation Beaver Cage

SLF Alpha (one of two now afloat with the Seventh Fleet) makes a landing into the Que Son Valley. BLT 1/3 and HMM-263 sweep the area through 12 May, accounting for 181 enemy killed and 66 captured. Marines casualties are 55 killed and 151 wounded.

8 May
Con Thien

North Vietnamese forces attack the Marine base near the DMZ on the 13th anniversary of their victory at Dien Bien Phu. Elements of 1/4 drive off the enemy, killing 197 and capturing eight at a cost of 44 dead and 110 wounded.

13 May
Khe Sanh

The 26th Marines headquarters and 1/26 assume the defense of the base. They launch Operation Crockett to prevent the NVA from building up forces in the area. It lasts until 16 July and kills 206 enemy. Marines losses are 52 dead and 255 wounded.

18 May
DMZ

Marine forces launch three simultaneous operations to make their first sweep through the southern half of the DMZ. SLF Alpha (BLT 1/3 and HMM-263) lands under the code name Beau Charger along the coast. 2/26, 2/9, 3/9, and 3/4 begin a sweep of the area around Con Thien under the code name Hickory. Two days later, SLF Bravo (BLT 2/3 and HMM-164) lands northeast of Con Thien under the code name Belt Tight. The operations wind up on 26 May. The Marines kill 447 enemy but lose 142 killed and 896 wounded.

Operation Rolling Thunder

VMA(AW)-242 flies the first Marine mission in support of Seventh Air Force's strategic bombing campaign in North Vietnam.

25 May
Operation Union II

The 5th Marines and the ARVN 1st Ranger Group conduct search and destroy operations in Quang Nam and Quang Tin Provinces. By the time it ends on 6 June, it accounts for 701 enemy killed. Marine losses are 110 dead and 241 wounded.

31 May
Commanders

Lieutenant General Robert E. Cushman takes over III MAF in place of Lieutenant General Walt.

23 June
Mishap

Twenty Marines die when two helicopters collide over Camp Lejeune.

30 June
Manpower

The strength of the Marine Corps on active duty is 23,592 officers and 261,677 enlisted.

Left: *Marines use Vietnamese sampans in January 1967. (National Archives)*

2 July
Operation Buffalo
1/9 conducts a sweep north from Con Thien and makes heavy contact. Both SLF Alpha (1/3) and Bravo (2/3) and 3/9 move to reinforce. By the time the battle dies out on 14 July, the Marines have killed 1,301 of the enemy and lost 113 dead and 290 wounded.

7 July
Manpower
To meet the need for captains, time-in-grade for first lieutenants to become eligible for promotion drops from two years to one.

15 July
Da Nang
More than 50 122mm rockets hit the airbase early in the morning, killing eight, wounding 175, and destroying or damaging 42 aircraft.

16 July
Operation Kingfisher
The 3rd and 9th Marines launch a series of sweeps in the vicinity of Dong Ha and Cam Lo that last through 31 October. At a cost of 340 Marines dead and 1,461 wounded, the operation killed 1,117 enemy.

24 July
Operation Rolling Thunder
Marine jets strike the Thai Nguyen power plant 30 miles north of Hanoi.

31 July
Training
In one of the largest amphibious landings ever conducted at Camp Pendleton, regular and reserve units conduct Exercise Golden Slipper to test the integration of the two.

1 August
Vietnam
There are now about 78,000 Marines in country.

19 August
Vietnam
Captain Stephen W. Pless, flying a Huey gunship, rescues four American soldiers from a beach where they are being attacked by dozens of Viet Cong. After driving back the enemy with low-level strafing runs, he lands and picks up the men, then strikes the water four times as he struggles to get the overloaded helicopter safely airborne. He subsequently receives the Medal of Honor for his intrepidity, while his three crewmen receive the Navy Cross.

28 August
Vietnam
The enemy makes heavy artillery and rocket attacks on Dong Ha and the airbase at Marble Mountain. Ten marines die and 49 aircraft are damaged or destroyed.

30 August
Phu Bai
An enemy mortar attack damages 18 helicopters and causes 57 Marine casualties.

September
Aviation
All CH-46s are grounded due to unexplained accidents, which turn out to result from structural failure in the aft rotor pylon. The situation is not resolved until December.

3 September
Dong Ha
A Communist artillery barrage destroys the ammunition dump and fuel farm and damages 17 helicopters of HMM-361. Thereafter no more helicopters are based here.

4–15 September
Operation Swift
A 5th Marines search and destroy operation in the Que Son Basin kills 571 enemy at a cost of 127 dead and 352 wounded.

18 September
Vietnam
Monsoon rains and resulting floods kill 10 Marines and make it difficult to supply bases near the DMZ.

Right: A M60 machine gunner takes the enemy under fire. (National Archives)

25 September
Con Thien
In one of the heaviest Communist barrages of the war, more than 1,000 artillery rounds strike the base. Although 202 Marines are wounded, only two are killed.

4 October
Vietnam
More Marine units shift north toward the DMZ when a brigade of the Army's 1st Air Cavalry Division replaces them in Quang Tin and Quang Ngai Provinces.

5 October
Mishap
Marine astronaut Maj Clifton C. Williams, Jr., dies when his T-38 jet trainer crashes in Florida.

24 October
Operation Rolling Thunder
Marine jets participate in a joint-service raid on Phuc Yen Airfield in North Vietnam. The attack destroys 10 MIGs.

27 October
Manpower
DOD announces a plan to double the number of African-American officers in the Marine Corps, from its present 155 (less than one percent).

GUNNERY SERGEANT JIMMIE E. HOWARD

Jimmie Earl Howard had made the all-state high school football squad in Iowa in the late 1940s. The 6-foot, 3-inch, 235-pound tackle earned a college scholarship, but dropped out of school after one year to enlist in the Marines just after the Korean War broke out in 1950. He performed so well at boot camp that he was promoted to PFC at graduation and made a drill instructor. He joined the 1st Marine Regiment in Korea in 1952 as a mortar forward observer. In 13 months of bitter trench warfare with the Chinese, he earned two Purple Hearts, as well as a Silver Star for bravery in the fight for the combat outpost at Bunker Hill. During the relatively peaceful dozen years that followed, he alternated tours in reconnaissance with stints coaching Marine football teams.

Staff Sergeant Howard joined Company C, 1st Reconnaissance Battalion, 1st Marine Division, in Vietnam in 1966. He was serving as an acting platoon commander when helicopters dropped him and 17 other men on a peak west of Chu Lai on 13 June. Their orders were to watch for enemy infiltration in the rugged area and call in air or artillery to strike the Communist formations. They successfully carried out that mission for the next two days, but a North Vietnamese battalion moved into position around the base of the mountain during the afternoon and evening of the 15th. Alerted to the danger by an Army Special Forces patrol, the recon team prepared for an onslaught that night.

The enemy launched their first attack at 2200. The Marines repelled that assault, and then another, but most of them had been hit by bullets or shrapnel by now. They also were running low on ammunition. Senior leaders in the rear arranged for strong aerial support, which arrived around 0100. Under Howard's direction and the light of flares, jets and Huey gunships alternated attacks on the hundreds of North Vietnamese arrayed on the slopes of the mountain. Bombs, napalm, rockets, and machine guns battered the Communist infantrymen. In the lulls between Marine air attacks, South Vietnamese artillery blasted the approaches to the summit.

Hit in the back by a bullet around 0300, Howard refused a morphine injection so he could stay alert and remain in command. He continued to encourage his men as he had all night. In between the first two major enemy assaults, he had urged his Marines to laugh out loud in response to the shouted threats and taunts of the surrounding Communists. When the Marines ran short of grenades, he had them throw rocks to simulate the explosive missiles. A little before first light, he called out to his surviving men: "OK, you people, reveille goes in 35 minutes."

A company from the 5th Marines landed by helicopter near Howard's Hill after sunrise. They quickly swept through scattered resistance to reach the peak, where the recon platoon commander directed their subsequent operations until the entire position was secure. Six recon Marines had died, along with two men from the relief company and two helicopter crewmen. But together, the Marine infantrymen and aviators had savaged a North Vietnamese battalion.

Cpl Jimmie Howard receives a Silver Star for bravery in the fight for Bunker Hill in Korea. Nearly 15 years later he would earn the Medal of Honor for more courage on another hilltop, this time in Vietnam. (Marine Corps Historical Center)

Ricardo Binns, John Adams, Jerrald Thompson, and Navy Corpsman Billie Don Holmes received Navy Crosses, while every other member of the patrol was awarded a Silver Star. Howard received the Medal of Honor in a White House ceremony. In praising the feat of the small band of Marines, President Lyndon Johnson harked back to the famous last stands of the Spartans at Thermopylae and the Texans at the Alamo. This time, though, the defenders had won. For his part, Howard gave all the credit to his men, "That's the guys who did it."

Howard volunteered to return for another tour in Vietnam in 1969. He retired from the Corps in 1972 and worked as a counselor for the Veterans Administration. He died in 1993.

1 November
Da Nang
During a visit to III MAF, Vice President Hubert Humphrey presents the presidential Unit Citation to 3rd Marine Division for its performance along the DMZ.
Operation Lancaster
The 9th Marines launches a series of search and destroy operations around Camp Carroll that last through 20 January 1968.

6 November
Operation Essex
A search and destroy operation by 2/5 in Antenna Valley near An Hoa kills 72 enemy at a cost of 37 Marine dead and 122 wounded.

8 November
Manpower
President Johnson signs a bill giving women equal promotion opportunity in the military services.

13–30 November
Operations Foster and Badger Hunt
3/7 and BLT 2/3 sweep the area west of An Hoa, killing 125 enemy. Marine losses are 21 dead and 137 wounded.

14 November
Mishap
Major General Bruno A Hochmuth, commander of the 3rd Marine Division, dies in a helicopter crash near Hue.

13 December
Khe Sanh
3/26 arrives at the base to reinforce it during a period of increasing enemy activity.

17 December
Vietnam
Captain Doyle D. Baker, flying an exchange tour with the Air Force's 13th Tactical Fighter Squadron, destroys a MIG-17 with cannon fire and a missile while escorting a bombing mission over North Vietnam. He is the first Marine pilot to score an aerial victory in the war.

26 December
Operation Rolling Thunder
Marine jets attack targets near Hanoi and Dong Hoi.

31 December
Vietnam
Of the 478,000 U.S. troops in country, 81,249 are Marines. III MAF has 114,158 personnel, of which

Left: "*Secondaries at Khe Sanh,*" *Larry Zabel, Naval Art Collection*

Opposite: "*Marine Bombers at Twilight,*" *John Steele, Naval Art Collection*

76,616 are Marines. Marine casualties during the year total 3,461 dead and 25,525 wounded. The III MAF effort to build a strongpoint barrier system along the DMZ, directed by USMACV, has consumed more 757,000 man-days during 1967.

Commandants

General Greene retires and is replaced by General Leonard F. Chapman, Jr., the 24th Commandant of the Marine Corps. He departs on 3 January for an inspection trip of Marine forces in Vietnam.

1968

6 January
Khe Sanh
General Westmoreland begins Operation Niagara, a plan to use heavy firepower to destroy enemy units building up around the Marine combat base.

8 January
Mishap
A CH-53 crash kills 36 Marines and five others in Vietnam.

11 January
Mishap
A Quantico-based transport crashes in Nevada, killing all 19 Marines on board.

16 January
Khe Sanh
2/26 flies into the base, placing the entire 26th Marines there.
Vietnam
The North Vietnamese state that they will not begin negotiations to end the war until the United States halts the bombing of North Vietnam.
Cuba
In a change of policy, 2/8 moves to Guantanamo Bay to become the permanent defense force. Instead of rotating battalions every 90 days, personnel will now be rotated into 2/8.

19 January
Khe Sanh
A platoon patrolling toward Hill 881 North has to withdraw in the face of strong enemy opposition. This marks the beginning of the siege of the remote combat base.

20 January
Khe Sanh
Company I, 3/26 kills an estimated 100 NVA and loses seven killed and 35 wounded in an attempt to clear Hill 881 North. The company is withdrawn after an NVA lieutenant comes into the main perimeter and reveals plans for a major assault beginning in the next few days.

21 January
Vietnam
General Westmoreland orders a temporary halt to work on the McNamara Line, the strongpoint barrier system along the DMZ. The 4th Marines begins Operation Lancaster II around Camp Carroll. The 3rd Marines begins Operation Osceola around the base at Quang Tri.
Khe Sanh
Company K, 3/26 defeats a Communist night attack on Hill 861. The NVA begins a bombardment of the combat base just before dawn. The Marines will receive incoming shells and rockets every day for the next 77 days. One shell sets off the main ammunition dump, raining exploding ordnance over much of the perimeter.

22 January
Khe Sanh
1/9 arrives to reinforce the 26th Marines.

23 January
Korea
North Korean naval forces seize the U.S. intelligence ship *Pueblo* (AGER-2) in international waters off their coast.

27 January
Vietnam
A seven-day truce begins for the Tet holiday. The ARVN 37th Ranger Battalion arrives at Khe Sanh.

30 January
Tet Offensive
Communist forces launch an offensive that spreads throughout South Vietnam by the next day. Attacks come against most major cities and province capitals. By infiltration and assault, they take control of most of Hue, the former imperial capital. An attempt to seize the U.S. Embassy in Saigon is thwarted by the Marine guards. Facilities at Da Nang are hit by rockets, mortars, and a ground assault.

1 February
Hue
1/1 and 2/5 begin operations to recapture the city. The Marines focus on the area south of the Perfume River, while the 1st ARVN Division is responsible for the Citadel, the old city north of the river. HMM-165 provides lift for ARVN forces into the city. The battle quickly devolves into typical building-to-building fighting.

5 February
Khe Sanh
Guided by ground sensors, Marine artillery blasts an enemy troop concentration, and shortly after Company E, 2/26 defeats a Communist attempt to take Hill 861A.

6 February
Hue
Marines capture the province headquarters building in Hue, pull down the Communist flag, and run up the Stars and Stripes.
Da Nang
Marines beat back another round of Communist attacks against installations and units in the area.

7 February
Khe Sanh
NVA forces using PT-76 amphibious tanks capture the Special Forces camp at Lang Vei, west of the Marine base.

8 February
Khe Sanh
Company A, 1/9 defeats an enemy attempt to capture a platoon outpost.

10 February
Hue
The 1st Marines (1/1 and 2/5) finish clearing the city south of the Perfume River. Marine casualties are 38 dead and 320 wounded, while the enemy loses over 1,000. 1/5 begins to reinforce the 1st Marines.

13 February
Hue
1/5 starts its attack on the Citadel and is soon joined by two battalions of Vietnamese Marines.

17 February
Vietnam
As part of a reinforcement package resulting from the Tet Offensive, the 27th Marines and 2/13 depart California for Vietnam.

24 February
Khe Sanh
In an effort to cut down the number of helicopters being hit by enemy fire during resupply missions to the hill posts, 1st MAW institutes the Super Gaggle.

It typically involves a KC-130 refueler, eight or more CH-46 helicopters carrying sling loads, up to 12 A-4s and four Huey gunships providing fire support, and a two-seat TA-4 with the backseater coordinating the mission. The attack aircraft would suppress enemy antiaircraft positions with napalm and tear gas, lay smoke on both sides of the helicopter path, then attack with bombs and guns anything that fired as the helicopters swooped in to drop their loads.

25 February
Hue
1/5 and Vietnamese forces complete the seizure of the Citadel, bringing the battle for the city to an end, except for mopping up operations. Total friendly casualties for the entire battle are more than 600 dead and almost 3,800 wounded, of which Marine losses are 142 dead and nearly 1,100 wounded. The number of enemy killed exceeds 1,000 and is estimated as high as 5,000.

27 February
Khe Sanh
A CH-46 is shot down near the base, resulting in 22 Marines dead and one wounded.

28 February
Khe Sanh
Two NVA battalions attempting to attack the 37th Ranger Battalion sector of the perimeter are hit by artillery fire and air support as they assemble.

6 March
Khe Sanh
Antiaircraft fire downs an Air Force C-12 transport, killing 43 Marines and five others.

10 March
Vietnam
1st MAW's fixed-wing aircraft are placed under the operational control of Seventh Air Force as the "single manager" for tactical aviation in Vietnam.

15 March
Force Structure
HML-167 is commissioned at Marble Mountain in Vietnam.

22 March
Manpower
The Marine Aviation Cadet program, which had allowed men without college degrees a chance to earn their wings, comes to an end.

30 March
Khe Sanh
Company B, 1/9 conducts a dawn attack against enemy trenches and bunkers, inflicting significant casualties. The siege is essentially ended as much of the NVA force has withdrawn. Marine casualties between 1 November 1967 and now total 205 dead and 1,668 wounded. Enemy confirmed dead are 1,602, with estimates of total casualties exceeding 10,000.

31 March
Vietnam
President Johnson announces a partial halt to the bombing of North Vietnam in an attempt to begin negotiations to end the war. He also declares an end to his campaign for reelection.

1 April
Khe Sanh
The 1st Air Cavalry Division and the 1st Marines launch Operation Pegasus to open a road link to the Marine base.

5 April
Civil Support
Three companies of Marines from Quantico and the Marine Barracks assist in quelling severe riots in Washington, D.C., following the assassination of Dr. Martin Luther King, Jr.

8 April
Khe Sanh
The siege is officially over when elements of the 1st Air Cavalry Division reach the area by road.

16 April
Force Structure
MAG-39 is activated at Quang Tri, Vietnam, as part of 1st MAW.

18 April
Khe Sanh
The 26th Marines is relieved by the 1st Marines and it moves back to Dong Ha and Camp Carroll.

30 April
Dai Do
BLT 2/4 attacks 4 NVA battalions dug in around the village of Dai Do and interdicting the Cua Viet River. The battle lasts until 3 May. Marines losses are 81 dead and almost 300 wounded, while estimated enemy dead exceed 500.

4 May
Operation Allen Brook
The 7th Marines begins a series of search and destroy missions to clear the area south of Da Nang. It last through 23 August and results in 1,017 enemy dead. Marine losses are 172 killed and 1,124 wounded.

5 May
Vietnam
In a miniature repeat of the Tet offensive, Communist forces launch rocket and mortar attacks against 119 towns and cities.

13 May
Vietnam
Peace talks begin in Paris between the United States, South Vietnam, and North Vietnam.

18 May
Operation Mameluke Thrust
The 1st Marine Division conducts search and destroy operations in central Quang Nam Province that last through 23 October, killing 2,728 enemy. Marine losses are 269 killed and 1,730 wounded.

21 May
Dong Ha
An NVA division makes an attempt to infiltrate south from the DMZ toward Dong Ha. In 10 days of fighting, the 3rd and 9th Marines drive the enemy back, killing more than 770 and taking 61 prisoners. Marine and ARVN losses are 112 dead and 446 wounded.

22 May
Technology
1st MAW makes the first use of the North American OV-10A Bronco, a light observation plane.

28 May
Khe Sanh
Companies E and F, 2/3 defeat an NVA attempt to take a hill along Route 9 near the base. At a cost of 13 dead and 44 wounded, the Marines kill 230 enemy. This is only one of a series of small battles around the base in the weeks after the siege.

1 June
Go Noi Island
In an effort to burn away the island's foliage in support of Operation Allen Brook, nine C-130s drop 31,000 gallons of fuel in drums.

26 June
Iwo Jima
The island is returned to Japanese control.

27 June
Khe Sanh
The Marine garrison begins to dismantle defenses and withdraw from the base, to be abandoned under a new operations plan for northern I Corps Zone.

30 June
Manpower
The strength of the Marine Corps on active duty is 24,555 officers and 282,697 enlisted.

1 July
Commanders
General Creighton W. Abrams replaces General Westmoreland as commander of USMACV.

Right: Echo Company, 2/7, during Operation Arizona south of Da Nang in June 1967. (National Archives)

LIEUTENANT VINCENT R. CAPODANNO, JR., USNR

The Capodanno family came from strong Italian roots. Vincent, Sr., arrived in the United States in 1900 at the age of 16, while the family of his wife, Rachel Basile, had immigrated two generations earlier. They married in New York in 1907 and moved to an Italian-American community on Staten Island. They had ten children. The last one was Vincent, Jr., born on 13 February 1929. Although Vincent grew up in a devoutly Catholic family, his initial ambition during his years in public school was to be a doctor. After graduating from high school in 1947, he went to work as a clerk with an insurance company and attended college at night. It was only in 1949 that he decided to become a priest. He was ordained in 1958 as a Maryknoll, becoming part of a society of priests dedicated to missionary work in foreign lands. It was a life that called for dedication and, not infrequently, bravery. He spent the next seven years in Taiwan and Hong Kong, mainly in remote villages.

In July 1965, he sought to join the Navy as a chaplain, specifically requesting service with the Marine units that had only recently deployed to Vietnam. He was not a complete stranger to the service, since all three of his older brothers had served during WWII, one of them in the Corps. After initial training in the Navy, and with the Field Medical School at Camp Pendleton, Lieutenant Capodanno reported to the 1st Battalion, 7th Marines at Chu Lai in April 1966.

Tall, wiry, quiet Father Capodanno wasted no time establishing a reputation as a field Marine and soon earned the nickname "Grunt Padre." As the only Catholic chaplain in the regiment, he spent much of his time rotating between the 12 rifle companies and accompanying them on operations. He explained at the time, "I want to be available in the event anything serious occurs, to learn firsthand the problems of the men, and to give them moral support, to comfort them with my presence. I feel I must personally witness how they react under fire—and experience it myself—to understand the fear that they feel." The tall, spare priest carried a load on the march just like the men. In battle, he had no hesitation in moving forward under fire to minister spiritually and physically to the wounded and dying. For numerous actions during his months with the 7th Marines, he subsequently received the Bronze Star. When he was not out in the field, he spent his time writing letters to the families of casualties and working with the villagers protected by Marine CAP units.

In December 1966, Capodanno was transferred to the 1st Medical Battalion and its field hospital near Chu Lai. Although he might have stayed exclusively in this somewhat more secure environment, he still spent a lot of time forward with combat units. Before the end of his tour in Vietnam, he requested and received a six-month extension. In July 1967 he transferred to the 5th Marines, then fighting in the Que Son Valley. Soon after he submitted paperwork for another six-month extension.

In the pre-dawn hours of 4 September, two companies of 1/5 became involved in a tough fight in Thang Binh District. By mid-morning, two companies of 3/5 helicoptered

Father Vince Capodanno, a Catholic priest and Navy chaplain, earned the nickname "Grunt Padre" for his selfless service with field Marines in Vietnam. (National Archives)

into position to reinforce the beleaguered Marines of 1/5. Chaplain Capodanno went out with them. As the men of 3/5 advanced from their landing zone to link up, they ran into strong enemy resistance. When one platoon was pinned down under heavy fire and in danger of being overrun, he went forward to their aid. He pulled a radio operator to safety, then proceeded to move through the fusillade to minister to the Marines. After being wounded in the hand, arm, and leg by mortar shrapnel, he refused aid and braved automatic weapons fire to drag a wounded sergeant to cover. Seeing a corpsman severely wounded by a machine gun just 15 meters away, Capodanno rushed forward to his assistance, placing himself between the enemy weapon and the casualty. Within moments, the chaplain was cut down and killed.

For his courageous devotion to his Marines that day, Lieutenant Capodanno was awarded the Medal of Honor, one of three Navy chaplains to receive the nation's highest decoration during the Vietnam War. He exemplified all those Navy doctors, chaplains, and corpsmen who have selflessly served the Corps.

Operation Thor
Air, artillery, and naval surface fires blanket the Cap Mui Lay area of southern North Vietnam in an effort to destroy long-range artillery located there. The operation continues through 7 July.

5 July
Khe Sanh
The combat base is closed and the last Marines depart.

22 August
Da Nang
Communist forces launch their third phase offensive with attacks on bridges, mortar barrages, and ground assaults in the area around Da Nang. They are driven off in each case before causing serious damage.

29 August
Operation Sussex Bay
The 5th and 7th Marines conduct operations to hunt down Communist forces involved in the recent attacks around Da Nang. The campaign ends on 9 September, with an estimated 2,000 enemy dead stemming from the initial Communist offensive and its aftermath.

5 September
Vietnam
Typhoon Bess strikes I Corps Zone with 50-knot winds and heavy rain. Operations are suspended for two days and defensive positions are washed out.

10 September
Vietnam
The 27th Marines begins departing Vietnam for Camp Pendleton. It is the first Marine unit to leave the war on a nonrotational basis.

16 September
Vietnam
Communist forces hit the command group of 2/26 with two mortar barrages, killing 22 and wounding 146.

29 September
Vietnam
Battleship *New Jersey* (BB-62) arrives on station off I Corps Zone and fires her first missions in support of Marines in the Vietnam War.

1 October
Manpower
Since the inception of the battlefield commissioning program in June 1965, more than 8,000 enlisted Marines have become officers.

3 October
Manpower
DOD announces that the Marine Corps will receive 2,500 of the 17,500 men to be drafted in December. This marks the first time since May that the Corps needed to resort to the draft.

5 October
Vietnam
The number of U.S. troops in country reaches 540,000, of which 84,000 are Marines.

6–19 October
Operation Maui Peak
The 7th Marines relieves the Special Forces camp Thuong Duc, in the process killing 202 enemy at a cost of 28 Marines killed and 143 wounded.

11 October
Space
One of the three astronauts on Apollo VII during its 11-day space voyage is Marine Reserve Major Walter Cunningham.

23 October
Operation Henderson Hill
The 5th Marines launches a series of search and destroy operations south of Da Nang. When the operation winds up on 6 December, the regiment has killed 700 enemy and lost 35 Marines dead and 272 wounded.

31 October
Vietnam
President Johnson announces a complete halt to the bombing of North Vietnam.

20 November
Operation Meade River
In support of a South Vietnamese pacification program, the 1st Marines launches a cordon and search operation designed to encircle the entire Dodge City area, 36 square miles of flat farming land south of Da Nang. The effort involves seven Marine infantry battalions. It ends on 9 December with 1,023 enemy dead and 123 prisoners. Marine losses are 108 dead and 510 wounded.

23 November
Operation Lancaster II
The series of 4th Marines search and destroy missions comes to an end. Reported Enemy casualties are 1,800, while 359 Marines have been killed and another 2,101 wounded.

9 December
Operation Napoleon/Saline
A 13-month-old series of search and destroy operations by the 3rd Marines in the northeast quadrant of Quang Tri Province comes to an end. The effort resulted in 3,495 enemy killed and 106 captured, while Marine losses totaled 395 dead and 2,134 wounded.

23 December
Korea
North Korea releases the crew of *Pueblo* after 11 months. Two Marines, Staff Sergeant Robert J. Hammond and Sergeant Robert J. Chicca, are part of the group.

28 December
Camp Carroll
Marines abandon the combat base, which they had been using for two years.

31 December
Vietnam
During the course of the year, III MAF inflicted 31,691 reported casualties on the enemy. Marine losses were 4,634 dead and 29,319 wounded. 1st MAW flew 47,436 fixed-wing sorties and 639,194 helicopter sorties.

6 January
Department of the Navy
President-elect Richard M. Nixon announces his selection of Rhode Island governor John H. Chafee as the new Secretary of the Navy. Chafee served in the Marine Corps during WWII and Korea.

22 January
Operation Dewey Canyon
The 9th Marines and supporting artillery units are helicoptered into the A Shau Valley for a search and destroy mission.

1 February
Force Structure
The 5th LAAM Battalion is deactivated at Yuma following the return of the 2nd LAAM Battalion from Vietnam.

25 February
Manpower
Since the summer of 1965, more than 30,000 Marines have voluntarily extended their tours in Vietnam for six or more months. That equates to a battalion a month. During December 1968, 3,200 of the 8,000 men scheduled to come home volunteered to remain in country.

28 February
Operations Kentucky and Scotland II
The 3rd Marine Division ends these two long-term operations. Kentucky had started on 1 November 1967 and focused on search and cordon operations in the area between Cam Lo, Dong Ha, and Con Thien. The division suffered 52 dead and 3,079 wounded while killing 3,921 enemy. Scotland II had begun on 14 April 1968 and encompassed the region around Khe Sanh. Marine losses were 463 dead and 2,555 wounded, most suffered in the numerous small battles after the siege. Communist dead numbered 3,311.

March
HQMC
Plans are finalized for a law enforcement branch in the headquarters to oversee training and other issues related to military police. It will come into existence during fiscal year 1970.

2 March
Vietnam
The South Vietnamese hold village elections throughout the country without serious disruption from Communist forces.

3 March
Technology
The Marines receive their first Sikorsky CH-53D, an improved model of the Corps' heavy lift helicopter.

Left: *"Northeast of the Rockpile,"* Ned Conlon, Marine Corps Art Collection

Opposite: *"The Hill At Thuong Duc,"* Col Charles Waterhouse, USMCR (Ret), Marine Corps Art Collection

9 March
Operation Taylor Common

The 1st Marine Division closes out an operation initiated on 7 December 1967. In the area southwest of An Hoa, Marine battalions killed 1,398 enemy and captured 610, while losing 156 dead and 1,327 wounded.

10 March
Dewey Canyon

Secretary of Defense Melvin R. Laird publicly confirms that some Marine units had crossed into Laos during the operation.

15 March
Manpower

The percentage of high school graduates among volunteer enlistees stands at 5.4 percent, while it is 71.5 percent among draftees. There are 1,071 college graduates in the Corps enlisted ranks.

18 March
Operation Dewey Canyon

The 9th Marines completes the operation, which results in 1,617 enemy killed, as well as the largest haul of Communist arms in the war. Among the items captured or destroyed are two 122mm towed howitzers, 66 trucks, 14 bulldozers, and hundreds of thousands of rounds of ammunition of all types and calibers.

26 March
Commanders

Lieutenant General Herman Nickerson, Jr., becomes the commander of III MAF. President Nixon names Lieutenant General Cushman, the previous MAF commander, the deputy director of the Central Intelligence Agency.

30 March
Vietnam

III MAF engineers and naval construction forces complete building a new Liberty Bridge across the wide Thu Bon River.

April
Technology

VMO-2 in Vietnam begins operating the Bell AH-1G Cobra gunship, the first true attack helicopter in the Corps' inventory.

3 April
Vietnam

American dead in the Vietnam War (33,641) now exceed those in the Korean War (33,629).

7–20 April
Operation Muskogee Meadows

The 5th Marines conducts operations to deny the rice harvest to Communist forces in the vicinity of An Hoa. In the process, the regiment kills 162 enemy at a cost of 16 Marines dead and 121 wounded.

17 April
Technology

The Marine Corps receives its first 175mm self-propelled guns in Vietnam, to replace its 155mm self-propelled guns.

22 April
Commandants

The Senate approves legislation granting four-star rank to the Assistant Commandant of the Marine Corps, as long as the strength of the Corps exceeds 200,000 at the time of appointment. The House already had passed the measure.

25 April
Training
American and Brazilian Marines conduct a combined amphibious landing at Vieques, the largest such maneuver involving the two countries since WWII.

27 April
Mishap
A grass fire near the ammunition dump at Da Nang ignites a store of unserviceable ammunition and spreads to other areas, destroying 38,000 tons of ground and air munitions and 20,000 drums of fuel, as well as closing the airbase for 18 hours. One Marine and a civilian are killed and dozens injured.

2 May
Operation Maine Crag
The 3rd Marines search and destroy operation south of Khe Sanh, begun on 15 March, results in 157 enemy killed. Marine losses are 21 dead and 134 wounded.

6 May
Vietnam
III MAF reaches its fourth anniversary. It commands the 1st and 3rd Marine Divisions, 1st MAW, Force Logistics Command, the Army's XXIV Corps headquarters, the Americal Division, the 101st Airborne Division, and the 1st Brigade of the 5th Infantry Division. It rivals the size of Tenth Army at Okinawa and is a field army in all but name only.

8 May
Operation Purple Martin
Begun on 23 February, this 4th Marines operation cleared the northwest area of Quang Tri Province, forcing an NVA regiment back into the DMZ. Marine losses are 79 dead and 268 wounded, while Communist dead amount to 252.

9–12 May
Arizona Territory
The 5th Marines conducts a search and clear operation using air and artillery that kills 230 enemy in the area northwest of An Hoa.

29 May
Operation Oklahoma Hills
The 7th Marines completes a search and clear operation south of Da Nang. The regiment killed 596 enemy in 60 days, at a cost of 53 Marine dead and 487 wounded.

2 June
Commandants
Assistant Commandant Lew Walt becomes the first in his billet to hold the rank of four-star general. It also marks the first time the Marine Corps has two four-star generals on active duty at the same time.

7–12 June
Arizona Territory
1/5 defeats several enemy night attacks and destroys an NVA battalion command group, inflicting over 300 dead.

8 June
Vietnam
President Nixon announces that he will withdraw 25,000 troops from Vietnam by the end of August. This will include the 9th Marines. American troops strength in country had reached 540,000 following the Tet Offensive.

15 June
Vietnam
The 1st Amphibian tractor Battalion begins redeploying to Okinawa.

23 June
Operation Cameron Falls
The search and clear mission headed by the 9th Marines and concentrated in the area southeast of Khe Sanh results in 120 enemy killed. During the 24-day operation, Marines losses are 24 dead and 137 wounded.

30 June
Manpower
The strength of the Marine Corps on active duty is 25,698 officers and 284,073 enlisted. This is the highest manpower total for the Corps since 1945. Of these, over 82,000 are in Vietnam. The reenlistment rate reaches its lowest level since before the Vietnam War, with 12 percent of first-term volunteers and only one percent of draftees signing on for another contract.

1 July
Force Structure
MAG-49 is activated as part of 4th MAW.

9 July
Operation Utah Mesa
This joint Marine-Army operation, begun on 12 June and conducted southwest of Khe Sanh, comes to an end. Marine losses are 19 dead and 91 wounded, while the Army suffers 94 casualties. Reported enemy dead total 309. This is the last operation of the 9th Marines in Vietnam.

14 July
Vietnam
1/9 sails for Okinawa, marking the beginning of the departure of the 9th Marines as part of the initial drawdown of U.S. forces in country.

16 July
Space
An element of the 2nd Amphibian Tractor Battalion stands by at Cape Kennedy in Florida as a secondary recovery team in case of a failed launch of Apollo 11, the mission that would place the first men on the moon.
Operation Virginia Ridge
The 3rd Marines wraps up a search and clear mission north of the Rockpile. Since its inception on 1 May, the operation has resulted in 560 enemy killed, at a cost of 108 Marines dead, one missing, and 490 wounded.
Operation Herkimer Mountain
The 4th Marines complete this operation northeast of Khe Sanh, which they had initiated on 1 May. The regiment suffers 25 dead and 219 wounded while killing 137 enemy.

20 July
Camp Lejeune
A confrontation on the base between racial groups results in the death of one Marine.

24 July
Space
Elements of HMX-1 accompany President Nixon on his trip to greet the Apollo 11 astronauts, while the Marine detachment of *Forrestal* (CVA-59) provides security for the Mobile Quarantine Facility temporarily housing the Apollo crew.

31 July
Sergeants Major
Sergeant Major Joseph W. Dailey succeeds Sergeant Major Sweet as the fifth Sergeant Major of the Marine Corps.

1 August
Legal
As part of the implementation of the Military Justice Act of 1968, Brigadier General Duane L. Faw and Colonel Ralph K. Culver join seven Navy officers and three civilians on the new Navy Court of Military Review.

13 August
Vietnam
HMM-165 flies from Marble Mountain to *Valley Forge* (LPH-8), the first 1st MAW element to depart the country as part of the reduction in forces. The 1st LAAM Battalion also begins to leave Da Nang for 29 Palms, while the last

elements of the 9th Marines board ship the next day for Okinawa.

18 August
Vietnam
HMM-362 departs. The last active-duty squadron flying the UH-34D, it will be redesignated HMH-362 and re-equip with the CH-53 upon arrival at its new station.

26 August
Vietnam
VMFA-334 relocates from Chu Lai to Iwakuni, Japan.

3 September
Vietnam
North Vietnamese leader Ho Chi Minh dies.

17 September
Vietnam
The United States announces a second troop withdrawal amounting to 40,500 personnel, of which 18,500 will be Marines.
Manpower
The October draft call will include 1,400 men destined for the Marine Corps, bringing its number of draftees for the year to 11,878.

18 September
Vietnam
USMACV decides that the Marine slice of the pending troop withdrawal will consist primarily of the 3rd Marine Division. Personnel transfers within III MAF would shift Marines with time left on their tour in country from this division to other units remaining behind.

21 September
Force Structure
Secretary of Defense Laird announces that the 5th Marine Division, with the exception of the 26th Marines in Vietnam, will be deactivated soon.

27 September
Operation Idaho Canyon
The 3rd Marines terminates a search and clear mission in the area southwest of Con Thien that has been going on since 17 July. At a cost of 95 dead and 450 wounded, the regiment killed 565 enemy.

Opposite: *Marine lieutenant, January 1968. (National Archives)*

Right: *2/5 Marines in gas masks in Hue. (National Archives)*

29 September
Manpower
The Marine Corps announces a cut of 20,300 in its active-duty strength.

1 October
Manpower
The Corps implements stricter reenlistment criteria, in particular with regard to disciplinary records.

10 October
Manpower
The Marine Corps reduces unaccompanied tours to units in Japan and Okinawa from 13 months to 12.

15 October
Force Structure
Nearly all units of the 5th Marine Division, with the exception of the division headquarters, are deactivated.

19 October
Vietnam
1/4 embarks on ship for transport to Okinawa. HMM-164 and HMH-462 depart the next day.

22 October
Vietnam
VMO-6 departs for Okinawa.

28 October
Force Structure
HMM-561 is deactivated at El Toro.

31 October
Force Structure
MAG-39 is deactivated in Vietnam.

1 November
Force Structure
With the 3rd Marine Division returning to Okinawa, 9th MAB is deactivated.

7 November
Vietnam
The last significant elements of the 3rd Marine Division sail for Okinawa. The 1st Marines terminates Operation Pipestone Canyon in the Dodge City and Go Noi Island areas south of Da Nang. Underway since 26 May, it resulted in 488 enemy dead at a cost of 54 Marines killed and 540 wounded.
Force Structure
I MEF is established on Okinawa to command all FMF units in Japan and Okinawa.

15 November
Vietnam
MAG-36 begins its transfer from Vietnam to Okinawa.

19 November
Manpower
At the request of President Nixon, Congress passes legislation basing the draft on a lottery system using birth dates. It goes into effect on 1 December

26 November
Force Structure
The headquarters of the 5th Marine Division is deactivated and is replaced by the 5th MAB, which will command remaining ground units at Camp Pendleton.

15 December
Vietnam
President Nixon announces a third round of troop withdrawals, to be completed by 15 April 1970.

17 December
Technology
Battleship *New Jersey* is decommissioned and placed into mothballs again.

31 December
Vietnam
The number of Marines in country is down to 54,559 (out of a total Marine strength of 301,675). Over the course of the year, 1st MAW provided 547,965 helicopter sorties and about 66,000 fixed-wing sorties. During these operations, the wing lost 44 helicopters, 34 fixed-wing aircraft, 92 Marines killed, 514 wounded, and 20 missing. Marine casualties during the year totaled 2,258 dead and 16,567 wounded.

1970

6 January
Que Son Valley
Fire Support Base Ross receives 250 rounds of mortar fire and a ground attack from a sapper unit. Marine units, primarily elements of 1/7, lose 13 dead and 63 wounded. Known enemy casualties are 39 killed.

8 January
Vietnam
III MAF establishes the Combined Unit Pacification Program (CUPP), a cousin to the Combined Action Program. Unlike CAP, Marine rifle squads deployed to villages under CUPP receive no special training and remain a part of their parent companies.

11 January
Vietnam
III MAF activates the Combined Action Force, a new headquarters to control the four Combined Action Groups of the CAP program. The CAP force mustered 42 Marine and two Navy officers, 2,050 enlisted Marines, and 126 corpsmen organized into 114 platoons.

18–25 January
Training
The 2nd Reconnaissance Battalion conducts Operation Snowfer in Camp Drum, New York, for environmental and cold weather training.

19 January
Training
Operation Springboard, a three-month exercise involving 110 ships and 260 aircraft from seven

Opposite: *Moving through the rubble of Hue. (National Archives)*

Right: *Echo Company, 2/7, during Operation Oklahoma Hills in April 1969. (National Archives)*

nations, begins in San Juan, Puerto Rico. It involves units from Brazil, Canada, Columbia, the Netherlands, United Kingdom, United States, and Venezuela.

19–23 January
Okinawa
The Okinawa Military Employees Labor Union's five-day strike is held without major confrontation. It does not seriously affect the continuation of essential Marine Corps activities.

24 January
Training
Recruit training increases from eight to nine weeks in length.

28 January
Vietnam
The third wave of withdrawal of U.S. forces begins. It will result in the permanent departure of 50,000 more personnel, including 12,900 Marines, by 7 April. The major Marine units involved are the 26th Marines, MAG-12, VMA-223 and 211, VMFA-542, and HMH-361.

31 January
Vietnam
Intelligence indicates that NVA traffic along the Ho Chi Minh Trail (the infiltration route from North Vietnam) increased during January to 10 times the level of September and October 1969.

1 February
Manpower
HQMC announces it is expanding its early-out program because of troop cutbacks in Vietnam. Only Vietnam veterans can apply for this program, which can release them from active duty as much as 14 months prior to original separation dates.

17 February
Vietnam
President Nixon declares that Vietnamization (the turning over of increasing responsibility for combat duties to South Vietnamese armed forces) is proceeding on schedule.

19 February
Iwo Jima
The United States and Japan hold combined ceremonies at Mt. Suribachi to commemorate the dead of both nations on the 25th anniversary of the battle. Major General William K. Jones, commanding general of the 3rd Marine Division, represents the Commandant of the Marine Corps.

23 February
Manpower
The Gates Commission recommends prompt pay increases for members of the armed services and other reforms to permit an end to the draft by 30 June 1971. The findings are referred to a White House study group for review.

24–27 February
Technology
The Marine Corps holds a Tactical Employment conference to begin establishing doctrine for the British-built Hawker Siddeley AV-8A Harrier, a revolutionary jet aircraft that could take of and land vertically.

9 March
Vietnam
In a reversal of roles, III MAF turns over operational control of American military forces in the I Corps Zone to the Army's XXIV Corps and becomes a subset of its former subordinate. This change in command took place because Marine redeployments from the area left Army forces in the majority there. III MAF still retained direct control of the 1st Marine Division and 1st MAW, maintaining the Marine air-ground team.
Commanders
Lieutenant General Keith B. McCutcheon assumes command of III MAF from Lieutenant General Nickerson.

13 March
Training
The Basic School is increased in length from 21 weeks to 26.

23 March
Civil Support
President Nixon authorizes the activation of Reserve units to assist the U.S. Postal Department in New York City during a strike. Units included are 2/25, 6th and 11th Communications Battalions, VMA-131, HMM-768, and Headquarters and Maintenance Squadron 49.

25 March
Civil Support
Three hundred Marine reservists are employed at the main post office, Brooklyn, New York. As of this date, 120 officers and 2,081 enlisted of the Marine Corps Reserve had been activated in the New York area. The situation is resolved the next day and the reservists are demobilized.

1 April
Reserve
Headquarters of the 4th Marine Division at Camp Pendleton assumes training responsibility for all Marine Corps Reserve ground forces. This training was formerly under the control of the director of the Marine Corps district in which the unit was located.

2 April
Vietnam
The number of Marines in country drops to 43,600.

10 April
Vietnam
Lieutenant Larry Parsons, a helicopter pilot believed killed in action near the border between Vietnam and Laos, is rescued after spending nearly 20 days in the Laotian jungle.

14 April
Training
The 11th MEB depart Okinawa enroute to Yang Po Ri, Korea, to participate in Exercise Golden Dragon, a combined USMC/KMC amphibious exercise.

20 April
Vietnam
President Nixon announces he will withdraw 150,000 more U.S. troops over the next year.

22 April
Caribbean
In response to a request by the Trinidad government, which is experiencing a military

mutiny, the United States dispatches 2,000 Marines to the area to stand by as a precautionary measure for the protection of U.S. citizens.

23 April
Caribbean
Lead elements of the Caribbean landing force, including BLT 3/2 and HMM-261, depart San Juan, Puerto Rico, for a position off the coast of Trinidad.

Opposite: *Helping hand, Dewey Canyon. (National Archives)*

Above: *Comforting a Vietnamese orphan. (National Archives)*

Right: *Final tribute. (National Archives)*

27 April
Vietnam
This is the first day in 1970 in which no Marines casualties are reported in Vietnam.

28 April
Caribbean
The Caribbean landing force depart the waters of Trinidad and resumes normal operations.

29 April
Cambodia
U.S. Army and ARVN units attack Communist base areas in Cambodia. Marine participation is limited to a handful of bombing missions and advisors with the VNMC.

30 April
Force Structure
The 26th Marines and 1/13 are deactivated at Camp Pendleton.
Civil Support
1/6, 3/6, and 3/8 deploy to Quonset Point, Rhode Island, to standby aid local authorities in handling a civil disturbance in New Haven. They remain there until 3 May, but are not employed.

1 May
Marine Band
The director of the Marine Band, Albert Schoepper, is promoted to the rank of colonel, the first Marine musician to attain this rank in the 172-year history of the band.

10 May
Civil Support
To counter possible civil disturbances in Washington, D.C., resulting from antiwar demonstrations, a Quantico-based battalion moves to the Anacostia Naval Air Station. The 6th Marines goes on six-hour alert for possible deployment to the area.

14 May
Training
The 3rd Marine Division begins a three-week operation, Exotic Dancer III, along the coastal areas of North Carolina. Over 60,00 troops from all branches of the armed forces are involved.

31 May
Peru
HMM-365 and a company of 1/2 are ordered to South America to conduct disaster relief operations after an earthquake. They proceed there on *Guam* (LPH-9). For 11 days Marines and sailors deliver food and medical supplies and evacuate the injured.

11 June
Vietnam
Communist forces begin a series of attacks, the largest since the Tet Offensive, against Marine Combined Action Program units and pacified villages in I Corps Zone. In some cases, the enemy kills numerous civilians in undefended villages.

18 June
Aviation
A Marine Corps KC-130 Hercules and its aircrew begin supporting the Navy's Blue Angels flight demonstration team.

24 June
Vietnam
The Senate repeals the Gulf of Tonkin Resolution by the vote of 81 to 10.

25 June
Force Structure
Marine Barracks Argentia, Newfoundland, is deactivated. Marines had manned this post continuously since January 1941.

30 June
Vietnam
The 1st Marine Division has had few major contacts in the first six months of the year. During the period it has killed 3,955 enemy at a cost of 283 Marines dead and 2,537 wounded.
Force Structure
VMFA-542 is deactivated at EL Toro, while the 3rd Anti-tank Battalion is deactivated at Camp Pendleton.
Manpower
The strength of the Marine Corps on active duty is 24,941 officers and 234,796 enlisted.

3 July
Vietnam
Vietnamese militia forces supported by Marine CAP units, helicopter gunships, and artillery defeat Communist attacks on several villages south of Quang Tri City. The allies lose 16 dead and six missing, while killing 135 enemy.

9 July
Vietnam
The fourth round of U.S. troop withdrawals begins. It will include 17,021 Marines, with the major units being the 7th Marines, 3/11, MAG-13, VMA(AW)-242, VMFA-122 and 314, HMM-161, and VMCJ-1.

15 July
Vietnam
Nearly 5,000 South Vietnamese troops begin a major sweep of NVA base camps west of Da Nang. Marine helicopters land the assault troops and their U.S. advisors. Elements of the 5th Marines begin Operation Barren Green to deny the corn harvest in the Arizona Territory to the enemy. The latter ends on 27 July, after Marine forces kill 18 enemy and destroy 10,000 pounds of grain.

16 July
Operation Pickens Forest
Remaining elements of the 7th Marines begin a search and clear operation southwest of Da Nang and soon uncover large food caches hidden by the enemy. The operation ends on 24 August and accounts for 99 enemy killed at a cost of four Marines dead and 51 wounded.

31 July
Force Structure
The 2nd Antitank Battalion is deactivated at Camp Lejeune.

8–13 August
Marksmanship
Marine shooters take 12 of 17 events during the 9th Annual Interservice Rifle Championships held at Quantico.

Opposite: *1/4 during Operation Scotland II. (National Archives)*

Above: *PFC Rex L. Brochet takes a break on patrol. (National Archives)*

Right: *A-4M Skyhawks of VMA-311. (National Archives)*

17 August
Training
Exercise High Descent is held at Camp Pendleton as a climax to two weeks of annual training for more than 19,000 reservists of 4th MAW and 4th Marine Division.

20 August
Manpower
A DOD study indicates that about 30 percent of U.S. service personnel have used marijuana or other illegal drugs.

22 August
Marksmanship
Marine individual and team shooters win 20 out of 24 matches in the National Rifle and Pistol Championships at Camp Perry, Ohio. For the first time in 14 years, the Marines win both the National Trophy Rifle and National Trophy Pistol matches.

27 August
Force Structure
3rd Force Reconnaissance Company is deactivated.

31 August
Operation Imperial Lake
Just after midnight, the 11th Marines opens the operation with one of the largest bombardments in its history: 13,488 rounds fired from 10 batteries for more than six hours on 53 selected targets in the Que Son Mountains. After an additional two

Left: *Marine mortarmen on a search and clear operation, June 1970. (National Archives)*

Opposite: *Mike Company, 3/3 near the DMZ in September 1969. (National Archives)*

hours of air strikes, elements of the 7th Marines move in to search for enemy forces and base camps. This operation will continue until the 1st Marine Division leaves Vietnam in 1971.

10 September
Technology
The Marine Corps Tactical Systems Support Activity is activated at Camp Pendleton. The unit will test, evaluate, and provide programming support for all the tactical systems and related equipment within the Marine Corps.

11 September
Jordan
Elements of the Sixth Fleet move into the eastern Mediterranean for possible evacuation of airline passengers in planes hijacked by Palestinian guerrillas and flown to Jordan.

13 September
Civil Support
President Nixon directs the military services to furnish 800 personnel (including 90 Marines) for Operation Grid Square, providing security for U.S. international passenger flights.

15 September
New York
A Navy-Marine Corps recruiting station in the Bronx was damaged by a bomb explosion for which the radical Weathermen group reportedly claimed responsibility.

18–21 September
Operation Catawba Falls
The 11th Marines begins the operation with 76 helicopters lifting 14 artillery pieces and 4.2-inch mortars and 10,000 shells onto a remote mountain top and turning it overnight into Fire Support Base Dagger. Four days of bombardment and bombing sorties are intended to deceive the enemy into preparing for a ground assault, while Marine ground forces redeploy unmolested near Da Nang.

19 September
Jordan
After the Jordanian government begins to suppress Palestinian armed groups in the country, the U.S. dispatches 8th MAB to the Mediterranean, where it will join up with BLT 2/2. 8th MAB arrives in the area on 2 October and remains until the end of the month. VMA-331 is also deployed on board *Independence* (CVA-62) during the crisis.

21 September
Vietnam
The Combined Action Force headquarters in Chu Lai is deactivated. The remaining CAP units, under 2nd Combined Action Group, now consist of 600 Marines and corpsmen and operate solely in Quang Nam Province.

1 October
Vietnam
The number of Marines in country has fallen to 29,600.

7 October
Chu Lai
The Marines turn over the base to the U.S. Army.
Manpower
The Department of the Navy tells a special House Armed Services Military subcommittee that more than 7,000 Marines and sailors will probably be discharged from the service in 1970 for drug violations.

12 October
Heritage
Retired Master Sergeant Paul Woyshner dies at the age of 75. Creator of many early recruiting posters, he coined the motto "Once a Marine, Always a Marine" for the Marine Corps League in 1917.

15 October
An Hoa
The Marines turn over An Hoa Combat Base to the South Vietnamese.

15–30 October
Training
Both U.S. and Philippine Marines conduct Exercise Fortress Light in the Philippines.

21 October
Philippines
SLF Alpha (primarily HMM-164) assists in disaster relief operations in the wake of Typhoon Joan.

30 October
Force Structure
The last of the Marine Corps amphibious artillery units is deactivated when the 4th Armored Amphibian Company furls its flag. Activated in 1952, the company was the only remaining one of its kind.

13 November
Force Structure
HMM-265 is deactivated at El Toro.

18 November
Mishap
A CH-46 helicopter crashes into a mountain near Da Nang, killing 15 Marines.

19 November
Training
The Marine Corps announces that it will resume its annual rifle squad competition at Quantico beginning in September 1971. The competition was discontinued in 1965 due to commitments in Vietnam.

20 November
Vietnam
A U.S. joint force (Army, Air Force, and Navy) conducts a heliborne raid at Son Tay, about 23 miles west of Hanoi, in an unsuccessful attempt to free American prisoners of war. The men had been moved a few weeks prior to the operation.

21 November
Force Structure
The Seventh Fleet's Special Landing Force Alpha is redesignated 31st Marine Amphibious Unit (MAU). Although the MAU (or MEU) designation has been used occasionally before, it now becomes the formal title for any Marine unit afloat built around a BLT and a helicopter squadron.

1 December
Force Structure
The 1st LAAM Battalion is deactivated.

15 December
Diego Garcia
The State Department announces that the United States will build a $19 million naval communications facility on the Indian Ocean island of Diego Garcia, a British possession.
Force Structure
MAG-33 is deactivated at El Toro.

22 December
Civil Support
The first military personnel are released from duty with Operation Grid Square.

24 December
Commanders
Lieutenant General Donn J. Robertson replaces Lieutenant General McCutcheon as commander of III MAF.

31 December
Operation Imperial Lake
In this ongoing campaign, the 1st Marine Division has lost 22 dead and 158 wounded while killing 196 enemy.
Manpower
The active-duty strength of the Marine Corps is 231,667, of which 25,394 Marines are in Vietnam. Marine casualties in Vietnam for the year total 535 killed and 4,278 wounded.

1971

4 January
Manpower
General Chapman announces that the Corps will not relax conduct and appearance standards but will adhere to its traditional rules: "We've decided that the Corps is going to be leaner, tougher, more ready, more disciplined and more professional than ever before."

6 January
Malaysia
After 100 inches of rain causes severe flooding, 31st MAU moves toward the Gulf of Thailand for possible disaster relief operations. It arrives on the 10th and remains in the area until the 25th.
Technology
The Marine Corps receives the first of its newest jets, the AV-8A Harrier.
Vietnam
Secretary of Defense Laird states that the U.S. program of Vietnamization is running ahead of schedule and that the combat mission of American troops would end by mid-summer.

Left: *An M60 team fires on a tree line in the Arizona territory. (National Archives)*

Opposite: *VMF(AW)-312 provides close air support in 1966. (National Archives)*

11 January
Operation Upsher Stream
1/1 and reconnaissance teams conduct search and destroy missions to deter rocket attacks on Da Nang. The operation lasts through 29 March, but results in minimal contact.

13 January
Vietnam
The sixth round of U.S. troop withdrawals begins. The number of Marines in Vietnam will be reduced by 12,198. The main units to depart will be the headquarters elements of both 1st Marine Division and 1st MAW, plus the 5th Marines, elements of the 11th Marines, VMFA-115, HMM-263, HMM-364, HML-167, and VMO-2.

19 January
Vietnam
While in night defense positions south of Hoi An, G Company 2/5 drives off a ground attack, killing 12 of the enemy.

20 January
Technology
The Navy announces that it will reduce the number of new amphibious assault ships of the LHA class from nine to five.

20–21 January
Vietnam
Company B, 1/1 loses 11 Marines wounded due to booby traps during Operation Upsher Stream. A CH-46 from HMM-463 on a medevac mission is hit by enemy ground fire and crashes, killing four Marines and a corpsman and wounding 16.
Cambodia
DOD reveals that Marine helicopters on *Iwo Jima* and *Cleveland* (LPD-7) in the Gulf of Siam are supporting South Vietnamese and Cambodian troops operating in Cambodia.

28 January
Manpower
President Nixon asks for a two-year extension of the draft and proposes a 50 percent pay raise for new recruits to achieve his goal of an all-volunteer military and an end to the draft by the mid-1970s.

30 January
Vietnam
South Vietnamese and U.S. Army forces begin Operation Lam Son 719 in Quang Tri Province.

2 February
Turkey
Ships of the Sixth Fleet set sail from Ismir, cutting short a scheduled visit, after anti-American demonstrations and incidents.

3 February
Manpower
The Marine Corps convenes a board to determine which lieutenant colonels, majors, and captains should be released from active duty to meet manpower reduction requirements.

7 February
Laos
In an expansion of Lam Son 719, South Vietnamese forces, supported by U.S. helicopters, fixed-wing aircraft, and artillery fire, enter Laotian territory to strike at Communist base camps. During the operation, VMA-311, VMA(AW)-225, and VMFA-115 fly 950 sorties into Laos. HMH-463, supported by the gunships of HML-367, flies 2,992 sorties during the operation and loses a CH-53 helicopter in Laos.

12 February
Vietnam
The 31st MAU takes station off the coast of North Vietnam, 50 miles east of Vinh. It remains there until 6 March to divert North Vietnamese troops during Lam Son 719.

16 February
Training
The Staff NCO Academy is officially opened at Quantico.

18 February
Vietnam
A CH-53D explodes in flight and crashes northeast of Phu Bai. All seven Marines on board are killed. Four AH-1J Sea Cobras arrive in Vietnam for combat evaluation and are assigned to HML-367.

27 February
Laos
VMA-311 Skyhawks destroy three NVA PT-76 amphibious tanks attacking a South Vietnamese firebase.

28 February
Force Structure
HMM-365 is deactivated at New River.

March
Vietnam
Marine aircraft fly 20,435 combat sorties during the month, nearly 1,200 by fixed-wing aircraft, including 160 into North Vietnam.

5 March
Manpower
Secretary of Defense Laird announces a major new program that will require every person entering the armed services to attend classes in race relations.

18 March
Manpower
Navy Secretary Chafee testifies before a Senate committee: "I would be less than candid were I to imply that we have the drug problem fully under control" in the Navy and Marine Corps. The secretary also indicated that racial tensions were growing within the two services.

30 March
Vietnam
The Marine Corps Reserve Civic Action Fund closes out. Marines and friends of the Corps had funneled $4,784,000 worth of help to the South Vietnamese people through this program.

7 April
Technology
The first Bell UH-1N twin-engine Huey is delivered to HMA-269 at New River.

8 April
Vietnam
Operation Lam Son 719 is terminated. Although the operation began in Quang Tri, the heaviest fighting occurred in Savannakhet Province, Laos. The operation had gone well until the planned withdrawal turned chaotic and many heavy weapons were abandoned.

Left: *Exiting a CH-53 on Charley Ridge. (National Archives)*

Opposite: *PFC Terry Perrigo reacts to enemy fire while on patrol. (National Archives)*

13 April
Vietnam
Defense Secretary Laird reaffirms that the U.S. ground combat role would end this summer, but that air and naval forces would remain indefinitely.
Force Structure
HMM-364 is deactivated at Santa Ana, California.

14 April
Vietnam
III MAF relocates to Okinawa. 3rd MAB is activated at Da Nang to command remaining Marine units in country. The MAB has 15,516 Marines and Navy personnel, concentrated mainly in the 1st Marines, 1/11, MAG-11, and MAG-16.
Force Structure
5th MAB is deactivated at Camp Pendleton and the 1st Marine Division assumes control of all ground forces there.

15 April
Vietnam
The CUPP program comes to an end after 18 months. During that time it had accounted for 578 enemy killed at a cost of 46 Marines dead.

16 April
Force Structure
Three AV-8A Harriers arrive at Beaufort and VMA-513 is activated to receive them, thus becoming the first Harrier squadron in the Corps.

23 April
Caribbean
A battalion landing team from Camp Lejeune rushes to sea ahead of schedule during Operation Exotic Dancer IV as part of a show of force designed to discourage Cuba from taking advantage of the political instability in Haiti following the death of president Francois Duvalier.

1 May
Civil Support
Marines from Quantico, Marine Barracks 8th and I, and Camp Lejeune deploy to Washington, D.C., to assist local authorities in controlling antiwar demonstrations. They remain there until 7 May.

7 May
Vietnam
3rd MAB ceases ground and fixed-wing combat operations.

11 May
Vietnam
The 2nd Combined Action Group is deactivated, bringing the CAP program to an end.

27 June
Vietnam
3rd MAB is deactivated as the last Marine units depart the country. There are 547 advisors and other Marines still serving in Vietnam, along with more than 240,000 other U.S. troops.

30 June
Manpower
The strength of the Marine Corps on active duty is 21,765 officers and 190,604 enlisted.
1 July
Force Structure
HMA-269 is commissioned at New River.

9 July
Manpower
The Secretary of the Navy grants exemption from disciplinary action and discharge under other than honorable conditions to those members of the Navy and Marine Corps who make voluntary disclosure of their illegal drug usage or possession.

9-10 July
Heritage
The first reunion of the WWII Navaho Code Talkers is held in Arizona.

15 July
Force Structure
MAG-56 is deactivated in southern California.

20 July
Manpower
The Cleveland Plain Dealer reports that the Marine Corps has the highest desertion rate of all the services, 59.6 men per 1,000.

6 August
Manpower
CMC's Advisory Committee for Minority Affairs holds its first meeting. Composed of 12 volunteer civilian leaders from across the country, its mission is to help ease racial tensions within the Corps and help recruit minority personnel.

7–12 August
Marksmanship
Marine shooters win 12 of 13 individual matches, the Interservice Rifle Team match, and the 1000-yard team match at the 10th Annual Interservice Rifle Championships.

11 August
Bases
The Secretary of the Navy issued a directive to Navy and Marine Corps base commanders instructing them to advise local government officials, community leaders, and private groups that failure to enforce open-housing laws would be a factor in any future decision to close bases.

13 August
Vietnam
The USMC Night Observation Gunship System detachment, flying two specially adapted OV-10s, completes the last of 207 missions conducted to test an integrated 20mm gun and an infrared target acquisition system.

26 August
Technology
The first production vehicle of the Corps' newest assault amphibian vehicle, the LVTP7, is delivered to the Corps. It hauls 25 troops and has a water-jet drive capable of pushing it through the ocean at 8.4 mph.

Left: *Marines rush to unload a CH-46 bringing in supplies. (National Archives)*

Opposite: *A Marine of India Company, 3/1, on patrol in 1969. (National Archives)*

28 August
Manpower
The Naval Training Center and the Marine Recruit Depot in San Diego announce they will begin testing new recruits for drug use.

19 September
Mishap
Two Marine recruits die within 12 hours of each other after apparently unrelated training exercises at Parris Island.

22 September
Manpower
The Marine Corps Human Relations Instructors School is inaugurated. Human relations training will be given to Marines of all ranks.

25–29 September
Okinawa
1st MAW aircraft provide disaster relief in the southern Ryukyus after the islands were hit by Typhoon Bess.

30 September
Force Structure
HMA-169, an attack helicopter squadron, is activated at Camp Pendleton.

9–22 October
Training
Exercise Deep Furrow, a joint and combined NATO exercise, includes amphibious landings in Turkey by Marines and forces from Great Britain and Italy.

11 October
Heritage
Marine Corps icon Lieutenant General Lewis B. "Chesty" Puller dies in Hampton, Virginia, at the age of 73.

3 November
Aviation
VMA-214 completes qualifications on board *Hancock* (CVA-19), the first time since the beginning of the Vietnam conflict that a Marine jet squadron has operated on board a carrier on the west coast.

10 November
Okinawa
The U.S. Senate approves a treaty to return Okinawa to Japan. After reversion, the U.S. would maintain military bases on Okinawa on the same basis as it now does on the Japanese home islands, in accordance with the U.S.-Japanese Mutual Security Treaty.

10 December
Indian Ocean
Elements of Seventh Fleet, including part of 31st MAU, depart Vietnamese waters, heading toward the Indian Ocean for possible rescue of American citizens as a result of the war between India and Pakistan. The ships will remain in the area through 7 January 1972.

14 December
Vietnam
VMA(AW)-224 deploys on board *Coral Sea* (CVA-43) on Yankee Station for potential aerial action against North Vietnam.

20 December
Mishap
Four Marines are killed when their helicopter crashes while on a flight from *Tripoli* (LPH-10) in the Bay of Bengal.

**21 December
Aviation**
The Marine Corps authorizes a Civilian Pilot Training program designed to attract more applicants and upgrade the quality of aviation students in the Platoon Leader Class commissioning program.

**26 December
Vietnam**
President Nixon orders a temporary resumption of bombing of North Vietnam as peace talks stall. VMA(AW)-224 participates in these aerial raids. There are 156,800 American troops in South Vietnam.

**30 December
Force Structure**
VMFA-334 is deactivated at El Toro.

**31 December
Vietnam**
Marine casualties during the year totaled 41 dead and 476 wounded.
Commandants
General Chapman retires and is replaced by General Robert E. Cushman, Jr., the 25th Commandant of the Marine Corps.

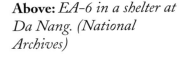

1972

**1 January
Manpower**
Reenlistment standards are raised to require a high school diploma or its equivalent.

**5 January
Civil Support**
Marine Air Control Squadron 7 is tasked to activate a radar site near Tucson, Arizona, in support of the Bureau of Custom's Operation Grasscatcher, an

Above: *EA-6 in a shelter at Da Nang. (National Archives)*

Left: *A 105mm howitzer at Khe Sanh. (National Archives)*

Opposite: *Khe Sanh Valley 1968. (National Archives)*

effort to detect and intercept illegal air traffic crossing the border with Mexico. Marines participate in the operation until 28 February.

12 January
Force Structure
After an 18-month hiatus, VMA-542 is reactivated at Beaufort and equipped with Harriers.

14 January
Manpower
DOD announces manpower cuts that will reduce military strength to its lowest level since 1951. Marine Corps strength will drop to 193,000.

7–27 January
Training
Elements of the 2nd Marine Division and 2nd MAW joined naval forces of the Atlantic Fleet in cold weather landing operations at Reid State Park on the coast of Maine in Exercise Snowy Beach.

8 February
Technology
VMA-513 conducts initial sea tests of the AV-8A Harrier on *Guam*.

10 March
Vietnam
The 101st Airborne Division, the last U.S. combat division in Vietnam, departs the country.

14 March
Vietnam
VMA(AW)-224 and *Coral Sea* depart Yankee Station.

23 March
Vietnam
The United States suspends the Paris peace talks following a long period of Communist intransigence.

30 March
Vietnam
North Vietnam launches its long-planned conventional assault on the South. Soon dubbed the Easter Offensive, it involves 14 divisions, 26 separate regiments, and hundreds of tanks and artillery pieces. It has three major prongs directed against Quang Tri

in the north, Pleiku in central South Vietnam, and the area around Saigon in the deep south. The campaign initially makes significant gains.

1 April
Vietnam
31st MAU and BLT Bravo (BLT 1/9) and their respective amphibious ready groups (ARGs) deploy off the coast of Vietnam to standby to evacuate American military advisors if necessary.
Force Structure
HMA-369 is activated at Futema, Okinawa.

2 April
Dong Ha
Captain John W. Ripley, a Marine advisor, blows up a bridge over the Cua Viet River in the face of intense enemy fire and a column of tanks. His actions stall a major Communist drive south on Route 1.

6 April
Vietnam
MAG-15 and more than two dozen F-4s of VMFA-115 and 232 deploy from Iwakuni to Da Nang to provide close air support to the South Vietnamese. A detachment of VMCJ-1 flying from Cubi Point also participates in aerial combat operations.

7 April
Vietnam
U.S. aircraft resume bombing operations against targets in North Vietnam.

8 April
Vietnam
The headquarters of the 9th MAB arrives in the Tonkin Gulf to command Marine amphibious forces in the waters off Vietnam.

11 April
Vietnam
33rd MAU is activated on board ARG Charlie with BLT 2/4 and HMM-165. BLT 2/9 is assigned to ARG Delta. When deployed with 31st MAU and BLT Bravo, this is the largest wartime deployment of Marine amphibious forces since the Korean War.

14 April
Vietnam
A dozen F-4s of VMFA-212 arrive in Da Nang from Kaneohe, Hawaii.

15 April
Vietnam
The United States conducts its first bombing missions against Hanoi and Haiphong in North Vietnam since 1968.

27 April
Vietnam
Peace talks resume in Paris between the United States, South Vietnam, and the Communists, but are suspended again on 4 May.

1 May
Vietnam
Quang Tri City falls to the NVA.
Force Structure
MAG-29 is activated as a helicopter group at New River.

8 May
Vietnam
American aircraft mine the main harbors of North Vietnam, including Haiphong.

12 May
Vietnam
HMM-164 lifts Vietnamese Marines for a raid behind NVA lines near Hue City.

13 May
Training
In the final stages of a NATO exercise, U.S., British, and Greek Marines conduct an amphibious landing in southern Greece.

15 May
Okinawa
The United States ends 27 years of American administration and transfers control of the Ryuku Islands back to Japan.

16–25 May
Training
Operation Exotic Dancer V, designed to test joint tactical doctrine, takes place in the Carolinas. Among the 50,000 personnel conducting amphibious and airborne operations are elements of II MAF, 2nd Marine Division, and 2nd MAW.

17 May
Vietnam
MAG-12 (Forward), 32 A-4s of VMA-211 and 311, and supporting units arrive at Bien Hoa Airbase near Saigon from Iwakuni.

Opposite: *Operation Meade River. (National Archives)*

Right: *HMM-265 CH-46. (National Archives)*

Below: *3/1 in Elephant Valley. (National Archives)*

June
Civil Support
Marine reserve units provide disaster relief following severe floods in Pennsylvania's Wyoming Valley as a result of Hurricane Agnes.

1 June
Manpower
Secretary of Defense Laird announces that the Marine Corps and Army would temporarily pay a $1,500 bonus for a four-year enlistment in a ground combat speciality. This is a test to aid in achieving the goal of an all-volunteer military.

15 June
Force Structure
VMA(AW)-225 is deactivated at El Toro.

16 June
Vietnam
The first Marine F-4s arrive at Nam Phong, Thailand, as part of a re-deployment of combat aircraft from South Vietnam. VMFA-115 flew the first Marine combat mission out of Nam Phong the next day.

20 June
Vietnam
VMA-533 and its A-6 Intruders begin arriving at Nam Phong from Iwakuni.

22 June
Vietnam
HMA-369, with seven AH-1J Cobras on board *Denver* (LPD-9), begins flying armed reconnaissance missions to interdict water-borne logistics craft along the coast of North Vietnam. These operations continue until 15 January 1973.

27 June
Vietnam
31st and 33rd MAUs conduct an amphibious feint off the coast north of the Cua Viet River to divert NVA forces resisting the South Vietnamese counteroffensive.

28 June
Vietnam
South Vietnamese forces begin a counteroffensive to drive back the NVA in the former I Corps Zone.

29 June
Vietnam
The U.S. Army's 196th Infantry Brigade, the last American ground combat force in country, departs Vietnam. Helicopters of 9th MAB lift two Vietnamese battalions into the rear of enemy lines south of Quang Tri City. Naval gunfire and Marine helicopters continue providing support to the South Vietnamese in the coming weeks.

Above: HMM-262 CH-46 in Que Son Mountains, December 1970. (National Archives)

Right: F Company, 2/7, trading fire with the enemy in Happy Valley. (National Archives)

30 June
Manpower
The strength of the Marine Corps on active duty is 19,843 officers and 178,395 enlisted.

8 July
Civil Support
2/6 is deployed to Homestead Air Force Base, Florida, for potential duty controlling disturbances during the Democratic Party national convention.

13 July
Vietnam
The Paris peace talks resume.

14 July
Vietnam
VMFA-333, embarked on America (CVA-66), begins flying combat missions when the carrier arrives off Vietnam.

22 July
Philippines
Elements of 9th MAB assist in flood relief operations. The effort lasts through 15 August.

24 July
Force Structure
The headquarters of 4th MAB is activated at

Norfolk, Virginia, to provide a command element for any contingency force sized between a MAU and a MAF.

31 July
Manpower
Commandant Cushman orders an end to "voluntary segregation" by race in living quarters at Marine Corps installations and on board ships.

12 August
Vietnam
Captain Larry G. Richard, an exchange pilot with the Air Force's 58th Tactical Fighter Squadron, downs a MIG-21 northeast of Hanoi. He is the second Marine pilot to claim an aerial victory in the war.

19 August
Civil Support
2/6 is again assigned to civil disturbance duty, this time in conjunction with the upcoming Republican Party national convention.

26 August
Vietnam
An F-4J Phantom of VMFA-232 is shot down by a MIG 70 miles southwest of Hanoi.

28 August
Manpower
President Nixon announces that there will be no draft calls after 30 June 1973.

1 September
Force Structure
MAG-43 is merged into MAG-49.

11 September
Vietnam
A VMFA-333 F-4 Phantom from *America* engages two MIG-21s, destroying one and damaging the other. It was the first MIG kill during the Vietnam War by an all Marine Corps team (Major Lee Lasseter and Captain John Cummings), and only the third overall.

11–30 September
Training
For the first time Reserve Marines participate in a NATO training exercise, Strong Express in Norway. This also marks the first overseas deployment of the new LVTP-7 amphibian assault vehicle.

15 September
Force Structure
HML-268 is activated at New River.

18 December
Vietnam
Following another stalemate in peace talks, the United States launches Operation Linebacker II, a heavy aerial bombardment of North Vietnam that dwarfs any prior aerial campaign against the North. The main targets are in Hanoi and Haiphong. The operation lasts until 29 December.

27 December
Heritage
The Commandant's House and Marine Barracks 8th and I are placed on the National Register of Historic Places.

31 December
Vietnam
American troop strength totals 24,200 personnel.
Force Structure
VMGR-216 (a fighter and attack squadron until 1962) is deactivated.

16 September
Vietnam
South Vietnamese Marines recapture Quang Tri City, which had been occupied by the NVA for 138 days.
Aviation
DOD reports that Navy and Marine aviators recorded their lowest accident rate in history in 1971.

24 October
Vietnam
The United States halts bombing attacks north of the 20th parallel due to progress in peace talks.

1 November
Force Structure
VMA-542 is activated at Beaufort.

1 December
Vietnam
The USMACV announces that during the last week of November no Americans died in Vietnam, the first week without fatalities there since January 1965.

4 January
Manpower
Due to the Supreme Court's recent upholding of a lower court decision, Secretary of Defense Laird orders an end to compulsory attendance at religious services at military academies and elsewhere in the armed services.

15 January
Vietnam
Citing progress made in the Paris negotiations, President Nixon suspends all bombing, mining, shelling, and other offensive actions throughout North Vietnam.

19 January
Civil Support
A Marine battalion from Camp Lejeune arrives at Naval Air Station Anacostia to provide assistance with riot control if needed during the upcoming presidential inaugural.

23 January
Vietnam
President Nixon announces that the United States has reached an agreement in Paris, "to end the war and bring peace with honor in Vietnam." Under terms of the accord, all U.S. prisoners of war will

be released and the remaining 23,700 American personnel in South Vietnam will be withdrawn within 60 days.

27 January
Manpower
Secretary of Defense Melvin Laird declares that peace in Vietnam allows DOD to begin a complete reliance on voluntary enlistment immediately.

Opposite, top: *Radioman on patrol. (National Archives)*

Opposite, bottom: *Manhandling a 105mm howitzer into position. (National Archives)*

Above: *A former prisoner of war, Marine Captain James V. DiBernardo comes home on 8 March 1973. (National Archives)*

Right: *Mortarmen of Hotel Company, 3/4, near Cam Lo. (National Archives)*

28 January
Vietnam
The cease fire goes into effect, with NVA forces still occupying enclaves in South Vietnam. Marine casualties during and after the Easter Offensive total 18 killed, 68 wounded, and 21 missing.

30 January
Vietnam
MAG-12 departs Bien Hoa for Iwakuni, Japan.

31 January
Sergeants Major
Sergeant Major Clinton A. Puckett succeeds Sergeant Major Dailey as the sixth Sergeant Major of the Marine Corps.

1 February
Manpower
The last four enlisted naval aviation pilots (NAPs) on active duty retire from the Marine Corps, bringing to an end a program that stretched back to 1923. The Defense Department announces a tightening of military disability standards to "cut substantially" the number of officers leaving the services with disabilities.

9 February
Force Structure
9th MAB is deactivated, except for its headquarters element, which remains in existence as a deployable command element within III MAF.

12 February
Vietnam
The first 116 American prisoners of war released by North Vietnam arrive at Clark Air Force Base in the Philippines. This group includes four of the 26 Marines held in captivity by Communist forces.

16 February
Vietnam
The Marine Corps ends its advisory program with the Vietnamese Marines and the last two advisors depart Quang Tri City.

22 February
Laos
Following implementation of a ceasefire between Communist and non-Communist forces in Laos,

the United States declares that it will discontinue all acts of force in that country.

23 February
Vietnam
Operation End Sweep, the Navy/Marine Corps minesweeping of North Vietnamese harbors and coastal waterways, begins. HMM-164 and 165 and HMH-463 assist in the effort. The operation continues through 18 July.

25 February
Cambodia
MAG-15, still based in Nam Phong, Thailand, begins flying combat sorties in support of Cambodian forces fighting Communist forces.

4 March
Vietnam
The second group of American POWs leaves Hanoi under terms of the Paris accords.

14 March
Vietnam
Sub Unit One, a detachment of 1st ANGLICO that has been providing support to South Vietnamese forces, is the last Marine unit to depart Vietnam.

18 March
Vietnam
A CH-53D of HMH-463 crashes into the water approximately 25 kilometers southeast of Haiphong while towing minesweeping gear. All personnel are rescued.

29 March
Vietnam
USMACV shuts down, the departure of all U.S. forces from South Vietnam is complete, and North Vietnam releases the last group of American POWs.

29–31 March
Tunisia
Helicopters of HMH-362 participate in disaster relief operations near Tunis.

April
Nicaragua
The U.S. Embassy in Managua is destroyed in an earthquake. Six Marine guards aid in rescue efforts and secure the compound.

5 April
Italy
A bomb severely damages the living quarters of the 13 Marines who guard the U.S. Embassy in Rome. There are no injuries.

26 April
Manpower
DOD increases the combat arms enlistment bonus for the Army and Marine Corps from $1,500 to $2,500.

14 May
Manpower
The Supreme Court rules that female members of the armed services are entitled to the same dependency benefits for their husbands as servicemen have always received for their wives.

29 May
Vietnam
Air Force Colonel Theodore W. Guy files charges against five Army and three Marine enlisted men, accusing them of misconduct while they were prisoners of war. The charges against the Marines are subsequently dismissed by the Secretary of the Navy.

25 June
Vietnam
Rear Admiral James B. Stockdale, a former prisoner of war, files charges against two other former prisoners, a Navy captain and a Marine lieutenant colonel. Although the Secretary of the Navy later dismisses the charges, he issues letters of censure and both officers retire.

Opposite: *A 2/9 81mm mortar crew near Vandegrift Combat Base. (National Archives)*

Right: *"Valor at Hue," Tom Freeman, courtesy of U.S. Naval Institute and U.S. Naval Academy Museum*

26 June
China
Marines raise the American flag over the U.S. liaison office in Peking during its formal opening following the establishment of diplomatic relations between the United States and Communist China.

30 June
Manpower
The strength of the Marine Corps on active duty is 19,282 officers and 176,816 enlisted.

31 July
Cuba
2/8 departs Guantanamo Bay and is relieved by a reinforced rifle company, marking the first reductions in security force requirements at the naval base since the 1960s.
Force Structure
After a hiatus of 11 months, VMA-231 is reactivated at Cherry Point and equipped with Harriers.

14 August
Indochina
Congress decrees the cessation of all funding for military operations in Southeast Asia. Marine air operations launched from Nam Phong, Thailand, against Cambodia, come to an end. MAG-15 begins to withdraw from Thailand on 25 August.

September
Manpower
The first selectees of the Marine Corps Enlisted Commissioning Education Program begin their study in September, with male Marines attending The Citadel and women Marines at the University of Washington, Seattle.

10–21 September
Training
Australia, Canada, New Zealand, and the United States conduct RimPac-73, a combined naval exercise in the Hawaiian Islands.

25 September
Space
Marine Lieutenant Colonel Jack R. Lousma pilots the record breaking Skylab II mission, which had begun on 28 July and ends this date setting a mark with 59 days in space.

17 October
Middle East
Arab nations institute an oil embargo against countries supporting Israel as it battles Egypt and Syria following their surprise attack on 6 October. The United States bears the brunt of the embargo as it rushes arms to Israel.

25 October
Middle East
U.S. forces world wide are placed on heightened alert following a Soviet threat to send troops to the Middle East. Later in the day tensions are reduced as an Arab-Israeli ceasefire takes hold. The alert is cancelled a few days later. 4th MAB, composed of BLTs 2/6 and 3/6 and HMM-261 and 264, is deployed in the Mediterranean during this time.

9 November
Department of Defense
The armed services implement strict energy conservation measures in response to shortages arising from the Arab oil embargo.

14 November
Technology
The Marine Corps adopts the M203 grenade launcher, which is attached under an M-16. One man in each fire team will now carry this 40mm weapon and double as a rifleman and grenadier.

16 November
Space
A new Skylab III team, commanded by Marine Lieutenant Colonel Gerald P. Carr, blasts off from the Kennedy Space Center atop the Saturn 1B rocket, for a 56-day mission.

1 December
Technology
The Navy launches *Tarawa* (LHA-1), the first general purpose amphibious assault ship.

5 December
Manpower
The Marine Corps becomes the last of the services to change its regulations in order to allow women to command units made up mostly of men.

1974

11 February
Reserve
Citing recent court decisions, Commandant Cushman announces that the Corps will permit reservists to wear short-hair wigs while drilling on weekends. Cushman said the prohibition on wigs was dropped because it was "no longer legally tenable," but that the decision "was not prompted by a desire to liberalize the Marine Corps standards of appearance and personal conduct."

Opposite, top: *UH-1E door gunner. (National Archives)*

Opposite, bottom: *"Roost at Eversharp Charlie," Maj A. M. Leahy, USCMR, Marine Corps Art Collection*

Above: *"Marble Mountain Patrol," John Groth, Marine Corps Art Collection*

14 February
Technology
Quantico and Camp Butler, Okinawa, are the first Marine bases to receive an innovative rifle range system known as SARTS (Small Arms Remote Target System).

1 March
Technology
The CH-53E makes its initial flight. The three-engine helicopter boasts twice the lift of the CH-53D.
Manpower
The Marine Corps selects 13 women Marines to be assigned billets in the 2nd MAW, Cherry Point, and the 1st Marine Division, Camp Pendleton. Women can now fill rear-echelon billets within FMF.

26 March
Aviation
DOD officials report that more than 5,000 Navy, Marine, and Air Force aircraft were not operationally ready because of shortages in spare parts and overdue maintenance.

30 June
Vietnam
The Marine Security Guard unit at the Saigon embassy is reduced from 174 to 57.
Bases
The Naval Disciplinary Command, Portsmouth,

New Hampshire, is deactivated. Marines serving long sentences are transferred to the Army Disciplinary Barracks, Fort Leavenworth, Kansas.
Manpower
The strength of the Marine Corps on active duty is 18,740 officers and 170,062 enlisted.

July
Australia
33rd MAU participates in the largest peacetime military maneuver ever staged in Australia.

Approximately 2,000 Marines joined elements of the U.S. Navy and Army, as well as forces from Australia, New Zealand, and Great Britain, for land, sea, and air exercises.

1 July
Manpower
The Marine Corps switches to a new aptitude test for recruits, the Armed Services Vocational Aptitude Battery.

Above: *A Marine holds a Vietnamese child while guarding a refugee ship in March 1975. (National Archives)*

Right: *A squad leader calls in the coordinates for an air strike. (National Archives)*

22 July
Cyprus
Following a coup and a Turkish invasion of the island, British Royal Navy and U.S. Marine (HMM-262) helicopters evacuate more than 400 citizens of the United States, Britain, and other countries from the British base at Dhekelia in southern Cyprus to *Coronado* (LPD-11), which transported the evacuees to Beirut.

27 July
Mishap
A Marine AV-8A Harrier crashes and burns at an air show in Milwaukee. The pilot survives after ejecting.

13 August
Force Structure
VMA-513 arrives at Iwakuni with 16 AV-8A Harriers. This is the first deployment of a Harrier squadron to the western Pacific.

19 August
Cyprus
Despite the efforts of a 15-man Marine Security Guard detachment, U.S. ambassador Roger P. Davies is murdered during a riot at the embassy in Nicosia.

21–28 August
Philippines
31st MAU helicopters assist in a flood relief effort.

1975

15 January
Manpower
The Supreme Court reverses an earlier decision by a lower court and by a 5-to-4 vote upholds a law that requires discharge of male officers who are twice passed over for promotion.

27 January
Cambodia
The Communist Khmer Rouge guerrillas surround the capital of Phnom Penh as government forces near collapse.

1 February
Manpower
The Marine Corps raises enlistment standards by placing greater emphasis on the general-technical score of the Armed Services Vocational Aptitude Battery. Sergeant Major Eleanor L. Judge reports to Headquarters Squadron of MCAS Cherry Point, becoming the first woman to be assigned to the top enlisted slot of a predominantly male unit.

23 February
Manpower
DOD announces that two-year enlistments will be eliminated by the end of the current fiscal year, making three-year terms the shortest available.

28 February
Cambodia
31st MAU (BLT 2/4 and HMH-462) deploys to the Gulf of Thailand for a potential non-combatant evacuation operation (NEO) as Communist forces gain the upper hand in Cambodia.

Above: *A recon Marine about to land in an LZ. (National Archives)*

Left: *Marines move away after setting a demolition charge in Quang Tri. (National Archives)*

March

The Marine Corps resumes urinalysis testing under a DOD program designed to identify and rehabilitate drug abusers.

5 March
Cambodia

The United States suspends its airlift of military supplies into Cambodia due to intense rocket attacks on the airport. In the Gulf of Thailand 1,500 Americans stand by on a helicopter carrier to hold the airport while U.S. nationals are flown out.

10 March
Vietnam

NVA units launch a large-scale offensive in the Central Highlands of South Vietnam.

17 March
Vietnam

South Vietnam abandons the central highlands provinces of Kontum, Pleiku, and Darlac to the NVA.

Left: *CH-53. (National Archives)*

Below: *A helicopter gunner adjusts the gun mount on a CH-46. (National Archives)*

Opposite: *On Mayaguez. (National Archives)*

22 March
Vietnam
HMH-463 at Kaneohe Bay, Hawaii, receives orders to load on board *Hancock* (CVA-19) and prepare for departure to Southeast Asia.

25 March
Vietnam
Hue City falls to an NVA invasion force heading south.

27 March
Vietnam
As the situation deteriorates in South Vietnam, III MAF stands up the Amphibious Evacuation RVN Support Group (BLT 1/4 and HMM-165), which sails soon after from Okinawa.

29 March
Vietnam
The Marine Security Guard detachment at Da Nang assists in the seaborne evacuation of the consulate staff, American citizens, and Vietnamese refugees the day before the city falls to the NVA.

1 April
Cambodia
President Lon Nol flees Phnom Penh for Indonesia with relatives and officials.
Vietnam
The Marine Security Guard detachment and the consulate staff at Nha Trang are withdrawn by helicopter to Saigon.

2 April
Vietnam
Marine security forces are assigned to four civilian merchant ships on charter to the Military Sealift Command as part of the evacuation of South Vietnamese refugees. One ship holds 16,000 people.

4 April
Vietnam
The Amphibious Evacuation RVN Support Group begins assisting refugees fleeing Communist forces in the vicinity of Cam Ranh Bay.

7 April
Vietnam
33rd MAU (BLT 1/9 and HMM-165) is activated in the Philippines.

9 April
Vietnam
NVA units penetrated Saigon's outer defense perimeter 37 miles northeast of the city.

11 April
Cambodia
HMH-463 and *Hancock* arrive in Cambodian waters.

12 April
Cambodia
31st MAU, reinforced by HMH-463, executes Operation Eagle Pull, the heliborne evacuation of

American citizens and other third-country nationals from Phnom Penh. BLT 2/4 provides security on the ground as the helicopters of HMH-462 and 463 pull out 287 people (including 84 Americans). There are no casualties, despite enemy fire directed at the landing zone.

17 April
Cambodia
Phnom Penh falls to Khmer Rouge forces, ending the civil war in that country.

19 April
Force Structure
9th MAB, recently activated and consisting of 31st, 33rd, and 35th MAUs, reorganizes in preparation for evacuation operations in Vietnam. MAG-39 is activated on board command ship *Blue Ridge* (LCC-19) to command the air units (HMH-462 and 463, HMM-165, HML-367, and HMA-369), while the BLTs (1/9, 3/9, and 2/4) are consolidated into RLT 4. MAG-39 remains in existence until 12 May.

20 April
Vietnam
Hancock arrives in South Vietnamese waters with HMH-463 on board.

24 April
Civil Support
Marine Barracks Guam participates in setting up and guarding a refugee camp on the island. The camps remain in operation until 30 October.

28 April
Civil Support
Camp Pendleton is designated as a refugee reception center. MAG-13 is assigned to begin building a tent city for some of the 130,000 Vietnamese fleeing Communism. The first of the refugees begins arriving the next day. The camp, holding a maximum of 18,000 people, processes a total of more than 50,000 before it closes on 31 October.

29 April
Vietnam
Prior to dawn, Communist troops launch a fierce rocket attack on Saigon, killing two U.S. Marines and destroying an American C-130 at Tan Son

Nhut Airfield. 9th MAB executes Operation Frequent Wind, the evacuation from Saigon of Americans, other third-country nationals, and some South Vietnamese officials and citizens. With a security force of more than 800 Marines protecting the landing zones and controlling the evacuees, 68 Marine and 10 Air Force helicopters airlift 6,968 people from Saigon in 17 hours. The last Marine helicopter lifted off the roof of the U.S. Embassy at 0753 on 30 April carrying Marine security guards. An AH-1J Cobra and CH-46 Sea Knight crash, with the loss of two Marines dead.

30 April
Vietnam
Saigon falls to the NVA and Vietnam is effectively reunited under Communist rule.

12 May
Cambodia
Communist gunboats seize the U.S. merchant ship SS *Mayaguez* in the Gulf of Thailand. President Ford warns of serious consequences unless the ship and her 40-man crew are released promptly.

14 May
Cambodia
Marines of Company D, 1/4, carried by escort destroyer *Harold E. Holt* (DE-1074), board and retake the deserted *Mayaguez*. Air Force helicopters land elements of BLT 2/9 on Koh Tang Island in the Gulf of Cambodia in an effort to recover the merchant crew, which is not there. The helicopters take heavy ground fire and several are destroyed or heavily damaged. Cambodian forces release the merchant crew and it links up with the *Mayaguez* by fishing boat.

15 May
Cambodia
Under cover of air and naval gunfire, nearly 200 Marines are extracted by helicopter from Koh Tang. Losses in the operation total 14 Marines, two corpsmen, and two airmen killed and 41 Marines, two corpsmen, and six airmen wounded. Another 23 airmen died in a related but accidental helicopter crash in Thailand.

21 May
Vietnam
Marine security forces complete their mission of

maintaining order on merchant ships crowded with thousands of Vietnamese refugees.

29 May
Sergeants Major
Sergeant Major Henry H. Black succeeds Sergeant Major Puckett and becomes the seventh Sergeant Major of the Marine Corps.

30 June
Commandants
General Cushman retires and is replaced by General Louis H. Wilson, Jr., the 26th Commandant of the Marine Corps.
Manpower
The strength of the Marine Corps on active duty is 18,591 officers and 177,360 enlisted.

October
Training
For the first time since WWI, Marines train in northern Germany, as part of NATO Exercise Autumn Forge.

10 November
Heritage
The US Marine Corps celebrates the 200th anniversary of its founding.

Opposite: *"Patrol Near the DMZ," Sgt Richard L. Yaco, USMC, Marine Corps Art Collection*

Above: *A crewman arms his CH-53 for the evacuation of Saigon. (National Archives)*

Right: *"Vandegrift Burning," Lt B. F. Long IV, USMCR, Marine Corps Art Collection*

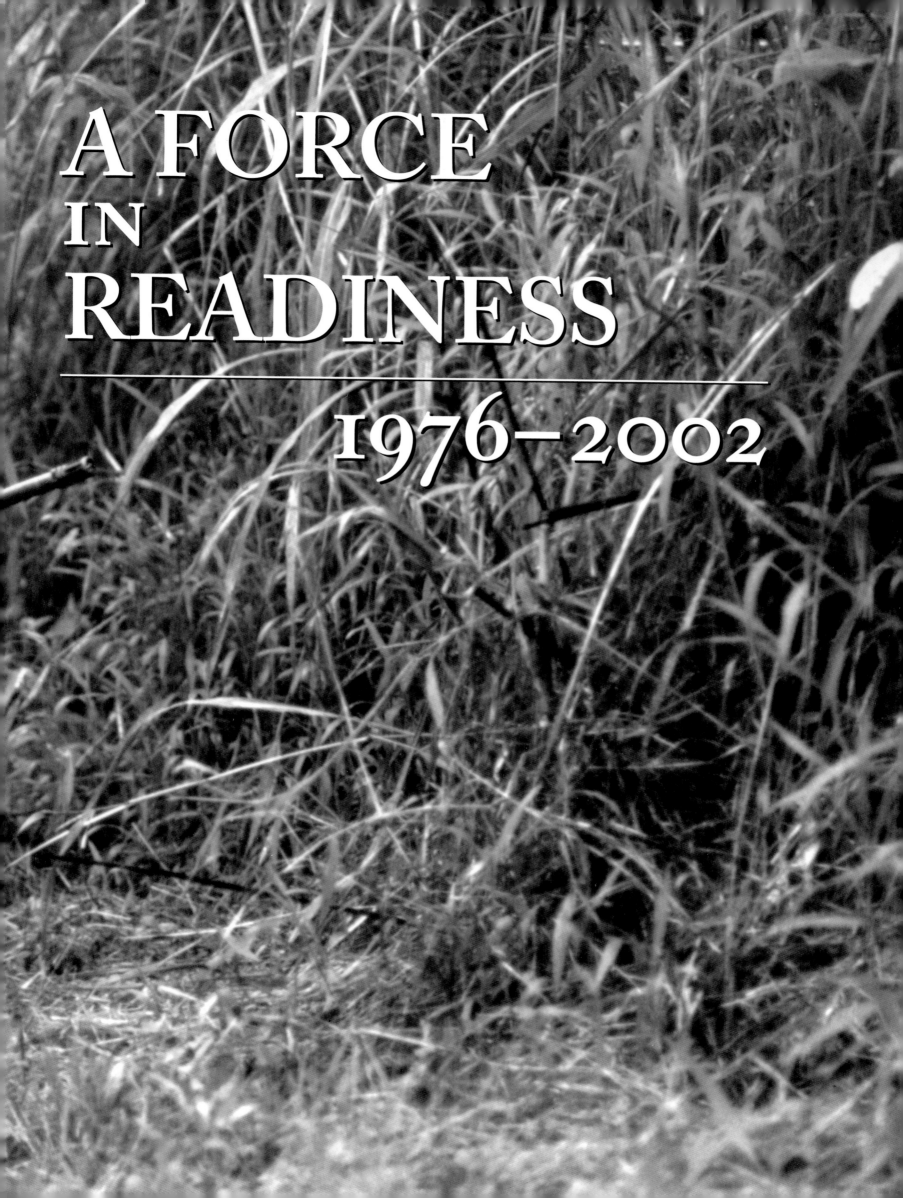

A FORCE
IN
<u>READINESS</u>

1976–2002

A FORCE IN READINESS

1976–2002

The Marine Corps had celebrated its 200th birthday on 10 November 1975, but it entered its next hundred years facing a number of tough challenges. Some of them reflected the difficult period that the nation itself was experiencing. The use of illegal drugs reached significant levels in the general population and in the military. Racial discord had been growing since the late 1960s. General distrust of the government and the military was making it more difficult to recruit quality personnel, a situation exacerbated by Vietnam-era decisions by the government to draft a large number of individuals with marginal intelligence into the services. The manpower problem, to include the difficulty of training unqualified people, came to the fore in early 1976 when a recruit in San Diego died of head injuries sustained in a pugil stick bout. All this was occurring at a time when the armed forces were trying to adapt to relying solely on volunteers.

As the other services often sought compromises or ways to make military life less challenging, the Corps made a conscious choice to advertise its toughness and elan, even if that meant taking in fewer people than it needed. There was no change in grooming regulations, no softening of boot camp. The Marine Corps even launched a war on drugs, and found the weapon to achieve victory when urinalysis gained legal sanction in 1982. Marines were thus in position to reap the most benefit when the American public

began to reassert its patriotism in the early 1980s. The quality of recruits and officer candidates soared, and the personnel problems of the 1970s became a distant nightmare.

Increased spending on the armed forces in the 1980s permitted the Corps to acquire new generations of weapons, replacing such old stalwarts as the M1911A1 pistol and the jeep. The Harrier, first acquired in 1971, was improved and the new version of the vertical takeoff and landing jet (the AV-8B) joined the equally new F/A-18 as the mainstay of Marine fixed-wing aviation. The Corps also began experimenting with tilt-rotor technology in the form of the V-22, which would revolutionize helicopter operations by flying faster and farther. The Navy chipped in by building a fleet of landing craft (the LCAC) that "flew" over the water on a cushion of air. The LCAC, the V-22, and a new advanced amphibian assault vehicle promised to dramatically enhance amphibious operations, though the latter two had not yet reached the fleet by the end of the century.

The Corps continued to innovate in areas beyond equipment. In 1978 it instituted a unit training program known as the combined arms exercise (CAX). The desert mountains and valleys of 29 Palms made a perfect place for all elements of the MAGTF to train in a demanding live-fire atmosphere. A year later, the Marines began pursuing the idea of maritime pre-positioning, which would place a brigade's worth of equipment and 30 days of supply on commercial vessels.

Three squadrons, stationed overseas, would allow brigades to fly to trouble spots and marry up in an amazingly short period of time with all they needed to fight. In 1985, MAUs began a challenging new pre-deployment training program that certified them as special operations capable. They thus could conduct a number of advanced missions, such as the boarding and seizure of ships at sea or short-notice amphibious raids.

There were no shortages of real-world operations to keep the Corps busy during the 1980s. The decade began with a debacle at Desert One in Iran in April 1980, followed by the truck bombing of the Marine headquarters in Lebanon in 1983. But Marines demonstrated their aggressiveness and agility in Grenada, just days after the Beirut bombing, as a MAU overran most of the island while airborne forces struggled with their limited mobility once they hit the ground. The Corps played a smaller but still useful role in air attacks against Libya in 1986, the Tanker War in the Persian Gulf starting in 1987, and the invasion of Panama in 1989.

The emphasis on maritime pre-positioning and the CAX produced a spectacular result in 1990 after Iraq rolled over oil-rich Kuwait in a single day. Within days, Marine brigades were heading to the Persian Gulf and soon after they were deployed and ready to defend Saudi Arabia. In the largest U.S. military operation since Vietnam, I MEF (composed of the 1st and 2nd Marine Divisions, 1st MAW, and the 1st and 2nd Force Service Support Groups) achieved far more than anyone expected. Assigned to create a diversion with a frontal attack on the strongest Iraqi defenses, the MEF broke through and liberated the Kuwaiti capital in four days.

The big war in the Persian Gulf gave way almost immediately to a long string of small wars and operations short of war. Marines helped rescue the Kurds in northern Iraq in 1991, provide disaster relief to Bangladesh the same year, feed the starving and protect U.N. forces in Somalia from 1991 through 1995, control refugees and then police Haiti from 1991 through 1994, and stem the genocidal activities of Serbian nationals in the former Yugoslavia from 1993 through 1999. Along the way there were numerous calls to evacuate Americans and other foreign nationals from troubled points around the globe. The Corps' high state of readiness and its expeditionary capability was just what the United States needed in a troubled world following the end of the Cold War. As a result, the Marines retained more of their structure than the other services that had focused much more on the vanished Soviet threat.

The threat of international terrorism grew throughout the last three decades of the 20th century and culminated in the deadly attack of 11 September 2001. The nation's response, as it has been for over 225 years, was to "send in the Marines." The Corps, as always, was ready and able to answer the call and carry its share of the burden of defending democracy.

A FORCE IN READINESS

1976–2002

1976

13 March
Mishap
A mentally deficient recruit dies from head injuries received in late 1975 during a pugil stick bout. As a result of the incident, Congress conducts investigations into Marine recruit training.

29 May
Technology
Helicopter assault ship *Tarawa* (LHA-1) the first ship of its class, is commissioned. In addition to carrying roughly 1,900 Marines and a squadron of helicopters, it has a well deck.

30 June
Manpower
The strength of the Marine Corps on active duty is 18,882 officers and 173,517 enlisted.

27 July
Lebanon
As fighting between factions threatens foreign nationals, the Marine Security Guard detachment in Beirut assists 32nd MAU in the evacuation of 160 American citizens and 148 other foreigners.

1 August
Force Structure
VMO-8 is deactivated at El Toro.

1 September
Uniform
Marines begin wearing the new camouflage utility uniform in place of the old sateen uniform.

7 November
Sports
The first annual Marine Corps Marathon is held in Washington, D.C.

1977

17 March
Mishap
A Navy landing craft carrying a liberty party of 34th MAU is struck by a Spanish freighter in Barcelona Harbor, drowning 24 Marines and 25 sailors.

31 March
Sergeants Major
SgtMaj John R. Massaro succeeds SgtMaj Black and becomes the eighth Sergeant Major of the Marine Corps.

Left: The six Marine-piloted RH-53Ds on their way from Nimitz *to the ill-fated rendezvous at Desert One in Iran in April 1980. (Defense Visual Information Center)*

Right: *LVTP-7 tracked landing vehicles of 32nd MAU splash ashore in Lebanon on 29 September 1982. (Marine Corps Historical Center)*

17 May
Heritage
The Marine Corps Historical Center opens at the Washington Navy Yard.

26 May
Manpower
The Basic School graduates its first class containing both males and females.

30 June
HQMC
The office of Director of Women Marines ceases to exist as female Marines are no longer categorized as a separate entity within the Corps.
Manpower
The strength of the Marine Corps on active duty is 18,650 officers and 176,057 enlisted.

1 September
Force Structure
HMM-265 is reactivated at Kaneohe Bay after a hiatus of seven years.

21 October
Mishap
A CH-53D helicopter crashes during an exercise on Mindoro Island in the Philippines, killing 23 Marines and one corpsman, and injuring 13.

17 November
Force Structure
BLT 1/4 arrives in California from Okinawa as part of the new unit deployment program (UDP),

which rotates units from the States to the Far East for six-month deployments to maintain unit cohesion, enhance combat readiness, and share out the hardship of unaccompanied tours.

1978

9–11 April
Training
5th MAB conducts Palm Tree 5-78, the largest exercise held to date at 29 Palms. The live-fire air-ground operation involves nearly 6,000 Marines.

6 May
Heritage
The Marine Corps Aviation Museum opens at Brown Field on board the base at Quantico.

11 May
Manpower
Margaret A. Brewer becomes the first female brigadier general in the Marine Corps.

30 June
Manpower
The strength of the Marine Corps on active duty is 18,388 officers and 172,427 enlisted.

6 July
Force Structure
Force Troops at Camp Lejeune is redesignated as 2nd Force Service Support Group. Similar name changes are made for Force Troops in Okinawa and Camp Pendleton.

21 August
Training
More than 2,000 reserve Marines participate in the first Combined Arms Exercise (CAX) at 29 Palms. The CAX will become a staple of Marine training for the next few decades, with units rotating through the base for the challenging air-ground live-fire operation.

1 September
Force Structure
MAG-39 is reactivated at Camp Pendleton as part of 3rd MAW.

20 October
Department of Defense
President Carter signs legislation that makes the Commandant a full member of the JCS.

1 December
Bases
Marine Corps Air Station Santa Ana is renamed MCAS Tustin.

16 December
Taiwan
With the announcement of normalization of U.S. relations with Communist China, a mob of thousands bombards the U.S. embassy in Taipei with bricks and stones. Marine guards drive them back with tear gas and nightsticks.

14 February
Iran
Two weeks after the Ayatollah Khomeini replaces the U.S.-backed Shah of Iran, demonstrators attack the U.S. Embassy in Teheran. Several Marines are abducted and held for over a week.

30 June
Manpower
The strength of the Marine Corps on active duty is 18,229 officers and 167,021 enlisted.

June–July
Nicaragua
Members of the Marine guard at Managua help evacuate 1,423 civilians during fighting in the city as Sandinista forces overthrow the Somoza dictatorship.

1 July
Commandants
General Wilson retires and is replaced by General Robert H. Barrow, the 27th Commandant of the Marine Corps.

15 August
Sergeants Major
Sergeant Major Leland D. Crawford succeeds Sergeant Major Massaro and becomes the ninth Sergeant Major of the Marine Corps.

19 October
Mishap
Typhoon Tip ruptures a 5,000-gallon fuel bladder at Camp Fuji, Japan. The gasoline pours downhill into the Marine base camp where it ignites and causes the death of 13 Marines of 2/4.

30 October
El Salvador
About 200 armed leftists attack the U.S. Embassy in San Salvador. The Marine security detachment holds them at bay with tear gas and warning shots until local authorities restore order. Two Marines are wounded.

4 November
Iran
A mob overruns the U.S. Embassy in Teheran. 65 Americans, including 13 Marine guards, are taken

hostage. Two weeks later, four Marines and nine others are released.

20 November
Pakistan
In Islamabad, a mob burns the U.S. Embassy as seven Marines defend the building and its 137 civilian occupants with tear gas. One Marine is killed during the attack.

21 November
Pakistan
A mob surrounds the U.S. Consulate in Karachi. Among the Marine security guard detachment are two of the 10 female Marines in the MSG Battalion. The wave of violence against American diplomatic compounds during the year soon results in an end to the pilot program to place women in the MSG program.

December
Doctrine
The Secretary of Defense announces that the Marine Corps will establish a Maritime Prepositioning Force. The MPF will have three squadrons, each consisting of five cargo ships filled with all the equipment and supplies needed to outfit a MAB for 30 days of combat. The Corps immediately begins outfitting six existing ships as a Near Term Prepositioning Force until the MPF is ready.

1 March
Force Structure
The Rapid Deployment Joint Task Force is established in Tampa, Florida. It is a headquarters designed to control highly responsive forces (primarily amphibious and airborne) committed to a short-notice contingency, with a focus on the Middle East. The first RDJTF commander is Marine Lieutenant General Paul X. Kelley.

24 April
Iran
In what becomes known as Operation Desert One, Marines pilot Navy helicopters in a failed attempt to rescue the hostages held in Tehran. Three Marines and five other servicemen die in an accident on a desert landing strip after the raid is called off.

3 June
Force Structure
HMM-365 is reactivated at New River after a hiatus of nine years.

30 June
Manpower
The strength of the Marine Corps on active duty is 18,198 officers and 170,271 enlisted.

Opposite: *A 22nd MAU Marine mans a .50-caliber machine gun in Lebanon. (Defense Visual Information Center)*

Right: *M-198 155mm howitzer in Beirut. (Defense Visual Information Center)*

MARINE SECURITY GUARD BATTALION

The Marine Corps' relationship with the diplomatic service extends well back into the early history of the nation. Perhaps the first instance of mutual support came in the oddest way, as the Continental Navy frigate *Boston* carried John Adams across the Atlantic in early 1778 to serve as a commissioner to the French government. When the Americans spied a British armed merchantman, they prepared to attack. Much to the dismay of the ship's captain, he discovered the diplomat armed with a musket and standing among the Marines poised for action.

For the next several decades, Marines participated in a number of actions on behalf of U.S. consuls, oftentimes protecting American lives and property in a troubled foreign land or avenging actions against the United States. The most famous of these expeditions, of course, was Lieutenant Presley O'Bannon's support of William Eaton in the seizure of Derna in 1805. The most unusual probably took place in 1903, when a captain and 19 Marines escorted an American consul to Abyssinia (modern-day Ethiopia). They brought back with them two lions, presents from the emperor to the president.

On a number of occasions ships' detachments went ashore with the express mission of providing local security to a legation. The most challenging of these assignments came in 1900, when the Marines of *Oregon* and *Newark* landed in China and moved overland to Peking during the onset of the Boxer Rebellion. They helped other foreign troops fight off the Chinese rebels for 55 days before an international relief force came to the rescue. For long periods in the first half of the 20th century,

Marines were assigned to guard the embassies in Peking and Managua due to the chronic instability of those countries. The frequent use of the Corps around the world on missions short of war led to a special relationship with the diplomatic corps—in the *Small Wars Manual of 1940*, the Marines even referred to themselves as "State Department troops."

After World War II, the State Department decided that it was time to cast off its previous policy of relying on hired civilians (American or local) to provide embassy security. Strangely enough, it turned first to the Army for support in 1947. Before those negotiations could bear fruit, someone recalled a provision in the Foreign Service Act of 1946 that allowed the Secretary of the Navy to assign Marines or sailors to embassy duty. There was no similar legal basis for the Army to do so. The official State Department request came on 22 June 1948. The Navy Department willingly agreed and President Truman approved of the deal on 5 November. The two agencies signed a formal memorandum governing the program on 15 December.

The first 83 Marines began three weeks of training at the Foreign Service Institute in January 1949, and the first 15 graduates departed overseas (for Bangkok and Tangier) near the end of the month. By May, over 300 Marines were on duty around the world. By 1953 the number had risen to nearly 700. In July 1954, Commandant Shepherd decided that more rigorous screening and schooling were needed. The first four-week course, run by the Corps, began on 4 November that year. Since then, the training syllabus has grown in length and difficulty. A significant organizational change in the program came on 19 February

1967, when the Corps formed the Marine Security Guard (MSG) Battalion to oversee the training of new volunteers and the administration of the far-flung detachments.

Although foreign governments are supposed to ensure the external protection of embassies and MSG detachments are primarily designed to provide internal security, on many occasions Marines have been called on to risk their lives to safeguard their embassies, fellow Americans, and foreign employees. A number of Marines have been killed or wounded in a wide range of hostile incidents over the decades. The first MSG Marine to die in the line of duty was Sergeant James Marshall, killed as he fought back against Viet Cong sappers attacking the U.S. Embassy in Saigon during the January 1968 Tet Offensive. Two more embassy Marines died in Saigon as the North Vietnamese Army overran South Vietnam in the spring of 1975. Corporal Charles McMahon, Jr., and Lance Corporal Darwin D. Judge were, in fact, the last Marines to die in that long war. In August 1977, Marines discovered a fire in the embassy in Moscow, evacuated the occupants, then accompanied Soviet firemen back into the building to safeguard classified material. Nine Marines were held hostage by Iran for 444 days following the seizure of the embassy in Tehran in November 1979. A terrorist bomb attack on the U.S. Embassy in Beirut killed Corporal Robert V. McNaugh in April 1983, six months before the destruction of the Marine headquarters at the airport.

More than a thousand Marines stand watch today at well over 100 U.S. diplomatic posts. Their pride and professionalism are often the most visible symbol of America to many people around the globe. For those who detest the United States and the values it supports, those embassies and their Marines also remain a primary target for hate and violence. The Marine Security Guard Battalion, recently made a part of the new 4th Marine Brigade (Antiterroist), will continue to be in the front lines of U.S. interaction with the governments and peoples of the world.

The Marine Security Guard Detachment of the U.S. Embassy at Moscow's Red Square. (Marine Corps Historical Center)

July
Force Structure
The Marine Corps activates 7th MAB headquarters at 29 Palms as the first force dedicated to the MPF mission. When fleshed out with subordinate elements, it stands ready to deploy by air to any port to link up with an MPF squadron.

1981

January
Norway
The Norwegian and U.S. governments sign an agreement providing for the prepositioning of supplies and equipment to outfit a MAB. An equivalent of MPF, these stocks will be maintained in special caves and allow a MAB to carry out the Corps' mission of reinforcing the Norwegian armed forces in the event of a Soviet attack.

20 January
Iran
The 52 American hostages held by Iran for 444 days are freed.

1 March
Force Structure
HMH-464 is activated at New River to fly the new CH-53E Super Stallion helicopters, which can refuel in flight and lift twice the load of earlier models.

13 April
Aviation
Two Harrier squadrons (VMA-231 and 542) deploy on board ship together to test a concept for augmenting fixed-wing aviation in the fleet during a contingency.

26 May
Mishap
A Marine EA-6B Prowler electronic warfare plane crashes while making a night landing on *Nimitz* (CVN-68). The four Marine aircrewmen and 10 others are killed, 48 are injured, and 20 aircraft are destroyed or damaged.

30 June
Manpower
The strength of the Marine Corps on active duty is 18,363 officers and 172,257 enlisted.

December
Technology
10th Marines receives the first of the new M198 155mm howitzers.

1 December
Manpower
Commandant Barrow announces his own war on drugs. Increased use of urinalysis testing will play a major role in the plan to decrease use of illegal drugs in the Corps.
Force Structure
HMH-465 is activated at Tustin.

1982

24 June
Lebanon
Marines of the 32nd MAU land in Lebanon to help evacuate 580 U.S. citizens from the port city of Juniyah following Israel's 6 June invasion to destroy the Palestine Liberation Organization (PLO). The mission is accomplished that day and the Marines return to their ships. A cease fire

between the Israelis, Syrians, and PLO finally takes hold, with Israel occupying the southern half of Lebanon and surrounding the PLO-occupied districts of west Beirut.

30 June
Manpower
The strength of the Marine Corps on active duty is 18,975 officers and 173,405 enlisted.

25 August
Lebanon
At the request of the Lebanese government, 32nd MAU (BLT 2/8, HMM-261, and MSSG-32) goes ashore and assumes control of the port of Beirut. It is part of a multi-national force with the mission of peacefully evacuating PLO forces and other Palestinians. 32nd MAU completes the mission and re-embarks on 10 September.

29 September
Lebanon
In response to massacres of Palestinian refugees by militiamen, 32nd MAU lands as part of a multinational force comprised of American, French, Italian, and British troops. The Marines take up positions at the Beirut International Airport.

18 October
Technology
The High Mobility Multipurpose Wheeled Vehicle (HMMWV) is announced as the replacement for the venerable jeep. The Corps will take its first deliveries in late 1985.

22 October
Technology
Completed field tests of the Meal Ready to Eat (MRE) show that Marines prefer the new field food to the old C Rations, which will be replaced by MREs as stocks are depleted.

30 October
Lebanon
The 32nd MAU is relieved by the 24th MAU (BLT 3/8, HMM-263, and MSSG-24).

9 November
Technology
The Commandant announces the fielding of the M16A2 rifle, a vastly improved version of the original M16 design.
Training
Following a two-day exercise in northern Somalia, 31st MAU participates in Exercise Jade Tiger 83, a four-day operation with Omani forces at Wahibah Sands, Oman.

7 December
Department of Defense
President Reagan approves the replacement of the RDJTF with Central Command, a new unified headquarters that will be responsible for the Middle East, southwest Asia, and the Indian Ocean.

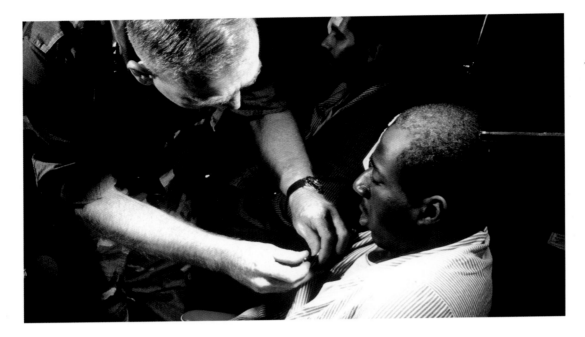

1983

7 January
Technology
VMFA-314 becomes the fist naval squadron to operate the McDonnell Douglas F/A-18 Hornet, which will eventually replace the F-4 and A-4 in the Corps.

February
Technology
The Kevlar helmet, shaped like the German WWII helmet, begins replacing the M1 steel helmet used by American forces since early in WWII.

2 February
Lebanon
Armed only with his .45-caliber pistol, Captain Charles B. Johnson steps in front of three Israeli tanks trying to pass through a U.S. checkpoint and stops them.

15 February
Lebanon
22nd MAU (BLT 2/6, HMM-264, and MSSG-22) relieves 24th MAU.

18 April
Lebanon
A car bomb placed by Islamic terrorists destroys the U.S. Embassy, killing 61, including 17 Americans (one of them a Marine guard).

26 April
Force Structure
HMM-266 is activated at New River.

30 May
Lebanon
24th MAU (BLT 1/8, HMM-162, and MSSG-24) replaces 22nd MAU.

28 June
Sergeants Major
Sergeant Major Robert E. Cleary succeeds Sergeant Major Crawford and becomes the 10th Sergeant Major of the Marine Corps.

30 June
Manpower
The strength of the Marine Corps on active duty is 19,983 officers and 174,106 enlisted.

1 July
Commandants
General Barrow retires and is replaced by General Paul X. Kelley, the 28th Commandant of the Marine Corps.

26 July
Force Structure
6th MAB is activated at Camp Lejeune as another headquarters dedicated to the MPF mission.

28 August
Lebanon
In one of many incidents since March, a Marine outpost comes under fire from opponents of the Lebanese government. For the first time, Marines return fire with small arms.

29 August
Lebanon
Marine positions at the Beirut Airport come under heavy bombardment. Casualties are two killed and 14 wounded. The Marines counter with their own artillery fire. This marks a major escalation in the fighting, with repeated exchanges of heavy fire thereafter.

8 September
Lebanon
In another escalation of the fighting, Marines call in naval gunfire from frigate *Bowen* (FF-1079) to silence a militia artillery battery in the Shouf Mountains above the airport.

12 September
Lebanon
31st MAU arrives off the coast from its normal station in the Pacific and Indian Oceans. It remains in the area until 1 October.

26 September
Lebanon
A cease fire goes into effect, but sniper incidents continue to inflict casualties on Marines, who return fire in kind.

21 October
Grenada
Following a Communist coup in this Caribbean nation, 22nd MAU is ordered to divert to the area to protect American citizens. It had just started its journey toward Lebanon.

23 October
Lebanon
A truck bomb destroys the building housing the headquarters of BLT 1/8. Marine casualties are 220 killed and 70 wounded, with 21 other American servicemen also dead. This is the highest one-day death toll in the Corps since WWII. A similar attack is made against the French position, killing

58. Elements of 2/6 begin deploying that day from Camp Lejeune to reinforce the BLT, while the Marine detachment of *New Jersey* comes ashore in the meantime.

25 October
Grenada
22nd MAU, Army Rangers, and elements of the 82nd Airborne Division invade the island to rescue over 1,000 Americans from factional fighting. Three Marine aviators die during the operation, which winds up on 2 November. Navy ships and Marine amphibian tractors and helicopters allow the MAU to secure a substantial potion of the island.

26 October
Technology
The Corps takes delivery of its first wheeled light armored vehicle, designated LAV-25.

6 November
Sports
Staff Sergeant Farley Simon becomes the first Marine to win the Marine Corps Marathon.

Left: *CH-46 on Grenada. (Defense Visual Information Center)*

Opposite: *A LAV-25 crosses the Bridge of the Americas in Panama. (Defense Visual Information Center)*

19 November
Lebanon
22nd MAU (BLT 2/8, HMM-261, and MSSG-22) relieves 24th MAU.

4 December
Lebanon
A heavy bombardment kills eight Marines and wounds two. This marks a resumption of heavy exchanges of fire.

14 December
Terrorism
A truck bomb hits the U.S. Embassy in Kuwait. Although dozens are killed and wounded, none are Americans. Marine security guards protect the damaged building.

1984

12 January
Technology
The Corps' first McDonnell Douglas AV-8B Harrier joins 2nd MAW at Cherry Point.

10–11 February
Lebanon
Following President Reagan's decision to withdraw most Marines from Lebanon, helicopters evacuate U.S. and foreign nationals from Beirut.

21–26 February
Lebanon
22nd MAU redeploys back to its ships.

24 March
Mishap
A CH-53 crash during Team Spirit 84 kills 18 U.S. and 11 Republic of Korea Marines.

4 April
Force Structure
The 2nd Light Armored Vehicle (LAV) Battalion is activated at Camp Lejeune.

2 May
Technology
Bell Aerospace Textron rolls out the first landing craft air-cushion (LCAC) in New Orleans. The Navy hover craft will bring new speed and range to amphibious operations.

30 June
Manpower
The strength of the Marine Corps on active duty is 20,366 officers and 175,848 enlisted.

14 July
Technology
Corporal Louis J. Hauge, Jr., the first ship designed specifically for the MPF, is launched in Maryland.

20 September
Lebanon
A suicide truck bomb explodes in front of the U.S. Embassy Annex in Beirut, killing 23 people and wounding numerous others, including four Marine guards.

28 September
Force Structure
HMM-364 is reactivated at Kaneohe Bay after a hiatus of 13 years.

30 November
Force Structure
HMH-466 is activated at Tustin.

1985

14 January
Technology
The 9mm Beretta 92SB-F replaces the M1911A1 .45-caliber pistol, which has been in service with U.S. armed forces for nearly 75 years.

6 May
Mishap
A CH-53D crashes in the Sea of Japan killing 17 Marines.

24 May
Training
A revised Marine Corps order increases the amount of combat-related training, to include marksmanship and defensive tactics, required of female Marines.

31 May
Force Structure
1st LAV Battalion is activated at Camp Pendleton.

14 June
Doctrine
Commandant Kelley directs a pilot program to train MAUs for some special operations. Following a lengthy training and evaluation program, 26th MAU is designated special operations capable and becomes the first MAU (SOC) in December.

19 June
El Salvador
Communist guerrillas fire on an outdoor café, killing 13 people, including four off-duty Marine embassy guards.

30 June
Manpower
The strength of the Marine Corps on active duty is 20,175 officers and 177,850 enlisted.

1 July
Force Structure
5th MAB headquarters is activated at Camp Pendleton.

13 September
Force Structure
HMM-166 is activated at Tustin.

15 October
Mishap
A CH-46 crashes off Camp Lejeune killing 14 Marines and a Navy chaplain.

27 November
Commanders
General George B. Crist takes the helm of Central Command, the first Marine ever to head a unified command.

1986

23–27 March
Libya
Freedom of navigation exercises in the Gulf of Sidra by three carrier battle groups result in the sinking of two Libyan missile boats. VMFA-314 and 323 and VMAQ-2 participate.

27 March
Technology
The Corps takes delivery of its first Bell Textron AH-1W Super Cobra attack helicopter.

1 April
Force Structure
The three attack helicopter and three light helicopter squadrons begin the process of re-organizing into six light attack (HMLA) squadrons, each with Hueys and Cobras.

14 April
Libya
VMFA-314 and 323 participate in air strikes against Libyan targets following a Libyan-sponsored terrorist bombing of a night club in Germany frequented by Americans.

30 June
Manpower
The strength of the Marine Corps on active duty is 20,199 officers and 178,615 enlisted.

29 August
Mishap
A CH-46 crash during an exercise in Norway results in eight Marines dead and 13 injured.

11 September
Force Structure
The 3rd LAV Battalion is activated at 29 Palms.

22 September
Training
The Commandant directs that senior SNCOs replace officers in running the SNCO Academies at Quantico, Lejeune, and El Toro.

1987

10 April
Department of the Navy
James H. Webb, Jr., a Marine captain in Vietnam and noted author, becomes the 66th Secretary of the Navy.

16 April
Force Structure
Marine Corps Security Force Battalion, Atlantic, is activated at Norfolk as part of a restructuring of Marine detachments afloat and Marine barracks.

26 June
Sergeants Major
Sergeant Major David W. Somers succeeds Sergeant Major Cleary and becomes the 11th Sergeant Major of the Marine Corps.

30 June
Manpower
The strength of the Marine Corps on active duty is 20,047 officers and 179,478 enlisted, the peak strength of the Corps since the Vietnam War.

1 July
Commandants
General Kelley retires and is replaced by General Alfred M. Gray, Jr., the 29th Commandant of the Marine Corps.

24 July
Persian Gulf
After an American-flagged oil tanker strikes a sea mine laid by Iran, elements of 24th MAU are dispatched to the gulf to assist Navy forces in securing the sea lanes for commercial shipping.

4 August
Technology
Amphibious assault ship *Wasp* (LHD-1) is launched at Pascagoula, Mississippi. It and its sister ships will replace the *Iwo Jima*–class helicopter carriers.

24 August
Legal
A court martial convicts Sergeant Clayton J. Lonetree of espionage and related charges involving his duties at embassies in Vienna and Moscow. He is the first Marine ever convicted of spying.

21 September
Persian Gulf
Marine helicopters assist in capturing *Iran Ajr*, an Iranian ship laying mines in the gulf.

8 October
Iran
With just 48 hours notice, Contingency MAGTF 1-88 is formed and sails on board *Okinawa* (LPH-3). Its mission is to relieve the detachment of 24th MAU on duty in the Persian Gulf. CM 1-88 remains on station until replaced by CM 2-88 on 20 February 1988.

9 October
Force Structure
Marine Barracks Portsmouth, New Hampshire, the second oldest post in the Corps, is deactivated after 174 years of service dating back to 1813.

6 December
Force Structure
Sea School, opened in 1923 at San Diego, is closed as part of the restructuring of Marine security forces.

Right: *A Marines sweeps the area outside the perimeter. ("Beirut Watch," Sgt Arturo Alejandre, USMC, Marine Corps Art Collection)*

1988

January
Manpower
Secretary of the Navy Webb decrees that Naval Academy midshipmen will now have to complete Officer Candidate School at Quantico in order to qualify for a Marine commission.

5 February
Force Structure
The titles of all MAGTFs are changed by replacing "amphibious" with "expeditionary" to reflect the wide range of capability they possess.

17 February
Terrorism
Lieutenant Colonel William R. Higgins, serving with a U.N. observer organization along the Israeli-Lebanon border, is abducted by terrorists. He is subsequently killed.

18 April
Persian Gulf
Marines of Contingency MAGTF 2-88 destroy the Iranian oil platform *Sassan* during U.S. strikes on sites used to launch attacks on ships in the Persian Gulf. A Marine Cobra helicopter and its two pilots are lost during the action.

May
Manpower
For the first time since the late 1970s, female Marines are authorized to become members of MSG detachments at American embassies.

23 May
Technology
Bell Textron rolls out the first V-22 Osprey, a revolutionary tilt-rotor aircraft that lands and takes off like a helicopter but flies like a prop-driven fixed-wing plane. It is designed to replace the aging CH-46 fleet.

30 June
Manpower
The strength of the Marine Corps on active duty is 20,079 officers and 177,271 enlisted.

9 September
Force Structure
VMGR-452 is activated as part of 4th MAW.

31 December
Force Structure
MAG-15 is deactivated at Iwakuni.

1989

7 January
Force Structure
HMA-775 is activated as part of 4th MAW at Camp Pendleton.

3 March
Force Structure
2/6 and 3/1 are placed in cadre status as part of a reduction of three infantry battalions and the addition of a fourth rifle company to the remaining 24 active-duty battalions.

17–20 March
Mishaps
The crash of a CH-46 and a CH-53D three days apart during Team Spirit in Korea result in the death of 17 Marines and one corpsman.

11 May
Panama
Following General Manuel Noriega's refusal to recognize the results of elections in his country, the United States deploys additional forces to U.S. bases there.

31 May
Mishaps
A CH-46 crashes during a night flight off *Denver* (LPD-9), killing 13 Marines and one corpsman.

30 June
Manpower
The strength of the Marine Corps on active duty is 20,099 officers and 176,857 enlisted.

11 July
Training
The Commandant establishes the Marine Corps Professional Reading Program for NCOs, SNCOs, and officers.

1 August
Training
The Marine Corps University is established to oversee a number of educational programs.

20 December
Panama
Four days after Panamanian security forces killed Marine Lieutenant Robert Paz at a roadblock, U.S. forces launch Operation Just Cause to overthrow the Noriega dictatorship, which has been implicated in illegal drug distribution. One company each of

infantry and light armored infantry, a Fleet Antiterrorism Security Team (FAST) platoon, and the Marine Corps Security Force company participate in the operation, which is largely complete the first day. One Marine is killed.

1990

30 June
Manpower
The strength of the Marine Corps on active duty is 19,958 officers and 176,694 enlisted.

5 August
Liberia
Elements of 22nd MEU(SOC) fly into the U.S. Embassy compound in Monrovia and begin evacuating Americans and other foreign nationals as a civil war rages in the country. Operation Sharp Edge continues until 30 November and pulls out over 2,400 civilians.

7 August
Operation Desert Shield
Five days after Iraq invades Kuwait, President George W. Bush orders U.S. forces to the Persian Gulf to contain further Iraqi aggression against oil-producing states in the region.

Opposite: *A VMA-513 AV-8B Harrier loaded for bear during Operation Desert Shield. (Defense Visual Information Center)*

Right: *A CH-53E lands on* Raleigh *(LPD-1) in October 1990. (Marine Corps Historical Center)*

LIEUTENANT GENERAL FRANK E. PETERSON, JR.

From the time he saw B-29 bombers flying out of the airfield near his hometown of Topeka, Kansas, during World War II, Frank Peterson wanted to fly. From his father, who ran an electronics business, young Frank learned how to repair radios, work hard, and challenge life. After he graduated from high school in 1949, he wanted to enlist in the Navy and see the world, but his father wouldn't sign the papers for the 17-year-old. Frank instead went on to Washburn University. In early June 1950, just three weeks before the Korean War broke out, he joined the Navy. After boot camp, he went to electronics school. In April 1951, he won the opportunity to become a naval aviation cadet. In October 1952, he earned his wings and opted for a Marine commission.

After advanced flight training, Lieutenant Peterson went to Korea in April 1953 and was assigned to VMA-212. Truce negotiations were ongoing, but the fighting intensified as the Communists sought an advantage to use at the bargaining table. In the few short months remaining in the war, he flew 64 combat missions. The most harrowing came on 15 June. In response to a request for close air support, he led a division of Corsairs against a mortar position in mountainous terrain. Despite damage to his plane from heavy anti-aircraft fire, he pressed home the attack at low altitude and dropped the first bomb, marking the enemy position for the remaining aircraft. He then joined in subsequent bombing and strafing runs that wiped out the target. For his actions that day, he received the Distinguished Flying Cross. By the close of the campaign, he also had earned six Air Medals.

Following the war, Peterson spent a ground tour as an air liaison officer with the 1st Marine Division. Back in the States, he flew with VMF(N)-542 at El Toro and successfully converted to a regular commission. Other flying and school tours followed, including the chance to complete his college education at George Washington University. In June 1968, now a lieutenant colonel, he took command of VMFA-314 in Vietnam and led it through a year of hard fighting.

In August 1968, Peterson and his radar intercept officer took off in their F-4 Phantom from Chu Lai, on a mission to provide close air support for a reconnaissance unit in trouble up near the DMZ. On his second pass at the target, anti-aircraft fire struck the left engine and it burst into flames. The plane was streaking north at the time and was already into air space over North Vietnam. Unwilling to bail out and risk becoming a prisoner, the two men stuck with their burning aircraft. Peterson brought it around, but as they neared the DMZ again, the other engine caught fire. Finally, when the hydraulics and controls quit working, the pilot gave the order to punch out. Although he did not know it for some time, he was injured in the ejection, suffering a herniated disk and a hairline fracture of the hip socket. Two days later, he was back in the air. His squadron ultimately received the Marine Corps Aviation Association's Hanson Award as the outstanding fighter squadron of the year. He departed Vietnam in the summer of 1969 with another 300 combat missions in his logbooks.

Back at home, he found himself in a new and entirely different sort of battle, as the first Special Assistant to the Commandant for Minority Affairs. At a time of high racial tensions in the armed forces and the nation, it was a challenging and difficult assignment. Over the course of two years, he helped lead the effort to solve widespread problems in the Corps related to racism, drugs, and indiscipline. After a year at the National War College, he went back to the FMF and helped reinvigorate the post-Vietnam Corps. He served as a group commander in 2nd MAW, chief of staff of the 9th Marine Amphibious Brigade, assistant wing commander of 1st MAW, commanding general of 9th MAB, commanding general of 1st MAW, and finally deputy commander of FMFLANT. In October 1985, he became the Silver Hawk, the Corps' longest-serving active aviator. Two years later, he added the title Gray Eagle when he became the senior naval aviator. He retired from active duty in 1988 after two years as the commanding general of the Marine Corps Development and Education Command in Quantico and went on to a civilian career as a corporate executive.

LtGen Frank Peterson stands in front of a Corsair, similar to the ones he flew over Korea as a young Marine aviator. (Marine Corps Historical Center)

10 August
Operation Desert Shield
7th MEB (RLT 7, MAG-70, and BSSG-7) begins flying from the United States to Al Jubayl, Saudi Arabia, where it will link up with its MPF squadron.

17 August
Operation Desert Shield
The first elements of 4th MEB (RLT 2, MAG-40, and BSSG-4)) sail from Morehead City for the Persian Gulf.

19 August
Operation Desert Shield
RLT 4 and BLT 1/6 begin loading on ships in Okinawa for deployment to Saudi Arabia.

20 August
Operation Desert Shield
Lieutenant General Walter E. Boomer, commander of I MEF, arrives in Saudi Arabia. His headquarters will command all Marine forces in the operation, except for those afloat.
Liberia
Elements of 26th MEU begin relieving 22nd MEU in Operation Sharp Edge.

22 August
Operation Desert Shield
President Bush orders the mobilization of reserve forces to support the operation. More than 31,000 Marine reservists will ultimately be mobilized for service around the world.

25 August
Operation Desert Shield
1st MEB begins flying out of Hawaii to link up with its MPF ships at Al Jubayl.

2 September
Operation Desert Shield
7th MEB deactivates and is subsumed into I MEF. 1st MEB follows suit a few days later. The major subordinate elements of I MEF (3rd MAW, 1st Marine Division, and 1st FSSG) take control of their respective parts of the force.

7 September
Operation Desert Shield
13th MEU(SOC) arrives in the Persian Gulf and remains afloat under Navy command.

17 September
Operation Desert Shield
The last elements of 4th MEB arrive in the Persian Gulf and remain afloat under Navy command.

8 November
Operation Desert Shield
President Bush announces that the U.S. will double the size of its forces in the Persian Gulf. The additional Marine elements will include 2nd Marine Division, 5th MEB, 2nd MAW, and 2nd FSSG. 2nd MAW will be composited with 3rd MAW. 1st FSSG will provide general logistics support to the MEF, while 2nd FSSG becomes the Direct Support Command operating in the immediate rear of the ground combat forces.

Left: *A logistics vehicle proudly flies the U.S. flag during Operation Desert Storm. (Defense Visual Information Center)*

Right: *An AH-1 Cobra supports AAVP-7s carrying the 1st Combat Engineer Battalion on 26 February 1991. (Defense Visual Information Center)*

1 December
Operation Desert Shield
5th MEB (RLT 5, MAG-50, BSSG-5), with 11th MEU(SOC) embedded, sails from California.

18 December
Technology
The first Marine Corps M1A1 Abrams tank is rolled off the assembly line. 2nd Tank Battalion will be the first to receive the new tanks and will deploy to the Persian Gulf with them.

1991

1 January
Operation Desert Shield
The 24th Marines (less 1/24) deploys from the States to Al Jubayl to assume the rear area security mission for I MEF.

2 January
Somalia
Elements of 4th MEB on board *Guam* (LPH-9) and *Trenton* (LPD-14) sail from the Persian Gulf area with the mission of evacuating American personnel from the U.S. Embassy in Mogadishu as a result of a civil war.

5 January
Somalia
Operation Eastern Exit gets underway at 0147 when two CH-53Es and a security force launch 466 miles from Mogadishu. Two in-flight refuelings from KC-130s are required to reach the objective. The dangerous, long-range mission is dictated by Somali looters attempting to invade the embassy compound. A return flight evacuates the first 61 civilians. Another 220 civilians, including the Soviet embassy staff, are lifted out the next day when the ships arrive off the coast.

10 January
Operation Desert Shield
The U.S. Army's 1st Brigade of the 2nd Armored Division (known as the Tiger Brigade) is attached to I MEF.

11 January
Operation Desert Shield
All II MEF elements have reached the theater and joined I MEF. 5th MEB arrives in the Persian Gulf the next day and joins with 4th MEB, forming the largest amphibious task force since Inchon in 1950.

16 January
Operation Desert Storm
Following the expiration of a deadline for Iraq to withdraw its forces from Kuwait, coalition forces (including 3rd MAW) launch offensive air operations against Iraq.

20 January
Operation Desert Storm
I MEF begins conducting artillery raids against Iraqi forces in Kuwait.

29 January
Operation Desert Storm
Iraqi forces launch three brigade-size night attacks across the Kuwaiti border. Two are repulsed. One captures the abandoned Saudi town of Al Khafji. eleven Marines die in these night battles, all in fratricide incidents.

1 February
Operation Desert Storm
Marine air, artillery, and observer teams assist Saudi and Qatari troops in retaking Al Khafji.

6 February
Operation Desert Storm
The Direct Support Command begins constructing a new forward logistics base. Dubbed Al Khanjar, the huge facility begins operations six days later.

23 February
Training
Reservists of 2nd MEB participate in Exercise Battle Griffin 91 and conduct the first full test of the Norway Airlanded MEB (NALMEB) concept—the prepositioned set of equipment and supplies created by a 1981 agreement.

24 February
Operation Desert Storm
The ground campaign begins before dawn, with 1st and 2nd Marine Divisions and the Tiger Brigade attacking toward Kuwait City through Iraqi obstacle belts. 5th MEB begins going ashore to become the I MEF reserve. Nearly all 3rd MAW sorties are in support of the MEF. I MEF strength, including attachments and 11,703 Marine reservists, is 84,515. Additional Marine forces afloat conduct deception operations to pin down Iraqi defenders on the coast.

28 February
Operation Desert Storm
President Bush declares a cease fire at 0800 Kuwaiti time. I MEF forces had reached Kuwait City, captured more than 22,000 prisoners, and destroyed hundreds of tanks, armored vehicles, and artillery pieces. Marine casualties for all of Desert Storm are 24 dead and 92 wounded. Five Marine aviators captured by the enemy are released soon after. Four Harriers and two Broncos were shot down, while five Hornets were damaged.

9 March
Operation Desert Storm
The first Marine units begin departing for the States. The last Marines will depart on 27 August.

15 April
Operation Provide Comfort
Following a failed revolt against Saddam Hussein's regime, two million Kurds are fleeing their homes in northern Iraq. A multinational relief operation

is underway, with 24th MEU(SOC) (BLT 2/8, HMM-264, and MSSG-24) moving inland to the Turkish town of Silopi. Within days, Marines move into northern Iraq to establish safe havens for returning refugees. Other Marine elements from around the world begin reinforcing the MEU, including Contingency MAGTF 1-91 from Okinawa. 24th MEU(SOC) remains part of Operation Provide Comfort until 19 July.

15 May
Bangladesh
Two weeks after a devastating cyclone strikes the country, 5th MEB (on its way home from Operation Desert Storm) arrives off the coast to support the international relief effort. 5th MEB participates in Operation Sea Angel through 28 May. It is replaced by Contingency MAGTF 2-91 from Okinawa, which remains through 7 June.

12 June
Philippines
Following the volcanic eruption of Mt. Pinatubo, Marines from III MEF and the barracks at Subic Bay begin assisting in relief work (dubbed Operation Fiery Vigil). The devastation results soon after in an early closure of damaged U.S. military facilities in the Philippines, including the naval base at Subic Bay, which had been home to Marines and sailors since 1898.

28 June
Sergeants Major
Sergeant Major Harold G. Overstreet succeeds Sergeant Major Somers and becomes the 12th Sergeant Major of the Marine Corps.

30 June
Manpower
The strength of the Marine Corps on active duty is 19,753 officers and 174,287 enlisted.

1 July
Commandants
General Gray retires and is replaced by General Carl E. Mundy, Jr., the 30th Commandant of the Marine Corps.
Force Structure
VMFA(AW)-225 is reactivated at El Toro after a hiatus of 19 years.

August
Force Structure
As part of the post-Cold War drawdown, the Marine Corps begins deleting the fourth rifle companies from its infantry battalions.

6 September
Commanders
The Marine Corps adopts a formalized screening process to select lieutenant colonels and colonels for command billets.

22 November
Caribbean
Elements of II MEF begin deploying to Guantanamo Bay, Cuba, to assist in processing thousands of refugees from Haiti, where a military coup has created political turmoil. The operation continues through June 1993.

1992

February
Force Structure
The Marine Corps begins deactivating its six permanent MEB headquarters.

31 March
Force Structure
VMFA-333 and 531 are deactivated.

1 May
Civil Support
More than 1,500 Marines from Camp Pendleton deploy to Los Angeles to assist authorities in quelling riots following the acquittal of four policemen charged with beating a motorist.

30 June
Manpower
The strength of the Marine Corps on active duty is 19,132 officers and 165,397 enlisted.

20 July
Mishap
Three Marines and four civilians are killed when a V-22 crashes near Quantico. Test flights are suspended while the accident is investigated.

18 August
Somalia
President Bush orders U.S. military forces to assist in famine relief efforts by flying food from bases in Kenya into Somalia.

1 October
Force Structure
VMA-331 is deactivated. VMAQ-4 is reactivated as an active duty squadron at Cherry Point.

10 November
Force Structure
Marine Barracks Guam is disestablished following almost-continuous operation since 1899.

24 November
Force Structure
Marines depart Subic Bay following the transfer of the base to the Philippines.

9 December
Somalia
After the famine worsens due to continued instability, President Bush orders direct military intervention to permit effective relief operations. 15th MEU(SOC) begins landing to secure ports and airfields for additional forces for Operation Restore Hope. Marine Lieutenant General Robert B. Johnson and his I MEF headquarters assume command of the joint task force, which will grow to 30,000 troops, including the 7th Marines, MAG-16, and elements of 1st FSSG.

1993

19 July
Balkans
VMFA(AW)-533 begins supporting Operation Deny Flight, designed to limit Serbian aggression against ethnic minorities in Bosnia. Marine squadrons will serve almost continuously in this capacity for the next several years.

28 April
Manpower
Secretary of Defense Les Aspin promulgates new policy that opens more occupational specialties and billets to servicewomen, to include pilots and crew of combat aircraft.

30 April
Force Structure
MAG-32 is deactivated at Cherry Point.

4 May
Somalia
Lieutenant General Johnston passes command of Operation Restore Hope to Turkish General Cevik Bir, as the U.S. role in the effort shrinks. The last I MEF Marines depart Somalia.

20 May
Force Structure
VMO-2 is deactivated at Camp Pendleton as part of the phase-out of the OV-10.

24 June
Somalia
24th MEU(SOC) deploys to Mogadishu in support of U.N. forces facing increasing fighting with Somali warlords.

30 June
Manpower
The strength of the Marine Corps on active duty is 18,430 officers and 159,949 enlisted.

1 September
Manpower
The DOD Bottom Up Review approves a strength of 174,000 for the Corps, as opposed to the 159,000 once projected as part of the post–Cold War drawdown.

30 September
Force Structure
VMO-1 is deactivated at New River.

7 October
Somalia
Following the death of 14 American soldiers in Mogadishu a few days earlier, the United States sends additional forces, to include the 13th and 22nd MEU(SOC)s.

1994

25 March
Somalia
24th MEU(SOC) oversees the withdrawal of the last U.S. forces, except for a Marine security platoon at the embassy.

12 April
Operation Distant Runner
11th MEU(SOC) evacuates 230 civilians, including 142 Americans, who are escaping ethnic fighting in the African nation of Rwanda.

26 April
Force Structure
VMO-4, the last OV-10D Bronco squadron in the Marine Corps, is deactivated.

Right: *Manning a Mk-19 grenade launcher during a weapons sweep in Mogadishu. (Defense Visual Information Center)*

15–23 June
Training
U.S. Navy and Marine forces conduct their first-ever exercise with Russian Navy and naval infantry at Vladivostok.

30 June
Manpower
The strength of the Marine Corps on active duty is 17,823 officers and 156,335 enlisted.

21 July
Force Structure
The 9th Marines is deactivated on Okinawa.

20 September
Haiti
Special Purpose MAGTF Carib (built around the headquarters of the 2nd Marines, 2/2, and HMM-264) goes ashore at Cap Haitien as part of Operation Uphold Democracy. This is an unopposed intervention designed to restore the authority of the elected president of Haiti. The MAGTF will remain in Haiti for 12 days.

24 September
Haiti
A Marine lieutenant and a rifle squad engage Haitian military personnel at a police station, killing 10 and wounding one, at a cost of one sailor wounded.

1 October
Force Structure
HMH-366 is activated at Kaneohe Bay.

1–3 March
Somalia
13th MEU(SOC), assisted by Italian Marines, provides security for the amphibious withdrawal of the last U.N. peacekeepers from the strife-torn country in Operation United Shield.

19 April
Terrorism
Two Marine recruiters are killed and four wounded in the truck bombing of the Alfred P. Murrah Federal Building in Oklahoma City, Oklahoma. There are also hundreds of civilian casualties.

24–25 May
Balkans
Marine aircraft participate in strikes on Serbian ammunition dumps in support of continuing NATO action in the troubled region.

8 June
Balkans
24th MEU(SOC) rescues Air Force Captain Scott O'Grady from Serb-controlled territory in Bosnia. His F-16C had been shot down by Serbian missiles six days earlier.

30 June
Sergeants Major
Sergeant Major Lewis G. Lee succeeds Sergeant Major Overstreet and becomes the 13th Sergeant Major of the Marine Corps.

Left: *Sgt C. Banks, Jr., of 2/2, distributes food in Cap Haitien, Haiti. (Defense Visual Information Center)*

Opposite: *Haiti. ("Getting Ready," Capt Charles Grow, USMC, Marine Corps Art Collection)*

1 July
Commandants
General Mundy retires and is replaced by General Charles C. Krulak, the 31st Commandant of the Marine Corps.

16 August
Manpower
In a change to the physical fitness test for female Marines, they are now required to run the same three-mile distance as their male counterparts.

29 August
Balkans
VMFA(AW)-533 at Aviano and VMFA-312 on board carrier *Theodore Roosevelt* (CVN-71) participate in the beginning of Operation Deliberate Force, an air offensive designed to force the Serbian government to end its brutal operations in Bosnia. The campaign continues through 21 December, when NATO forces are fully deployed in Bosnia to enforce peace.

26 September
Manpower
First Lieutenant Sarah Deal completes the training syllabus for the CH-53E and is assigned to HMH-466, thus becoming the first female Marine pilot.

30 September
Manpower
The strength of the Marine Corps on active duty is 17,831 officers and 156,808 enlisted.

1996

17 January
HQMC
The Commandant and other major elements of HQMC move into the Pentagon from the Navy Annex, where they have been located for more than five decades.

27 March
Manpower
Marine Major General Carol A. Mutter is the first female nominated for three-star rank in any of the services. She is promoted on 23 July.

April
Force Structure
The Chemical Biological Incident Response Force (CBIRF) is created to provide a Marine capability to deal with terrorist acts involving chemical or biological agents.

20 April
Liberia
Elements of 22nd MEU(SOC) fly into Monrovia and begin a weeks-long evacuation of thousands of Americans and other foreign nationals in the face of an ongoing civil war.

10 May
Mishap
A mid-air collision involving a CH-46E and an AH-1W over Camp Lejeune results in the death of 12 Marines, one sailor, and one soldier.

21 May
Central African Republic
Another element of 22nd MEU(SOC) flies into the country to evacuate Americans and assist the MSG detachment in protecting the embassy during an army mutiny.

30 December
Manpower
Female Marines begin reporting for the first time to Marine Combat Training, a post-boot camp program that provides infantry training to Marines destined to serve in non-infantry specialties.

1997

31 January
Force Structure
VMFA-451 is deactivated.

1–14 March
Doctrine
The recently activated Warfighting Lab conducts Hunter Warrior, an exercise at 29 Palms testing futuristic doctrine and technologies.

13–26 March
Albania
26th MEU(SOC) evacuates more than 900 Americans and other foreign nationals during chaotic conditions following the disintegration of the Communist government.

29 May
Zaire
22nd MEU(SOC) begins evacuation of civilians escaping a civil war. Over the next five days, the MEU pulls out more than 2,500 people, including 450 Americans.

30 September
Manpower
The combined strength of the Marine Corps on active duty is 174,873 officers and enlisted.

1 October
Bases
The Marine Corps takes over Miramar from the Navy as a replacement for El Toro.

1998

31 January
Force Structure
The Marine Corps begins deactivating the last of its ships detachments.

14 June
Force Structure
VMFA-235 is deactivated at Miramar.

25 July
Manpower
As part of an increase of flag officers in the armed services, the Marine Corps is authorized an increase from 68 to 80 generals, giving it one more than it had during WWII.

30 July
Training
Commandant Krulak announces changes to recruit training. The most significant will be the Crucible, a 54-hour event near the end of the boot camp cycle that will challenge the mental and physical endurance of recruits and mark their transformation into Marines.

30 September
Manpower
The combined strength of the Marine Corps on active duty is 174,049 officers and enlisted.

3 February
Mishap
A Marine EA-6B on a training mission in Italy flies through a cable and sends a ski gondola crashing to the ground, killing 20 people.

6 June
Eritrea
KC-130s attached to 11th MEU(SOC) evacuate civilians following border clashes between Eritrea and Ethiopia.

7 August
Terrorism
Truck bombs explode at U.S. embassies in Nairobi, Kenya, and Dar es Salaam, Tanzania. More than 250 are killed, including one Marine security guard. FAST platoons deploy to secure the sites.

30 September
Manpower
The strength of the Marine Corps on active duty is 17,892 officers and 155,250 enlisted.

16 December
Iraq
31st MEU(SOC) and VMFA-312, on board *Enterprise* (CVN-65), participate in Operation Desert Fox, an air campaign launched in retaliation for Iraq's obstruction of a U.N. weapons inspection program. The operation lasts for four days.

24 March
Balkans
NATO launches Operation Allied Force, an air campaign to force Serbian withdrawal from the ethnic Albanian province of Kosovo. Harriers of 24th MEU(SOC) participate.

30 April
Balkans
Elements of 26th MEU(SOC) go ashore in Albania to provide security and assistance to a camp housing refugees from Kosovo.

14 May
Technology
The Marine Corps takes delivery of its first production MV-22 Osprey.

20 May
Balkans
VMFA(AW)-332 and 533 begin flying in support of Operation Allied Force from bases in Hungary.

Opposite: *LAV in Operation Provide Comfort. (Defense Visual Information Center)*

Right: *Marine Hornet about to launch from* Enterprise. *(Defense Visual Information Center)*

10 June
Balkans
Operation Allied Force is suspended when the Serbian forces begin withdrawing from Kosovo. 26th MEU(SOC) begins deploying to the province to enforce the peace agreement. It remains ashore through 6 July.

28 June
Sergeants Major
Sergeant Major Alfred L. McMichael succeeds Sergeant Major Lee and becomes the 14th Sergeant Major of the Marine Corps.

1 July
Commandants
General Krulak retires and is replaced by General James L. Jones, Jr., the 32nd Commandant of the Marine Corps.

2 July
Bases
The Marine Corps closes El Toro and Tustin as part of a reduction in military bases.

30 September
East Timor
31st MEU(SOC) helicopters support the deployment of Australian forces restoring peace in the region following post-election violence by armed gangs. 11th MEU(SOC) takes over on 26 October and remains on station through 7 December.
Manpower
The strength of the Marine Corps on active duty is 17,897 officers and 154,744 enlisted.

2000

---

8 April
Mishap
A MV-22 Osprey crashes near Tucson, Arizona, during a training exercise, killing 19 Marines.

30 September
Force Structure
HMH-366 is deactivated.
Manpower
The strength of the Marine Corps on active duty is 17,938 officers and 155,383 enlisted.

12 October
Terrorism
A boat bomb blasts a hole in the side of destroyer *Cole* (DDG-67), killing 17 sailors and injuring 39. Marines of 2nd FAST deploy to secure the ship in the harbor of Aden, Yemen.

Left: *Marines of Bravo Company, 1/8, wait inside a MV-22 Osprey for the start of a training mission. (Defense Visual Information Center)*

11 December
Mishap
Four Marines are killed when their MV-22 Osprey crashes near Jacksonville, North Carolina. The second crash of the year leads to an indefinite suspension of MV-22 flights.

2001

---

11 September
Terrorism
Members of the Al Qaida terrorist organization hijack four jetliners, crashing one each into the Pentagon and the two towers of the World Trade Center in New York City. A fourth crashes in rural Pennsylvania. Marines in the Pentagon participate in rescue operations.

30 September
Manpower
The strength of the Marine Corps on active duty is 18,057 officers and 154,878 enlisted.

October
Department of Defense
General Peter Pace becomes the first Marine ever to serve as the Vice Chairman of the JCS.

7 October
Operation Enduring Freedom
U.S. forces begin an air and special operations campaign against Taliban and Al Qaida forces in Afghanistan. VMFA-251 and 314, on board carriers *Roosevelt* (CVN-71) and *Stennis* (CVN-74), and the Harriers of 15th MEU(SOC) participate in the aerial campaign.

Left: *MV-22 silhouetted against the morning sky as it lands on* Wasp. *(Defense Visual Information Center)*

Below: *LtGen Anthony Zinni, commander of Marine forces that secured the withdrawal from Somalia. (Defense Visual Information Center)*

10 October
Force Structure
4th MEB (Antiterrorism) is activated. It consists of existing forces: Marine Security Force Battalion and its two FAST companies, Marine Security Guard Battalion, CBIRF, and an interim antiterrorism battalion.

1 November
Operation Enduring Freedom
Task Force 58 is activated in Central Command to control the 15th and 26th MEU(SOC)s.

25 November
Operation Enduring Freedom
15th MEU(SOC) elements begin landing in Afghanistan more than 400 miles from the coast and taking control of Forward Operating Base (FOB) Rhino. Marine air and ground forces begin patrolling the region in search of Taliban and Al Qaida fighters.

7 December
Operation Enduring Freedom
In the largest Marine fire fight of the campaign, a patrol kills seven enemy and destroys three vehicles while interdicting a road. Aircraft destroy several more occupied vehicles.

11 December
Operation Enduring Freedom
Elements of 26th MEU(SOC) secure the long-abandoned U.S. Embassy in Kabul, Afghanistan. They are soon replaced by Marines of 4th MEB(AT).

Right: *Marines man an entry control point outside Kandahar, Afghanistan, in January 2002. (USMC)*

Below: *Weary Marines return from a nine-day patrol in Afghanistan. (USMC)*

14 December
Operation Enduring Freedom
Elements of 26th MEU(SOC) advance overland and take control of Kandahar Airfield. It soon becomes the primary detention facility for captured enemy personnel of key interest to the United States. Marine helicopters also support joint and coalition forces from this base.

24 December
Operation Enduring Freedom
15th MEU(SOC) begins redeploying back to its ships. FOB Rhino is closed on 3 January 2002.

2002

---

9 January
Operation Enduring Freedom
A KC-130 of VMGR-352 crashes in Pakistan, resulting in the death of seven Marines.

11 January
Operation Enduring Freedom
Detainees begin arriving at Camp X-Ray at Guantanamo Bay for interrogation and holding. Marine elements from II MEF are part of the task force running the facility.

19 January
Operation Enduring Freedom
U.S. Army forces begin relieving Marine elements at Kandahar Airfield. 26th MEU(SOC) is back on board ships by 8 February. A CH-53E crashes, killing two Marines and injuring five.

26 February
Operation Enduring Freedom
TF 58 is deactivated.

This book is an expanded update of the official Marine Corps chronology. As always, the staff of the Marine Corps History and Museums Division provided access to their invaluable materials. Jack Dyer, curator of art and a former combat artist, gave his sage advice in selecting illustrations. Reference historians Dan Crawford, Bob Aquilina, and Lena Kaljot made available their extensive files. Evy Englander, the librarian, never failed to find a book needed to fill in a missing link. In addition, Gail Munro (curator of the Navy Art Collection), Jim Zobel (archivist of the MacArthur Memorial), Paul Culp (curator of the Thomason Collection at Sam Houston State University Library), and Jim Ginther (archivist at the Gray Research Center), were of great assistance in mining material from their respective collections.

Colonel Jon T. Hoffman, USMCR, has spent his entire career as an infantry officer and military historian. During his 17 years of active duty, he has commanded two companies in an infantry battalion, taught history at the U.S. Naval Academy, and served as the deputy director of the History and Museums Division. He has published dozens of articles and two books. His first book, *Once a Legend: 'Red Mike' Edson of the Marine Raiders,* received the Marine Corps Heritage Foundation's 1994 Greene Award. His most recent volume, *Chesty: The Story of Lieutenant General Lewis B. Puller, USMC,* earned the 2002 Greene Award and was *The New York Times* bestseller list. In 1998 he was honored as a *Marine Corps Gazette* Distinguished Author.

INDEX